CHRÉTIEN

CHRÉTIEN

—— *Volume 1* ——

THE WILL TO WIN

LAWRENCE MARTIN

LESTER

PUBLISHING

Canadian Cataloguing in Publication Data

Martin, Lawrence, 1947–
Chrétien

Includes index.
Contents: v. 1 The will to win – v. 2 The patriot.
ISBN 1-895555-75-2 (v. 1) – ISBN 1-895555-83-3 (v. 2)

1. Chrétien, Jean, 1934–   .   2. Canada – Politics and government – 1963–1984.*   3. Canada – Politics and government – 1984–1993.*   4. Canada – Politics and government – 1993–   .*
5. Prime ministers – Canada – Biography.   I. Title.

FC636.C47M37 1995   971.064'8'092   C95-931567-5
F1034.3.C47M37 1995

Lester Publishing Limited
56 The Esplanade
Toronto, Ontario M5E 1A7

Printed and bound in Canada
95 96 97 98 5 4 3 2 1

To the daughters of my dreams,
Katie and Kristina

CONTENTS

AUTHOR'S NOTE

I N WRITING about a political phenomenon such as Jean Chrétien, an author begins with some unusual advantages. There is a uniqueness about not only him, but also the entire Chrétien family that comforts the writer. The Chrétiens are direct people. When they talk to you, their eyes don't shift.

For this volume, the prime minister and his brothers and sisters were generous with their time. But this biography is not, nor should it be, one that uses the family as the dominant sources. My approach was to start at the periphery and work towards the centre. Of the more than 250 interviews done for volume one, all but a handful were on the record. The recollections and impressions of friends, adversaries, and colleagues were blended with the Chrétien family's own assessments to try to arrive at a semblance of reality.

I am acutely aware, as all biographers are, of the tricks that memory plays, of the varieties of self-interest of the protagonists, of the "spin" that can be put on any story. My approach was to try to position myself as a relatively neutral observer. Many argue persuasively that objectivity is unattainable. If that is the case, one can at least strive for balance and perspective.

In many cases, conflicting versions of the same event were put forward. The Chrétiens themselves sometimes offered widely varying recollections of important developments. In such instances, I have tried to get as close to a consensus as possible.

Personal interviews are the driving force of this volume. In his book *Mulroney: The Politics of Ambition*, John Sawatsky departed from the traditional, academically inspired style of writing about our prime ministers. He eschewed the common practice of drawing heavily on already published material and, through the sheer mass of interviews he conducted, painted a strong, legwork portrait. In the Chrétien biography, I have undertaken the daunting challenge of trying to follow suit and have tried to improve on the approach in two respects: by gaining access to the subject and his family, and by naming virtually all the sources used.

Chrétien, of course, has already given his own version of events —in the form of his major best-seller, *Straight from the Heart*. Despite its many strengths, this was more a memoir than a biography, and it left large gaps in the story.

Volume one of this book takes Chrétien's story to the late 1980s, when he arrives—after twenty-five years in the trenches—at the threshold of power. Volume two will open with him gaining the leadership of the federal Liberal Party, and then will follow his difficult years in Opposition and his first term as prime minister of the country.

Writing a biography of this sort is a frightening enterprise because the author is so dependent on the corroboration of key people in the subject's life. I was blessed with the cooperation of the great majority of people I approached.

I am particularly fortunate to have had the advice of the publisher Malcolm Lester and the editor Janice Weaver. To encase all of Chrétien's life and political career into one volume would have been unwieldy. They devised a manageable and, for the reader, much more accessible two-volume formula. Malcolm Lester's supervision of the project was enlightened and judicious. Ms. Weaver, who has a superb eye for error, frequently rescued the manuscript from technical folly.

Gordon Robertson is owed a big debt of gratitude for the striking and powerful design of the volume. I had some good research assistance, particularly from Richard Latour, who delivered crates of press clippings and assorted other materials on Chrétien's background. I am also grateful to Marie Isaac for her terrific help in providing government documents under the Access to Information Act; Stephanie Myles for research assistance; Richard Cleroux for help in translating some of my French interviews; Paul Hornbeck for proofreading; Diane Comeau for volunteering documents on Chrétien's period in Indian Affairs; and all those at Lester Publishing and Key Porter Books for their efforts.

As this was oftentimes an around-the-clock project, I owe special thanks to Maureen, Katie, and Kristina for their patience and understanding.

Lawrence Martin
Ottawa
August 1995

CHAPTER ONE

SURVIVAL OF
THE FITTEST

AT THE SUMMIT of the working-class village of La Baie Shawinigan, the graveyard reveals a large black tombstone bearing the names of the Chrétiens who didn't make it. Between 1910 and 1936 Wellie Chrétien and Marie Boisvert had nineteen children. Nine of them survived infancy and led engaging lives. The histories of the other ten are written on the granite stone: Joseph Chrétien, 1910–1910; Madelaine Chrétien, 1916–1916; Albert Chrétien, 1920–1921; Gisèle Chrétien, 1921–1922; Jeanine Chrétien, 1924–1924; Jean-Guy Chrétien, 1925–1926; Marie Chrétien, 1926–1926; Gilles Chrétien, 1928–1928; Jean Chrétien, 1930-1932; Willie Chrétien, 1932–1932.

Some died following premature birth, others of the croup, still others of afflictions unknown. The boy named Jean, second last among the dead, was a big, thrashing pink baby, so large in comparison with the other infants that they called him Gros Jean. He had survived into his second year, thus bringing hope to the family that he might be among the ones to last. But the hope died one day, as the family and their doctor looked on, in the living room of the Chrétien home.

Big Jean, who they feared had diphtheria, was naked on the table in the centre of the room, intermittently hollering and gasping for air. Marcel, one of the Chrétien brothers, picked him up

I

and tried to comfort him. But the baby, unable to draw enough breath, couldn't be helped. He was placed back on the table and, as the others looked on in despair, soon passed away. There would be no Big Guy from Shawinigan.

That same year, the Chrétiens had another baby, but this one died in infancy. Then, in the Depression year of 1934, two years after Gros Jean's death, Marie Chrétien gave birth to child number eighteen. This boy had ears so big that they could flap in the wind, but otherwise was very small. Marie and Wellie named him Jean, and it was only fitting that he soon was called Ti-Jean or Little Jean.

Ti-Jean was a common Québécois name. The "Ti," as in *petit*, was a sign of affection as much as size. But it didn't do much for a boy's self-esteem to have his smallness proclaimed every time someone pronounced his name, so Jean's parents did not encourage its use. They sensed, as Jean was growing up, that he was becoming sensitive about his height. Others in the family came to suspect this too, but he wasn't the type to talk about it, or for that matter, the other handicaps he faced. No one thought too much about his size problem until one day—as best as could be remembered, he was fourteen—when Jean went downtown, all by himself, to visit the doctor.

The doctor was his eldest brother, Maurice. He was a gynecologist, a very serious man, twenty-four years Jean's senior. When he opened the door and saw the little guy, dark moons sagging under his eyes, he had no idea what could be the matter. Maurice knew it was in his young brother's nature to meet problems head-on. This was characteristic of all the Chrétiens. But Jean had never turned up at his office alone like this.

Jean got quickly to the point. He explained in quite an angry manner that he was the smallest kid on the block, that even his younger brother Michel was taller than he, that it was terrible to be so small. He was eating his food, he said, and going to bed on time. How could it be? Why wasn't he getting bigger like everyone else?

Jean went on in this vein for a couple of minutes, getting more worked up as he did. Then, with great indignation, he declared, "You're the doctor! Give me something to make me grow!"

Maurice's eyes widened. "I beg your pardon?"

"Give me something to make me grow!"

Maurice laughed to himself. He was not about to disillusion young Jean by telling him there were no miracle remedies for shortness. So he reached into his cabinet, took out a bottle of pills, and without telling him they were only vitamins, said, "Jean, you take one of these every day."

The little guy was only too happy to do so and, as coincidence would have it, things began to get better for him. He not only started to grow; he shot up like a beanstalk. Before too long, he had gone from the shortest in the family to the tallest. That brother of his, he soon believed, could work miracles.

When Jean wasn't around, family members often joked about this visit. To be sure, it was unusual for someone to do what he did. But there were circumstances that helped explain this incident, as well as other episodes, some even more bizarre, that were to follow.

To begin with, the very nature of the town he lived in placed an unusual emphasis on size. In the Shawinigan of the 1930s and 1940s, brawn, not brains, ruled the streets. Size was a key to survival. That the Chrétiens lost half their children in infancy wasn't terribly unusual. Other families suffered similar losses, and from this tragic state of affairs, the message was clear enough. The strong advanced, the weak fell off. The biggest were the best of the breed. Competitions like the tug-of-war matches among the factory workers took on great meaning in the town. So did arm-wrestling bouts between Chrétien family members. Ti-Jean often got beat by a nephew, Raymond, which infuriated him.

Just as pressure from outside the Chrétien home favoured the strong, so too did the push from inside. What counted for the Chrétiens, however, was superiority built on success. Physical

3

strength was important, but there was probably nothing that meant so much to Jean's parents as achievement. It was a matter of pride.

The family, as Jean's mother so clearly demonstrated, had to have status. Marie Chrétien, who was an attractive woman despite having carried nineteen children, had too much self-esteem for the village she lived in. It was customary in La Baie Shawinigan for the women to sit out on their row-house porches, shelling peas. Mrs. Chrétien preferred not to be seen doing that. She shelled her peas out back, out of sight.

The big day in the company town was payday. The wives of the labourers waited anxiously for it, then stampeded into neighbouring Shawinigan to shop and stock up on supplies. The Chrétiens, like the others, lived from one payday to the next. But Mrs. Chrétien was not seen among the rabble, rushing out of the village. She always waited a day or two, then got dressed in her finest and went into Shawinigan by herself. It wasn't only that she didn't want to be seen with the others, said her daughter Giselle. "Our mother didn't want people to think she had been waiting for that money."

She picked up some of her hauteur, a trait the other townspeople came to view as snobbish, from a neighbouring family, the Comtes, who were from France. They taught her elite French mannerisms, how to prepare French dishes, and the joys of a touch of wine. She always had wine in the home for celebrations. Gilles Argouin, a friend of Jean's, fondly remembered a day when they were just kids, eight or nine years old, and they won a little-league hockey tournament. Mrs. Chrétien invited some of them over for a party. She took out a bottle of wine, gave each little champion a glass, and toasted them all.

One side of her personality undoubtedly came from her father, Philippe Boisvert. Jean Chrétien's maternal grandfather was a large, handsome figure, with a moustache that spanned all provinces and an infectious *joie de vivre*. It was he who gave the Chrétien family its important pan-Canadian flavour. Early in the new century he moved his family out West, to northern Alberta, leaving Marie behind to marry Wellie Chrétien. Each year he would return from the Prairies, descending on *bas Canada,* as he called it, with gifts and song and tales of the Wild West. Judging Wellie Chrétien too austere for his taste, Philippe would venture out to neighbours who enjoyed a good whack of whisky. When he returned, invariably a bit sotted, he'd tell the Chrétiens that he had just happened to be visiting friends who liked to have the odd nip, "so I had to have a few myself to make them feel comfortable."

He'd write letters from Alberta in such incoherent French that the Chrétiens had trouble deciphering them. But once, wishing to announce that he'd sold his land and now had enough money to drink full-time, he managed, in the true spirit of the *bon vivant,* a fine rhyming couplet. "Marie," he wrote, "j'ai vendu ma terre, puis je bois de la bière."

Marie, resplendent in a flower-laden hat with a brim that reached beyond her shoulders, married Wellie Chrétien in 1909. She was only seventeen years old and perhaps it was her girlish innocence that compelled her to choose a man so cheerless and dull. In taste and temper, the two of them seemed such opposites. Wellie brought a spartan chill to a household Marie wanted to be warm. He approached the business of living with dire seriousness. If there was a single word to define him, it was "disciplined." He went to work on his father's farm at age eleven, then got a job helping to build one of the first paper mills in what was to become La Baie Shawinigan. He was kept on by the company as a machinist. Later, he supplemented this work with two other part-time jobs. He was the superintendent for those homes in the town that were owned by the mill, and he sold life insurance. Though he was left with virtually no free time, he accepted this without complaint. It being his philosophy that only work made things better, all his hours were devoted to it.

He was square of build, short, with darkish hair and bold, direct eyes that never veered from their target. Always exacting, always demanding, he was respected by his children but was too cold to be loved. His words were few. One of the more common scenes around the household had Jean and the other children playing on the *salon* floor while Wellie sat in his chair, reading the newspaper. If the noise level rose beyond the permitted decibel range, Wellie's arm shot up from behind the journal. He'd hold it firmly in position, finger pointed skyward, until all the kids had run upstairs to their rooms. Precise regulations had to be followed at the dinner table. If one of the children left a knife or fork in the wrong position at the table, they heard the father's reprimand. "You have no excuse! Me, I wasn't taught these things. I didn't learn them. But you! You have no excuse."

There weren't many books in the home, just some encyclopedias, the odd adventure story, and a book on Wellie's hero, Wilfrid Laurier. The Chrétiens went to church on Sunday, but they didn't say grace before Marie's delicious meals. Nor did they partake of another widespread religious practice—reciting the rosary. Wellie Chrétien was too pragmatic to believe that anyone should rely on Providence.

His rigorous ways left the children to wonder whether he ever enjoyed himself. They thanked their lucky stars that Mom, with her good humour, was around for counterbalance. She frequently hid their misdeeds from Wellie, so as to deny him his scorn. At the same time, however, the children could only admire their father's discipline, his capacity for hard work, and his sense of purpose.

While he differed in so many ways from the kinder Marie, they both shared the same deep pride. Marie's could be seen in the way she carried herself, while Wellie's was manifest in his unrelenting efforts at self-improvement. He was a man, said son Gabriel, "who always wanted to learn something." At forty-three, in an era when adult education was uncommon, he enrolled in math courses at the Shawinigan Technical School. He dutifully took part, also in middle age, in an English-language correspondence course administered from Great Britain. His three jobs left him with few unfilled moments, but he faithfully carried out the requirements of the program. At the same time, he continued to make diligent efforts to speak better French than the *joual* heard in La Baie Shawinigan, and he scolded his children for their malapropisms.

His utter devotion to betterment, to work, and to learning were uncommon in a place where attitudes were imprisoned in milltown ritual. It was his great gift to Jean and the other children to break from that ritual and see beyond the limited possibilities that La Baie Shawinigan yielded.

La Baie was not a place where stars were supposed to be born. It was a town of modest people with modest expectations. They lived beside smokestacks, worked the mill, went to church, reproduced, voted, and died. Premier Maurice Duplessis and God be willing, they went to heaven.

Situated about two hours by car northeast of Montreal, La Baie Shawinigan, in the 1930s, had approximately two thousand inhabitants, almost all Catholic, almost all French. Shawinigan proper, the "big city" next door, had twenty-five thousand, none of whom thought much of La Baie. Trois-Rivières, population sixty thousand, was twenty miles down the road, located off the major highway, halfway between Montreal and Quebec City.

Though nestled right up against Shawinigan, La Baie had its own identity because it was the first to be settled. Hubert Biermans, a Belgian, opened the town's first mills at the turn of the century, giving La Baie the memorable official birth date of 1900. Its ruggedly spectacular geography added to its distinctive personality. The town was built against a steep, heavily forested hillside that plunged sharply into the rushing St-Maurice River. The river in turn opened onto the picturesque bay, before jutting east to meet up with the St. Lawrence at Trois-Rivières.

On the river's edge, smack against La Baie Shawinigan's main

street, clamoured the giant paper mills and power plants. Their in-
cessant racket and malodorous exhausts blanketed the workers'
ghetto. So accustomed to the rhythm of the roars did the inhabitants become that on the rare occasions when the factories shut
down, they had trouble sleeping. It was too quiet.

Almost all the townspeople owed their lives to the mills. The
mills employed them, the mills owned their homes, the mills set
their careers, their schedules, their lifestyles, their vocabularies.
The sense of belonging was inescapable.

The majority of residents lived right at the bottom of the hillside on the main street. Others were stationed at the top, in a district that was owned by the Belgian and appropriately named
Belgoville. The Chrétiens lived alternately below, above, then
below again. Jean was born at the bottom, across from the Belgo
mill, then spent his boyhood and early teen years up on top on rue
Biermans.

To call the atmosphere claustrophobic was to be understated.
Wellie Chrétien lived in Belgoville, worked at La Belgo, and resided
on rue Biermans. Beyond the Belgian's omnipresence, there wasn't
much else of consequence in the labourers' enclave. There was a
park, a grocery store, a church, a restaurant, a school, a town hall, a
pool hall, and the graveyard where all the Chrétien infants lay.

The place had an air of forebodance about it, with the mood,
perhaps owing to the town's harsh landscape, easily turning melan-
choly. If the geography of La Baie was unrefined, so was the mind-
set. Raymond Chrétien, Maurice's son, often visited from Shawinigan proper, gaining a sense of its flavour. "In La Belgo culture,"
he said, "physical strength would protect you from everything.
People would not bother you, they would not make jokes about
you. They would respect you."

"That's why," he continued, "Jean was so scared. He was thin,
he was called Ti-Jean. He was small and he was living in a world
where physical strength meant so much."

In neighbouring Shawinigan, the inhabitants looked condescendingly on La Baie, with its low-grade homes, its coarse spoken French, its roughneck mentality. The foul odours emanating from the town's waters and mills prompted Shawinigan residents to coin a special nickname for their dour little suburb. They called it La Baie de Puants: The Bay of Smells.

Given the state of the air in their own town, it was a rather galling appellation. Wafting through Shawinigan proper was usually an offensive industrial aroma of some kind, the flavour depending on the direction of the breezes. If the winds were blowing in from the paper mills, there came the gagging odour of sulphur. From the southeast, the gusts brought the soot and grit of the electric furnaces at the carbide plant. From other directions, one could sniff the noxious chlorine from the CIL company or the stench from the great belches of the coal furnaces at Shawinigan Chemicals.

Still, while La Baie had only a backwater reputation, Shawinigan proper could boast of some successes. Built among hills and valleys of the rough landscape lining the St-Maurice, it was one of Canada's first industrialized cities. By the 1950s it had become one of the most prosperous small cities in the country.

Growing up in La Baie, Jean Chrétien could look next door and see industry booming all around him: pulp-and-paper plants, paint and chemical factories, electrical companies, rubber plants, oil companies, aluminum factories. They'd all come, as the century opened, following the arrival of the Shawinigan Water and Power Company. The company harnessed the surging waters of the St-Maurice to produce cheap electricity. With cheap power, there was cheap land and, until the unions got tough, reasonably cheap labour. These were draws that were hard to ignore. Employment in Shawinigan was plentiful. Its people ate at good restaurants, bought cottages on the nearby waters, and shopped at some fine stores on Fifth Street. The postwar economic boom brought cars, fur coats, jobs for all, and as long as the French Canadians could tolerate their second-class status, a degree of satisfaction.

Until 1958 the city, though largely French, had a decidedly

English name—Shawinigan Falls. Since the 1920s the French had repeatedly tried to change it, but the English barons of industry always prevailed, arguing that it would be against their interests to de-Anglicize the name. This rationale held until the nationalist St-Jean Baptiste Society finally led a successful counter-campaign.

The anglophones, only 5 to 10 per cent of the population, dominated the top executive positions at virtually all major companies in the city. They lived in the best homes along Maple Street and had an English high school for their sons and daughters, an English newspaper, and all-anglo curling, social, and golf clubs. They made it difficult for the Chrétiens and other francophones to use their posh golf club in neighbouring Grand'Mère, and while they were only a small minority in the area's other golf club, the Shawinigan Country Club, they held the majority on its board. Religion added to the divide. The anglos were Protestants, attending the Anglican churches, and the francophones were Roman Catholic.

Some degree of friction was inevitable. Palle Kiar, a man of Danish descent, lived with his English friends on George Street. "To get to the candy store, we'd have to cross rue Champlain. If you had a nickel, you had to round up three or four of your anglophone friends to go over in convoy. The [francophone] kids on rue Champlain would throw rocks at you and call you names. And if they crossed over to our side, they'd get rocks thrown at them. That was just sort of the normal situation." Road-hockey games between French and English sometimes got fractious. The kids played with horse buns that had been dropped from the coal carts or milk wagons of the period. Towards the spring the buns began to thaw and the idea, when a boy had a shooting opportunity, was to aim high.

But despite the passions of adolescents—the Chrétien boys believed, for example, that all those anglo Protestants would literally burn in hell—and despite the apparent subjugation of the francophone majority, serious conflict was avoided. When the economy was performing well, the English dictatorship was viewed as benign. And even when times were tough, Wellie Chrétien and his sons saw no great injustice being perpetrated.

"Some francophones were angry, yes," said Gabriel Chrétien, the third eldest son. "But you had to admit—and I am a French Canadian and I admitted it—that the English were the ones who had the right education. We had no mechanical engineers in the province of Quebec. And so when the big companies had to do some hiring for top jobs, they had to get people from the western provinces. So I wouldn't say they were refusing us those kinds of jobs. We couldn't do those jobs."

Wellie Chrétien was respectful of secular authority, be it English or French. He believed that he had been treated well by the English company managers at the mill and that he had no right to complain—even though, after decades of conscientious work, he was never promoted to a managerial position. His humble station at the mill was something of a sore point with him. Once he was asked, in the presence of eldest son Maurice, why he had never been promoted to foreman. Maurice saw a sad look come over his face. "It's because my English wasn't good enough," his father responded. But he wasn't angry at the anglo bosses, Maurice recalled. He only regretted the circumstances. "That's why I learned English," explained the eldest son. "To be equal! Instead of fighting it, you learn. Learn, learn, learn. Then you become somebody."

The distinctly favourable attitude of the family towards the other Canadian solitude had a number of influences, probably none more important than Wellie's father, François. Jean never met Grandpa François, who died before his grandson was born. But as family members saw it, a good measure of François lived on in both Wellie and Jean.

François, a defiantly proud Liberal politician, was a tough character who was always prepared to challenge the establishment. He pursued three occupations, working like a slave at each. He was a farmer, a lumberman who measured wood for the nearby paper mills, and the long-time mayor of St-Étienne-des-Grès, a small village a short distance from Shawinigan. Grandson Maurice found him distant and driven. "When you're a boy of nine or ten, you want to play with your grandfather. But he was not that type of man. He was working from early in the morning until sunset and coming home with the oil lamp and reading his newspaper and going to bed."

With massive hands and arms from lifting the logs and working the fields, Grandpa Chrétien was considered the strongest man in the village. His strength benefited him as a politician. When he was shouted down as a *maudit rouge*, which was often enough, he wasn't one to turn the other cheek. Instead, he would descend from the podium and beat the offending loud-mouth into submission. He stayed away from drink most of the time because he could get violent enough when sober. "If I have more of that stuff," he once told a fellow villager, "I'll kill somebody."

Besides the physical power, François enjoyed another advantage over the locals: he was educated enough to be literate. Townspeople came to his home with letters they couldn't read or requests for responses they couldn't write. His assistance usually paid off on voting day.

He was a political organizer in the Shawinigan area from the early post-Confederation days, and anyone who doubted his commitment to the Grits need only have considered the election campaign of Hubert Biermans. The 1900s had just begun and Wellie Chrétien was working at Biermans's paper mill. Biermans decided to run in the provincial election as an independent candidate. Though Wellie was an ardent Liberal, he decided that for obvious reasons he had better support his boss. But he worried about his father. François Chrétien's word carried so much weight that he could be a decisive force in the outcome of the election. Indeed, ignoring his own son's anxiety, he directed his political machine against Biermans. Maybe Biermans was a millionaire, he declared, but that didn't make him a more worthy man. His forceful campaigning sent the owner of the town down to defeat. Wellie feared losing his job but held on.

Jean's grandfather's devotion to the Grits was never matched with any such devotion to the church. He was an early proponent of the separation of church and state, and became so critical of the clergy he was almost excommunicated. His free-minded reform spirit was characteristic of many Québécois Liberals of this period, who fought strongly against the established powers in the province, the Roman Catholic Church and the aristocracy.

François died, as Chrétien legend had it, of his own volition. Confined to a hospital bed, life-support tubes sticking out of his body from one ailing end to the other, he could take no more. In a fit of rage he yanked out the tube lines and passed away shortly thereafter. Among those attending his funeral was a rising star in the region's political firmament, Maurice Duplessis.

Wellie Chrétien's Liberalism was as immutable as his father's, but his allegiance sprang not just from ancestry. He had experiences of his own to draw on.

The company for which he sold insurance was L'Association Canado-Américaine, headquartered in Manchester, New Hampshire. He made frequent trips there, eventually achieving, despite his uneducated, blue-collar background, the rank of board member, a position he held for three decades. New Hampshire had a large French-speaking population, and over the course of his visits, Wellie saw what was happening to it. The culture was vanishing. Unlike the French in Canada, the French in the United States fell prey to assimilation in the great American melting pot.

It was an important lesson, one that he passed down to his sons and daughters. It was clear, he told them, that the Canadian federalist system, as advocated by the national Liberal Party, worked to their advantage because it preserved the French language and culture.

His thoughts on the contrasting attitude of the Americans,

who favoured absorption of the French, were borne out in the correspondence of the period. In a letter to Prime Minister Mackenzie King in 1942, President Franklin Roosevelt wrote approvingly that the New England French "no longer vote as their churches and societies tell them to do. They're inter-marrying with the original Anglo-Saxon stock." The "positive development" should be extended to Canada, the president continued, with the objective of "assimilating the New England French Canadians and Canada's French Canadians into the whole of our respective bodies politic. There are many methods of doing this."

For most of his trips back and forth to New England, Wellie was driven by Émilienne Godin of Trois-Rivières. Her husband, also a board member, accompanied them, sleeping in the back seat. They drove all night, through Montreal, Quebec's Eastern Townships, and the mountains of Vermont and New Hampshire. While Mr. Godin snored away in back, Wellie Chrétien jabbered on up front to keep Mrs. Godin awake at the wheel. She found Wellie to be an exceptionally upright man who spoke correct French, dressed meticulously, sat straight up in the car, and was unfailingly polite. Mrs. Godin sensed that, like Mrs. Chrétien, Wellie didn't really belong in the town he lived in. He was a cut above.

Mrs. Godin—the very proper Wellie never called her by her first name—often fretted during the trips about losing her way. Wellie always had ready advice. "You see the railway tracks over there, Mrs. Godin? You can never go wrong if you follow the railway tracks." During one trip he expanded on his approach to life. "When I get up in the morning," Mr. Chrétien explained, "I say, 'This is one day and I am going to work my very hardest and make the best of this day. I'm not going to worry about tomorrow because it's not here yet and there's nothing I can do. I will solve today's problems and I will move on.'"

Mrs. Godin wondered why Wellie worked during almost all his spare hours, leaving him little time to spend with his family. He agreed it was sad that he didn't see them much, but his time away working was for a noble purpose, he explained. He didn't want them to face the limitations he had. He had to provide them with an education so they could become something in life.

He talked at length about all his children and how they were progressing in their schooling. Most of them got favourable evaluations from Wellie, but he was concerned about the small one, young Jean. He kept getting bad notices from the teachers about him, and it seemed he was becoming a major discipline problem. The other children, Wellie told Mrs. Godin, were more conventional, tending to be more tolerant of things. But Jean, Mr. Chrétien said, "He's different from the rest. He has a will of his own."

CHAPTER TWO

THE LITTLE GUY

MAURICE liked what he saw of his little brother at first. "Jean was trying to help his younger brother Michel by teaching him to do good. 'Don't do that, Michel. That's not right. Come with me.' That kind of thing." Jean's sister Giselle thought he was adorable. She remembered the day she went shopping for a new coat and, finding one she loved, brought it home to ask permission to buy it. Mrs. Chrétien liked it, until she saw the price. "I'm sorry, Giselle," she said, shaking her head. "This is too much." Ti-Jean was sitting at the table as the scene unfolded. When he saw the crestfallen look on his sister's face, he piped up. "Don't worry, Giselle. You can get the coat. I will give you all the money in my piggy bank so you can get it." He had $4.58.

There were other moments like this, moments when, like most anyone else at that age, he was hard to resist. But soon the rascal in Jean Chrétien took over. He became an impossibly stubborn little brat, throwing public tantrums until he got his way. His brother Marcel took him to the barber shop once, but he refused to get in the chair, running from one end of the shop to the other. Marcel gave chase, picked him up, and threw him in the seat, but Ti-Jean was out of it in a second and gone again. Marcel finally gave up and dragged him home.

At the toy store one day, Ti-Jean's face lit up with joy at the sight of a tricycle with a wagon attached. He got on it and started racing up and down the aisles like an ambulance driver. He demanded that Marcel buy it for him. When Marcel, who didn't have the money, refused, Ti-Jean had a fit, kicking and screaming and causing such a ruckus in front of the other customers that Marcel had to ask if he could buy the bike on credit. He did—and later returned it.

Jean insisted on getting his own way among his friends as well as his family. Out on the street, though, he faced less opposition. On rue Biermans, when he and his friends, six, seven, and eight years old, played soldiers, Chrétien was always the commandant. He would simply appear and assume the role, no questions asked. It was as if it was in the natural order of things.

Because it was a tough neighbourhood, the kids often held tests of endurance and strength. Despite his small size, Chrétien organized them and gave out the grades. When the kids played hockey, Chrétien assumed the role of manager, coach, and captain. For baseball, it was the same.

One of the soldiers and ball players was Jean's neighbour, Yvon Boisvert. Boisvert was struck by his friend's determination. Chrétien bled determination, he said. "It was he who was the boss of everything, and with him you had to win. It wasn't for fun. You simply had to win." Another infantryman on rue Biermans was Gilles Marchand. Taller and tougher than his commander-in-chief, he was still not about to challenge his leadership. "That was part of his person," said Marchand. "It was something innate in him. You have that kind of thing or you don't. Chrétien had it from the first day."

The first school Chrétien attended was the Jardin de l'Enfance, a boarding-school run by Dominican nuns. It was here that five-year-old Jean—blond, short-cropped hair, deep-set eyes, big elephant ears—developed a hatred for boarding-schools that remained with him throughout his erratic educational career.

The Jardin was located in central Shawinigan, only a short bus ride from La Baie. Yet Jean sometimes went weeks, even months, without setting foot in his home. His mother visited him occasionally on weekends, but his father rarely came at all. When he did get leave to return home the odd Sunday, he pleaded with his parents not to send him back. Scenes of high drama, tears, fights, and bitterness unfolded every time he had to board the bus for the return trip. He so badly wanted to attend an ordinary day-school like the other boys in La Baie and play sports in his free time and eat his mother's cooking and receive her loving care. But his stringent father wouldn't allow it. Wellie believed that the demands of the boarding-school regimen were good for him. There were other considerations as well. Their home in Belgoville was a small, semi-detached brick unit, with only three bedrooms upstairs. Space was tight with so many children in the house. Moreover, Marie Chrétien's health was often in question. Having the kids away at school gave her time to rest.

The day at the Jardin started with a wake-up call at 5:30 a.m. In the darkness the kids marched single file to St. Pierre's church, which was across the way. Chrétien loathed this little journey, as did the other students, especially in the deep cold of winter. Their whole day was strictly regimented, with classes, study periods, meals, one break period, and bed at 7:30 in a dorm room that slept a hundred. Meals consisted of porridge or soup, milk, bread, and other basics. There was no toast, and cereal was considered a big treat.

Jean was rebellious from the moment he got to the Jardin. Time and again, the nuns belted him across the hand with the strap or ordered him to sit at the front of the class. But as hyperactive as he was, his surges of nervous energy could not be harnessed. He constantly talked, he bugged his neighbours, he got in scraps with any student who challenged him. Even class picture day was a trial. He detested it because he was so short that he had to stand in the front row with all the other small students.

After six years of earning indifferent grades and resisting the confinement and the rules, he got relief. The Jardin's curriculum extended no further, so he was transferred to the local school, Sacré-Coeur, in La Baie Shawinigan. He would fondly remember his two years there. They marked the only ones from the time he was five that he lived year-round with his family and enjoyed the normal life of a young boy.

While the change to the day-school made him happier, it didn't change his behaviour. The obstreperousness continued. The teachers could never shut him up, recalled Gilles Argouin. "He was always in trouble. Even though I was older, I was in the same class as he was. I remember once, when the bell rang to end classes and we had to get in a line-up. Well, Jean was in front of me, yacking away as usual. The teacher told him to stop it, but Jean continued yacking anyway." So the teacher came after Chrétien with eyes blazing, Argouin explained, but Jean, "a quick little bugger," ducked just in time. The teacher's arm shot over him and whacked Argouin right in the eye. "As you can imagine, Jean got a big laugh out of that one," recalled his classmate. He was one of the many friends of Jean's youth who thought that, given his ungovernability, Chrétien wouldn't amount to much.

"He was so undisciplined," said Normand Déry, another schoolmate. "Once, a teacher, St-Laurent, had to pull him by the ears to get him to behave." This form of discipline, a good yank on the hearing apparatus, was employed sparingly by the teachers and loathed by Chrétien. He'd recoil like a terrified cat. News of St-Laurent's punishment soon got back to Jean's parents. Though they normally wouldn't challenge the school's disciplinary measures, this time they marched down to Sacré-Coeur and demanded to see St-Laurent. They told him he wasn't going to do that to their boy any more.

Jean's parents were particularly upset because it had become apparent by this time that their son had hearing difficulties—that he had probably had them since birth. There had long been hints of the defect. There were moments at dinner, for example, when

Wellie would address a question to Jean and the boy would continue eating, face in his plate, completely oblivious to his father's words. Unfairly, Wellie concluded Jean was deliberately ignoring him. "What's the matter?" he would bellow. "Can't you hear?"

Eventually they got him looked at and learned he was deaf as a wall in the right ear. How this had affected his ability to learn was hard to judge, but family members did observe another peculiarity. In trying to pronounce words, Jean often made unusual errors. Whether this was related to his hearing defect, they didn't know.

He had been in an accident at the local Amateau Creek. While family members thought it unlikely that it had caused any permanent damage, it was a harrowing experience. The creek, bordered by rocks, was deep in some places and shallow in others. One day Guy Chrétien, who was four years older than Jean, and Guy's buddy, Gilles Lefebvre, were kibitzing with Jean by the water's edge. The older boys were teasing him, as he was not a good swimmer, about being afraid to go in. After more taunting, Guy and Gilles took him by the feet and the arms and, with a few heave-hos, hurled the terrified little guy into a spot where they thought the water was deep. His body entered swiftly, cutting the water like a knife, and Guy and Gilles had a good laugh. When seconds passed and nothing happened—no Ti-Jean scrambling angrily to the surface—the laughter died. Guy and Gilles then noticed that at Jean's point of entry, the water was changing to a deep reddish colour.

Jean surfaced, bloodied and in a state of shock. They rushed him home to sister Juliette, who was minding the house while Mother visited her relatives out West. An examination by the family doctor revealed that Jean had smashed his head against a rock at the bottom of the creek. Stitches to repair the laceration left an enduring scar under the eye.

Jean was a leathery, rugged kid who, frantically busy organizing sports, had no time to brood over aches and pains. From commandant of the soldiers, he became captain of the local teams. It was a precocious performance. At eleven and twelve, the only years he was out of boarding-school, Chrétien was manager and coach of a hockey team in the bantam division of the district little league. The bantam division included boys as old as fourteen and was usually coached by kids in their late teens or parents. But in deference to Chrétien's leadership abilities, bigger, older boys willingly came under his supervision. He became the region's first under-age hockey coach.

The team the eleven-year-old built was extraordinary. He went after the best skaters and hitters in the area, and if the rules needed stretching to get them, Chrétien was prepared to stretch the rules. He desperately wanted Gilles Argouin on the club. Argouin, rugged and skilled, was all-star calibre, but he was also over-age and therefore ineligible. Chrétien, worried the team couldn't win without him, devised a strategy to circumvent the age requirements. He instructed the elder Argouin to masquerade as his younger brother. If anyone asked any questions, he told Argouin, "just show your brother's birth certificate."

The scam held up wonderfully all season long. Gilles the Imposter was a star, bashing opponents into the boards, scoring goals, and leading Jean's team to victory. The older coaches were getting whipped by a team coached by a kid who, when standing behind the bench, could barely see over his players' heads.

In the playoffs, however, the under-age coach with the over-age player saw his luck run out. Chrétien's team faced off against Shawinigan-Sud, Gilles Argouin's home town. People there knew his age. After losing the game, a couple of players from that team squealed to the league directors. Argouin was suspended for two years, while his friend, the instigator of the subterfuge, faced no charges. Jean Chrétien was back behind the bench the very next season.

Victory itself was vital for Chrétien, but it also had to be appropriately commemorated. Once, he arranged a little local hockey tournament for which there were no formal prizes. His team made it to the final. Since there was no trophy, and triumph without the spoils wouldn't do, Chrétien came up with one. From the mantel-piece in his home, he took a big bronze prize one of his brothers had won and stuffed it in his hockey bag. Before the game, Chrétien took it out and showed it to his team. "You see this tro-phy, boys?" he said. "If we win the game, we get to keep it. But if we lose, don't worry, guys. It stays in the bag."

Chrétien was impulsive, always ready to start a fight if he didn't get his way. Gilles Marchand remembered him as bull-headed, with "an atrocious temper." Chrétien's sister Giselle put it in more euphemistic terms. "When Jean wanted something, he was deter-mined to get it. He wouldn't let go." Both on the diamonds and on the ice, fights were common. "Jean was too small and thin then to be real tough," recalled Argouin. "But he was tough with his mouth. He intimidated with his mouth. He talked, talked, talked."

Like most eleven- and twelve-year-old boys, Jean and his best friends—Yvon Boisvert, Gilles Argouin, Wilson Prescott, Gaston Pronovost, and Gilles Marchand—were sports crazy. Athletics were the chief source of status, of ego-gratification. For all the Chrétien boys, none of them terribly bookish, the games were what counted. When Jean found he couldn't be the star player— he was good but too small to be top rank—he decided he'd be the star at the management level. If winning meant leaving his best friend, the musically inclined Yvon Boisvert, off the team, Yvon Boisvert was off the team.

By his early teens, Chrétien had acquired an encyclopedic knowledge of baseball. He knew the name of every player in the big leagues and the position he played. His brother Guy tried to stump him on occasion but always failed. Whenever a baseball game was on the radio, even during family get-togethers, Jean would run up to his room to listen. When he played the game, it was often at sec-ond base. But for Jean, who always wanted in on the action, one position was rarely enough. Boisvert recalled one time when he was playing shortstop. A pop fly was descending directly into his glove, but Chrétien came scurrying over from second, called out that he had it, climbed halfway up Boisvert's back, reached his glove over the puzzled boy's face, and missed the ball completely. It crashed violently into Boisvert's nose, almost knocking him out. Teammates carried him off the field, laid him on the bench, and administered ice to a sniffer that had swollen to three times its normal size.

At play, Chrétien insisted on hanging around with the older, bigger kids so he could feel important. While this wasn't unusual for boys Jean's age, with him it was more like an obsession. Relatively minor affronts about his size, such as having to stand in the front row for school photos, bothered him immensely. In the neighbourhood pick-up hockey games, for example, nobody wanted to play goal. One time, recalled Jean Harnois, a classmate of Chrétien's, they decided to put the smallest kid in the nets. The smallest kid, of course, was Ti-Jean. Although Harnois couldn't remember much about the games they played back then, one thing stood out clearly—the look on Chrétien's face when they told him he had to be the goalie. He was being singled out as the little guy from Shawinigan. And for young Jean Chrétien, there was nothing worse than that.

Jean's friends loved his spirit and sense of adventure. While some wished they had his drive, others felt he was too driven. They sensed there was something pushing him, an anger inside. All the Chrétien boys, observed neighbour Normand Déry, had more desire to succeed in life than the others in the town. But none, he said, craved it more than Jean. For Jean, it was a race to the summit, a fight for status. There was a world out there to conquer. As the novelist F. Scott Fitzgerald had put it, "Life was something that could be dominated, if you were any good." Chrétien would show them just how good he was.

Because he was born in 1934, he was too young to have a good sense of the war years. But he was aware of his father's strong views on Quebec's role in the war effort. If there were ever any doubts where the head of the Chrétien clan stood on the question of Quebec nationalism, they were addressed during what came to be known as the conscription crisis. In April 1942 the Mackenzie King government held a plebiscite asking Canadians to release it from its promise not to introduce conscription for overseas military service. English Canada voted overwhelmingly in favour of compulsory service—by a margin of four to one. Because Quebeckers felt, among other things, betrayed by the government's about-face, they registered an abjectly contrary sentiment—72 per cent against to 28 per cent for. Among the few francophones who voted for making it mandatory to send their sons to battle was Jean's father. He had three boys eligible to be drafted.

Wellie was a war hawk. He believed that those francophones who fled their home towns and hid out in nearby forests for fear of being conscripted should be hunted down and suited up. He felt nothing but disdain for them and didn't seek to camouflage his opinion. Rumours quickly spread that he was an informant for the war authorities, turning over the names of draft dodgers and telling recruiters where they were hiding. His sons, though not disputing his clearly held bias, later denied he ever engaged in any such activity.

Jean Chrétien remembered his father telling the older boys that they were not to wait for conscription; they had to volunteer. Only one, Gabriel, was accepted. Maurice was turned down because he was a doctor and Marcel because he had poor eyesight. Gabriel enlisted and became an artillery captain, but he never got his wish to serve overseas. Nevertheless, Wellie Chrétien put a star in the window of his home to show everyone in the village that unlike most of them, he had a boy in the service of his country.

Wellie Chrétien, it was clear, was a Canadian first, a French Canadian second. His bold stance during the conscription crisis hardly enhanced his or his family's popularity. His family also found itself up against establishment beliefs on other issues. Being of long-standing Liberal, federalist stock, they were categorically on the wrong side of the provincial political machine, run by Maurice Duplessis's Union Nationale. The premier's corrupt tentacles reached into almost every corner of Quebec life, bringing favour to the faithful and disadvantage to the rest. Duplessis was first elected in 1936, on a platform that ironically included integrity in government. His party was thrown out in 1939 and brought back in 1944. The Union Nationale, a strongly nationalist, exclusionary voice, then remained in power until 1960. Its system of patronage and favouritism was more an extension of previous Liberal abuse than a new phase of corruption. Still, the Duplessis regime, which enjoyed its full sweep of powers during Jean Chrétien's formative years, was a prototype patronage machine that excluded all but its devotees.

To oppose Duplessis was also to be pitted against the great power that was in league with him—the clergy. All in all, given these factors, given Wellie's financial constraints and the low regard in which La Baie Shawinigan was held, the circumstances were not ideal for getting a start in life. But against the many disadvantages Jean and his siblings faced, there were some important counterweights. They had unusually ambitious parents who were intent on giving their children an education that would get them off La Baie Shawinigan's treadmill. They had, in Maurice, a brother who was charting a new course, breaking free of blue-collardom. And though they were wearing the wrong political stripe provincially, the Chrétiens were on the big team federally.

In their modest community, they also numbered among the better off. While certainly not wealthy, they didn't lack any of the basics. Nine children constituted a burden, but Wellie worked hard and Maurice was soon contributing from his substantial earnings. The Chrétiens had a large garden, and there was always plenty of food on the table and plenty of sports equipment for the kids. Gabriel Chrétien was one of the first French boys in La Baie to own a pair of skis. Dad had an automobile, off and on, as early as the late 1930s. Mom would never realize her dream of visiting

Europe, but she was able to afford long trips to western Canada to see her relatives.

The finances were at times more plentiful than others. During the Depression, Wellie lost his main job, and as a result, Gabriel was not able to get the education he wanted. In the 1940s the three youngest boys, Guy, Jean, and Michel, shared an allowance of a nickel a day. The boys often got by on hand-me-down clothes, but the three daughters, naturally more fussy, were always presentable. Giselle might not have got the new coat she wanted that day Jean offered her his piggy-bank money, but she and her sisters did well by the standards of the time. Carmen, the eldest, once got a racoon coat from her father. It cost a hundred dollars.

Mrs. Chrétien was the family treasurer. Her bank was a curlicued candy dish, lime green in colour, which she kept on the mantel in the *salon*, open and visible to all. Whenever anyone needed money, banker Mom went over to the green dish and checked the balance. It got so low sometimes that it caused concern among the older boys. They suspected an emergency fund was hidden away somewhere, and indeed, Maurice uncovered it. He didn't mention it to anyone, however, not even his brothers.

The hidden bank kept, among other things, the all-important education fund. Both parents had a very basic message for their children. In Maurice's words it was, "Be good and be educated." The difficulty was that meeting the educational requirement of this, the first Chrétien commandment, involved more money than Wellie ever knew. To help his children break from La Baie Shawinigan's follow-your-father-to-the-factory routine, he realized that what was needed was access to Quebec's finest educational offering: the eight-year classical program at the seminary colleges. This was the proven route to the esteemed occupations—lawyer, doctor, educator, clergyman. The program was much too expensive for a man of Wellie's means, however. A stroke of luck was needed or his dream of creating a family of professionals would be forgotten.

He was fortunate enough to have a first son who was a cut above. As well as being a top student, Maurice was a terrifically ambitious youth with an eye for opportunity. Few of the French kids, for example, saw the need, even though Shawinigan was owned and operated by anglophones, to learn English. Maurice was driven to do so as the result of a trip he took with his father to Westfield, Massachusetts, in 1922. Maurice, then twelve, loved sports and wanted to play baseball with the American kids. But unable to communicate in English, he stood alone watching, glove in hand, as the other boys played the game. He returned home annoyed and determined to learn the language so that it wouldn't happen again.

In Shawinigan he met a girl named May Walsh who was fully bilingual. She got him started on English, and on dancing as well. He practiced the language hard, jumping into conversation with any English speaker he could find. Within a few years he was one of the few bilingual people in La Baie Shawinigan.

Tall, strong, and aggressive, Maurice, in his own words, was "a straight talker and a fighter, not afraid of anybody." He played defence in hockey. "As you know, playing there you have to knock over a lot of other guys. Well, that was a good lesson I learned."

By his teens, he was ready to make the break with La Baie, but there was still the problem of money. Then came the stroke of luck he and Wellie had been hoping for. The insurance company Wellie worked for began offering a scholarship to the most promising student among all the families on the company's client list. The prize was a healthy two hundred dollars, enough to meet most of the financial requirements of a year at a classical school. Wellie anxiously put in an application for his son. Maurice won the scholarship, which meant his father could send him to the seminary college in nearby Joliette.

He excelled there, winning more scholarships and imagining many career possibilities would open up to him. But the limitations of the solitude he lived in blocked the route to his first choice, chemical engineering. Shawinigan was home to one of the biggest chemistry labs in the country, but it was an all-English club. Engineering was not considered a suitable occupation for Québécois. When Maurice made inquiries about the profession, he got cold, quizzical responses that as much as said he was in the wrong place. Disappointed, he pursued his second choice and attended medical school at Laval University in Quebec City. To help pay his way, he got a job in the sports department of the newspaper *L'Événement*. The sports editor needed someone to translate stories from the English wire services into French. Because he had made himself bilingual, Maurice Chrétien could do the job.

He did well at Laval and soon developed a thriving medical practice. His success in school inspired his brothers, as did his success in his career. With the profits from his practice, he was able to help get some of them out of La Baie and into Joliette.

Young Jean would get more than a bottle of vitamin pills from Dr. Maurice. He'd get the means to make a new start.

CHAPTER THREE

THE JOLIETTE
YEARS

N O ONE knew for certain, but the medical authorities felt that it had happened on the wedding day of his sister Giselle.

That day, February 16, 1946, was the coldest one of the year in Shawinigan. Jean Chrétien, who would turn twelve years old that month, was unable to stay at home the night before the wedding because guests from out of town were using his room. He slept at his brother Maurice's and faced a long walk to the church in the morning. The walk froze him half to death. The fierce gales, cutting icily from the north, struck the left side of his face the hardest. When Chrétien arrived at the church, his cheek was as numb as concrete.

Nevertheless, he served as an altar boy at the wedding mass for his sister and her handsome groom, Jacques Suzor. Though the cold was a major topic of conversation—"My God, it's turned the flowers brown," muttered the guests—no one seemed to realize the severity of young Jean's frostbite.

By evening his face was still numb. His mother mentioned it to the bride and to several wedding guests, but in the week that followed, Jean didn't complain about any pain. His face started to look better. The matter passed.

Over the next few months, however, a deformity began to appear in the area where the cold had hit. It looked at times as if Jean's mouth had shifted laterally. When he talked loudly, his lips pulled up and to the left. When he laughed, no such pull occurred. The abnormality caused no physical pain, but it was horribly humbling for a boy entering his teen years. He also faced the disturbing possibility that it could get worse. What if the malady continued to work its way, grotesquely, up the cheek?

That didn't happen. But for a kid as sensitive as Jean, his was a distressing state: deaf in one ear, malformed at the mouth, no taller than a baseball bat. The gods, it appeared, had not chosen Jean Chrétien to smile on.

Maurice Chrétien thought the hearing problem was at the root of the disfigurement. Jean had always favoured his left ear, the good one, and this constant emphasis on one side of the face, the doctor reasoned, resulted in the pull. But many other doctors, as well as a neurosurgeon, discounted the possibility. They concluded that the frostbite had damaged a facial nerve, causing a muscle paralysis known as Bell's palsy. The condition usually occurred in young men, and often cleared up in a matter of weeks. In a small minority of cases, however, the paralysis was permanent.

The sudden appearance of Jean's disorder added weight to this diagnosis. It was only after Giselle's wedding that it began to show. It was only then that other youngsters started to mock him, calling him "crooked face" or taunting him with comments like "Talk straight, Baie boy!" Chrétien would later recount having a ready response to the gibes: "I may have a crooked mouth but not a crooked mind like you." Others couldn't recall his being so clever. They said he'd tell his tormentors that he liked his face the way it was, and they could go to hell.

The malady, which was a sensitive matter for him despite his outward bravado, unfortunately coincided with the start of his classical training at the seminary college in Joliette, an hour's train trip from his Shawinigan home. Joliette would be traumatic enough for Jean Chrétien. He didn't need added burdens.

In effect, the eight-year seminary college program rolled a high-school and university education into one. The curriculum for this, the prized educational route in Quebec, accentuated traditional disciplines such as mathematics, science, religion, literature, Latin, and Greek. No females needed apply. The schools were all-male bastions, thick concrete fortresses not unlike the penitentiaries to which their occupants often compared them.

The clergy running these institutions, particularly in Jean Chrétien's day, imposed tyrannical discipline. For modest infractions—tardiness, untidiness, talking out of turn—students were strapped, pulled by the ears, forced to kneel for hours at a stretch memorizing Latin passages. A worse form of punishment was arguably the endless isolation. Educational philosophy of the period held that learning required sequestration. Jean Chrétien, and thousands of boys like him, left home in September, returned at Christmas, then left again for the five months until the summer break. Telephone communication was permitted only for pressing matters. Sunday was the only visitors' day. Students remained confined, shut off from female companionship for ten months of the year, from ages thirteen to twenty-one. Rules required lights out and bed at 8:45 p.m., even if it was spring and the sun was still streaming down. It didn't matter if a student was twenty-one and had reached adulthood; he was treated the same as a fourteen-year-old. It didn't matter if logic defied this type of confinement; it was the system, and it didn't tolerate rebels.

Joliette was not quite as Draconian as some of the other seminary colleges. Ste-Anne-de-la-Pocatière, for example, was worse. So was Trois-Rivières. Joliette provided the students with more cultural and sporting relief from the militaristic regimen than did most. It was run by the Clairs St-Viateur, an order that did not enjoy as strong a reputation as that of the Jesuits who taught Pierre Trudeau, but that was still well up on the scale. Wellie Chrétien had sent Maurice to Joliette, and he was determined that the tradition continue—this despite the distressing fact that Joliette was a conservative stronghold, a breeding ground for Maurice Duplessis's Union Nationale. It was under the watchful eye of Duplessis, himself a seminary college graduate, that these educational establishments thrived. It was at his feet that the religious establishment knelt.

Jean Chrétien followed his brother Guy to Joliette. Guy had not earned a distinguished reputation in his three years at the institution. With a personality that drew mostly from the high-spirited Boisvert side of the Chrétien family, Guy suffered from what was clearly a character flaw in the eyes of the Joliette clergy: he enjoyed having a good time. Having often crossed swords with the master of discipline, Father Alphonse Galarneau, he earned the priest's lasting enmity one day by daring to challenge his dictatorship. Guy was officiating at a school hockey game, with Galarneau looking on. He made a bad call, or at least one Galarneau didn't agree with, and the priest leaned over the boards to tell Chrétien what a fool he was. Guy snapped back that Galarneau should mind his own business. The Chrétiens' reputation, as Jean arrived, was hardly enhanced.

Jean was not made for these places. There was too much mischief in him. He had already shown, at the Jardin de l'Enfance, that he wasn't an order-taker and now, at Joliette, he would show more of the same. He wanted to defy the rules the moment he arrived. He couldn't remain still or quiet, and he often displayed a defiant, sarcastic edge. It was all too evident on the day he was ordered to leave the class. The expression was one he heard often: "Chrétien! Prenez la porte." Literally, it meant "Chrétien! Take the door!" On this occasion, Chrétien replied, "Yes, Father. And where would you like me to put it?"

He drove them mad. Decades later the clergymen who had taught him would talk about Jean Chrétien as if there had been demons racing about inside him. His English teacher, the even-

34

tempered Father François Lanoue, could recall only one time, in his fifteen years of teaching at Joliette, that he was pushed to the point of taking a student by the ears. It was such an extraordinary moment for him that almost a half century later the memory was still vivid. "I could show you the very place where I did it, the very desk where he, Chrétien, was sitting." Chrétien, he said, was creating so much havoc and was so oblivious to Lanoue's reprimands that the priest couldn't help himself. In a fit of anger, he grabbed Chrétien. "I pulled his right ear, because his lips are on the left side."

Unlike Lanoue, Father Galarneau didn't initially realize that Chrétien was deaf in one ear. In the study room one day, when the demons in Jean were out of control again, Galarneau approached from behind, took him by both ears, and lifted him as if he were about to hang him from a clothesline. Chrétien recoiled with a degree of fury that Galarneau, having manhandled hundreds of students through the years, had never seen.

"He had a bit of a complex about his health," Galarneau recalled. "He suffered from it." Time after time, Jean could be found in the college's infirmary. He was often ill, or as many priests suspected, pretending to be ill. His trips to the school hospital became so regular that his instructors began referring to him as "Aesculape," the god of healing.

Following Jean's first year at Joliette, he was joined by his younger brother Michel. Fourteen-year-old Jean was terribly jealous of his brother. He had, in his own words, "a complex about it." Despite being two years younger than Jean, Michel, who had skipped a grade, was still much taller. He had spurted to almost six feet. Michel was also a better hockey player, so good that he was being watched by big-league scouts. His school grades were excellent, his physical condition tops. As well as towering over Jean, Michel looked older and more mature, as was evident when they went to the movies one day. They let Michel in but sent older brother Jean home because he looked under-age.

35

While it may normally be good to have a brother to lean on, Michel's presence at the school only made it more difficult for Jean. The competition between the two of them extended even to the boxing ring. On rainy days, when the students spent their break time inside, boxing was the big event. Chrétien vs. Chrétien, brother vs. brother, held the promise of so much wrath and raw-boned slugging that it was a feature attraction. Because Michel was the bigger of the two, he held the advantage. He also had better co-ordination, a fluidity that could be observed on the hockey rink, in the ease with which he pivoted and weaved. Jean, by contrast, was thin. The boxing gloves hung from his arms like bowling balls. The only edge he held, besides a couple of years in age, was a burning, competitive hunger. But that wasn't enough, as Michel made clear one day. With a roaring crowd of students gathered around, Michel pounded at Jean mercilessly. The smack of the leather against Jean's body tolled throughout the gym. When it was over, Michel had left his older brother with yet another disfigurement to add to the growing list—a broken nose.

After two years at Joliette, Jean began thinking of ways to get out. Even beyond all the hardships he was facing in the quarantine-like conditions, he couldn't really see the purpose of this form of education for him. He fancied himself a future engineer or architect ("I was very good in science") and reasoned, therefore, that he should be at the Shawinigan Technical Institute. There he could get a diploma and then move on to university. The added beauty of the technical school was that it was a regular day-school in his home town. He could come and go and live a normal teenage life, while pursuing the career path he preferred.

The regulations at Joliette decreed that if a student missed two months of school, for whatever reason, his year was forfeited. That got Chrétien thinking. If he could come up with a way to miss that period of time, he could perhaps convince his father to enrol him in the technical institute.

He needed a plan, a fantastic deception. Executing the great escape would be far more difficult than other scams, such as getting an over-age hockey player on his team. This time he would have to hoodwink the authorities at school, along with his uncompromising father and an older brother who was keeping a close eye on him.

He knew a student who had missed a lot of school when he'd had his appendix removed. From him, the idea came. Chrétien would put his acting ability to a severe test. He would fake appendicitis.

He'd seen the student's symptoms, the laboured movements, the pained expressions, and decided to talk to him to find out more. Where was the exact spot the pain was felt, or was supposed to be felt? What questions did the doctors ask? What was the appropriate reaction when the doctor touched the sensitive area? In effect, Chrétien took a crash course on the affliction. It had a major advantage over others he might have concocted: doctors more or less had to go along with the sufferer's story. There was no test to determine with certainty whether the patient had the disorder. If Chrétien could display the correct symptoms, the physicians would probably have to take his word for it. Since he had already missed some time at school, reaching the two-month point wouldn't be difficult.

Phase one of the plan—a manifestation of abdominal pain—was undertaken. Jean Chrétien buckled over in agony in the hallways of Joliette. He evinced magnificent pained expressions and sounds of anguish. Clergymen and classmates alike looked on with varying degrees of concern, if not alarm.

He was taken to the infirmary, where the school's medical staff examined him and where, having been well tutored, he splendidly followed the script. When the doctor touched the designated tender spot, the one that was supposed to trigger a wrenching cry of *douleur*, Jean Chrétien was up to the task. The doctor concluded that, indeed, he appeared to have the symptoms of appendicitis.

With sadness in his voice, he informed Jean that he would have to leave school and go home for rest and further examinations.

Chrétien managed to restrain his joy. He had perfectly executed part one of the great appendicitis hoax. Phase two, the bamboozling of the family, would be a bigger challenge. The two brothers at Joliette weren't a problem. Jean hadn't told Guy about the plot in advance, but Michel knew and covered for him. Guy soon found out and did the same. If asked, they said their brother was in terrible pain.

Wellie and Maurice, Jean knew, would be suspicious. Both were aware of Jean's chequered past, his hatred of boarding-school, and his capacity for deception. After a few days at home, he grew nervous, fearing the scheme would unravel.

Mrs. Chrétien phoned Maurice and asked him to examine Jean. Maurice did a check-up and the patient, rehearsed by now, reacted just the way he had with the doctor at Joliette. "He was a good actor," Maurice would recall.

Their concern mounting, the Chrétiens summoned a specialist, Dr. Justin Trudel. Dr. Trudel did numerous tests, taking Jean's X-rays and his white blood count. These turned up no further symptoms. Nor did Jean have nausea or a fever, other tell-tale signs. But these weren't present in every case, and Trudel found Chrétien otherwise convincing. The last thing he wanted to do was send the boy back to the school and have an emergency unfold—a rupture could lead to death—without Jean near a hospital. The medical rule of the day, especially on the appendix, was "When in doubt, take it out." Trudel decided there was no use running a risk. Better to take Jean to the hospital and perform surgery.

Unfortunately, no camera was around the Chrétien household to record young Jean's reaction to this announcement. Of the various scenarios his fifteen-year-old mind had envisioned, surgery wasn't among them. Clearly he had overplayed his hand. He should have eased off on the anguish and told Maurice things were getting better.

It seemed perfectly obvious that his one recourse was to come clean, to tell Trudel and the family and the administrators at Joliette that it was all a crass fiction, that he had made it all up, that, in fact, he was as healthy as a peach. But Jean was too terrified to own up. He was so scared that he could hardly talk. He simply could not bring himself to end the charade. With Dr. Trudel and big brother Maurice at his side, he went to Shawinigan hospital for the surgery.

At the hospital they cut him open, they probed, they examined, they looked again. The condition of an appendix was not something that could be easily ascertained, even in the full glare of the operating chamber. But Trudel and Maurice were sure enough. There was nothing wrong—not even an inflammation. Trudel could only wonder how the boy had been feeling such pain. A glowering Maurice knew the answer to that, but he wasn't about to say anything under the circumstances.

Having cut into Jean, Trudel decided there was no use leaving the non-vital organ in there. And so, though it was in mint condition, they took it out. When Jean came to, he got the news. His body was now minus one high-quality, tiny perfect appendix. Caught in his own trap, hoisted on his own outrageous petard, he went home to recuperate from one of the most gratuitous pieces of surgery Shawinigan had ever seen—and to prepare himself for the gallows.

Quite naturally, he feared that his severe father, when informed of the sham, would go berserk. Wellie had seen Jean perform some bad acts in his day, but nothing to match this. And if there was one thing he couldn't tolerate, it was lies.

The plot, however, had not offered up its final twist. By special providence, in the form of good brother Maurice, Jean was saved from whatever his father might have done. In the past, for fear of Wellie's rancour, Maurice had joined with his mother in preventing incriminating information about the boys from reaching him. Once, the director of Joliette sent a letter to the Chrétiens saying that their three sons had become such discipline problems at the college that he didn't want to see any of them back—not even Michel, whose grades were excellent. Marie Chrétien, who fortunately saw the letter before Wellie got home, conferred with Maurice. Hiding the letter, she dispatched him to Joliette to try to repair the damage. Maurice's intervention got the boys reinstated, and Wellie didn't hear a word of what had happened. It wasn't until several decades had passed, after Marie had died, that he found out. Going through the family papers one day, he came upon the note from the principal of Joliette.

After the appendectomy, Maurice realized what Wellie's reaction would be if he discovered the truth. So he substantially doctored the news of what had happened at the hospital, telling Wellie that it was probably a good idea to take out Jean's appendix. Jean's father would never hear the truth. Nor, for that matter, would the public at large. When the time came to enter politics, Jean Chrétien's years at Joliette were left out of the official biographies his campaign team distributed to newspapers. When the time came to write his memoirs, Jean Chrétien wrote of Joliette that he "missed a year of school because of sickness."

Though Wellie Chrétien had been steered into believing that Jean had done nothing wrong, his son still did not get to register in a new school. He had, as he had hoped, missed so much of his third year at Joliette that the college would not take him back for the rest of it. But when he asked his father to send him to Shawinigan Technical Institute, he got a flat refusal. It so happened that a new classical college, Séminaire Ste-Marie, had opened in Shawinigan that year. "You're going to Ste-Marie," Wellie said. That meant that Jean would not only be going back to a boarding-school, but that he would have to repeat a year he had already taken at Joliette. "I've already passed that grade," he told his father.

"You repeat it," Wellie commanded.

Because their father was kept unaware, the appendix scandal didn't take on the significance around the Chrétien home it otherwise might have. It did, however, convince Maurice, who was becoming more and more concerned about Jean, to take on added responsibilities. He became, in a sense, a second father, or, as John Maloney, a classmate of Jean's and later a psychologist, described him, "Jean's emotional father." Wellie was not a man with whom Jean could discuss heartfelt problems. Maurice, said Maloney, filled the void.

The eldest brother lectured Jean about his college performance. He told him sternly that his parents were making sacrifices to put him through school, and they weren't going to do it for nothing. He grew so angry one day that he grabbed Jean by the shoulders and violently shook him, demanding that he straighten himself out. Wellie, meanwhile, had taken to calling him the "black sheep." Every family had one, the father said, and Jean was theirs.

Jean's parents kept pointing to Maurice as an example: "If you don't study, you will not be like Maurice. You will never be a professional." Maurice, as Jean remembered him, issued threats. "If you don't behave, when you need my help I won't be there." But Jean would always tell him he didn't want his help anyway.

He had asked Maurice for help, however, the day he marched into his office and demanded something to make him grow. His coincidental growth spurt soon afterwards took him from his bantam height to a lean, mean six foot one. Until that point, Maurice hadn't realized the degree to which the height issue had troubled Jean. Of course he didn't think the vitamin pills would have any effect. When they apparently did, Jean thought Maurice was the greatest doctor since Banting. He had a friend who was also terribly short and terribly rankled by being so. Jean, of course, had the perfect remedy. "Go see my brother," he told the small boy. "He'll fix you up in no time."

Eventually, Jean's height would bring new confidence, bravado, and physical strength. For now, though, he was back at boarding-school at Ste-Marie, repeating a year he'd already taken and giving up on his idea of a career as an engineer or an architect. It had become clear to the Chrétien boys that their father deeply hoped one of them would become a lawyer and perhaps move from there to politics. A legal career would likely have been Wellie's own choice, had circumstances allowed him to go beyond the first few years of elementary school. Because of Michel's superior grades, Wellie had big hopes for him. But Michel, like Jean, had his own career dream: he wanted to become a hockey player. While at Joliette, he was offered a good junior hockey contract, which might have opened doors to the pros. He excitedly telephoned home with the news, but his father ordered him to reject the contract and complete his classical college education.

Wellie still had not given up on his so-called black sheep. He had not failed to notice how others looked to Jean to take charge. He was impressed by his son's organizational ability, particularly as it related to sports. With his energy level and leadership talents, Jean would be wasting his time in engineering or architecture, his father told him. He had already engaged him in several minor election tasks, such as putting up posters, passing out leaflets, and a common activity of the day, distributing twelve-ounce bottles of whisky with the Liberal Party label attached. Soon Wellie noticed that Jean had a particular relish for political activity and didn't need much pushing.

Though sports still intrigued him, it was obvious he'd never be a superior athlete. So he turned his attention to the other calling that put men on pedestals—the even bigger game of politics. When Jean came home for the summers, he began attending political speeches in Trois-Rivières. He and his friends Yvon Boisvert and Gilles Marchand were still just kids, and politics was an adult enterprise. But Jean would convince them that it was of the utmost importance that they go. They'd get the bus into downtown Shawinigan, then another to Trois-Rivières, then a third to the location of the rally. There they'd listen with rapt attention to Maurice Duplessis or Maurice Bellemare, the federal MP from the area, or the Trois-Rivières mayor, J. A. Mongrain, who could deliver the great stemwinders.

"Find me another fourteen-year-old kid who will travel thirty miles to go to a political speech," said Boisvert, recalling the days. "I tell you, sir, with him it was an obsession." From each speech the young Chrétien always took one lesson, one idea to chew over and store away. Gilles Marchand sensed that the orator who influenced him most was Mongrain, the Liberal who once unsuccessfully challenged Duplessis for his seat. "Mongrain was fantastic. He could speak for hours without a text and command attention. This is what Jean learned from him—speaking without a text."

During this time, the Chrétiens moved down the slope, from Belgoville to the street that fronted the factories. Now they lived right next door to the political nerve-centre of the town—the pool hall. Many a row between political partisans was fought there. Now, in the middle of the uprisings, a new kid appeared, a little hothead named Jean Chrétien. With his quick temper and adolescent bombast, he levelled broadsides at all comers, even the fierce Duplessis partisan Léonard Paquin. Paquin was a massive brawler who stood six feet tall and weighed 220 pounds. Once, the two got in an argument so vociferous that the spectators feared Jean would get badly hurt. His brothers rescued him that time and on several other occasions.

He began a friendship with Robert Lamothe, the son of a local jeweller. Lamothe was many years older than Jean, but that was part of his appeal. Lamothe was also dating Jean's sister Juliette, for whom the competition was tough. "I came by Jean's place a lot," he remembered. "I was afraid of his father. He was too strict, and so I didn't let myself get too close to him. But the girls were nice." He sometimes cruised the streets (on bicycles) with Jean or went to parties, where Chrétien was usually the first one to get things going, breaking into either song or a political debate. "Jean wanted everyone to know what he thought. All the time he was talking about politics, shouting about politics. It got so that we were teasing him about it. But it was obvious. He wanted to lead."

Chrétien had developed a slim, ramrod physique. His once blondish hair had darkened, and he favoured a pulled-back, pompadour look that, with his shadowed eyes, gave him a rather Frankensteinish mien and added to his alert, imposing presence. He was still too young, however, to have formed mature political opinions. Most of the spare time he had enjoyed in his early life had been given over to sports, not reading. But he had more familiarity with the political themes of the period than the average teenager. He had heard his father's pitches, made his bus treks to the political rallies in Trois-Rivières, and was now rehearsing his lines at the school for the blunt—the pool hall. His early rudimentary posturings reflected his father's tastes. He was four-square against the rampant patronage of the Duplessis machine, opposed to the political interference and wide sway of the clergy, and in keeping with his pro-conscription dad, less nationalist than great numbers of his Quebec brethren.

There could be no doubting where his allegiances lay. The family was of solid Liberal stock dating back to Confederation. Grandfather François was a powerhouse Liberal political organizer as well as a mayor. Wellie, who had become secretary-treasurer of La Baie Shawinigan, was a tireless foot soldier for the party in their election campaigns. Once, in Trois-Rivières, he had shaken the hand of his hero, Wilfrid Laurier. He told Jean about this special moment in his life, and Jean remembered it when he first shook the hand of a prime minister. When Louis St-Laurent passed through Shawinigan in 1949, Jean met him at the local arena. He walked away a proud boy.

All Wellie's sons became ardent Grits, with the exception of Marcel, who voted Union Nationale in a few elections. Besides having close friends who were running for the party, Marcel also owned a shoe store. So pervasive was the Duplessis machine that

Marcel believed that if he showed himself to be a Liberal, he wouldn't sell any shoes. Wellie could tolerate the odd vote of dissent, explained his son Michel, but he would never have allowed any member of his family to join another party.

Jean didn't displease him when, with his buddies from La Baie, he went to meetings of the Union Nationale to heckle. Once, at the back of a hall packed with the political enemy, sixteen-year-old Jean began a loud, impromptu pro-Liberal speech that caught the attention of those in the last rows. He carried on for three or four minutes before he and his young friends were unceremoniously led out into the street.

Jean returned to Joliette after doing his repeat year at Séminaire Ste-Marie. He had had another scholastically unproductive season. Since he was doing the year over again, he didn't feel he had to try very hard. Raymond Langevin, the director of Ste-Marie, said Jean was a lively boy whose interests were elsewhere. "He did nothing more than the minimum." His performance in language studies, in French and in the little English they taught, was undistinguished, Langevin recalled, "because he didn't push himself." Classmate Réginald Savard got the impression that "the quality of French was not important for Jean. He never attached much significance to speaking good English or French." But it was hard to blame him for his poor performance in English, said another classmate, Gabriel Houle. "The priest who taught it didn't know much more than we did."

At Joliette, Chrétien discovered that being Liberal wasn't easy. The great majority of faculty and students were Duplessistes. One of the few Liberal students was August Choquette, a future federal member of Parliament. "To be a declared Liberal in those days," Choquette recalled, "was almost an act of courage." But Choquette was not averse to challenging Joliette's ways. Once, he'd hopped the seminary fence to go to a restaurant, only to run smack into Father Galarneau on his return. Galarneau grabbed him by the ears, pulled him in front of his class, and had him stay on his knees for the entire period, memorizing the *Iliad*.

In the run-up to the 1948 provincial election, Choquette, whose father was a Liberal candidate, made it his mission to defend the Grit cause. One day he was lambasting the Duplessis machine right in front of Galarneau's office. He had gone on for some time, and was seeing only cold stares and being told that "we're all Union Nationale!" when suddenly, out of the pack came the voice of a younger student he hardly knew. The boy, Jean Chrétien, declared, "No, I am a Liberal too!"

Choquette was struck by Chrétien's boldness in baring his opinion in such a situation. It was a memorable political moment for Choquette, though not as memorable as a remark made sometime later by Father Galarneau. The obvious target of the comment were Liberals such as Chrétien and himself. "Imagine," Galarneau said, "these are the boys who think they might be our representatives someday."

But Jean had more on his mind than Father Galarneau's nasty observations. Because he had had to repeat a year, he now found himself in the same class as Michel. The pairing was a disaster for him, rekindling all his old insecurities. He initially kept pace academically, but soon fell further and further behind. Because Jean kept his jealousies secret, and wouldn't reveal how pained he was by his insufficiencies and handicaps, Michel didn't realize he was part of the problem. He attributed Jean's struggles to focusing too much on leading outside the classroom instead of in it. He became known as a rebel, someone who was always trying to change the system. If there was one thing the priests couldn't tolerate, recalled Michel, it was that.

Jean had become a constant source of worry for his mother. She visited him as often as she could, making the return bus trip to Joliette on Sundays. On the way home, she'd often stop by her son Gabriel's home to have tea with his young wife, Françoise. "I remember Mrs. Chrétien on those days," Françoise said. "She'd come off the bus and she'd be all dressed up and she'd come in and she would be so depressed. She would say, 'Jean, he isn't working at school. He's not going to make it through.'"

After completing his fourth year of an eight-year program, he was asked to leave Joliette. He'd continued to fall short of the standards of the school. Notes from the principal and meetings with Maurice and Mrs. Chrétien helped convince them that part of the problem was having three boys together at the same college, two of them in the same year. The Chrétiens didn't fight the decision this time. They agreed it was probably a good idea to transfer Jean somewhere else.

One school that was close, so they could keep an eye on him, was Duplessis's alma mater, the St-Joseph seminary in Trois-Rivières. There the level of discipline was severe, and Jean would be without his brothers. He'd be able to make a fresh start.

So, with a degree of hope, the Chrétiens enrolled their son in the giant, forbidding garrison twenty miles down the road. Had they been able to foresee what would happen his first day there, they might have thought better of the decision.

CHAPTER FOUR

ALINE

CHRÉTIEN had a friend at Joliette, a blustery, obstreperous hell-raiser named Marcel Chartier. As his personality would suggest, Chartier found it easy to get along with Jean. Their academic records were equally unimpressive, and Chartier, caught with questionable literature in his possession, had also been kicked out. He then moved on to the seminary college at Trois-Rivières, but he quickly fell into disfavour there as well. By coincidence, on the same day Jean Chrétien arrived at the school, in September 1951, Chartier was on his way out the door. He'd been expelled again.

On the face of it, his departure could have been viewed as a good omen by those wishing to see Chrétien's turbulent ways reformed. It meant there was one less bad guy to fall in with. But there was something else to consider. There was a little piece of patrimony Marcel Chartier was leaving behind.

Chrétien had arrived with all his luggage in tow and was heading down the corridor, ready to make his new start. From the other end of the hall appeared Chartier, who was known for his language, rich and foul. "Chrétien!" he shouted. "What the f—k are you doing here?"

The two scoundrels exchanged greetings and memories of the bad old days, then Chartier prepared to part. He pulled his hand from his pocket, shook Chrétien's, wished him well, and was off to look for a school that would have him. Chrétien felt something in his hand. He looked down, eyes widening with astonishment as he did, to find a key. On further inspection he determined that this wasn't just any key. This was the passe-partout. The master-key. The key to every door in the compound.

He arrived at Trois-Rivières a much taller young man than he had been at Joliette. He looked almost twice the size. He was thin but strapping, and more confident than he had ever been. He'd also begun fostering his "street fighter" image. The place his family had moved to—the row-housing section of La Baie, where the road fronted the factories and the St-Maurice River—was more rugged than up top in Belgoville. With the pool hall right next door, Jean got entangled in a few brawls and, by his own recollection, fared "very well" in them.

"The Chrétiens were known as a strong group of guys, and Jean was a good fighter," recalled Gilles Marchand. But he was all too ready, as Marchand saw it, to settle a dispute with fists instead of reason and all too ready to make decisions based on impulse instead of logic. Marchand got the better of him in a few scraps. "Jean and I weren't always on the same wavelength. We got in lots of battles when we played hockey and baseball. I wasn't too easy to push around, nor was he. When he didn't get his way, he was ready to go at it. But there were times he took the hits himself. He was a leader, but that didn't mean he could push everybody around."

Chrétien realized that at these seminary colleges, most of the students came from wealthier backgrounds than he and were not schooled in the lesser arts of muscle and might. Aware of his advantage, he readily displayed it. In his first days at Trois-Rivières, he inflicted a brutal beating on a tall, blond-haired student. When an argument at the front door turned mean, Chrétien erupted, levelling the poor kid with a series of lightning shots to the head that left onlookers dumbfounded. "I really socked it to him bad," Chrétien recalled. "In front of everybody." He was proud of himself for doing so. He believed he'd sent up a red flag, a warning to the others—"Don't mess with Chrétien."

Many of the students, Georges Trepannier for one, were stronger than Chrétien but lacked his streetwise know-how, those tricks of the trade that can mean triumph or disaster. Trepannier was a weightlifter, and though he was short, he had biceps like cement blocks. One day Chrétien got in a rhubarb with him in the gymnasium, and it wasn't long before the disagreement moved beyond words. Chrétien was at a disadvantage because he had injured his leg. The lower portion had been in a cast, which had been removed that very morning, leaving him tenderfooted and inhibited.

As the quarrel with Trepannier moved to the brink, Chrétien recalled an old fighter's ruse he'd seen enacted just a few months earlier in a pool hall Donnybrook in La Baie Shawinigan. In that fracas the fighting had spilled out of the hall into the parking lot— in full view of Chrétien who, sitting on his family's porch, was for once an innocent bystander.

The brawl's main participants were two of the town's foremost greasers. One of them was looking scared, backing off, favouring an injury of some kind. Sensing this, the other was overconfident, grinning, not realizing he was leaving himself open to the retreating party's sucker punch. That punch was the knockout blow.

Back in the gym in Trois-Rivières, with one leg out of commission, Chrétien now faced Trepannier, who was brazenly moving in on him. The summertime vision of the pool-hall battle came just in time. Chrétien, favouring his bad leg, sheepishly back-pedalled, looking as if he wanted no part of the showdown. Then, in a meteoric flash, bang! bang! bang! Trepannier's face was purple, and the bout was a rout.

"Oh, it was a fantastic thing!" Chrétien remembered. "He didn't fall over, but he slid against the wall, you know, and he was shaken. And after that he got up, and I knew how to box, so I caught him in two or three places."

Trepannier, spilling blood and humiliated, still tried to come at

Chrétien. But the street fighter told Trepannier's friends to take him away or he would put him out for good.

The next day Chrétien was called to the director's office, where he explained that he was only defending himself. "Well, maybe," the director said, "you can defend yourself a little less the next time." Georges Trepannier didn't soon forget the incident. In the school yearbook each graduate listed his favourite hobby, his favourite saying, and so on. Under *cauchemar* (nightmare), no one was surprised at what Trepannier wrote: "To be hit by a punch from Chrétien."

Chrétien loudly celebrated Trepannier's defeat, making sure his brothers back home heard all about it. In the Chrétien clan, such victories were the source of bragging rights, and Jean wanted to be certain everyone, but especially those like young nephew Raymond, knew. He thought the boy was getting, as they said in those days, a little too big for his breeches. Raymond was physically strong, which was part of the problem, but more than that, Maurice had been able to offer his son a lot of the material advantages that were not present in Wellie Chrétien's household. Raymond represented a new, more upscale breed of Chrétien, and he sensed a bit of uneasiness, even jealousy, on the part of Jean.

Raymond's father had emerged from a blue-collar environment to become a member of Quebec's professional class. Jean and everyone else could readily see the benefits: the beautiful cottage, the long holidays, the good clothes, the fancy car. The effect, Raymond believed, was to prick Jean Chrétien's ambition, to hasten and harden his desire to have those same advantages.

Jean and other members of his family sometimes visited Maurice's handsome cottage on Lac des Piles, north of Shawinigan. Those visits left no doubt in Raymond's mind that Jean too would have it all some day. The look on his face—"I'm just as good"—said as much, and there were other indications. Once, when Maurice had the two of them out doing chores, Jean made clear his disapproval. "Later in life I won't have to do this crap," he said pointedly. "I'll have somebody to do it for me."

Although he was as comfortable in a pool hall as anywhere else, few doubted Jean Chrétien's desire to be something in life. Raymond certainly sensed it, and so did Jean's younger brother, Michel. Jean surprised him one day, at age sixteen or seventeen, when he announced that he planned to go to Harvard and get an MBA. The other teenagers from his insular company town had hardly heard of the big American schools, much less talked about attending them. But Jean had now left thoughts of the Shawinigan Technical Institute far behind. He had new dreams mapped out. He'd get a law degree from either Laval or the University of Montreal. Then, to be one up on the others, he'd supplement it with a Master of Business Administration. In Quebec such degrees were supposed to be the preserve of the wealthy and the ruling class. But Jean Chrétien was the street fighter who wanted Harvard.

It was at this point that someone entered his life who could help him make it all happen.

Guy Chrétien, four years older than Jean, was the first to spot her. "I used to see this lovely girl passing by our house. I noticed she was probably the prettiest in town. I didn't think in terms of Jean going out with her. Never thought of that. But I probably told him how nice she was. She was a little young for me."

She had dark hair and big, round Virgin Mary eyes. She was slender, well-proportioned, and serene. Though hardly a girl of privilege, there was a sense of refinement about her. She looked not unlike the 1950s photographs of Jacqueline Kennedy. There was an air about Aline Chaîné that set her apart.

Her family was of even more modest means than the Chrétiens. Aline was the eldest of Yvonne and Albert Chaîné's six children. Her mother, a hairdresser, and her father, a labourer, had a difficult relationship. A touch of scandal hung about the household because, rare as it was in those days, the Chaînés were separating.

Aline was quiet, detached, and unusually ambitious. She wanted to study languages in Europe but, as was the case with most wishful girls her age, the nature of the society she lived in constrained her. At sixteen she attended the Shawinigan Business College, enrolling in a one-year accelerated program to become a bilingual secretary. Of the thirty-five students in the class, she finished first. "She was an excellent student," recalled a classmate, Claudette Germain. "She was smart and discreet. She dressed very simply but very well. She was always taking care of her smaller brothers and sisters. The river wasn't polluted at that time, and Aline would take them down there to play and swim."

The Chaînés lived two blocks down the street from the Chrétiens and, in the context of the modest offerings of the town, saw the Chrétiens as high up on the ladder. Mrs. Chrétien had her aristocratic leanings, befriending not the lowbrows in La Baie but the finer families in Shawinigan proper. There was a doctor in the family, a respected father who was secretary-treasurer of the village, and sons and daughters who were going to good schools. For an ambitious girl like Aline, this was important. It made the prospect of going out with a Chrétien boy all the more attractive.

When they met on a bus one day in the summer of 1951, Aline was fifteen and Jean was seventeen. Jean didn't know her well and hadn't seen her in some time. Like him, Aline had been very short but had quickly sprouted, and Jean was both surprised and impressed. "Are you *la petite* Chaîné?" he asked. They chatted and he told her he was planning a dance with some friends. While not suggesting he was asking her out personally, he said she might like to come along. Aline requested permission from her mother, who said it was all right as long as she had an escort. Aline phoned Jean and told him she could go, but only as his date. Unfortunately, Jean had already arranged female accompaniment for that evening and had to say no. Soon he was back to Aline, though, asking her to go to the movies.

He had, as his friend Lamothe recalled, good luck with girls.

Many liked him, including Lamothe's sister, who claimed to have been deeply involved with him. But whatever his past associations, Jean quickly became serious about Aline. "I was not interested in girls until Aline, really. I was shy and an awkward dancer, but there were parties. Some loved little parties and they would invite me. I had a series of girls who came dancing with me, but they were never girlfriends."

That summer, to help with the finances at home, Aline was starting work as a secretary for a chemicals plant. Given the family's domestic disharmony, her responsibilities were onerous. Though she and Jean went out a few more times, he soon had to return to "prison." They promised to write.

Chrétien still had three years of schooling left at the seminary college. He would be there, if he could accomplish the unlikely feat of avoiding expulsion, until he was twenty-one. He could see her in the summers, however, and there was also the possibility of masterminding some great escapes from the seminary during the school year.

Their relationship meant survival would now be easier for him than for many of the other students. In the later years at these colleges students found the isolation more and more absurd. Deprived for three-quarters of every year of normal social interaction with the female sex, the college boys, liberated in the summer, chased girls as if they were the only game in town. They grew up, so many of them, without time to play the field, and often ended up staying with the only girl they had ever had a chance to court. They also had to be on the alert—these were the years before sex scandals involving abusive masters became public knowledge—for wayward priests. Classmates would warn others of potential molesters. Chrétien had one teacher at Joliette "show an inclination for that." He noticed none at Trois-Rivières.

Because the sequestered form of education was the accepted elite method throughout the province, Jean and his friends weren't inclined to confront its dated and Draconian ways. They found themselves at times bitterly opposed to its precepts, but they also bore in mind that they were among the privileged few, that this was the best education the province had to offer, and that the system, supposedly tried and true, dated from the previous century. Long after they graduated, many of the students would use the word "unnatural" to describe their upbringing, especially in cases like that of Jean Chrétien. He was among those who were sealed off from their real homes not only for the high-school and university years, but for most of the years since he was five.

The impact of being quarantined under religious dictate for so long varied from student to student. Some emerged more hardened and independent, some socially and sexually backward, some religiously brainwashed, some credulous and shy, and some time bombs ready to detonate on the day freedom came. "We didn't have the right to have feelings or to express them," said John Maloney, the future psychologist who was a classmate of Chrétien's. How much better it would have been, he felt, to attend such institutions on a day-school basis, as some students did. "It was very severe, but we had to accept it. It was part of the game, a difficult game at our age."

Many admired the sanctity and devotion to learning of their teachers, but others found them hopelessly narrow. Their word was law, and opportunities for dissent were rare. "I remember Jean and I had a professor who was teaching us the history of Canada," said Laurent Déry, who attended classes with him at Trois-Rivières, "and he was extremely nationalist on the subject of Quebec. I would say that by today's standards, he was a separatist. His name was Plante, Herman Plante. He was so nationalist that our group, Jean and I and the others, were very reluctant to adopt what he was teaching us." The student who complained most bitterly about Plante, said Déry, was Jean Chrétien. He ranted about him, though always outside the classroom. "If you were resistant publicly to some of these teachings," said Déry, "they would say, 'You don't belong in this place any more.'"

Among the school's future stars was the brainy André Bureau, later head of the Canadian Radio-television and Telecommunications Commission (CRTC). He treasured his years at the seminary college for the grounding he got in philosophy, Greek history, and languages, as well as for the lasting friendships he formed, including one with Jean Chrétien. "Jean was already a fighter, in the sense that he was prepared to stand up strongly for what he believed in. He was never neutral. He made his feelings clear to everyone, whatever the consequences. He was never preoccupied with strategy or diplomacy. His code of values was such that the truth had precedence over everything."

Intellectually, because of this very directness, Chrétien was viewed as uninteresting. "He never used 'camouflage' to dress up his arguments," said Bureau. "He never pretended to be someone he was not. We had friends who were playing that intellectual game, and they were pretty superficial. Jean never pretended to be an intellectual and, in fact, would joke about it."

Though Chrétien detested the seclusion, the seminary atmosphere did play to many of his strengths. To survive, students were forced to develop and maintain friendship networks. Chrétien the extrovert, the reflex politician, the big mouth as some, less charitably, would have it, was the right fit. Because the students were thrown together morning to night, because they ate together, slept in huge dorms together, watched no TV together, they had to rely on interpersonal skills, which were political skills, skills Jean Chrétien had in abundance.

He found himself, as he had on rue Biermans, playing the role of *rassembleur*, the one who brings the rest together. Students liked him because, especially in the pre-Aline years, he brought life to an otherwise bleak atmosphere. In debates he got so worked up that he sprayed saliva around the room like a kid with a garden hose. In the graduates' newspaper, this gauche habit was referred to as Chrétien's "fetish."

He was not the star, not academically, politically, athletically, or socially. A far more articulate, charismatic, and learned figure, to take just one example, was his friend Jean Pelletier. This future mayor of Quebec City and top Chrétien adviser had the air of a young Jean Béliveau in his school pictures and was mature beyond his years. His ambition, as noted in the yearbook, was to have "une correspondence plus vaste que celle de Voltaire." He moved comfortably among the students, held forth on the major national and international issues of the day, and displayed a panache that the unpolished Chrétien could never hope to attain.

Although he was from the upper stratum of Quebec society, Pelletier was attracted to Chrétien because of their mutual interest in politics and because Chrétien was "full of pep." What most impressed him were Chrétien's instincts, so sound, and his drive. "Jean is a fighter. He must win." They did differ, in these college years, because Pelletier was more nationalistic. He attributed this to the fact that he and others had grown up in the more exclusively French environs of Quebec City, while Jean, in Shawinigan, was more exposed "to the Anglo-Saxon reality."

When Premier Duplessis came to his alma mater to meet the graduating class, Pelletier and Chrétien were there. Each student was introduced. When Duplessis heard Jean's name, the premier said, "From Shawinigan?"

Chrétien said yes.

"Your father is Wellie Chrétien?"

"Yes."

"Your grandfather was François Chrétien, mayor of St-Étienne-des-Grès?"

"Yes."

"Then you're a damn *rouge*."

Chrétien dined out on the story for years, always making it sound as if the premier was scolding him. Jean Pelletier remembered it differently. Duplessis was having fun, only teasing Chrétien, he said. "You know, it's amazing. Jean didn't like his regime. But Jean liked the man personally. . . . Duplessis himself was a charming man."

Chrétien surrounded himself with impressive friends like Pelletier, André Bureau, and Pierre Garceau, a theatrical *bon vivant* who was an intellectual with a keen interest in politics. Pelletier, Bureau, and Garceau were the student-politician equivalents of Trudeau, Jean Marchand, and Gérard Pelletier. Chrétien, by contrast, was the philistine of the group but was always too imposing to be pushed aside.

In the roughneck world of politics, nuance of thought was less important than the qualities he possessed: conviction and a forceful way of getting his point across. Back home in Shawinigan, the Junior Chamber of Commerce held a public-speaking contest for the youth of the region. Chrétien won it. Gérard Dufresne, a local businessman and one of the judges, gave his first-place vote to Chrétien because he was in command of his material, sure of himself, and "clear about the message he wanted to impart." Dufresne went home that night and told his wife, "Honey, this Chrétien boy is going to be somebody."

When the Chrétien family moved down the hill, they found themselves directly across from the municipal hall where politicians staged their rallies. In the summers Jean rounded up the crowds. Sometimes, before the principal speakers arrived, he was trotted out to do a warm-up act, delivering a blistering spiel of his own. From the very start he was spontaneous and unfearing in front of crowds, all instinct and reflex and emotion.

The college in Trois-Rivières did not stage an official model Parliament like many universities did. But a history professor did organize a mini-Parliament in his class, and Jean played Liberal leader. He began following federal politics closely in these St-Laurent years and also kept an eye fixed on the United States, not only for baseball, which he still avidly followed, but also for politics. The Democratic Party—"To err is Truman," said the president's opponents—was finally surrendering the White House after a run of sixteen years.

To those outside his circle, students like Robert Bilodeau, Chrétien was already "a servant of the Liberal Party." A Union Nationale partisan, Bilodeau admired Chrétien's forthrightness but saw little else that would take him places. He was too much of a carnival barker, said Bilodeau. There were no ideas coming from him, just noise.

Bilodeau was one year younger than Chrétien and, as one of the victims of his flash temper, had good reason to find fault. Chrétien, Bilodeau discovered, had a strange way of introducing himself. Having come up in the class a year after him, Bilodeau inherited Chrétien's desk. He was putting his supplies in it when he noticed that a book had been left behind. He began to leaf through it to see if it was Chrétien's. As he did, he felt a looming presence behind him. Before he could turn around, Chrétien had seized him and violently delivered a knee to his gut. "What are you doing with my goddamn book?" Chrétien shouted, ripping it from Bilodeau's hands. "That's my goddamn book!"

The volume, a Latin text filled with answers to the professors' tough questions, was not one Chrétien was supposed to have. Presumably, Bilodeau reasoned, he had not wanted to be discovered with it. Physically smaller and younger, Bilodeau did not try to resist or counter the assault. Because he was a strong Quebec nationalist, he later found himself in constant disagreement with Chrétien. But he didn't want to challenge him verbally either. It was too intimidating a task. Chrétien's vocal tactics, straight from the Shawinigan pool hall, were as aggressive as his physical ones. He drowned out Bilodeau and other opponents in a loud, brash torrent, never giving them a chance to speak. In Bilodeau's phrase, Chrétien was "une machine à parler." A talking machine.

He was also the keeper of the key—and that was no small treasure. Though sneaking out of the establishment meant running the risk of expulsion, many students took the chance. They wanted to see their girlfriends, have a drink, go to a movie, or simply find relief from the tedium and the incarceration. Because the school doors were locked so early, engineering an outing usually required a key. Chrétien didn't want the whole school to know he had it, for fear the secret would get back to the authorities, so he worked the game subtly. When the key was needed, messages were passed to him through intermediaries. Moreover, so the key could never be discovered in his possession, he had a secret hiding place—right next to the director's office. Embedded in the wall was a compartment that held the fire hose. The hose was folded into several layers. In between the third and fourth layer, Chrétien slid the passe-partout.

The key not only allowed free movement in and out of the building, but also gave access to forbidden rooms inside. The *curés* of the establishment, for example, were known to smoke some fine cigars. Chrétien's key allowed him to get into the cigar sanctum and make off with some high-quality stogies for the likes of his friend Pelletier. There was also a special priests' cafeteria, which featured better food than the detestable goulash served the inmates. That too was raided by the Chrétien brigade.

The choicest act of daring, however, was the nocturnal breakout. After the lights were off and everyone was supposedly fast asleep, the boys of intrigue tiptoed down the corridors, followed the key-man out the door, padded softly across the grass, and hopped the fence. Then, free under the stars, which was heaven for them, they ran downtown and installed themselves at the Blue Bird, where they enjoyed the booze, the smokes, the food, the girls, and the prospect of the even bigger challenge that awaited them: re-entry. Getting back into the college without getting caught was even more nerve-racking than getting out. The truants didn't know, for example, if an inspection of the beds had been made in their absence, if another student had ratted on them, or if the director of discipline would be waiting at the door.

But once safely back and tucked in, what a relief! "Oh," said Chrétien, "that was the thrill. You come back after an escape like that, and you get in your bed, and you have a great feeling that you have escaped once more." The next morning was just as fabulous. There was the post-mortem, the replay, when they, the daredevils, got to brag about it to all the guys.

Chrétien was always, as he said, "the guy who liked to play with danger," the one seeking the adrenalin rush. That was a big part of life for him, "The thrill [of being] outside of the rules."

He got away with it a lot in his initial years at Trois-Rivières, but in 1952, just before the final exams, he was caught and summarily thrown out of school. Being expelled didn't, in and of itself, overly concern Chrétien. His high-risk attitude prepared him for such eventualities. The real fear, however, was the prospect of facing his father. Wellie Chrétien had heard this type of news about son Jean too many times before, and Jean didn't want to break it to him again now.

He phoned his brother Guy in Shawinigan. Guy agreed that he could not turn up at the door with another pink slip, that a cover-up of some kind was in order. He told Jean that he had a friend in Montreal with an extra room in his apartment. Perhaps Jean could hide out there until the school year ended, then show up at home with an innocent look on his face.

Guy wanted to help because Jean had often come to his assistance, generously so. There was the time, for example, when Guy was studying medicine in Montreal so he could become a pharmacist. While visiting Jean at Trois-Rivières, Guy had let him know that the night-life on rue Ste-Catherine was taking its toll. He was out of cash. Jean reached into his pocket, pulled out a small wad, and handed it to him. "He knew I wasn't going to buy a book with it," recalled Guy. "He knew it was for *la belle vie.*"

Knowing Jean as he did, Guy had to wonder how he had come to have the money. His brother said it only took a little imagination. He had become an entrepreneur, he explained, working the school's black market. He was selling chocolate bars to hungry students, desperate for anything that didn't taste like potatoes. A friend got the bars wholesale, then passed them to

Jean, who peddled them in the corridors and took his cut of the action. Since the school officially outlawed the practice, the challenge, as was the case so often in Jean's early life, could be encapsulated in three words: avoid getting caught. Finding a place to store the chocolate bars was the trick. Fortunately, he had a jacket, a red windbreaker, with plenty of lining. He cut the lining just enough to allow him to slide in the thin Caravan bars. When he was accused of engaging in the activity, which was more than once, he pleaded innocent, telling the *curés* they could even check his locker. That they did. But when Chrétien opened it up for them, his red jacket, lined with the goods, drooped harmlessly from a hanger. "You see," Chrétien would say, "there's nothing here."

Guy's friend in Montreal was Léonce Gallant, and he agreed to take Jean in. Gallant lived on Laurier Street and had a landlady who, coincidentally, was also named Laurier. Jean enjoyed the irony of hiding from his father, the great Laurier admirer, in Madame Laurier's home on rue Laurier.

After waiting until the completion of the exam period, he returned home as if nothing had happened. "My dad did not know anything. So I told him a few weeks later, 'I'm not going back to Trois-Rivières. I want to go elsewhere.'"

He let it be known that a school in Charlottetown, Prince Edward Island, interested him, and his father said he would consider it. But that summer, all other interests were overtaken by the girl. He was falling in love with Aline. The prospect of moving hundreds of miles away from her to go to school was now out of the question. That left Joliette, but this college, like Trois-Rivières, didn't want him back.

The dilemma deepened. His father, unaware of Jean's expulsion, didn't think there was a problem. He could simply return to Trois-Rivières. Before Jean had to face the prospect of telling the truth about what had happened at the school, his brother Maurice again came to the rescue. Without telling his father, Maurice went to the directors at Trois-Rivières and got Jean reinstated. He was back in school, his father none the wiser, with Aline close at hand.

As he moved out of his teens and into his senior years at the college, Chrétien gradually became more responsible, the main factors being his ambitious spirit, Maurice's positive example, and most of all, the sobering influence of a girlfriend who herself was a model of sobriety and responsibility.

Jean made the short hike from Trois-Rivières to Shawinigan to see Aline as often as possible. He stayed at the home of a friend, Jean-Pierre Plante, so his parents wouldn't find out he was in town. Sometimes he used his brother Gabriel's home as a base, asking him and his wife, Françoise, to cover for him. But there was soon no need for Jean to camouflage anything about his relationship. His mother became enchanted with Aline. She appeared to recognize immediately that Aline could be the force to change his ways. In those years, "Mom was taking care of me more," he said. "She was afraid that I was going to turn bad. . . . Aline was my girlfriend and Mom encouraged it very much. . . . My mother loved Aline. She said it was a blessing when Aline arrived in my life."

On Sundays Mrs. Chrétien and Aline travelled together to Trois-Rivières. Though those were visiting days, the boarding-school countenanced no visits from girlfriends. "But Mom would take the bus . . . to Trois-Rivières with Aline and get me out of the college. [She] let me spend two or three hours with Aline, and we would go to the movies or places like that. After that, she would get on the same bus and go back with my girlfriend. And Mom would not have seen me for more than ten minutes."

When the other students saw Mrs. Chrétien get off the bus with Aline, leave her on the sidewalk and head to the principal's office, then come out of the school with Jean in tow and turn him over to his girlfriend, they were incredulous. Recalled Chrétien: "The guys said, 'What a woman she is!'"

Classmate Laurent Déry, for one, would never forget those moments. "I was so envious of Jean. He had this very pretty, fragile girl and he could see her every week. Every week! Me, I had a girlfriend too, but she lived farther away and I could only get out every two months or so to go and see her."

On non-visiting days, when Aline was in Trois-Rivières and Jean couldn't get out of the college, he would go to the gate to meet her. They could be seen holding hands through the linked fence, whispering to one another. His spare moments and spare thoughts turned more and more from adolescent hi-jinks to her. He began to realize that if he was to get to law school and fulfil his dreams of going to Harvard and making it to the professional class like his brother, he had to dedicate himself to work.

This was a critical point in his life. The rogue was becoming responsible. "I realized at that time that I wanted to marry Aline eventually, and I had to behave to be able to find a good job and have a home and all that." He was driven by the desire to build a successful life for himself and the girl he was planning to marry. "I became obsessed by that—that I had to succeed in order to become a lawyer, to become a politician, to have a family, and so on. That made me think about serious things. The fun was over at that time, you know. Real life had hit me."

Déry soon began noticing the change. He was shocked once when, with revelry on his mind, he went to see Chrétien, the most likely candidate for it. Déry had got his hands on the key to a vault that not even Chrétien's passe-partout could open—the wine cellar. He'd accidentally come upon it while eating with some nuns in the cafeteria. The wine cellar teemed with prizes, some of them of cheaper quality for use at the Eucharist, others of impeccable vintage for visits by the premier of Quebec. Déry and friends raided the cellar one night, stole off with a few cruets, then ran to round up some celebrants. The party was to start right after the surveillance priest took his leave.

Having made a dash to Chrétien's quarters, Déry excitedly put the news to him, only to get a jolting response. "No thanks," he said, "I'd rather not." The party went on without Chrétien, who had concluded that the risks were too great.

Déry was soon back with another proposal. He told Chrétien he and a group of friends were planning a midnight escape to the Blue Bird. Again, Jean turned him down. He had some studying to do.

Chrétien's new attitude led to higher grades. He was soon scoring above average, just missing the top rung. In his last years at Trois-Rivières he received honourable mentions in several courses: Canadian literature, eloquence, Canadian history, geology, physical education, astronomy, and social doctrine. The honourable mentions indicated that he had finished just below the top three students in each of the disciplines.

Though some had thought him fine with fists but frail of mind, he was beginning to prove otherwise. His grades were high, the friends he kept were intellectually impressive, and the courses he took were the same. Each student at Trois-Rivières had a spiritual director, the clergyman to whom he took his personal problems. One year, Chrétien, who would normally have been expected to choose the hockey coach, surprised his fellow students by selecting a literature professor, Louis Martel. No one else chose Martel. A brilliant and witty intellectual who didn't suffer fools gladly, he was too daunting for most and tended to intimidate those not hovering up in the stratosphere with him. He was not keen on advising Chrétien at first, but the two of them eventually got along, and Chrétien would describe the experience as having a significant impact on him. It helped him realize there was more to life than bats and balls.

Chrétien's curriculum that year included an in-depth study of philosophy—Hegel, Marx, Kant, Aristotle, and Plato. He studied the writings of St. Thomas Aquinas, the thirteenth-century Christian theologian whose teachings underpinned Roman Catholicism. Logic, morals, and metaphysics were drummed in. In letters, he read Racine, Molière, and Corneille. Then, as if the faculty had political careers in mind for their students, the school taught speech composition and delivery in the fifth year of the eight-year program. Jean Chrétien's work in these two areas was responsible for his high grade in the part of the curriculum that went under the title "eloquence."

While strong in some areas, the curriculum had major gaps in others. The course on Canadian history might well have been renamed French-Canadian history, so perfunctory was the coverage of English Canada. The history of Europe was taught, but almost everything focused on France. An egregious oversight was the United States. The school's program virtually ignored American history and politics. Also absent were courses on economics and commerce. Graduates were therefore highly ignorant about the superpower to the south and the lifeblood economic links Canada had to it. Chrétien's group filled in some of the blanks through close attention to the media, and they took a strong interest in current events at the provincial, federal, and international levels. When the Duplessis government's Tremblay Commission brought down a major study on immigration, for example, Jean Pelletier read it in its entirety and discussed it with Chrétien and the others.

The school put considerable emphasis on teaching the French language. Two periods a week were also given over to English. To the surprise of many, Chrétien continued to show no special enthusiasm for learning English, despite his Harvard ambition and his plans for a public career. His parents sent him for some private lessons one summer to help him along, but back at school he again found himself with an English teacher from whom it was difficult to learn. Henry Boudreau, an American francophone, was a man respected for his knowledge but without classroom skills. He could exert no authority over the students, and his lessons soon dissolved into chaos. If Boudreau turned to the blackboard, hoots and hollers filled the air, and pens and pennies smashed against the windows. Whenever there was order enough, Boudreau had students come to the front of the class and make a speech in English, either from memory or from a text. Because Chrétien liked to talk in public so much, the teacher had him up to the front frequently. As Boudreau remembered it, Chrétien performed better than most. The embattled language teacher would be surprised, years later, when Chrétien arrived in Ottawa claiming to know very little English.

Wellie Chrétien, who had worked hard to learn proper French and who had taken a correspondence course in English, maintained a close watch on his children's progress in the languages. He expected much from his boys because they were going to exclusive schools. But he frequently had to chastise Jean for using street French at the dinner table. "I'm not sending you to these schools to speak like that," he'd tell him.

Not many of Chrétien's classmates took note of the rough quality of his French. These were the days before the Quiet Revolution, and the calibre of French spoken outside the classroom was not the issue that it became later. None of Jean's friends were telling him then that he spoke the language of Molière poorly. No one, not even the precious Aline, was joking then that the only thing worse than his second language was his first.

CHAPTER FIVE

JEAN FIDÈLE

J EAN'S MOTHER was ill off and on through 1953 and early 1954, but no one in the family was unduly concerned. Her setbacks didn't seem overly serious. She had only turned sixty, and was still physically strong and warm of spirit. The hypertension she suffered did necessitate a slower pace. But she was told to relax and get a lot of rest.

Marie had had more free time since her kids had grown up, and she looked forward to one day realizing her dream of visiting Europe. She had derived so much pleasure from her trips west, in particular one to Banff National Park in the early 1940s. It left her with a deep appreciation of Canada and its beauty. "This probably affected us as children, her family being in Alberta," said Michel. "When she returned from her trip, she had just a few pictures to show, but I remember the great lengths she went to in describing the beauty of the park. I was just a boy, and I listened to every word about everything she saw. She went on for so long, for hours it seemed. And I remember when I finally went to that park myself, it all came back to me. All the words she said, all the detail."

The children, had they any idea that time was so limited, would surely have pooled their resources and given her that longed-for trip to Europe. Marie Chrétien wasn't the type to complain, though, so no one really knew how sick she was.

"My mother would say there was always something positive in any situation," remembered Michel. "We were raised in that spirit." All her children had fond memories of her, whether she was serving wine to Jean's young hockey champions, or hiding her sons' bad behaviour from their stern father so they wouldn't get in trouble, or simply carrying herself in that noble way she had, bringing pride to them all.

All she wanted was that her children be good and that they be educated. By 1954 she could be satisfied that they were both those things. But for so many of them, the best years were still ahead and their mother would never live to see—and this is what hurt her sons and daughters the most—the real fruits of her efforts.

Friday, April 15, began as a warm spring day. Mrs. Chrétien had been back from a hospital stay for quite some time and was feeling reasonably well. Son Guy had, by this time, taken his degree in pharmacy and was an intern at a pharmaceutical store in the town. The night before, he'd gone to a show with friends, stayed for a few drinks, and got home very late. He decided to sleep downstairs in the *salon* so he wouldn't disturb anyone. In the morning he awoke to find his mother taking his cover and gently tucking it in around him. This was the last thing he remembered of her. "She tucked me in like a little baby," Guy recalled forty years later, choking back tears at the memory. "Just like she always did."

Maurice Chrétien was at his doctor's office, where the patient load, as always, was heavy. His mother called him early in the afternoon. "Son, I don't feel too good. Maybe you could come over." Because it was so warm, Maurice found her sitting on the porch. She was weak and in some pain, but when she tried to describe what was wrong, she was vague. Maurice himself was puzzled about the nature of her condition. He talked to her for a moment, then suggested she go inside and lie down.

She was a big woman who had become heavier with the years. While supporting her and offering words of encouragement,

Maurice led her inside and upstairs to her bedroom. He was gently helping her on to the bed when he suddenly felt her go limp and pass out in his arms. She was dead by the time her head touched the pillow.

Maurice tried to compose himself, then began the horrible task of alerting the family. He found his father at Marcel's shoe store. Never a man to show emotion, Wellie remained stoic on hearing the news.

Gabriel, following Marcel into the business, had opened a shoe store in nearby Louiseville only a week earlier. His mother had made the trip for the grand opening, and he remembered how happy she had been. When the phone rang, the shoe store was busy and Gabriel was sitting on a stool fitting a customer. He was called over to the phone and heard Maurice tell him in a cracking voice, without mentioning the word "death," that something terrible had happened to Mother. Gabriel hung up the phone and, dazed, went back to the stool and continued fitting the shoe. Seconds later, a great well of tears burst through his eyes. He got up from the stool and barely made it to the back of the store.

One of the daughters, Giselle, was in Montreal. A few hours before her call from Maurice, she had received a letter from her mom. In it, her mother thanked Giselle for spending so much time with her when she was sick. She was feeling better now, she said, but wanted Giselle to know how grateful she was.

Michel was still at Joliette. They let him finish writing his chemistry exam before telling him. When he went up to the front to hand it in, the teacher told him the director of the school was waiting in the corridor with a message. Michel too had just received a letter from his mother that sounded promising. After conferring with the director, he boarded the seven o'clock train for Shawinigan.

Jean was one of the closest to his mother. Concerned for his well-being, she had spent more time with him than the others. Like his brothers and sisters, he knew she was not well but had no idea of the gravity of her condition. He was at the college in Trois-Rivières when the phone call came. He received the news and went straight to the chapel. He then went to the director's office to get permission to return home.

The family gathered around the bed where Marie Chrétien's body lay. Françoise Chrétien had driven in from Louiseville with her devastated husband, Gabriel. "Their mother was still in the bed," Françoise recalled. "They hadn't changed her position. All those six boys stood around the bed. I saw all of them just cry like kids, looking at their mother with all the love they had." Wellie, meanwhile, continued to show little emotion. "He had a very straight face," said Françoise. "He wouldn't say a word, and I remember Maurice was always around him."

Doctors determined the cause of death to be a massive hemorrhage in the wall of the heart. At the funeral, family members were proud that the turnout was so large—especially since none of the children was yet in politics, and people therefore weren't coming out of duty. Gabriel lost control when the coffin was being placed in the ground and had to be escorted away. Jean managed to maintain his composure, but the wound was very deep. He had much preferred his mother to his father. While she was certainly as ambitious for Jean as his father was, and insisted on schooling and manners and the rest just like Wellie, she had done it with warmth. His mother had had what his father lacked: a sense of humour and an understanding spirit. She was a Boisvert.

After Marie's death, the message from Wellie was that everyone had to push ahead as hard as if not harder than before. "My father lived all his life for his children," said Michel. "He wanted us to continue to go to school, and he would support us." Bleak months followed her death, but soon Jean was able to bring his father great news. He announced his intention to pursue the one career that Wellie valued most highly and had dearly hoped one of his sons would follow—law. When Jean told him he was enrolling at Laval, Wellie's face transformed. "It was the very best thing for him that Jean could ever have done," said Guy. "It was like a dream for him."

Jean had first shown his passion for the law in the Trois-Rivières graduates' yearbook. He wrote that his ambition was "To become a disciple of Thémis" (the Greek goddess of law) and to have his own hockey club, complete with uniforms. His favourite song was "Blue Moon," his favourite spot the Blue Bird, and his favourite activity "To go parking in the graduates' parking lot." The yearbook editors gave summary comments on each student. For Chrétien they wrote, "A future lawyer who will bring great service to his community, thanks to his sense of equity."

He chose Laval over other law schools for two reasons. First, it was the traditional law school for students from the Shawinigan–Trois-Rivières area. Many of his friends were going there. Second, Quebec City was the political nerve-centre. The provincial legislature was within walking distance of the campus and daily treks to Question Period were practically part of the curriculum. Premier Duplessis and many top political figures lived in the Château Frontenac hotel, which was close to the school. Prime Minister Louis St-Laurent also had his home and law offices in the city.

When Jean arrived in Laval, a friend, the notorious Jean-Claude Ladouceur, had already arranged an apartment for him. Ladouceur was known as Le Chat (the cat), because he was always on the prowl. He was legendary at the law school for holding the record for flunking out more times than any student in Laval's history.

Le Chat's father was a former school chum and political confidant of Maurice Duplessis. Ladouceur revered Duplessis, and the premier, ever eager to keep his sycophants happy, gave him good reason. There were nice little gestures, such as the one on Le Chat's birthday. The day before it, he received a call from Duplessis's secretary. "The Boss wants to see you," she said. "Tomorrow. Two p.m." Ladouceur was worried, thinking he'd done something wrong. Once he had been seen on campus with the Liberal

August Choquette. A ranking Union Nationale member told him that he wasn't helping his career prospects by being seen in such company.

At the appointed hour, Le Chat came to Duplessis's office, where he found the usual group of officials milling around. He walked in, and the premier greeted him. "Jean-Claude, have a seat. How are you?"

Le Chat nodded. "Fine," he said.

Duplessis looked at him solemnly. "Tomorrow is your birthday?"

"Yes."

Duplessis reached behind his desk. "I have a present for you." He pulled out a framed portrait of himself, dedicated to Ladouceur. Le Chat offered his deepest thanks and left, thrilled beyond belief.

Le Chat liked to cultivate friendships among Liberals for reasons, given his close relations with the Boss, many of the Grits came to suspect. When he heard that Chrétien, whom he had known in Shawinigan, was enrolling at Laval, he found him an apartment next to his own and in the perfect location—on Quebec City's most famous street, the Grande-Allée—right between the campus and the Legislature, a short walk to both.

Laval University was a century old. Located in the *quartier latin*, Quebec City's old quarter, the school enjoyed a special status among Canadian universities. None featured such a marvellous blend of high culture, redolent history, and quaint beauty as Laval. Its twisting, sliver-thin streets, rising and cascading against the backdrop of the St. Lawrence and the Château Frontenac, evoked previous centuries. Its grey stone architecture was eternal yet cosy. Not much had changed at Laval. Students still stayed in ancient rooming-houses, with cafés and bistros below. In language, manners, and attitude, it was everything La Baie Shawinigan was not. If the symbol of survival in Chrétien's hard-nosed home town was strength, in the Latin Quarter it was finesse.

When the tall, lean, hollow-cheeked form of Jean Chrétien first set foot on the cobblestones in 1955, Quebec was entering a period of profound transition. The old-fashioned power system, which was dominated by a bossist political culture in league with the clergy, was giving way to a sweeping modernization and enlightenment that would come to be known as the Quiet Revolution.

Chrétien was twenty-one years old, an age when most boys with his background had started full-time careers. Yet he had four years of law school ahead of him, and was thinking of more post-graduate studies in business. Though he struck others as impatient with detail, he had a good record in technically oriented school subjects. "You know, I was thinking law, because of my dad, but my mind was more scientific. . . . My brothers were all in science. And I have to tell you that I was very good in mathematics and physics." At Trois-Rivières, out of a possible 20, he had scored 18s and 19s in these disciplines. "So it was always in my mind that it would be easier for me to go into a scientific branch than law. But Dad was pushing me in law. So I was thinking [that] if I was to be a lawyer, perhaps I could work to be, at the same time, a graduate in business. It would be a good match."

The law school at Laval was among the nation's easiest. The workload was less than onerous, the atmosphere casual, and the attitude of the professors, most of whom had more consuming jobs as lawyers, relaxed. Classes were from eight to ten in the morning and four to six in the early evening. For the hours in between, students headed off to restaurants, political clubs, the Legislature, home for a nap, or in a minority of cases, to the library to do some work.

Having lived through a youth of boarding-school confinement, Jean Chrétien now stepped into the daylight of liberty, an atmosphere free of rules, free of clergy, free of the disapproving glare of his father. He arrived at Laval with much of his college group intact. Pelletier, Garceau, and Bureau enrolled in the first year of law school with him. The rabble-rousing Marcel Chartier was there, as was August Choquette, another character who could be relied upon to bring life to the proceedings.

One of the school's first orders of business was the selection of a president for the class of about fifty first-year students. Chrétien checked out the field of potential candidates. He knocked on Garceau's door, confirmed that his friend was not entering, and declared his own interest. He campaigned door-to-door among the students, gave speeches wherever groups of them were assembled, and distributed literature outlining his favourite Liberal Party themes—the need for more aid for students and more democracy in the educational system.

His hard campaigning won him the election, and he set off on a course of political activism. In those days to be a Liberal at Laval was, by definition, to be anti-establishment. The law faculty tended to lean towards the Union Nationale. Many teachers were working lawyers who realized that to get ahead, to get that judgeship or sinecure or big client, they had to flatter the ruling clique. Students affiliated with the Liberals found it much harder to get government grants, bursaries, and favours than the Duplessis backers. The latter, for example, received free of charge an essential resource book—the *Revised Statutes of Quebec*—while Liberal students had to pay ten dollars for it.

Chrétien wanted to address this problem, so he and Garceau decided they would go right to the top: Duplessis. Chrétien had experienced that memorable moment with the premier at Trois-Rivières, and Garceau's family knew both him and his secretary. They worked up enough courage to knock on his door and were ushered into an office of flowers, Krieghoff paintings, baseball and boxing souvenirs, and the forceful, sparkling eyes of the premier himself.

As a simple matter of democratic rights and fairness, the two young Liberals argued, all students should get the same deal on the statutes book. But Duplessis didn't like the word "rights." To be university students was a matter of privilege, he countered. They could afford it, and they were therefore privileged. He further explained that the students who supported his government had faith. "So they are rewarded for their faith. You, Chrétien and Garceau, don't have the faith."

Too young and naïve to be intimidated, Chrétien and Garceau maintained an aggressive posture and ultimately a compromise was offered. Duplessis told them he was glad they had come to see him, and he gave them a deal on the books—five dollars each instead of ten. The two students could hardly wait to get back on campus to tell the others of their exploit. "We were so proud of this," Garceau said. "We told everyone."

Chrétien soon joined the campus Liberal organization, quickly asserting himself at their monthly meetings at the Reform Club. He was also making himself known among the senior Liberals in Quebec City. Garceau remembered him going to their offices or homes and simply introducing himself: "I'm Jean Chrétien, a law student at Laval and member of the Liberal Club. If you have a moment, I want to get to know you." When fellow students wondered how he could do this, he'd say, "Why not? If the guy doesn't want to talk to me, he'll shut the door."

Social life for the students in Chrétien's circle had its focal point at Chez Houde, a restaurant-bar where the political debates were hot, the girls were chic, and the meals were served at fifty-nine cents to avoid a tax that applied to anything that cost sixty cents or more. Chrétien appeared at Chez Houde only occasionally and usually left one beer later. He had tried drinking a few times at parties in Shawinigan and had made a fool of himself, so he tended to avoid the urge. This behaviour also reflected the influence of Aline Chaîné. Aline, whom he was seeing virtually every weekend, was abstemious. She hated drinking and forcefully made her views known to Jean. So he didn't drink very much, and he didn't smoke. Wellie had given Jean permission to smoke, but he tried it and didn't like it. Free of two of the vices that enhance student life, Chrétien also swore off on the third: chasing women. He had vowed to Aline before leaving for Laval that all other girls would be considered forbidden fruit. He was so faithful to this pledge that his friends at Laval started calling him Jean Fidèle.

Garceau and the others made many attempts to shake him from his temperance, but Chrétien was the new responsible man. No longer troubled by the lack of discipline that plagued his adolescence, he moved towards the other extreme. Attendance at classes was not compulsory. Many students slept in, missing the morning session, while others got too comfortable in the bars and skipped the four-to-six lectures. For Chrétien, however, the same Chrétien who skipped out whenever the possibility arose at Joliette and Trois-Rivières, attendance was sacred. "Never missed a class," said Garceau. "Never. And he did his homework. Serious? Oh, he was serious. He was too damn serious. He was boring at times."

Through much of his youth, Jean Chrétien had broken rules to escape the bounds of confinement. Now came the fine irony. With the arrival of freedom, he was imposing those bounds on himself. Louis Batshaw, an anglophone student, shot pool with Jean Fidèle at the Reform Club, and occasionally had dinner at his apartment. He discovered Chrétien had an interest in classical music and lent him some of his records. "I saw him as an ambitious and able person. He was aggressive but warm. He was shrewd, nobody's fool." Of all the bunch that hung around together at law school, he said, "Jean Chrétien was probably the most serious."

Students divided themselves not only along political lines, but also more pointedly along social lines. There was the bourgeois class of law student, the young men from the wealthy families of Quebec City. Then there was the country crowd from La Mauricie, the area around Shawinigan and Trois-Rivières. As a member of this second group, Chrétien, like the others, resented the categorization that came with it. They were looked upon by some of the Grand-Allée types as uncultured hicks of lesser intellectual aptitude.

Voting for student positions frequently divided more along social lines than political ones. To a large extent, the political classification fit neatly with the social one: down-home Grits vs. upper-class Duplessistes. The Union Nationale supporters taunted rivals with put-downs like "You should feel lucky we even let you bastards vote."

One of Chrétien's Shawinigan pals was Guy Germain. Because the group already had one member known as Le Chat, it was only fitting that another be called the Dog. Germain was Le Chien and, like Le Chat, he too was a Union Nationale man. Some testiness between him and Chrétien could therefore be expected. One night at Chez Houde the cheap beer was flowing, the rhetoric was impassioned, and the Dog was in fine form, taking the measure of Jean Fidèle at every opportunity. Germain fancied himself the stronger debater. Once, he had chided Chrétien with a story about Cicero, the renowned Roman orator. He described how Cicero had practiced speaking with pebbles in his mouth. If he could make himself heard through pebbles, Cicero reasoned, how wonderful he would sound upon removing them. "Jean," the Dog offered, "your problem is you never got the pebbles out."

At Chez Houde that night Chrétien finally decided that his friend had levelled one too many broadsides. It was time to fire back. "Germain!" he shouted bitterly across the table. "The only reason why you, you bastard, are at Laval today is because you kiss the ground that Duplessis walks on!" The insult was loud and froze the room into silence. It was obvious from the reaction of the rest of the group that Chrétien's blast had overstretched the bounds of appropriate polemics. Embarrassment crept over him. Slowly, normal conversation resumed, and eventually Chrétien made his way over to Germain and explained that he hadn't really meant what he had said. They shook hands.

Around this time, Chrétien met a fellow student who would have a significant impact on his thinking. Most of his friends had seen little of Canada beyond the small corner they lived in, but Guy Lebrun was different. Lebrun was a young man with a national vision. He was from St-Tite in La Mauricie but had spent much of his youth in English Canada, first in New Brunswick and then at a seminary college in the then very English nation's capital, Ottawa. When Chrétien met him, he was a vocal anti-nationalist, with opinions on Quebec roughly paralleling those of Pierre Trudeau. Quebec, he agreed, merited a broader presence on the national stage, but he attacked Quebec-firsters as parochialists who knew nothing about the rest of Canada, not the language, not the geography, not the people. There was perhaps no greater federalist at Laval than Guy Lebrun, and he and Chrétien quickly began a lifelong friendship. "I told Jean and the others very often that my country is Canada. I don't want to say I was the main influence, but I think Jean was impressed by the vision."

The other end of the spectrum was represented by a future leader of the Union Nationale, Gabriel Loubier. Loubier had wealthy parents and drove around the *quartier latin* in a sumptuous, creamy convertible, sometimes with Jean and Aline as passengers. Loubier believed that the autonomist-leaning Union Nationale was the vehicle to win back the powers that the federal government had taken from Quebec in the Second World War. The Union Nationale could assure Quebec of its grand place because, Loubier argued, it was the only provincial party not tied to a federal one. It was the party, in his view, that spoke to Quebeckers' hearts, that grouped together all the political and social tendencies, Left and Right, as one bold instrument. This, the autonomous, inward-looking, proud Quebec, was one vision of the province's future. The other was that of a stronger, more open Quebec, enhancing its unique status within the Canadian landscape.

Loubier often debated with Chrétien at Chez Houde. He found Chrétien to be a driven, committed youth, so palpably a politician. "You knew it then. You knew he was a politician of the future. You just had to look at him. It was obvious. It bore a hole in your eyes." During their debates, Chrétien would rant against the injustices and the corruption of the Duplessis system. "He made it clear to anyone he talked to," said Loubier. "He was a fighter. He was brutal in what he was saying."

Chrétien had no shortage of targets for his harangues. In Quebec so much was determined by favouritism. Party affiliation and patronage decided, as Chrétien put it, "if your village got an asphalt road, if your organization got a grant to hold a sports event, if your restaurant got a liquor licence, and if your university got funding. Duplessis seemed omnipotent. His enemies, such as Pierre Trudeau, were denied teaching jobs; his friends' illegalities were overlooked by the police; and corruption was so much a part of the system that most people just came to accept it and hope for a piece of the action."

To prove the point, the Laval gang decided to set up a summer job for Le Chat's cousin, Jean Ladouceur. Since he was a good Union Nationale man, they knew it would be easy to arrange something for him. The group's great impersonator, August Choquette, picked up the phone and took on the voice of one of Duplessis's cabinet members, Solicitor-General Antoine Rivard. He called one of the pillars of the patronage system, who recognized the Rivard voice without Choquette's even having to state the lie. "I have a young man here," Choquette intoned, "a good party man who needs work for the summer so he will be able to pay his school fees next year. His name is Jean Ladouceur." Ladouceur was called within days and given a make-work job, the most strenuous aspect of which was the weekly trek to an office to pick up his cheque.

Chrétien neatly apportioned his time among the three things that now counted for him: Aline, his legal studies, and politics. His first sortie against Duplessis had been his visit to the premier's office with Pierre Garceau. Now he organized a bid to disrupt a session of the legislative assembly with a student call for more democratic rights and increased aid for education. He rounded up a few dozen students who, armed with pamphlets listing demands, headed to the visitors' gallery. There they intended to chant slogans and hurl the literature at the seated members. Someone leaked the plan, however, and on arrival at the gallery the students found it blocked by the premier's constabulary. There were more policemen in the gallery than Chrétien had students. The demonstration flopped.

Fingers immediately pointed to Le Chat as the informer. He was so well placed among the Liberals that he was always a ready target of suspicion. He had even managed to wangle his way into a job as a summer clerk at Louis St-Laurent's law firm. The story took on more notoriety when friends learned of Ladouceur's visit to Duplessis to ask the premier's advice on whether he should take the position. The premier gave his assent, making light reference to the "Saint" in St-Laurent's name. "Take the job," Duplessis told Le Chat. "You'll be with St-Laurent two hours a day, but you will be with St-Maurice the other twenty-two."

Chrétien concluded that Ladouceur was not the one who had leaked the plan for the raid. But he had sufficient evidence in other cases to confront Ladouceur and accuse him of acting as an informer. He found out, for example, that the Cat had found information on several students in a newspaper, a low-level scandal sheet, and passed it on to the premier. Ladouceur, of course, hotly denied any spying charges.

Hoping for greater success than his aborted raid on the Legislature, Chrétien next helped organize a general student protest in front of the building. The demonstration, a decade before student protests were in vogue, saw about a thousand Laval students march on the assembly demanding reform of the system for financial aid for education. The students hurled eggs and tomatoes at the seat of government, attracting headlines—"Hundreds Bombard Quebec Legislature"—and the like. Union Nationale sympathizers, some of Chrétien's friends among them, mocked the proceedings. Gabriel Loubier and Le Chien sat atop Loubier's convertible, hurling insults while draining a bottle of Scotch. Newspaper reports did not specifically identify Chrétien as a ringleader, but fellow students knew what he was up to.

While getting his law-school education, he returned to La Baie Shawinigan in the summers to live at home with his father and work at the Belgo mill across the road. He was so engrossed with Aline, however, that family members didn't see him often. "He was with Aline," said Gabriel, "and that was it. Politics, now that was something different. But socially, he was a loner."

Friends noted the effect of his constant exposure to her. She was gradually turning his negative aggression into positive aggression. She didn't do this by trying to assert the upper hand in the relationship or by setting out any specific agenda. It was primarily a matter of leading by example. He came to understand that to command her respect, he had to be a responsible citizen. André Bureau, who was earning top marks among the law students, thought Aline arrived just in time. Chrétien's many rough edges, he noted, could well have crippled his career. "I'm sure, I'm absolutely certain, that his life would have been quite different. She was not imposing anything. She never gave that impression. But you knew very well that Jean wasn't allowed to do this or that. She made him more responsible, more serious, a better student."

One thing she couldn't curb, though, was his rock-solid partisanship. For a man so young, Chrétien appeared to have his mind already made up. People said the same thing of his father. If he had a shortcoming, it was the complete inflexibility of his political beliefs. Liberal or nothing.

Jean Chrétien's obstinacy caused some problems for Bureau. His own father was a strong Liberal federally, but at the provincial level he supported Duplessis. This was enough to make André Bureau suspect in Chrétien's eyes, and Bureau became a little bothered by his black-and-white view of the world. There was not enough room for compromise with Chrétien, he thought, not enough shades of grey. His firm commitment on principles was a fine quality for a leader to have, Bureau reasoned, but if ideas were lodged too solidly at too young an age, how could there be room for intellectual growth? Students surely needed an open mind, he insisted, one that searched and explored and wondered, not one given to mechanical, reflex action.

Chrétien had begun communicating more frequently with his father, a shift that could only reinforce his Liberal bent. Wellie's interest in Jean, now that he was fulfilling his father's dream of having a son at law school, was naturally keen. And now he had more time on his hands. He had lessened some of his own workload, including giving up his job as secretary-treasurer of La Baie Shawinigan, a post he had held since 1932. It was a minor post in a minor place, but the clout of the Chrétiens was such that his departure in 1957 merited a feature article in the area's major newspaper, *Le Nouvelliste* of Trois-Rivières. The article, as if put together by an advertising agency, was one of fulsome adulation, describing Mr. Chrétien as "a prodigious worker, a model citizen, a father of an exemplary family." He had, it said, a fantastic memory and a wonderful vigour; he had raised sons and daughters who were all successful and respected citizens.

Jean's father lined up his son's summer jobs easily enough because it was company policy to hire the sons of men the mill employed, especially if they needed financial help to pursue their studies. Jean made about $1.50 an hour, a good wage for a summer employee. He spent his first summer at the Belgo mill rolling four-by-two logs along the plant floor and stuffing them into a grinding machine. His co-workers took pride in their great strength, but Jean was too skinny to compete in that department. At the annual company picnic he was left off the tug-of-war team. Other summers he worked on the paper machines, as what was called a "broke hustler." When a breakdown occurred on the big continuous reel, Chrétien's job was to gather all the refuse and dump it into a pulper. He was the sixth man on a six-man team. It was terribly hot and loud and the machines broke down frequently. The noise level, worrisome for someone with only one good ear to begin with, was so bad that workers began wearing ear covers as buffers.

Chrétien went at the job with an unrelenting enthusiasm that pleased co-workers and that his foreman, Ole Kiar, found just short of overbearing. His extroverted personality struck everyone as extraordinary. Although he was just a junior at the plant, he had the chutzpah to gather groups around him and preach the Liberal gospel. At election time he gave speeches in the cafeteria, in the washrooms, and standing up on the huge paper rolls. He presented himself as a man of the people, even though he was now going to law school and rising above the ranks of the traditional Baie workers. Watching him, Georges Cossette, one of the workers, saw "a born politician. He was saying things everybody liked to hear. He was a friend of everybody there. He tried to convince the people that we needed good social programs and better working conditions, and he was good." When he launched into his anti-Duplessis themes, he drew scorn from some. But most were impressed by his energy, passion, and bravado. "He was indefatigable," explained Maurice Poirier, who worked with him. "Guts," said Roland Corriveau, another co-worker. "The kid had guts."

Strikes plagued the Belgo mill in the mid-1950s, but Chrétien readily crossed the picket line. "The guys were all massed on the line," recalled Guy Chrétien. "They were really worried about scabs. But Jean would show up, yack with them a little bit, and they would let him through. On the way out, he would stop and gab some more." The workers knew the Chrétien boys and knew they could use the money, Guy reasoned. "But Jean could talk his way past anybody."

The mill men could see Chrétien's early ambition at work. They saw him making the rounds, meeting the workers in the other departments, and filing their names away, never to be forgotten. Both outside and inside the factory, his speeches during this period were largely in support of the provincial Liberal member for the Shawinigan area, René Hamel. Hamel was a dazzling orator who first ran federally in 1945 as a member of the Bloc Populaire, the left-wing Quebec nationalist party. He became a virulent opponent of Duplessis, winning for the Grits provincially in 1952 and 1956. He won again in 1960, after losing the party leadership fight to Jean Lesage. Defiant in his support of the working man and his desire for clean government, Hamel and his politics attracted the Chrétien family, and Jean became one of his warm-up acts. He was effective at this, and other politicians in the area began to take note. In 1956 the provincial Liberal leader, Georges Lapalme, came to Shawinigan to campaign. Jean Chrétien, now twenty-two, was master of ceremonies for the evening and delivered such an impressive stemwinder to open the show that the Liberal candidate in the adjacent constituency approached one of Chrétien's brothers afterwards, demanding that Jean come to his riding to speak for him.

One reason for his effectiveness was that he would hurl charges of scandal and corruption on slivers of evidence. Hamel didn't want to make such charges himself, so he trotted out Chrétien to do it for him. Chrétien began to sound less like a thinking politician and more like a wind-up attack dog. He fed off the excitement. The crowd would cheer him on, and he would give them more.

"He wasn't aware sometimes of the meaning of what he was saying," said Gilles Marchand, who also worked at the mill at this time. "He didn't think of the consequences of his words or acts." Jean's brother Gabriel had a similar view. He went to him one day and said, "Jean, they're making you say anything. Be careful."

CHAPTER SIX

THE SIXTIES CLUB

JEAN CHRÉTIEN married Aline Chaîné on Monday, September 10, 1957, at Sacré-Coeur, the church in La Baie Shawinigan. He'd completed two years of his four-year law program and had told his fiancée, "I'll enter politics someday—but not before I'm forty."

Jean was twenty-three and Aline was twenty-one. They had been seeing each other for almost six years, but for much of that time Jean was sequestered in boarding-school or at Laval University. He once told Aline that since he was away so much, it wouldn't be fair of him to ask her not to see other boys. Aline never had any interest in others, however. Her girlfriends made fun of her for being so faithful, warning her that like most boys who go off to college, Jean would forget about the girl back home. But their cautions had no effect. She waited—"I never thought of another man, ever"—and Jean never forgot about the girl back home.

They were, as a friend put it, "like two fingers on the same hand." Everyone thought Jean had made a wonderful choice. From an industrial ghetto in backwoods Quebec, he had plucked a diamond, a subdued beauty who was smart, responsible, and eager to chart a big life beyond the small town where she began.

They both had a quality that set them apart. For so many, the learning process stopped at the end of the school years. They settled, had children, laboured away at their jobs-for-life, and watched the children grow. Jean and Aline, by contrast, had an abiding capacity for self-improvement. Jean was always examining himself, comparing himself with others, trying to ascertain where his faults lay. After speeches, he demanded evaluations from friends. Aline was the same way. She worked hard on her English and Spanish, worked hard at her music lessons, and worked hard on her appearance. She did some modelling for clothing stores in Shawinigan, learning how to present herself in just the right way.

She was looking beyond Shawinigan. "Our parents didn't have very much, so I was ambitious to know everything, to travel, to know about the world, to learn, to be successful," she told an interviewer. "We were both ambitious. But I was less driven. We had the same values. We understood each other. We came from similar backgrounds." She could readily see his ambition, she said, but what impressed her was that it was an ambition that went beyond simple ego-gratification. "What struck me was that he wanted to help people, that he was not a selfish person."

She had travelled no farther than Ottawa, where she'd been once as a member of an organization for young Roman Catholics. Her English had improved because she'd been able to practice it with the managers of the plant where she worked as a secretary and then a payroll manager. She knew from experience that bilingual Quebeckers advanced more readily in their careers, but she had a hard time, as did others, convincing Jean of this. He maintained the same attitude towards the English language that he had had since his early days in school. Not interested.

In keeping with the culture of the time, Aline was fully prepared to play the traditional support role. But she was hardly a wallflower. Her bold, dark eyes betrayed a firmness of purpose that Jean respected. Their friends realized, as they watched Aline place a restraining hand on his shoulder or take him away early from parties where the drinking was uncontrolled, that she was a unique force in his life—nothing less than his guardian angel.

The wedding date was chosen for financial reasons. Jean

worked weekends at the mill, sometimes double shifts. He didn't want to schedule the wedding for a Saturday and miss the big payday, so they held the ceremony early Monday morning. He had worked sixteen hours at the factory the day before, and didn't finish until midnight. Under the circumstances, it was hard to work up any anticipation. Moreover, the celebration was smaller than they might have liked. "It was a very simple ceremony with a few friends," he recalled. "It was a very small affair because my wife's family had no money, and I didn't want to impose anything on them."

Jean's three sisters had all been married in coloured gowns. Aline wore a traditional white dress, cut short just below the knees. Her hair was cropped more closely than she later wore it. She was slim and, though twenty-one, could have easily passed for seventeen. In keeping with the style of the day, Jean had his hair brushed abruptly up and back, which made his features look more severe instead of softening them. His friends who attended were Pierre Garceau, from Laval, and Guy Suzor and Jean-Pierre Plante, from Shawinigan.

Normally it would have been the parish priest, Father Auger, who performed the wedding mass, but the Chrétiens detested Auger, and Auger held similar feelings towards them. The priest was thoroughly *bleu*, bound tightly to the old patronage system. To him Liberals were ungodly, and since the Chrétiens were the big Liberal family in the parish, he constantly sought to sully their image, even spreading rumours of the boys' dating practices. "We had an automobile then, and Papa lent it to us," said Gabriel. "Auger was saying we were using it to go out with the girls—and that we got the girl in the car and went parking in the woods." The priest, Gabriel added, even told Wellie Chrétien about this supposed high crime. Father Auger, meanwhile, drove around in a big Oldsmobile and, if the stories had any truth to them, was committing the odd nefarious parking deed himself. Rumours and allegations had implicated Auger in a myriad of scandalous activities.

These included womanizing—he supposedly made off with attractive members of his flock to a summer camp at Lac des Piles, ostensibly for business purposes. Fraud—he was reputed to have amassed, through unique bookkeeping practices, a personal fortune from the collection plate. And political skulduggery—he worked as a Duplessis pawn to besmirch the reputation of all good Liberals.

To no one's surprise, Jean Chrétien brought in a substitute to do the wedding: Abbé Bourassa.

After the ceremony, the party moved to a *salon* atop the Hotel Shawinigan. In keeping with Quebec custom, Wellie was the best man and said a few words at the reception, as did Jean. Then, before the high-powered festivities began out at Maurice's cottage on the lake, Jean and Aline drove off to a blaze of horns for a three-day honeymoon at Lake George in upstate New York. Gabriel let Jean take his new car for the trip. It was a 1957 Pontiac convertible, white and powder blue, with a high-charged engine and a body that extended half a block. Gabriel worried that his newlywed brother, without insurance, would smash it up, but the party at Maurice's probably served to drown his fears. It was, by all accounts, a great bash. The booze flowed like a river, fully clothed guests were thrown into the lake or jumped in voluntarily, and no one stopped celebrating until the stars ceased to twinkle.

Following their half-week honeymoon, Jean and Aline moved into a one-bedroom basement apartment on Quebec City's rue Geneviève, in the shadow of the Château Frontenac. Aline continued working as a secretary for some insurance underwriters and did a bit of modelling at the hotel, but she was soon pregnant. If Jean's social appearances were rare before, he became even more of a phantom now. Since there were no classes between ten in the morning and four in the afternoon, Jean took over many of the cooking and cleaning duties. He could even occasionally be seen hanging out laundry—a deed that earned him the admiration of the landlady.

They were, by all accounts, happy, sometimes exultant, newlyweds. Jean was blessed with a sweet wife, a group of ambitious, fun-loving friends, and the challenge of a career to build and a country to conquer. He had the capacity to see himself in a realistic light and make plans accordingly. He was almost always discreet in talking about his ambitions, but he told his friend Lamothe that politics was on his mind and that if he entered the game, it would be to win. "I'll become number one," he said. "I won't be there to finish second."

His days of school-yard capers weren't totally behind him. One day he, Garceau, Pelletier, and some others happened upon a young lady with luxuriant blonde hair, pouting ruby lips, and eyes that could stop a train. She was a ringer for Brigitte Bardot, the French movie star who was then in her sensuous prime. In a bid to liven up the town, Chrétien and his cohorts decided to try to pass her off as the real thing—Bardot on a secret rendezvous in the Quebec capital.

They persuaded the girl to play the part. They rented a limousine, scouted out the Château Frontenac, and called the newspapers. Chrétien's apartment served as the base for the caper. "Jean was the dispatcher, the ringleader, organizing the whole thing," recalled André Bureau. "I was the chauffeur for Bardot and the bodyguard. And quite frankly, I wasn't built like a bodyguard."

Chrétien leaked the news to the media. His friend Garceau, complete with white scarf and affected accent, whirled about as Ms. Bardot's assistant. The paparazzi arrived, and the bluffing Bardot, breathtaking in a mink stole, paraded by them, protected by a coterie of law students masquerading as Parisien bodyguards.

The plotters, fearing savvy newsmen would spot the caper for the canard that it was, instructed the girl not to give interviews. "Mademoiselle Bardot ne veut pas parler," Garceau told the press.

One exception was made, however. St-Georges Côté, the provincial capital's celebrated news anchorman, had dispatched a reporter to the scene, and Brigitte purred a few lines for him. It was, the reporter thought, an exclusive! Not only did Côté run her quotes on his show, he thought the event so important that he interviewed the newsman himself. "Tell us about the atmosphere," he asked him. "What was it like to be in the presence of the starlet?"

Chrétien and his merry schemers gathered back at his apartment to listen to the show. When they discovered that St-Georges Côté had been completely taken in by the prank, they fell over with delight. Said Chrétien, "We laughed like crazy."

Ultimately, after her picture appeared in the papers, the ruse was uncovered. "It worked out almost too well," said Bureau. "It was a real success, but we could have ended up with big problems. Some of the major names in journalism in Quebec City were really annoyed. You know, they were on the air saying they had seen her, and then they find out it isn't true."

Having fashioned a make-believe Bardot, the Laval gang had no trouble arranging the phoney Senate appointment of a pretentious professor. One of Chrétien's friends got on the phone to the professor, imitating the voice of a federal cabinet minister. "My heartfelt congratulations, sir," he intoned. "I've just come out of a cabinet meeting and am pleased to inform you that you have just been named to the Senate." The professor swallowed the bait. "I am delighted," he said.

As André Bureau recalled the prank, the professor was told to keep the good news secret for a while. "So then we called the newspaper and told a reporter, 'He's just been appointed, and you can call his home to confirm it.'" Just as the Chrétien gang hoped, the journalist called and got a long interview. In the next morning's newspaper Quebec City residents read all about their new senator.

Despite numerous denials from August Choquette, everyone believed he was the culprit—including his law professors. One of them, who wasn't satisfied with Choquette's grades, raised the issue in class one day. "You know, Choquette," he said, "you can do an imitation of the prime minister of Canada, you can imitate the premier of Quebec, and you can imitate the teacher speaking to you right now. Let me make a suggestion. Instead of forever screwing around, why don't you try imitating the top student in this class?"

More serious business for the Chrétien gang was the federal Liberal leadership convention in January 1958 to pick a successor to Louis St-Laurent. By this time, Chrétien was president of the Young Liberals of Quebec, a position that gave him full delegate status. Before the Grits' convention, the federal Progressive Conservatives had convened to choose John Diefenbaker as their new standard-bearer. A young Brian Mulroney, who like Chrétien was from a small pulp-and-paper town in Quebec and who would soon be on his way to Laval, had been a delegate to the Tory congress. Seen frequently at Diefenbaker's side, Mulroney made his presence felt.

The Liberal convention didn't promise much drama; Lester Pearson was considered the automatic choice. But Chrétien's Laval delegation was keyed up. "We were all excited about going," said Louis Batshaw, one of the group, "because Pearson was world famous. He'd just won the Nobel Peace Prize. Paul Martin didn't have a chance, but he was giving out a lot of free drinks." Chrétien's clear intent on arriving in Ottawa was to support Pearson. But he met Paul Martin in the lobby of the Château Laurier, was impressed by him, and began to feel sympathetic because few of the delegates were approaching him.

The latter factor was enough to make him change his mind and move into the Martin column. If most delegates were basing their judgements on traditional factors such as policy positions and electoral winnability, Chrétien made his on the basis of the candidate's loneliness. "It was clear that Pearson was going to win, that Paul was the underdog. And when I saw that he was the underdog, I said 'Goddamn it, I am going with him.' So I switched and went with Paul, and I got my guys and said, 'We have to be with him.'"

He felt comfortable with the decision because it was always his preference, he said, to be on the side of the outsider.

Because he was only a youth delegate, he did not make a prominent display of his new partisanship. But in policy sessions, some of his interjections registered on the party elders—and on the media. The most notable was his attack on the Quebec patronage system as it affected college students.

Chrétien's own experience had taught him something. His ascendancy to the presidency of the Laval young Liberals had been effortless because no one else wanted the job. Most students, dependent on grants or loans from the government, feared reprisals from the Duplessis machine. The governing party in Quebec had made it known that such aid might not be available to active Liberal Party supporters. Chrétien, unlike others, didn't have to worry. He had won a private bursary—just like his brother Maurice twenty-five years earlier—that paid five hundred dollars a year. He also worked summers at the paper mill. He didn't need the largesse of Mr. Duplessis.

His attack on the Union Nationale's nepotism brought headlines—"Liberal Quebec Students Go Underground" and the like. He was featured prominently in these reports and drew satisfaction from them. Even though he could barely read the stories, he was seeing his name in the English press for the first time.

At the convention he also worked to promote a cause that he had been fighting for in demonstrations on campus: free access to universities for all students, no matter what the income bracket. The convention passed a resolution to this effect. Between sessions, while other youth delegates partied at the seedy hotels in which they were billeted, Chrétien worked the Château Laurier suites, making himself known. One of the other young Liberals present was a highly ambitious student from Toronto named Jim Coutts. Coutts was taking down names of Liberals he thought noteworthy. One of the names he wrote in his little black book was Jean Chrétien's.

Later in the year, Chrétien was elected vice-president of the Canadian University Liberal Federation. While he didn't often involve himself in the debates played out on the pages of the Laval University student paper, *Le Carabin*, he was sufficiently angered by an article suggesting that young Liberals didn't pull any weight with the anglophone party hierarchy that he fired off a letter. He had discovered that he could have some say at the national party level, whatever its domination by the English. In considerable detail he laid out the party structure, noting that at the federal convention the university club had three votes, the same number accorded each riding in the country.

Chrétien was elected president of his law class for a third successive year. The biggest prize, however, was the position of student president of the entire law faculty, a post that enabled the winner to represent the students at meetings of the university's governing bodies. The contest, held at the end of his third year, coincided with a province-wide student protest, including the boycotting of classes, over the issue of increased aid for education and Duplessis's refusal to receive a delegation of students on the matter. For the first time, students across the province had come forward in a display of unity against the premier's dictate.

Chrétien was persuaded by Liberal students and professors to seek the presidency. The Duplessistes put up Bernard Flynn as his opponent. Flynn had looked warily on the growth of the anti-establishment movement on campus. When he spoke out against the pending student strike, he became an instant favourite of the Union Nationale supporters.

The campaign thus turned into a battle between the old order and the new. Cabals formed, the candidates made speeches, and political colours were declared. "This was the beginning of the Quiet Revolution," recalled Flynn. "The division of opinion was quite sharp. In the context of the times, I can now see how conservative I was." Chrétien, he noted, if not a leftist, was far more avant-garde. He was also a *rassembleur*. "He was the type of guy who rallied people around him. He was like Mulroney in that respect. You'd never see Mulroney standing alone somewhere." When he was at Laval, Mulroney was the favourite to win the school presidency, but he declined to stand for the position.

Chrétien had solid support from his own class, but less among the first- and second-year students. The election ended up in a draw. The next day a run-off was held, and Flynn won by a couple of votes. Chrétien had suffered the first defeat of his political career, and it stung him deeply. Losing to the status quo party was upsetting enough, but Chrétien was also hurt by the way it happened. At this early stage of his career, he was already the type of politician who cherished loyalty. In this campaign he felt the golden rule of loyalty had been violated.

After agreeing to run for the big post instead of seeking another mandate as class president, he strongly backed a replacement candidate for his own job. The candidate got the position. Chrétien then assumed he could count on this student's support in his own election bid. But the student felt that given his new rank, he should remain neutral. He abstained. Since the first ballot ended in a tie, the abstention cost Chrétien the victory. It was a breach of trust he would never forget.

Nevertheless, he had to try to put the disappointment behind him, because he soon faced another significant challenge: the third-year exams. These were considered the most difficult of the program, and though Chrétien had been diligent all year, never missing a class, he didn't consider that to be enough. He and two classmates repaired to a hideaway for a marathon cram session. Armed with questions from old exams going back three decades, they drilled one another for three days. Chrétien went into the exams prepared and scored well, not in the top rung but, as usual, above average.

In the summer that followed, he took a step that demonstrated unusual foresight and shrewdness for a man of his young age. He gathered together three of his closest Shawinigan friends—Marcel Bérard, Guy Suzor, and Jean-Pierre Plante—and told them he planned to start a club. The other clubs in town—the Richelieu, a businessmen's club called the Pic, and others—were white-collar clubs, Chrétien explained. Why not put together an organization that included blue collars like the people he had grown up with in La Baie Shawinigan?

The four men formed the Club de Soixante, the Sixties Club, named because the 1960s were around the corner and because they estimated they would have about sixty members.

In appealing to the working classes, the club satisfied Chrétien's penchant for the underdog, but it also served many other purposes. Comprising mainly young people who were Jean Chrétien's friends, the Sixties Club acted as a school for self-improvement, a socio-political club designed to do good works and help its members realize their ambitions. It could almost have been the brainchild of Dale Carnegie, the author-lecturer whose book *How to Win Friends and Influence People* gave instructions on personal betterment and vied with the Bible for all-time best-seller status.

Since boyhood Chrétien had been envious of anybody bigger or better. He'd been impressed by the status institutions like Harvard. He'd been determined to improve himself. Now he was creating something that was consistent with this side of his personality but wholly at odds with the other Chrétien, the street fighter. He was graduating from the school for scandal to the school for polish.

More important, while it was never overtly stated, Chrétien was forming a club that could one day be the core of his political machine. The men of the Sixties Club (there were no women members) were almost all Liberals, Liberals who liked Jean Chrétien. "It was Jean's idea," said Bérard, one of the club founders, "and in his mind it was for politics. He wanted to have a group of friends around him for political purposes."

Chrétien had spent three years away at law school, but his clout and popularity in Shawinigan were strong enough to rally the group around him. "We were so humiliated by the patronage that was so thick in politics," said Jean-Pierre Plante, another founder, "that we wanted change." The consensus was that Chrétien offered the best hope of realizing that change. Chrétien, they concluded, was a natural-born leader. He had a level of commitment that the others didn't have, and his upfront style of communication appealed to them. Already he was "a fantastic orator," said Plante.

The Sixties Club launched several inaugural activities: a campaign to raise money to fight cancer; a program to invite guest speakers to enlighten club members; and with the help of a local firm, an investment group whose earnings would be used for an education fund. Additionally, members taught one another the importance of public speaking, political organization, and presenting oneself for maximum effectiveness. Several members of the club, along with Chrétien, had worked on Liberal election campaigns, provincially and federally. Those who hadn't, learned from those who had.

Because Chrétien still had a year to complete at law school, he did not become the club's first president. The honour went to Bérard, who had attended elementary school with Jean. For the club's first guest speaker, Bérard invited Dr. Maurice Chrétien, who had become the director of the Canadian Association of Francophone Doctors. He gave a presentation on life in Scandinavia, where he had spent some time. In subsequent meetings, the club heard speeches on seeing the Soviet Union through a Canadian's eyes and on understanding Batista's Cuba, given by a speaker who was introduced by Guy Chrétien. Jean Chrétien returned from Laval at Christmas to present the club with its first constitution. He succeeded Bérard as president and immediately switched the focus of the presentations from the experiences of world travellers to lessons in the operation of businesses, which was more in keeping with his own interests. His guests gave talks on the secrets of the stock market, the administration of a business, company law, and financing new enterprises. By now, because of his marriage, his family—a daughter, France, was born in 1958—and his need to earn a living, he was less inclined to supplement his law degree with an MBA from Harvard. But learning how to make a dollar, as he had done with his black-market chocolate business, was still a major priority for him. He was a man who watched over every penny. "Threw nickels around like manhole covers," they said of him. "Very often he had no money in his pockets," recalled Bérard. "You'd go to a restaurant with him and he'd say, 'Oh, I have no money.' So someone else would have to pay."

One of the early members of the club was Georges Cossette. A Shawiniganite from a wealthy family, Cossette saw Jean Chrétien even then, at age twenty-four, as the future leader of the country. Though Chrétien had informed close friends like Robert Lamothe that he would be going for the top if he entered politics, he was really not one of those political prodigies who went around telling people he would be prime minister of Canada someday. "He usually stopped at cabinet minister," said Guy Suzor, one of the few people Chrétien confided in. Suzor applied the brakes then anyway. "I told him that his chances of becoming PM were about the same as me becoming pope." Most of his friends, like Suzor, saw a political future for him, but none thought he had the stuff to go all the way. For one thing, he wasn't any smarter than they were. For another, he was too close to the ground; he lacked an aura.

Cossette, whose nephew was the precocious young Conservative Hugh Segal, was the exception. He saw Chrétien as the one. At a club meeting, where Chrétien's name was being bandied about, Cossette interjected, "I'm telling you people, that guy is working so hard he's going to be prime minister of Canada someday." Chrétien, he said, wanted it and would get it. His prediction prompted laughter from one in the group. No one was prepared to

99

support his view. But Cossette held firm. He'd seen Chrétien performing at the Belgo mill, standing on the huge paper rolls during the breaks, saying the things people wanted to hear.

Chrétien began cultivating friendships with area businessmen, such as the wealthy lumber company owner Jean-Paul Gignac, and with local workers, like the vocal union boss Fernand D. Lavergne. In the official Sixties Club booklet, which included brief biographies of its executive members, Chrétien was listed as a businessman as well as a lawyer. Also mentioned, in a lighter vein, was his prowess as a dancer. In this, the era of the twist, Chrétien had become one of note, winning a club twisting competition.

He did much of his socializing in Shawinigan with Suzor, a sharp political operator and good beer drinker who worked for Du Pont Chemicals and was related to Jean through marriage. Suzor and Chrétien and their wives often went out together on Saturday nights, usually to one of Shawinigan's three movie houses or dancing at the Shawinigan Country Club.

The spring and summer of 1958 had been especially eventful for Chrétien. The period brought the birth of his daughter, the formation of the Sixties Club, and the collapse of his cherished Liberals. In the March election, John Diefenbaker's evangelism captured Canadians' imaginations and returned the Chief to power with a record 208 of a possible 265 seats. One of the few Pearson Liberals to survive the Tory onslaught was J. A. Richard, a veteran Quebec Grit of no particular distinction. Chrétien campaigned for Richard, although by this time it was already in the back of his mind that this was the seat he wanted himself.

Chrétien got more political bad news when the candidate he supported for the Quebec Liberal leadership, Shawinigan's René Hamel, was defeated by Jean Lesage. Having a close friend in Quebec City as leader and perhaps premier would have been a great plus for the budding politician. But it would probably have seen him launch a provincial political career instead of a federal one.

He always found himself on the opposition side in these

years—in school politics, in provincial politics, and now, with the election of the Tories, in federal politics. The role fit his underdog temperament. Despite his keen interest in business, he clearly saw himself as "a left-wing Liberal." His goal before moving to politics, he noted, was "to be a lawyer to the unions. That was very much my desire. My social ambition was to be on the populist side, not on the side of business."

CHAPTER SEVEN

THE YOUNG LAWYER

J EAN CHRÉTIEN was called to the bar in June 1959. A Shawinigan newspaper noted the event with the comment that "this young lawyer has never failed to make an impression wherever he has been."

He was faced with several decisions on graduation. One was whether to supplement his lawyer's credentials with a business degree from a prestigious American university. He dropped that idea, however, in part because of a chance meeting with Louis St-Laurent. Chrétien, still at an impressionable age, asked the eminent gentleman for advice on his career path. In a voice deep and rich and resonant, St-Laurent stated the obvious: "Young man, if you want to be a successful lawyer, practice law."

He also had to decide where to make his home. He and Aline were charmed by Quebec City but not enough to consider remaining there. Chrétien's political base was his home town, he was a better cultural fit for Shawinigan, and most of his law school friends were returning to La Mauricie. More important, Jean's father expected his son to come home. Though he would never tell him this, Wellie was finally developing a measure of pride in his fifth son. Gone were the days when, as he told Mrs. Godin during their long car trips to New Hampshire, "you would open the door and there was Jean with his suitcase. He had been expelled again."

It was a more contented father who went to a clothier in Montreal to rent his son's graduation gown. But owing to the clerk's hesitancy to accept his cheque, he almost didn't get it. By fortunate coincidence, however, Jean's friend Le Chien, Guy Germain, was in the store at the same time, picking up his own garment. When he heard the squabble at the front desk, he went over and said to the clerk, "Sir, if Mr. Chrétien's cheque isn't honourable, there isn't a cheque in all of Quebec that is honourable."

Though Chrétien was now twenty-five years old, his father's word still weighed heavily on him. Jean felt, as he would categorically state in later years, that his father "drove" him into law and politics. His insistence on this point was curious, however, because he appeared to relish his political outings and had quite enjoyed law school. He gave no one the impression that he was being compelled to do things he did not wish to do.

While preparing to open his own law practice, Chrétien received a job offer. The oldest legal firm in Shawinigan, Lafond, Gélinas, invited him to join. It was a good offer, but Chrétien would have to think about it. Alexander Gélinas was a well-known supporter of Duplessis, and Joe Lafond, though not actively partisan, was a Quebec nationalist. Joining the firm would mean teaming up with the other side.

Lafond and Gélinas had set up their general practice in 1921. Lafond's son, Jean, joined the firm in 1953, and it was he who sought out the new lawyer. The young Lafond sensed Chrétien had a keen interest in law, was impressed by the precision of some of his observations, and knew of the Chrétien family's excellent reputation. The possibility that Jean Chrétien might have been using law as only a springboard to politics did not cross Lafond's mind. "In the conversations I had with him, he never showed an interest in pursuing a political career."

Jean Lafond was leaving Shawinigan for Quebec City to be a municipal law specialist in the bureaucracy. He convinced his father that the firm needed new blood and should make an offer to Chrétien. Eventually, Chrétien decided to hold his political nose and join the firm.

Some, like Raymond Landry, who later became a member of the firm, found it peculiar that Chrétien could team up with these establishment *bleus*. But while angry political debates with his partners ensued, Chrétien didn't worry much about the affiliation. He was determined to carve out his own identity in the legal community.

The first year was usually a tough one for lawyers. Wellie Chrétien worried that his son would find business hard to attract and that he would become disillusioned with the low profitability. He'd heard that other lawyers had struggled terribly at the start. But if Mr. Chrétien fretted much, he was underestimating the type of boy he had.

His son had his first case before he even moved into his office. A neighbour whose house was being expropriated by the city came to him for help. Working out of his own home, Chrétien was able to get the city's offer bumped from $10,000 to $15,000, a 50 per cent increase. He sent the client a bill for $250—5 per cent of the amount he had gained for him. To Chrétien's complete surprise, the neighbour complained about the bill, saying he thought Chrétien had taken up the matter as a friend. He thought he was doing it free. Chrétien responded that it wasn't yet Christmastime. "I've got to make a living, you know."

The neighbour's next ploy angered Chrétien even more. He went off to ask the good counsel of none other than Father Auger, the same man who loathed everything Liberal, especially the Chrétiens. Auger, not surprisingly, sided with the neighbour. He came to the Chrétiens and said it would be a good deed if Jean didn't charge the villager. He would even make mention of this kind act from the pulpit come Sunday, if Chrétien agreed to it.

But Chrétien wanted the money. He told Auger there could be no deal. The clergyman responded with an angry, blanket condemnation of the profession Chrétien had joined. Lawyers are all a bunch of crooks, he said. "You mean," replied Chrétien, "that you don't know one honest lawyer?" In fact, there was one, Auger responded—Robert Lajoie of Trois-Rivières.

Chrétien's legal debut was so far a source of considerable aggravation. Having performed a service, he was being condemned for expecting a small recompense. And now he'd been drawn into another confrontation with the parish priest. He thought about dropping the matter, but it wasn't in his character to do so. Instead, he went to Trois-Rivières to see Lajoie, a barrister who did enjoy an impeccable reputation. Chrétien explained the case and the fee he had charged. After reviewing it, honest Bob Lajoie determined that Chrétien *was* at fault—he was guilty of underbilling! "You should be charging a 10 per cent commission," Lajoie said, "Not 5."

A delighted Chrétien had Lajoie send a letter with his recommendation to the client and to the clergyman. If Lajoie, the most honest lawyer around, wanted 10 per cent, what did that make Chrétien, who was only asking half that sum? Auger ate crow and the neighbour, some months later, came forward with the smaller payment.

Chrétien went at his legal business with vigour and enterprise. Maurice's medical practice provided him with an example of how to make a success of one's profession. One key was discipline. That meant no alcohol, bed early, in the office every morning by eight, out every evening after six. A second key was to get a head start. Chrétien learned to exert a maximum effort for the first two hours, the most important hours of the day. He would accept no interruptions during this time, no casual phone calls, no office small talk, no escapes for coffee and doughnuts. The big lead was crucial.

Following the expropriation dispute, Chrétien got a case from another former neighbour. Gilles Marchand was vice-president of the union representing more than a thousand workers at the Belgo mill. The workers, most of whom knew Jean Chrétien, had clashed with management on the question of overtime pay. Because Chrétien was fresh out of law school, some of the mill men didn't want to hire him to represent them. Marchand persuaded the workers to give him a chance, arguing that Chrétien, having been one of them, understood their situation better than any other lawyer in town. Moreover, he said, Chrétien had the guts to take on management. As a summer student, Chrétien had once protested the awarding of supervisory jobs to anglophones. He also, Marchand might have added, crossed picket lines.

Since the union executive was dominated by young workers, Marchand found it easier to sell his candidate. He was helped in this by another executive member, Georges Cossette, the same Cossette who was going around saying that young Chrétien would be prime minister someday. Chrétien got the case and was excited by it. He told many friends that having the opportunity to represent working people was what motivated him both as a lawyer and as a politician. Soon the union had won the right to overtime pay, and in not too long a time, Chrétien had expanded his affiliation with the "little guy." He became his region's lawyer for the Confederation of National Trade Unions (CNTU).

In his first month Chrétien made $60, in addition to the $250 owed him on the expropriation case. In his first year his earnings were $6,000, an excellent sum in those days for a rookie lawyer.

His practice included criminal work. Most every new criminal lawyer dreamed of a crack at a murder case, and it was Chrétien's good fortune to have one before his practice was a year old. An acquaintance from La Baie, Gilles Huard, went to Trois-Rivières, booked into a hotel, got in a fight with a prostitute over her fee, and strangled her to death. Huard then called up the only lawyer he knew—Jean Chrétien.

Chrétien was ready to take the case when, once again, the parish priest intervened. The Huard family had sought the advice of the church on their son's plight. Father Auger solemnly heard them out, told them what prayers were in order, then offered another suggestion: they might be better off with a different lawyer. So the Huards asked the highly regarded Alex Bastien to take the case. Bastien agreed, but Gilles Huard balked, saying he wanted to stick with his original choice. Bastien phoned Chrétien, explained what had happened, and turned the case back over to him. The priest ate crow again.

With the help of his friend Pierre Garceau, who was working at a legal firm in Trois-Rivières, Chrétien made the case that Huard was drunk, that it was his first time with a hooker, and that she provoked him by stopping in the middle of the act and demanding more pay. At that point, Chrétien argued, Huard completely lost control.

At the outset, it looked as though Huard was facing life imprisonment or a very long sentence. By making the provocation defence stick, however, Chrétien got him off with only a few years.

The trial attracted a lot of newspaper coverage and helped make Chrétien a name lawyer in the region. He also learned what he felt was a valuable lesson in how the machinery of the justice system operates against clients without financial means. Huard could not afford the legal fee required for hiring an investigator. In this case Chrétien and Garceau, with a lot at stake as new lawyers, did it themselves. At other times, Chrétien well knew, penniless defendants were not so fortunate.

Having quickly established himself in the region's legal community, Chrétien was named a Crown prosecutor. It was only a part-time position, one that supplemented his regular legal work, so Chrétien didn't regard it as very significant. Besides, he preferred to be on the side of the accused, not the accusers. Nonetheless, the appointment, which came after only a year in the business, was indicative of the respect he was earning. Friends who predicted his legal work would come second to the advancement of his political interests were reshaping their opinions.

Raymond Landry, a newly minted lawyer from the University of Montreal, worked next door to Chrétien at the firm. He got a good look at how the private Chrétien compared with the public one. He discovered that the differences were pronounced.

The office atmosphere, said Landry, was spartan and deadly serious. If the public Chrétien was forever pumping hands, rushing here and there, putting on a friendly show, in the office he was quite the opposite. "He was the type of guy who worked by himself," said Landry. There was no banter, no cheer. Chrétien worked long hours, went home for lunch, and came in on weekends. He didn't like to spend money—not on the office, not on the employees, not on himself. So serious was Chrétien about his work that Landry wondered when he ever took time to enjoy himself. Occasionally, he did play a round of golf with Landry, but it was only nine holes, at which point Chrétien usually said he had to get home to Aline. When he did go into the clubhouse with Landry or other playing partners, it was just for one quick drink.

Chrétien's style was to attack each new file with energy, immediacy, and commitment. He was not the type to linger around the office, taking measure of complex legal issues or citing historical analogy. Instead, he was given to rapid accountings fashioned with plenty of momentum and clear-cut conclusions. By reputation he was a straight shooter, aggressive and technically efficient. Everything was by the book—the cold, clear, pragmatic book of Wellie and Maurice and François Chrétien.

Although the office atmosphere was rigorously businesslike, Landry did not find Chrétien inconsiderate. Landry's first big case involved a serious automobile accident in which several were killed. Landry was nervous; he'd never handled anything so important. Moreover, the trial was out of town, in La Malbaie, meaning there would be no one to fall back on. Sensing his apprehension, Chrétien decided to accompany Landry on the trip. For three days he stayed with the rookie lawyer in La Malbaie, guiding him through the case. Landry was most appreciative, especially because he knew how rare it was at this stage of his life for Chrétien to spend time away from Aline. He expected to find a sizeable cut in his fee on the case, but he was surprised in this as well. His tight colleague didn't bill him a penny.

Chrétien was disappointed when the CNTU, one of his major clients, decided to turn its legal work over to friends in Montreal. With most of his union work gone, he had to look elsewhere for clients—including the management side. This was a difficult adjustment for Chrétien, who prided himself on union work. "It was kind of an ideological switch," he said. "I was not good enough for the unions, but I was good enough to be against the unions." In law school, with the idealism typical of a student, he had told his brother Marcel that making a lot of money would not be important to him. "I would rather work with the unions and change society," he told him. Marcel could only laugh when his young brother began making very good money from very big customers.

In his criminal law file the workload grew heavy. The region's criminal courts were in session only on Fridays in Trois-Rivières. Chrétien, who had taken over the defence client lists from lawyers who had become full-time Crown attorneys, would frequently show up with more cases than any other lawyer in La Mauricie.

Despite his success, he drove a small car, lived a frugal lifestyle, and wore inexpensive suits. He parcelled his life neatly among his family, the law office, and politics. But while the turn towards the disciplined life was continuing at good measure, it wasn't—if it ever would be—complete.

Jean's brother Guy appeared at a lawyer's party in Shawinigan once to find him so drunk that he couldn't get to his feet. Guy ranked among the more accomplished imbibers in the Chrétien clan, so was not one to scoff at this sort of behaviour. He was worried, however, about Aline's reaction. She was already seeking a pledge of abstinence from Jean. If she saw him like this, Guy reasoned, there was no telling what she would do.

So when his besotted brother mumbled incoherently that he'd better be taken home, Guy strongly disagreed. Just as he'd arranged shelter for Jean in Montreal when he was expelled from college, he'd find a safe haven for him now. It was a mild autumn evening, and Guy knew of a well-wooded park nearby. He decided that rather than roll Jean along the apartment corridor to his wife, he would let him sober up for a few hours in the great outdoors. So he carried him out to his car and drove him to the local forest. The ground was covered in red and brown and golden leaves, and Guy made a cosy bed of them in the great dark shadows of the oaks. He tucked Jean in and told him he would be back before the morning birds sang. In no condition to disagree, Jean dozed off under the moonlight.

In the early morning hours, Guy returned as planned and took his now ambulatory brother home. Aline was none the wiser, but for Jean, the episode was another learning experience. Even if he wanted to, he realized that he couldn't drink with the best or even the worst of them.

Alcohol was probably only partially to blame for his next transgression, one far more egregious than the bed-of-leaves affair. Chrétien attended a meeting of the bar association at a Trois-Rivières club with the peculiar name of Ki-8-Eb. The entire legal community turned out, including the wives. Chrétien and Marcel Chartier, the old seminary college friends with a total of five expulsions between them, entered into drink-leavened conversation at the bar. A boozer of some renown, Chartier was known to get belligerent around about the seventh belt and start peppering his political partisanship with blunt put-downs of anyone within earshot. In talking to Chrétien, his banter was only marginally offensive until an eminent Liberal, J. A. Mongrain, happened by. Chrétien regarded Mongrain as a lion among the Liberals and the best orator he had ever heard. But Chartier, a Union Nationale man, had no use for him, particularly since Mongrain had belittled UN followers in a recent speech.

He took to mocking the old man, and as he did, the decibel level rose. Insults between him and Chrétien, who were about the same in size, followed rapidly, one upon the other. Bystanders sensed that as long as the discussion remained political, it could be contained. But soon the exchange took a personal turn, quickly diminishing the odds of civility. Chartier knew that Chrétien was doing well as a lawyer and was proud of it. But there was still the odd whisper about town that it was his eldest brother who, by providing financial help, had got him going. Nothing, Chartier knew, infuriated Chrétien more than this insinuation.

So now, with piercing broadsides ringing through the salon, Marcel Chartier sharpened his dagger on the ultimate calumny and plunged it in. "At least I," he roared, "didn't need a big brother to get my start in life!"

In the next instant blood was streaming across the floor, women were screaming, and swarms of lawyers were trying to bring Jean Chrétien under control. In a rage, he had unleashed a volley of punches, one of which struck Chartier brutally. Chartier had no time to get in a response. As he keeled over, his head angled directly towards the sharp edge of a glass table. Chrétien was in control enough to see this and, for a brief second, feared the worst. Fortunately, Chartier just missed the table. He lay dazed on the floor, occasioning more shrieks from the female contingent, some of them the wives of chief justices.

Marcel Chrétien was in attendance. "The guy was out on the floor in a minute," he said of the mêlée. "I never had a chance to say a word. I just remember seeing the guy lying flat on the floor, blood streaming from his nose. The women were crying."

Word spread that Chartier had provoked the altercation by insulting Chrétien's wife. Both men denied that. Chrétien, for one, would never be enthusiastic about discussing the battle. He was stung, he recalled, by Chartier's accusation that he needed a brother to lean on. At the same time, he worried about Chartier's injuries. "It was not a very nice conversation," he said.

Chartier admitted defeat. "Chrétien had it on me," he said. "He won the fight—that's a fact." He remembered being left dizzy but not seriously hurt. Chrétien, he said, "was a very good fighter, very good, ready to fight at any time. He was always the first one with the fists in the air. No doubt about it. And he was good.

"I had another fight with his law partner, Raymond Landry. That one was even, I guess."

Jean Chrétien was no longer a kid when the brawl occurred— he was twenty-seven years old. Since he was the undisputed as- sailant, in full view of credible witnesses, he could well have been charged with assault. But while Chartier might have had the grounds to lay a charge, he never gave a moment's thought to doing so. Such fights—at least in Chartier's case—were not uncommon, and among the old law school group, no grudges were held.

News of the fracas never got far beyond Trois-Rivières. Chrétien's friends were still trying to keep the story under wraps decades later, and not surprisingly, the scene did not make it into the memoir Chrétien wrote about himself in 1984. The fight did at least serve to enhance his reputation as a scrapper. He had entered the professional class and had begun spending more time with the elites, but the image of himself as a blue-collar guy was still the one he wished to cultivate. He liked the money he made as a lawyer and, despite any protestations to the contrary, wanted to make lots of it. But he also knew that, by nature, he was too much of a street fighter to make the transformation that Brian Mulroney was in the course of making. Mulroney, who had similar modest origins and working-class roots, left them far behind as he became more infat- uated with the ruling class. With his honeyed voice, handsome profile, and beautiful suits, it was a class to which he could easily aspire. While Chrétien returned to Shawinigan to practice law, Mulroney left his Baie Comeau home for an establishment legal firm in Montreal.

Nevertheless, Chrétien had his own considerable hubris to at- tend to, a proud spirit that said he was as good as the intellectuals and upper classes. This led to some interesting internal conflicts. He liked being in the presence of the powerful and the influential, and resented being categorized as backwoods and lowbrow. Yet the street-fighter image was his political ticket, and he took pains to emphasize his working-class beginnings. By 1960 he was already living the dichotomy that would mark his political life.

Political tradition set the boundaries: there were blue collars and their populists and upper classes and their establishment men. Politicians were supposed to be in one bracket or the other. The difference with Jean Chrétien was that he didn't believe people who said he couldn't have it both ways.

One look at the friends he kept made it clear that Chrétien wanted to cast the widest of nets. They were a strange mix. To begin with, there was Shawinigan's leading leftist or, as many would describe him, Communist. Fernand D. Lavergne was an uneducated but brilliant father of eight. Two decades older than Chrétien, he was a successful union organizer and a spear in the side of the establishment. He was a friend of Pierre Elliott Trudeau's, a peripatetic labour lawyer based in Montreal. Trudeau became an admirer when he first represented Lavergne's union. Trudeau would come to Shawinigan, said Lavergne, and "he wasn't speaking of good wines and dancers then." Instead, he'd tell the workers of the misery he had encountered on his world travels. After a time, Lavergne noticed Trudeau wasn't billing him for his legal work. When he asked Trudeau about this, the lawyer told him that if he wished, Lavergne could forward an amount equal to the basic hourly wage of the average factory worker in Shawinigan. As for the number of hours worked, Trudeau, who had come into a big inheritance from his father, suggested Lavergne send in his own estimate.

When the union leader, a biting, sarcastic, and wonderfully humorous public speaker, contested the 1957 federal election, running in Shawinigan for the CCF (later the NDP), Trudeau came to his nomination meeting. The campaign saw Lavergne stridently attacking the Quebec judicial system, claiming that judges were prostituting themselves before the Union Nationale establishment "to save their jobs." His blasts resulted in death threats to his wife and threats of prison for himself. He was labelled a Communist and pilloried by the religious establishment—led, of course, by the ubiquitous Father Auger. At the schools his daughters attended, the nuns asked the children to pray that Lavergne lose the election. Lavergne finally took the matter up with the bishop, lecturing him on the differences between church and state, but gaining no satisfactory response.

That Lavergne was accused of ungodly communism, hated by the clergy, and loathed by the business establishment were credentials impressive enough for Jean Chrétien. Despite the differences in age, Chrétien cultivated a friendship with him that was close and enduring. He joined hands with Lavergne in fighting the province's retrogressive religious enthralment. As Chrétien put it, the Roman Catholic Church and its political brethren "shared an interest in keeping Quebeckers poor, rural, uneducated, and bound to the Church teaching that life on earth is just a grim passage to heaven." Maurice Duplessis had once told Chrétien it was a privilege, not a right, to attend university. The premier had fashioned, Chrétien believed, the whole province on such a model.

In their own parish, Chrétien and Lavergne faced not only religious dictatorship, but also depravity. The handsome blond Auger was allegedly sexually abusing young girls. "We were revolted," said Gilles Marchand, referring to the stories he and his friends were hearing from the young women. But in the name of the Lord and the premier, Auger dispensed blessings and favours, making sycophants out of so many that even while the evidence of his immorality piled high, public opinion remained on his side. Because the political divisions were so rigid, Auger was defended by Union Nationale partisans like Marcel Chartier, no matter what the charges. It was probably true that he was fondling women of the parish, said Chartier. But that, he added, didn't make him much different from many other priests who were likely doing the same thing.

If friends like Lavergne put Chrétien firmly in the left-wing camp, he still managed to make himself very respectable to those on the establishment side of the ledger. He befriended many of the top industrialists and businessmen in the city; he was a leading member of an establishment law firm; he had his own organization, the Sixties Club, which was a school for the upwardly mobile; and he was, with a sharp eye for business investments, set on becoming one of Shawinigan's nouveau riche.

A leading French-Canadian industrialist in Shawinigan was Jean-Paul Gignac, one of the city's richest men. Gignac built a lumber business from scratch and turned it into a major enterprise. He and Chrétien became good friends, though Gignac, like Lavergne, was many years his senior. Before too long, Chrétien found himself in Gignac's limousine, accompanying his new friend on his frequent trips back and forth to Montreal. He would go from learning maverick politics from the socialist Lavergne one day to limo politics from the industrialist Gignac the next.

Though he was Liberal to the core, Chrétien always extended an olive branch to conservatives. He maintained a friendship with Chartier, despite the violent clash, and with Ladouceur, despite having labelled him a Duplessis spy. He once surprised Ladouceur, who never did graduate from Laval, when he spotted him in his brother Guy's drugstore. It was 1960, and Chrétien was on his way to the opening of Jean Lesage's election campaign in Louiseville. "Why don't you come along?" he asked Ladouceur. Given his political affiliation, Le Chat felt a little awkward but agreed. Chrétien kept him at his side throughout, introducing him to all his good Liberal friends. It was Chrétien's way, said Le Chat. "He never wanted to lose a friend."

One Duplessis backer on the make in Shawinigan was Gabriel Buisson, whose parents had been proud supporters of R. B. Bennett in the dirty thirties. Buisson worked in the Shawinigan chemical

(above) Jean (front row, far right) posed in front of Sacré-Coeur Church in La Baie Shawinigan. The armbands symbolize that he and his friends have just received the Catholic rite of confirmation. Gilles Argouin is in the second row, on the far left, and Yvon Boisvert is in the middle of that same row. [Courtesy of Yvon Boisvert]

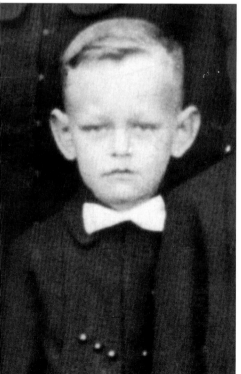

(left) Ti-Jean is shown here at his dreaded first boarding-school, the Jardin de l'Enfance. Although the school was only a short bus ride from his home, young Jean sometimes went weeks, even months, without seeing his parents. His experiences at the Jardin instilled in him a hatred of boarding-schools that dogged him throughout his erratic educational career. [Courtesy of Jean Harnois]

Twenty-year-old Jean (second row, far right) played all sports but was crazy about baseball. He closely followed the major leagues, memorizing the names and numbers of every player on every team. [Courtesy of the Chrétien family]

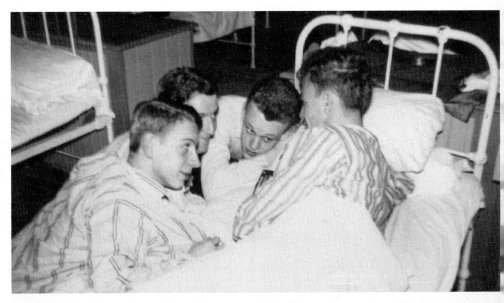

In this 1954 photo, Jean and his friends are engaged in an activity that was absolutely forbidden at the Trois-Rivières seminary college they attended—they are listening to a radio. Although Chrétien bridled at the regimentation, the seminary atmosphere did play to many of his character strengths. [Courtesy of the Chrétien family]

(left) In this forty-year-old photo, a beaming Jean and Aline have been named king and queen of the local corn roast. [Courtesy of the Chrétien family]

(below) In keeping with the style of the day, Jean liked to wear his hair brushed abruptly up and back, which made his features look more severe instead of softening them. [Courtesy of the Chrétien family]

Twenty-three-year-old Jean Chrétien and twenty-one-year-old Aline Chaîné were married in a simple ceremony in La Baie Shawinigan on September 10, 1957. They were wed on a Monday because Jean often worked double weekend shifts at the local pulp-and-paper mill and didn't want to miss the big payday. The day before his wedding, he had worked sixteen hours, finally finishing up at midnight. [Courtesy of the Chrétien family]

(left) Jean and Aline got out their finery for the 1959 law student ball at Laval University. Although Jean had had a rebellious youth, he settled down as soon as he met Aline. Friends eventually took to calling him Jean Fidèle. [Courtesy of the Chrétien family]

(below) This photo of forty-three-year-old Maurice Chrétien, taken while he was practicing medicine in Shawinigan, gives some sense of his strong personality. Twenty-four years older than Jean, he became, in a sense, a second father to the boy, playing a role Jean sometimes resented. In 1954, the year this photo was taken, Maurice was named a Fellow of the Royal Society of Canada. [Courtesy of Maurice Chrétien]

The most important quality Jean and Aline shared was an ambitious spirit. Both wanted to experience the world beyond the constricting confines of the small town they came from. As a federal member of Parliament, Jean was able to give Aline opportunities they might otherwise never have had. Here they pose with some Aborigines during a trip to Australia. [Courtesy of the Chrétien family]

Aline posed with their children, (left to right) Michel, France, and Hubert, for this 1977 promotional shot. The family was not without its difficulties. Michel, who was adopted in the Northwest Territories as a baby, was often withdrawn and uncommunicative, and Hubert suffered from dyslexia, a learning disorder. [Canapress]

(above) Chrétien never lost his love of sports. As an MP, he played goal for the House of Commons hockey team. Also shown are William Rompkey (far left), Warren Allmand (fourth from right), and David Dingwall (far right). [J. M. Carisse Photo]

(left) Despite moving to Ottawa to serve in Parliament, Chrétien never really left La Mauricie behind. One of his favourite spots was his cottage at Lac des Piles. Whether he went there to relax, to escape, or simply to enjoy the surroundings, he was always happiest at the lake. [Courtesy of the Chrétien family]

From the moment they met, Jean and Aline seemed perfectly suited to each other, and their relationship only got stronger with time. They were so close that a friend once described them as being "like two fingers on the same hand." [J. M. Carisse Photo]

research lab for five years, took courses in chemical engineering, then struck out on his own, forming a small chemicals company. Though Chrétien was a Liberal, Buisson liked his aggressiveness, the ease with which he worked up a head of steam. He hired Chrétien to write up his first company charter.

The company got its start producing paint for highway lane markers. Just before the 1960 provincial election a Union Nationale party boss came to Buisson with an order for one thousand gallons of paint and promises of more to come. The implication was clear: Buisson should get to work backing the local Union Nationale candidate, who was trying to unseat one of Chrétien's favourite Liberals, René Hamel. Buisson did what was expected of him, taking out a full-page newspaper advertisement and contributing heavily to the conservative's campaign. When Hamel held on to win the riding in the election that brought Lesage's Liberals to power, Buisson appeared to have played his cards poorly. Shortly after the vote, Chrétien came to his office to tell him he had made a bad mistake and, lest he never see another government contract, had better make amends. They went to see Hamel in Quebec City. On Chrétien's urging, Hamel decided to make a friend of an enemy. What had started as a mission of mercy turned into a massive payday. Buisson walked out of the meeting with the promise of an order for ten thousand gallons of road paint. He was on his way to a multi-million-dollar business and eventual status as Shawinigan's richest man—thanks in no small part to Jean Chrétien.

No one thought Chrétien had much in common with Buisson, but Chrétien knew he was a big comer. As he always would, Chrétien took special enjoyment out of being with people who had made it. Buisson thought this was one of the keys to Chrétien's success. He knew "how to make good connections, good friends. He had a way with people."

He also had a way with money. He was doing very well as a lawyer, making an outstanding $35,000 a year by 1963. At the same time, however, he was looking to sweeten his pot through business deals. He and Sixties Club co-founder Guy Suzor picked up a tip that a section in the northern part of the city was about to undergo a real-estate boom. It would be a good investment, but he needed at least $11,000, money neither he nor Suzor had. "But Jean talked me into going down with him to see the bank manager," Suzor recalled. "He talked his way into his office. The manager turned us down flat. But Jean kept talking. We walked out of that bank at 8:30 on a Friday night with the money." He and Suzor bought the land, built their own houses on the choice lots, then began selling off other chunks at a sizable profit. Chrétien's new home on rue Guillemette was a cube-shaped, flat-roofed bungalow, fashionable though not ostentatious.

With Ole Kiar, his old boss from the Belgo mill, and a few others, he bought one of the city's principal hotels—the Hôtel des Chutes. It was a house of ill repute that had fallen into ill repair. Chrétien and friends made the investment partly to help a friend who was losing badly on the building. They wanted to turn it into a first-class facility, fix all the rooms, bring in a good chef, and get rid of the prostitutes. Chrétien acted as the lawyer on the deal and, along with Kiar, went to Quebec City to get approval for building modifications. The trip left Kiar with vivid memories of Chrétien. "What I recall is watching this guy just cut through those bureaucrats like they were butter. He had them eating out of his hand. There was no question about having to wait. He told them that he hadn't driven this distance to sit around and that underlings wouldn't do. He wanted the deputy minister, if not the minister himself."

He was developing a keen interest in the economy of the city. By 1960 Shawinigan had passed its peak and was entering a period of decline that would see industries leave *en masse*, the population drop rapidly, and politicians scramble to save it. Technology was the root cause of the fall. With the arrival of petrochemicals, the Shawinigan chemical industry became outmoded. Du Pont's cellophane-producing plant was closed down because of the appearance of polyethylene. The town's strong labour movement made costs much more prohibitive than they had been, and the nationalization of the province's private power companies under a new Quebec cabinet minister named René Lévesque reduced the city's competitive advantage. Most damaging of all, however, was the arrival of the modern transmission line. "When they invented the aluminum cable," said Jean-Paul Gignac, who became a Hydro-Quebec executive, "that was the end of Shawinigan." In the days when electricity was transported along copper wire, it made sense for companies to locate close to big dams, such as those in Shawinigan. The new fantastically efficient power lines economized the process to such an extent that there was no longer any need to locate at the source.

Chrétien was kept abreast of economic developments through guests of the Sixties Club and a growing number of high-powered friends. Many people, seeing the speed and skill with which this young man moved, felt that had he stayed in either law or business, he would have reached the very pinnacle of his field.

But other plans were in the making. "I had a big [law] firm for Shawinigan," he recalled. "I had the biggest firm within a few years, and I was doing very well. But when the opportunity came for election, I said to hell with it."

CHAPTER EIGHT

THE WILL TO WIN

E VEN BEFORE he waged his first remarkable federal election campaign, one in which his chances of victory seemed so impossible, the foundation stones of Jean Chrétien's political character were well in place.

Ever prudent with the dollar, raised in a family where all the pennies counted, he was a fiscal conservative. If he had a profligate side to him, it was with words, not money. A law partner noted, when Chrétien left to enter politics, that if he maintained the nation's books in the frugal way he presided over the law firm's treasury, the country would be in sound financial order.

Though cautious in his spending habits, Chrétien was a social-policy liberal. In his fiery summertime speeches at the paper mill, he advocated greater social protections and union power. At Laval he marched to the Legislature, demanding universal access to post-secondary education. Education was a right, he argued, not a privilege. As an apprentice politician, he peppered his rhetoric with calls for fairness, equal opportunity, help for the disadvantaged.

A third cornerstone of the Chrétien construct was his instinctive federalism, the ocean-to-ocean concept of Canada that had its roots far back in family history. Since boyhood Jean had heard his parents and grandparents talk of the greatness of his country. He had seen his father line up against the francophone majority in voting to send his brethren off to war.

Still, there were times when he flirted with the other side. He was so thoroughly exposed to nationalist gospel from so many of his law school friends that he could hardly help it. Jean Pelletier jumped directly from law school to the Union Nationale premier's office, serving as an assistant to Duplessis's successors. Gabriel Loubier became a star in the Union Nationale firmament. Le Chat and Le Chien were card-carrying conservatives, as was the bellicose Marcel Chartier. As well, Liberal Party brethren like René Lévesque, a politician Chrétien then deeply admired, were preaching a more vigorously nationalist message.

For a while—until he was firmly rebuked by a friend—Chrétien was beginning to sound just like them. The dressing-down came at a lunch at the Château de Bois hotel in Trois-Rivières, where he and his lawyer friends congregated every Friday. Chrétien was discussing a controversy that had erupted in 1961, when Ottawa civil servant Marcel Chaput was fired for spouting his strongly held separatist beliefs. Chrétien defended Chaput, and by extension the sovereigntist movement. Guy Lebrun, the most ardent federalist among Chrétien's Laval friends, bore down on him like a tornado. How can you sit there and condemn what's going on in English Canada, he demanded of Chrétien, when you don't know anything about English Canadians? "You don't even know how to speak English. You've hardly ever been in English Canada. You've spent all your life in Shawinigan and Quebec. Why don't you learn something before you go talking through your hat?" The blistering attack unsettled Chrétien, who vowed to get back at Lebrun. On the drive home to Shawinigan he swore at the empty passenger seats, but by the time he arrived, he had calmed down, realizing his friend was not far off the mark. Soon he was back on the federalist road again. "Finally," said his ex-roommate Garceau, "Jean made up his mind and said those guys, the separatists, are losers and the big game is the Canada game."

Having spent three years as a lawyer, building a highly successful practice and putting his stamp on the legal community of La

Mauricie, Jean Chrétien was now ready to undertake what his life had been pointing towards for years. Law was interesting enough, and had certainly provided him with a comfortable standard of living and prestige in his community. But Jean Chrétien wanted more. Bernard Ducharme, a Shawiniganite who was at different times a classmate of both Chrétien and Brian Mulroney, saw the young men as sharing a quality that set them apart. They were both "frenetically ambitious." Neither would be content without action, influence, and power. For them, life, as Malcolm Muggeridge put it, was a drama, not a process.

Chrétien was ready to make the jump—and it was with deadly seriousness that he did so. The provincial route was a possibility, but two factors made federal politics more likely. First, his father, the great Laurier patriot, was pressing for Ottawa. Second, the federal seat for the Shawinigan area was more readily available. The provincial incumbent, René Hamel, had become a cabinet minister in Jean Lesage's government and showed promise of holding the riding for some time. Federally, Chrétien's prospects were brighter. In 1962 J. A. Richard, the sitting Liberal for St-Maurice–Laflèche, was seventy-two years old. He had sat in the House of Commons since 1949, and when local Liberals spoke of him, they liked to emphasize the word "sat." In his thirteen years in Parliament, they said, Richard only got to his feet once—to ask the Speaker to open a window.

Many Liberals wanted "the old coot" to step down to make room for Chrétien. When the Diefenbaker government called an election in 1962, Chrétien rushed over to see Richard, only to be informed by the veteran that he wanted to "sit" for another term. At twenty-eight, Chrétien was younger than Richard's youngest son. The MP told him to slow down. "Next time," he said. Chrétien believed he had enough support to defeat Richard at a nomination meeting, but demonstrating unusual restraint, rejected advice to push the MP forcibly aside. Richard was a friend of the family's.

In the June election, Richard was trounced by Réal Caouette's Social Credit Party, losing to Socred candidate Gérard Lamy by almost ten thousand votes. Led by the incendiary Caouette, the Socreds were a rural Quebec movement promoting nationalism, old-fashioned religion, and an economic theory that advocated printing millions of dollars in new bills to ease the poor man's plight. In the 1962 election, the party won over half a million votes in Quebec and twenty-six of the province's seats. Chrétien got wind early of what they had done to poor old Richard and personally informed him of the rout. He had warned him that it would be a tough election for a fellow his age. Now he felt vindicated. Richard reacted calmly. "Oh, I'm very sorry for you guys who have worked so hard," he said.

The Liberal nomination was now open but, given the rush of events in the nation's capital, hardly desirable. By early 1963, the Diefenbaker minority government had collapsed, and new elections were called for April. Great majorities could easily be overcome in the normal four or five-year period between elections. But in this instance, there were only nine months. Gérard Lamy had hardly a chance to find his seat in the Commons. Any challenger in the coming election would face the prospect of reversing a ten-thousand-vote majority overnight.

Chrétien consulted many friends, all of whom advised against running. The electorate had just thrown out the Grits, they reasoned, so they weren't about to vote them back in. Chrétien was inclined to agree but continued sampling opinion, and eventually got around to visiting René Hamel. Hamel's view was perhaps the most important because he controlled the riding's electoral machine.

He surprised Chrétien by telling him he should enter the race. "You won't win," he deflatingly added, but running in an election did wonders for one's law practice. As Hamel knew from experience, the free publicity was a windfall. In addition, Hamel added, Chrétien would be able to cut into Lamy's margin by about three thousand votes and thereby lay the groundwork to beat him the next time.

Chrétien, who never hesitated to knock on the doors of people he did not know, visited Claude Ryan, the editor of Montreal's prestigious newspaper *Le Devoir*. Ryan, who was impressed by Chrétien's overall good judgement, encouraged him strongly. If he had any hesitation, it was because of Chrétien's depth. "I told him he didn't seem to have the breadth that some others have," recalled Ryan, "but that he had the stuff of realism."

The endorsements from Ryan and Hamel were encouraging. Slowly, the young lawyer warmed to the idea, particularly since, as Hamel had explained, even a loss could be considered a win. The next step was to contact the key players in the political machine. Did they want him? If so, how hard would they work for him?

He approached one of Hamel's chief organizers, Robert Beaulieu, at a meeting of the provincial riding organization. Beaulieu, already an admirer of Chrétien's, was standing with Hamel when Chrétien came by. "Here's the future federal member from Shawinigan," Beaulieu announced. For the rest of the evening, Chrétien, having heard the comment, trailed Beaulieu around the hall. When Beaulieu left, Chrétien followed him out the door. He stopped him and said, "Bob, what you said earlier, that tempts me."

They arranged a meeting at Chrétien's home with two other top organizers for the following Friday night. Then, the week after that, they had another session at Chrétien's—this time with fifty organizers. Everyone liked Chrétien and pledged their full support. Before they adjourned, they made two strategic decisions. First, they determined that Chrétien should not be rubber-stamped for the Liberal nomination. "There were no other candidates for the nomination," recalled Beaulieu. "We decided a competition was needed to increase interest. Therefore, we had to find another candidate." In addition, they decided to make sure a Conservative Party candidate entered the election. "The Tories didn't have a name up yet," said Beaulieu. "We knew there were at least two thousand Conservatives in the constituency who would never vote Liberal, but who would take away votes from the Socred. So we had to find a Conservative candidate if one did not come forward."

At the same time this was going on in Shawinigan, Liberal Party pooh-bahs from Ottawa and across the province met in Quebec City to discuss strategy and the allocation of campaign resources. Because the Créditiste lead in St-Maurice–Laflèche was so imposing, they wrote the riding off, deciding that only a token Liberal effort was justified. Riding representatives challenged the view, arguing that they had a young man capable of staging a miracle upset. Their listeners were unsympathetic, and the meeting adjourned.

Two opponents faced Chrétien for the Liberal nomination, one put up by the party machine for the sake of media interest. He backed down before the vote, and Chrétien crushed the other. And so, Jean Chrétien's first campaign—a smart, dirty, and determined campaign—was set to begin. Few observers gave him any chance of winning. The period between this election and the last was simply too brief. But Chrétien believed he could cut into the Socred majority and, as Hamel said, set the groundwork for a victory the next time.

Four days after the nomination, Lester Pearson, the party leader, visited Trois-Rivières for a rally of all Liberal candidates in the region. He laid out the major campaign priorities—the reduction of unemployment, decreasing dependence on the United States, putting the country's two solitudes on an equal footing—then watched as the candidates made their own pitches. As Jean Chrétien's name was announced, a working-class man at the front of the crowd jumped to his feet. This man didn't want to hear any talk of Chrétien's not being able to win. He held up a poster so large that no one in the hall could fail to see it. "We're Voting for Jean Chrétien," the placard declared, "Our Future Prime Minister!" Lester Pearson took notice. When Chrétien completed his remarks, Pearson pointed it out to Jean. Then he laughed.

The impassioned supporter was Claude Lacoursière, a Shawinigan labourer who was a relative of Chrétien's and used to play baseball with him. To many, his action had the look of a put-up job, something Chrétien organizers had arranged in the back rooms to draw attention to their man. Lacoursière, however, claimed he did it of his own volition. He later made two other great banners with similar messages and strung them across the top of Shawinigan's main thoroughfares.

The leader's visit proceeded more successfully than Chrétien's own debut in La Baie Shawinigan. The local priest, Father Auger, damned if he was about to see a Chrétien victory, scheduled a last-minute general meeting of all parishioners for the same evening as the Chrétien launch. The gambit, which was obviously intended to leave Chrétien with a half-empty hall, did diminish the turnout, but the candidate still had enough supporters to avert embarrassment. He struck back at Auger later in the campaign. In case the priest couldn't hear his blasts condemning the church for meddling in political affairs, Chrétien made it easier. The town hall, where Chrétien gave many of his speeches, was located next to Auger's church. Chrétien had his workers install large speakers outside, facing right at Auger's windows.

His platform closely followed the Pearson line. One important exception, however, was his hesitation over his leader's stance on nuclear arms. In a reversal of traditional party policy, Pearson had agreed to the American desire to locate nuclear warheads in Canada. The switch drew the wrath of many young Liberals in Quebec, including Pierre Trudeau. Chrétien fudged, saying he didn't like the turn-about but wanted to research the question further to see if Ottawa had in fact made a commitment to NATO on the issue.

But this was never a campaign that would pivot on the issues, nor did Chrétien have any intention of making it one. This campaign would be won on personality, energy, and youth. Past elections had belonged to the old crowd, to old tactics, to old traditions. Inspired in part by the success of John Kennedy, the Catholic American president whose image captivated so many, Chrétien ran a campaign infused with the spirit of youth and the ideals of public service.

His foresight in forming the Sixties Club five years earlier was now becoming abundantly clear. The club became his electoral machine, pushing aside, sometimes indelicately, the old order. With their dark suits, narrow ties, and cropped hair, the Chrétienites had the look of a Kennedy youth troupe. Jean's elegant wife, Aline, carrying herself with Hyannisport chic, fit the mould, as did his dictatorial father, Wellie, looking over everyone's shoulders from afar. With his dark, sunken eyes and his hair shooting back as if he'd stuck his fingers in an electrical outlet, Chrétien himself, however, hardly looked as if he had stepped out of Camelot. Nor was there that easy-money look to his Sixties Club friends. They would carry out their campaign in distinctly un-Kennedyish fashion, doing it on the cheap. Wellie Chrétien was no Joe Kennedy. Of young Jack's first campaign, the senior Kennedy once declared, "With all the money I spent, I could have elected my chauffeur."

Chrétien was not gifted with any undue amount of charisma, but he had the quality from which leadership often takes its cue. He had willpower. It was emblazoned in him. There was an aura about him that said he could do things. This surging sense of the possible gave the campaign its exceptional energy level.

In the microcosm of the riding of St-Maurice, the waves of a generation fell in behind him. "I never saw anything like it," said Roger Caron, a Chrétien campaigner. "All the youth came out. Today you have difficulty attracting volunteers. Not then. It wasn't the money involved. It was the joy of participating, the joy of winning."

"It was a new-style politics," said Guy Suzor, Chrétien's campaign manager. "In the past, politics here were dominated by the old crowd." This was the easiest campaign Suzor would ever run. "You didn't have to ask people to do anything," he said. "They were out there before you called."

The riding had forty-four thousand voters. They divided themselves principally among four municipalities, three of which—Shawinigan, Shawinigan-Sud, and Grand'Mère—were clumped together. The fourth, La Tuque, another paper-mill town, was a ninety-minute drive north of Shawinigan. Together these centres accounted for all but about 10 per cent of the vote for the riding. The constituency, roughly speaking, was 90 per cent French, 90 per cent Roman Catholic, and 90 per cent blue collar. Voters were fickle. Federally, they elected a nationalist Bloc Populaire candidate in the 1940s, swung to Richard and the Liberals in the 1950s, then elected Lamy of the Social Credit in 1962.

Chrétien saw his first task as dispelling the assumption that the Socreds could not be overtaken. "In order to win," he told his organizers, "we have to create the impression that we are winning." He needed imagination and some surprise elements in the campaign, but not having a sizeable treasury made extraordinary measures difficult. What little financing he did have came from brother Maurice, the lumber-company owner Jean-Paul Gignac, and the wealthy family of Chrétien's friend Georges Cossette. In thinking of novel ideas that could draw crowds and still be carried out on the cheap, someone suggested bean fests. Baked-bean dinners. Everyone liked beans and they were a quarter a can. The candidate endorsed the proposal and the dinners became one of the feature attractions of the campaign.

They were organized right down to the ketchup man, Sixties Club member René Prévost. Beans were ladled from giant pots, with coffee and little white cubes of cake served for dessert. The fêtes were advertised as special "Canadian dinners." Personalized invitations went out from Mr. and Mrs. Chrétien, and Shawiniganites and workers in other communities came out by the hundreds, sometimes the thousands. Jean and Aline worked their way through every table, serving the beans themselves. For a warm-up act there was the pugnacious and witty oratory of Fernand D. Lavergne, the union man who, if the candidate was late, could roll on for two hours at a stretch and still keep the folks entertained. The incumbent Socred Gérard Lamy, a furniture maker and former barber, was a father of fifteen. With that many children, he boasted, he was the one, not the inexperienced Chrétien, who knew the problems of the average Quebecker. Lavergne took him to task. "Jean Chrétien is only twenty-nine years old," Lavergne asserted, "and in our religion, since we are allowed only one wife, it would not be well viewed if he had fifteen children." Yes, Mr. Lamy was a fine reproducer, Lavergne shouted. But what the voters needed was not a *reproducteur* but a *législateur*.

The bean feasts were helping to instil in the campaign some of the positive psychology that Chrétien wanted. But he still needed something extra—and here the strategists became more imaginative. Nothing created confidence so much as a willingness to match words with money. So the Chrétiens gathered their resources, primarily from among themselves, turned them over to Guy Suzor and the other campaign managers, and sent them off to the taverns. Over beers, they started debate among the factory workers by arguing that the Liberals were on their way to victory. When the inevitable response—"Chrétien hasn't got a chance"— was forwarded, the Liberal worker pulled out a wad of bills and offered a bet. If the drinker across the table wanted to put a wager down but didn't have the cash, another campaigner was usually on hand to cover for him. Suzor and company placed bets in virtually every tavern in the riding.

Soon word of the Chrétien camp's cockiness had spread throughout the constituency. A winning psychology was being set in place. Casino politics was working. If Chrétien wasn't in front, the voters reasoned, why were his supporters making all those bets? "If you have ten guys watching two guys arguing about politics," recalled Jean Chrétien, "and the Chrétien supporter offered to bet five dollars, and the other guy who was against Chrétien doesn't cover the bet, the other guys who are watching say, 'Jesus! Chrétien is winning.'"

Though it was not a campaign driven by a particular issue, Chrétien spoke repeatedly of the need for more French power in Ottawa. With industries beginning to leave Shawinigan, the town was seeking help from outside. Ottawa therefore had to become active in Quebec and Quebec active in Ottawa. The Liberal candidate pledged more public works, better forms of social assistance, and the creation of special municipal banks offering low interest rates to get new businesses up and moving. "What's necessary," he said, "are men who will fight to put French Canadians at the top of the country, and it's in Ottawa where that battle is taking place and must be won." He also promised, though without going into detail, to reform the British North America Act to reflect relations not among the ten provinces but between the two solitudes.

While his Sixties Club movement might have envisaged a nobler form of politics, while in fact it was corruption under Duplessis that was among the driving imperatives for the formation of the club, Jean Chrétien did not hesitate to resort to low-grade tactics himself to battle his Socred opponent. Against Gérard Lamy, he waged a sometimes dirty, sometimes misleading campaign. He ran hyperbolic attack ads in the newspapers, insulted the intelligence of his opponent with name-calling, angered his own staff with insensitive treatment of them, and published a campaign biography of himself that, lest anyone be reminded of past transgressions, was strategically doctored. The biography, which was printed in the *Shawinigan Standard,* left a four-year gap—his dark years at the seminary in Joliette.

Ridiculing his opponent became one of Chrétien's favoured weapons. "Canada is at a turning point in its history," he said in one speech, "and it's not the time to send buffoons to the House of Commons to represent French Canadians." The slurs were coupled with vile newspaper advertisements predicting the destitution that Social Credit economics would inflict on the average citizen.

In preaching his party's funny-money theory, Lamy claimed that the problem with the economy had nothing to do with production. There was a surplus of production. All one had to do was look at all the goods available in the stores. The problem, rather, was purchasing power. The people didn't have enough money to buy the goods. The solution then was obvious: print more money, piles of it. Make $5 billion available on easy terms and people would buy more and factories would hum to fill the orders and unemployment would be erased.

While fundamental economics taught that such an infusion of freshly printed money would devalue the currency, hike the price of imports, and bring on ruinous inflation and high interest rates, the leader of the Créditistes, Réal Caouette, claimed otherwise. He appealed to simple rural folk who had large families to raise, not economics texts to read. Caouette was born in Shawinigan. He roared through his home town, his voice screeching like rubber on a sharp turn, preaching religious and economic fundamentalism that left the locals in awe. "There's not enough money in circulation because some stubborn banker in Ottawa won't start the printing machine," he cried. "To those who say Socreds will lead you to economic chaos, ask the half million unemployed today if there is not chaos already." An aircraft firm, Canadair, had put thousands of workers on the streets. Why not, cried Caouette, open a car-manufacturing plant for them?

To discredit the Créditistes, Chrétien's Liberals dug into the photo files of 1922 Germany to find victims of an inflation so savage that it took a wheelbarrow full of money to purchase a loaf of bread. They ran these pictures, coupled with photos of similar penury from Hungary in 1946 and France in 1948, in full-page advertisements. In a display in *L'Echo de St-Maurice*, the pictures were under a headline that blared, "Le Crédit Social, c'est la misère." (Social Credit, It's Destitution.) Under the photos quotes from prominent Liberals, including René Lévesque, savaged the Socred policies.

These tactics and the sometimes dictatorial manner in which Chrétien ran the operation offended some on his campaign team.

One of them, Georges Cossette, finally confronted the candidate and, in what one worker called a bitter quarrel, told Chrétien he had to adopt a new attitude. "I told him," remembered Cossette, "that he should spread his powers through the organization more." His style was so brusque, recalled Suzor, "that it wounded the egos of people."

"Chrétien was doing things that weren't right in that campaign," said Gilles Marchand. Though it was true, he said, that the Quebec political tradition was heavy on foul play, Chrétien's politics were supposed to signal a turn for the better.

Whether Chrétien even needed devious tactics in his campaign against Lamy was unlikely. The Socred was an extraordinarily weak candidate. Though he enjoyed the built-in advantage of having such a big lead from the previous election, if there was anyone capable of squandering such a lead, it was Lamy. In truth, as he would say years later, he really didn't care to win. In his few months representing the Socreds in Parliament, he found he had nothing to do. "I didn't like the life we had in Ottawa. It bored me to death." More significantly, given the meagre ten-thousand dollar MP's salary, he couldn't afford to be one. "With fifteen children, you can't get by on that. I couldn't let them starve."

However, having just won a victory for the party and being a grand admirer of Caouette, Lamy didn't feel it was right to drop out after only a few months. "But I didn't campaign that second time. It didn't interest me at all. I let them put up my name as a candidate just for form. I made very few speeches. I let him win."

No official constituency-wide polls were taken in St-Maurice–Laflèche as the campaign wore on. So, riding his big lead, Lamy remained confident, even while hardly campaigning. A survey in La Tuque, which was not Chrétien territory, showed Lamy getting 85 per cent of the vote. This led him to predict that Chrétien was going down to such a horrid defeat on April 9 that he wouldn't even get his deposit back. At least J. A. Richard, he said, had been able to do that. "It's too bad that an honest young lawyer will have to take such a fall just because he happens to be running for such a rotten party."

But Chrétien wasn't concerned about Lamy, who was regarded by the educated voters in the riding as a nutcake. Much more worrisome was the ringing voice of Caouette, which seemed to linger in the streets long after he had left town. Because the Socreds were populist themselves, it was difficult for Chrétien to strike his "little guy" pose. He desperately wanted to sell this image because he felt the Liberals had become elitist in recent years, thus causing them problems at the polls. But the Socreds were harping on this very theme. "It's the intellectuals [who] have brought the country to its knees," Lamy alleged. "And now the little guy must suffer."

Though emphasizing his youth, Chrétien was also trying to reach out to all voters. His statement "Je suis le candidat de tout le monde" (I am the candidate of everyone) was characteristic of his approach to politics. While he was on the left side of the party at that time, he hated categorization. "I want to bring together all the classes of society," he said in the campaign. "I'm prepared to sacrifice my law career to give myself over to the interests of this constituency." He dwelled on his working-class roots, painstakingly emphasizing these over his lawyer's credentials. "Nobody can understand you as well as I can. . . . I am the son of a labourer and have worked in plants and overcome many obstacles." Much of his oratory was splattered with factory slang. His look was anything but slick, and he would keep it that way. He lost a button on his coat while campaigning, but whenever one of his workers pointed this out, suggesting he might want to get it fixed, he shooed them away. The button would stay off.

He promised that he would visit every single home in the constituency and maintained a furious pace in trying to do so, occasionally sleeping in his car in the rural districts. To remind voters that this was a new Liberal Party, he made frequent reference to the dynamic young Liberal on the provincial scene, René Lévesque. Here was a man typical of the new breed, said Chrétien. He saw himself in Lévesque's light because Lévesque too had the interests of the workers at heart. "We need men at the federal level like René Lévesque has been provincially, someone to bring back to the party its leftward dynamism."

One flaw the campaign exposed was his inability to communicate in the English language. The riding had a significant chunk of English-speaking voters—about four thousand—and the party staged a rally expressly for them on the night of March 19. Chrétien embarrassed himself, stumbling over English words, mispronouncing them, putting the accent on the wrong syllable, halting, faltering, pausing, stopping. His family members, most of whom had learned English and had talked to him of its importance, shook their heads in dismay.

At the conclusion of his speech, a feeling of relief swept through the chamber. "I didn't understand anything he said," recalled Guy Suzor. "The English didn't understand anything either." After the speech, as Chrétien worked the room, some voters made him promise that if they were to vote for him, he would learn their language.

The single biggest event was the all-candidates meeting in Grand'Mère two weeks before the election. Though only twenty-nine, Chrétien was politically seasoned enough to know that the winning formula was to pack the hall. As the only well-organized candidate, he had no trouble doing so. Grand'Mère was Lamy's home town, but Lamy had no supporters at the meeting and, when introduced, was lustily booed and became visibly offended. In his remarks, Chrétien, cheered at every syllable, toyed with him. He noted that Lamy had made but one speech in the House of Commons, then added sarcastically, "He's obviously a very important MP." Returning to the Socred's boast about having so many children, Chrétien said, "If it was a question of kids, my father, Wellie, should be prime minister, because he and my mother had nineteen."

The Chrétien Liberals had not had to find—not this time anyway—a fake Conservative Party candidate to help their campaign.

A Tory, Bruno Pellerin, entered the race of his own accord. He and Martial Laforest, the NDP candidate, had only marginal support at the meeting.

Speaking last, Lamy was introduced to another torrent of boos. Targeting his main challenger, he asserted, "If you want to have continued unemployment, vote Liberal." But he was barely into his final oration when the catcalls got so loud that he could hardly be heard. The Chrétien supporters were sabotaging him, he charged, and they were being paid to do so. "This is a travesty!"

Chrétien came to the microphone to ask his campaigners to calm down. "Ladies and gentlemen, Mr. Lamy is your member of Parliament. Will you listen to him, please? In two weeks no one will have to listen to him any more."

News of Lamy's disaster at Grand'Mère spread through the town. The Liberals regarded it as a windfall for Chrétien, whose momentum was now palpable. The Lesage government chipped in with an announcement late in the campaign that it was building a $6-million hospital in Shawinigan-Sud. Early on, Chrétien had begun to feel that Hamel was wrong in saying that this could only be an election to lay the groundwork for future efforts. Now he was highly confident of triumph. He predicted to family members that he would win by two thousand votes.

In the days before the vote, the betting in the taverns picked up. Maurice, who was covering most of the bets himself, had hundreds of small-bill wagers on the line. Suzor and company had wagered over $12,000. But the big test was still to come. A Shawinigan businessman, a big bettor who spent a lot of time at the racetracks, failed to see that any strong Chrétien trend had developed. He came forward with a wager that threatened to make a mockery of the casino politics the Chrétiens had so successfully played. He put up five thousand and said, "Match that."

The Chrétiens were rocked by the size of bet, but couldn't afford to back off. It would be a certain signal they had lost faith, and in small towns word spreads quickly. So Jean put up some money. Wellie, who had never bet a penny in his life, contributed no less than five hundred dollars, and Maurice took on much of the rest. They covered the bet.

The night before the election the family congregated at the home of Marcel, the shoe salesman. The phone rang and Gabriel picked it up. "I want to talk to a Chrétien," the voice said. "Any Chrétien will do."

"Well, I'm a Chrétien," said Gabriel. "What do you want?"

"Well, I'm sorry to have to tell you this," the voice said, "but tomorrow, you and your family will have the humiliation of your life."

No humiliation was forthcoming. The people of St-Maurice–Laflèche came to the polls in great numbers on April 8. Of the 43,816 eligible voters, 36,168 or 82.5 per cent cast ballots. The early poll results showed a slight Chrétien lead, and this lead built slowly throughout the evening. Chrétien had predicted a 2,000-vote win. He was wrong by 56 votes. He won, as a later count would show, by 1,944. His final tally was 16,358, less than 50 per cent of the total vote. Lamy's non-campaign brought him 14,414 votes. He won La Tuque and the rural areas of the riding, while Chrétien won the three main principalities: Shawinigan, Shawinigan-Sud, and Grand'Mère. Conservative candidate Pellerin took 3,018 votes, and Laforest of the NDP 1,983.

Chrétien was humble and modest in his acceptance speech. He called it "a victory of mutual confidence," and his father raised his arm on the platform. After media interviews and a victory celebration with Sixties Club friends and others, he returned to his home where his wife and sisters, Giselle and Juliette, had a little party for him in the *salon*. They sipped wine until 2:00 a.m. The former black sheep of the family was happy but subdued.

CHAPTER NINE

THE WIDER GAME

H E TOLD his brother Gabriel, on entering Parliament in 1963, that he would be a politician for ten years, then start a third career. Gabriel cautioned him that it didn't make much sense to be planning so far ahead. But career plans, especially during his long daily walks to deplete his hyperactive edge, always churned in Jean's head. He had told his wife that for his third career, he would become a judge. They'd return to Quebec City, where their love had soared in the Laval years, and he'd sit on the bench.

On arriving in Ottawa, he felt a rush of exhilaration. It was different then. To be a politician carried some honour and prestige with it. To be elected to the House of Commons was to be made to feel important, especially if you were as young as the new member from St-Maurice–Laflèche, and especially if, unlike many other Quebec politicians, you saw service in the federal government as a higher calling.

When he walked under the Peace Tower for the first time, Chrétien was emotionally moved. He thought first of his mother, who had died nine years earlier, and how proud she would have been, she who worried so much about whether he would amount to anything. If there were regrets regarding her absence, they were softened by his awareness of how his father felt. Dad had hoped so much that one of his sons would become a politician.

The whole family was proud of him. They saw that politics and Jean Chrétien were a natural fit. His younger brother Michel viewed him as a quick thinker and a great man of action, though perhaps a little too stubborn, his mind being "a very strong one which you cannot influence very much." But Michel marvelled at his capacity for integrating the information presented to him, grasping the kernel, and running with it. What a fine skill, he felt, for politicians to have. Having watched him in the campaign, his other brothers and sisters could also see that—even though he was less articulate than all of them—he possessed a unique ability to communicate. It was quite a paradox. The more inarticulate he was, the more effective he became. His coarse rural blasts punctured the air with purpose and genuine feeling. Getting the message across didn't have to mean speaking in neatly packaged, flowing sentences. Fragments—choppy, raspy, resonating fragments—could serve one well, as they had John Diefenbaker.

Though so young, so unilingual, so untravelled, and so unfinished, Jean Chrétien brought to Ottawa a quality he'd had since he was a boy. He was still as cocky as when he'd played soldiers with his friends on his street, naturally assuming the post of commandant. His blood coursed with a rebellious confidence that kept pushing him forward, no matter the shortage of skills. He was so young when he set foot in Ottawa, but he didn't feel nervous. "When I arrived, I looked around and I said, 'I can make it here.' It took me a couple of days, after I met the newcomers and so on, and I said, 'I know better than that.'"

Though he was aware, often acutely so, of his weaknesses, he was just as aware that weaknesses could be overcome. He had that quality that set him apart, the capacity for growth. If someone told Chrétien he didn't know anything about a certain subject, his attitude would be "Well, then, I'll learn it. In a couple of years you won't be able to say that."

In Ottawa he found he sometimes had free time on the weekday evenings. Most of the new MPs liked to play cards or drink or find some other way of wasting time. Chrétien wasn't interested, so he enrolled in a post-graduate course in law at the University of Ottawa. One of his classmates was another newcomer to the capital, Jean-Luc Pepin. The course exam unfortunately fell in the same week Chrétien's wife gave birth to their second child, Hubert. He had to return home, and was unable to write it and get his passing grade.

In Parliament's West Block, the MPs who shared the same floor of offices with Chrétien observed his degree of discipline. "He was a very circumspect fellow," noted Rick Cashin, a new member from Newfoundland. "He wasn't the hail-fellow-well-met type. He was serious, more serious than the others in the group. A straight sort of guy."

There was so much hunger in him. In sports the well-known adage was that when you put people on the field with roughly equal abilities, the winner would be the one who wanted it most. Of the big new flock of Quebec MPs who arrived in Ottawa in 1963, it was Jean Chrétien who wanted it most. He was hungry for knowledge, for power, for prestige, and though it was something he might not want to acknowledge, for wealth. He would later write of having left a healthy law practice for the meagre MP's wages, but in fact, he continued for several years to work at his law practice while in Parliament and draw a handsome retainer. Bernard Ducharme, the classmate of both Chrétien and Mulroney, noted that while Mulroney had headed for a big Montreal law firm and Chrétien had returned to his small-town roots, the difference in their tastes was not as pronounced as those forks in the road might suggest. Ducharme, who had drawn up the Sixties Club logo for Chrétien, was another who observed that he always tried to surround himself with men of power and financial importance. Another friend believed that this was the Achilles' heel of Jean Chrétien: he would never be the true tribune of the people, the friend said, because he would never turn his back on the money men.

In 1963 he was still very much a parochial youth. In his twenty-nine years he had rarely been out of Quebec. This narrow backdrop was why some, like Raymond Chrétien, the ambitious son of Jean's eldest brother, Maurice, preferred Jean's opting for federal over provincial politics. It would broaden his perspective. Raymond also made a decision at this time that was consistent with the wider federalist vision of the Chrétien family. He left Quebec to join the Canadian public service, the diplomatic corps. Not many Quebeckers were taking such a route. "In those years for a man from Quebec to become a federal public servant," recalled Raymond, "was almost an abdication of responsibility."

One look at the picture Chrétien hung up on his office wall in the nation's capital suggested that while cooped up inside his province, he had kept at least one eye on the outside world. The new MPs had to share quarters for a short period, and Chrétien's office-mate was the great mimic from his Laval days, August Choquette. Choquette was surprised to see that Chrétien, the country lawyer, put up an elegant photo of John and Robert Kennedy. He had spoken often to Sixties Club friends about his admiration for the Kennedys. In his early days as an MP, he would unsuccessfully propose that an important government centre (one he had in mind was the CBC building) be named in memory of the president.

Having gone the classical seminary college route and earned a law degree from Laval, Chrétien had academic credentials that were more than respectable. But the mere fact that he was from Shawinigan made him susceptible to the charge that he was an intellectual lightweight. More than in English Canada, the Quebec culture, as in France, encouraged classification of this sort. To be rural was often to be philistine. Michael Pitfield, the emerging Trudeau confidant, had academic qualifications no more impressive than Chrétien's (a B.A. from an unknown New York state college, a law degree from McGill, and a night-school diploma in public law), but he was viewed, being of the Outremont caste, as a high-level intellectual. To be sure, rural Quebec had sent many weak MPs to Ottawa, which only encouraged the typecasting. Chrétien, while seeing himself as superior to the stereotype, was still sensitive to it. He couldn't claim to be an avid reader or an ideas man—he was more Roman than Greek—but the notion that he didn't have the intellectual baggage, said Marcel Bérard, his friend from grade school, "upset him very much."

Possessing appropriate intellectual *gravitas* was an important qualification in 1960s Ottawa for earning a cabinet posting. While Lester Pearson's own academic career was not terribly distinguished, he did emerge from an academic background. He had taught at the University of Toronto and had also, though he was not elitist like many of them, spent several years in the diplomatic corps. In looking for rising stars from Quebec, he and his advisers focused on scholastic and intellectual credentials. Chrétien was rural, without polish, and lacking any kind of worldly experience that would impress a prime minister who was a Nobel Prize winner.

While he understood that his populist style counted for little among the literati, Chrétien also knew that political appeal and effectiveness bore modest relation to the number of poets one could quote. His friend Fernand D. Lavergne saw a much more important quality in Chrétien: judgement. "To read books enriches the mind," said Lavergne, "but it doesn't provide the reader with good judgement." Chrétien was not profound, observed Jean-Yves Morin, a Shawinigan professor of political science. But since when, he asked, did politics demand depth? "Le profondeur?" remarked Morin. "Ça donne quoi?"

Nonetheless, the hurdles Chrétien faced were considerable. Ottawa was flooded with new Liberal MPs from Quebec, many ambitious like himself. In the early 1960s it was still an English capital. The government operated largely in the one language, and Chrétien spoke little of it. He was exceptionally young and green, and his populist stock was not favoured. To enhance the stature of francophones in the Liberal Party, Pearson was cultivating establishment and academically distinguished figures like Guy Favreau, Maurice Lamontagne, and Maurice Sauvé. And there were others on the horizon, wise men like Pierre Trudeau, Gérard Pelletier, and Jean Marchand.

Chrétien knew few MPs from outside Quebec when he arrived, but his friend Lavergne had suggested he make contact with Doug Fisher, the NDP member who had defeated Liberal giant C. D. Howe in Port Arthur. Fisher's name was known to Chrétien because he had made headlines in Quebec with his harsh critiques of nationalists like René Lévesque and Marcel Chaput. Fisher also wrote a newspaper column and was viewed as a politician worth knowing. When they were introduced, Chrétien, struggling with his English, got the pronunciation wrong, calling him "Dog." Fisher took him to the Commons and, pointing to a back row of pews, politely informed the young Quebecker that this was where he would be sitting. Pointing in the direction of the front row, Chrétien said, "Yes, Dog, but someday I be sitting up there."

Fisher found him direct and "so damned practical, a guy who learned the ropes quickly and grasped how power was exercised." He was, along with newcomers like John Munro, a young MP from Hamilton, a man on the make. "You could say that," said Munro. "We were both thrilled by it all and wanted to get in the cabinet and do something."

For Chrétien, being on the make meant separating himself from the Quebec grouping. What Fisher, Munro, and others noticed instantly was that the young French Canadian didn't hang back in familiar territory with his Quebec colleagues. He began making alliances with MPs from all regions of the country. He also made a point of spending time with the anglophones so he could learn more English. "Most of us spoke a little bit of French," said Joe Macaluso, an MP from Hamilton West, "but when we tried it with him he said, 'No, don't speak French to me. You must speak English. I have to learn it.'" He befriended, among others,

Macaluso, Newfoundland's Cashin, Donald Macdonald from Toronto, and "Mo" Moreau of British Columbia.

Having been told of the importance of English on innumerable occasions, Chrétien was finally getting serious about learning his second language. "I have to tell you," he would explain one day, "that for me, I didn't learn English because I was never very much interested by it. . . . For me, studying was not important. Sport was important. Arguing about politics might have been important. But studying came late. And by the time I started to be serious with my studies, we were not learning English any more." For his brothers and sisters, he said, the opportunities were different. Guy studied in P.E.I., Michel studied in Montreal and at Harvard, Gabriel was in the armed forces and learned English there, and Giselle worked for English managers in several Shawinigan industries. "But I didn't think about it. I thought of politics, but I didn't know if it was to be provincial or federal politics."

It wasn't only in the area of language that Chrétien made strides towards English Canada. On a whole range of matters, he set about playing a wider game, making himself the national man, doing things, as Doug Fisher noted, that Quebec representatives did not normally do. In short order, he would insinuate himself into the English milieu, make friends across the country, attack nationalists in Quebec with vigour, become parliamentary secretary to an anglophone minister, and tackle a dossier—economics—that French Canadians traditionally ignored.

It was as if the patriotic hand of his father was leading the way. The two of them continued to exchange letters frequently, and Wellie found his son to be a good listener. "I don't know why it is," he mentioned to Mrs. Godin one day, "but Jean follows my instructions most of the time."

Chrétien's initial ambition, as sensed by his office mate August Choquette, was to become the first francophone minister of Finance in Canadian history. Some had spoken of the smooth Jean

Lesage as a possibility when he was a federal MP in the 1950s, but Lesage had left Ottawa for Quebec politics. Chrétien had a non-economic mind and a non-economic background. Neither his classical education nor law school had embraced the subject, and he had no experience on Bay Street or with a major business. On the surface the ambition appeared unreasonable and unreachable.

His eye for power had told him, however, that the men of influence were those who controlled the purse-strings. He had once wanted to go to Boston to study business, he had looked with envy on the comforts money had brought his brother Maurice, and he had begun, with mixed results, making investments himself. At the time of his election he and four friends invested $200,000 each in the purchase of the Shawinigan Transport Company. Chrétien had been the lawyer for the owner when the company went into bankruptcy. To prevent him from being totally stripped of his assets, Chrétien found investors to buy the company, telling them the bargain-basement price was an excellent deal. If it was so good, the investors said, why don't you come in with us? To his regret, Chrétien did.

When the five men took over the transport company, they found it had lost most of its major clients. The owner had phoned them all after signing it over and told them he was no longer in business. Most had quickly found other haulers. "So the guy had really screwed me," Chrétien recalled, "when I really, you know, saved him. Normally I would not have done it if I had not been busy with my campaign." André Grenier, who had his own trucking business, headed up the new group of owners. He, Chrétien, and the rest quickly bailed out, and Grenier found a new purchaser. By selling when he did, Grenier felt he saved Chrétien's $200,000 investment. "I sold it before it got unsellable." The politician, he noted, kept a low profile throughout, not wishing to be identified with a losing venture.

For his first two years in Ottawa, Chrétien kept his family in Shawinigan and returned every weekend. These were trying times at home. Aline lost two infants to miscarriages, each late in the pregnancy. One baby was already seven pounds, and it was Maurice, the gynecologist, who tried unsuccessfully to save it. Jean and Aline had been telling five-year-old France for months that she would soon have a baby sister or brother.

"I was in the hospital for ten days and we just cried the whole time," recalled Aline. "Jean was so afraid to tell France that there was no baby. We saw all of the other women in the hospital with babies, and when we went home, Jean went through the door and, right away, France was asking, 'Where is my baby?'"

Finally, a baby brother did come in the person of Hubert. Aline had to stay in bed virtually the entire pregnancy. To keep herself occupied she continued to study English and Spanish, eventually becoming fluent in both.

Jean was home a lot when Parliament was not in session. When it was sitting, he would try to supplement his weekend trips with a mid-week visit to Aline, if she was healthy. They would meet in Montreal.

Chrétien made many friends in the Shawinigan business world, one of them the esteemed man of finance, class, and athletic prowess, Jean-Paul Gignac. In the 1960s Gignac, who had moved on to Hydro-Quebec, worked in Montreal and, every Monday morning, had a limousine drive him the two hours from Shawinigan to the big city. Not long after the election of 1963, he had a companion on those drives. Chrétien rode as far as Montreal in Gignac's limo before catching the train to the capital. It was quiet and they would talk the entire two hours about a wide range of subjects—but mainly economics and business.

"He wanted to know what was going on in business and how my business developed and operated, the basics of what I was doing," recalled Gignac, who was twelve years Chrétien's senior. "He wanted to know why I was doing it this way and how I could make money out of that. In those days we [in Quebec] didn't have any grants or subsidies. We were on our own. We had to use our imagination and work like hell." Gignac told Chrétien that big business was an English bastion, that no help for French Canadians was coming from Ottawa. "The French Canadians didn't have much of a chance. This I experienced and told him. And I told him it would have to change." Gignac, who had helped Chrétien financially in his election campaign, tried to impress upon the young politician the extent of the discrimination. He told him, for example, how he used to have the freight for his lumber company shipped by Canadian Pacific, which was headquartered in Montreal. Though Gignac could speak English, he was insulted that in dealing with the national headquarters, he could not use his native French. Eventually he switched to Canadian National, because the people there spoke French to him.

Chrétien listened intently. Gignac was impressed by his curiosity, his memory, and most notably, his sense of purpose. "I was sure he would succeed, because he knew what he wanted. He had fixed objectives."

One day Chrétien informed Gignac that it was time for him to state his preference for a parliamentary committee. Gignac suggested he select Finance because of the lack of expertise among Quebeckers in this field. Chrétien, who shared in this lack, saw it as a good idea. During his campaign he was puzzled by the Social Credit's funny-money theory. Despite condemning it with every term imaginable, he hadn't understood the economics of it and wanted to learn. He volunteered for a Finance assignment and, as Prime Minister Pearson informed him, was the only Quebec MP to do so. He sat on the House Banking and Finance Committee, which helped set the stage for an important career development.

His maiden speech in the Commons, delivered on May 23, 1963, was a somewhat pedantic effort, occasioning a comment in the Quebec press that its author was obviously "no intellectual meteor." As a primary theme, Chrétien chose the ageless question of Quebec and Canadian unity. "Mr. Speaker, since I have been elected, many of my English-speaking colleagues have asked me questions on a problem of the day and wanted to know what I thought of the separatist movement in the province of Quebec.

"Mr. Speaker, I believe we should not give too much importance to that situation.... I am confident that the present separatist movement is not serious." He noted the discrimination against French Canadians in Quebec in the fields of industry and commerce, emphasizing that francophones, as Gignac had told him, were "too often left in the background." The federal government should recognize that Quebec "may wish to be more independent from Confederation than in the past. The government of our province must be given the means to solve its own problems. The federal government will have to adopt laws on biculturalism that are adequate and recognize, on a national scale, that during the next one hundred years, Canada, a country where there are two languages and two cultures, will be different from the United States."

The speech was harmless enough to this point, but then he raised the nuclear issue. After becoming embroiled in the controversy during the election campaign, tilting against the announced Pearson plan to station American warheads in Canada, Chrétien had turned around and voted with his party on the issue in his first days in the House. He had decided to support the policy if he could find proof that the Canadian government under Diefenbaker had committed itself to the weapons as Pearson claimed. He first asked Lucien Cardin, the associate minister of Defence. Cardin provided Chrétien with confidential documents that substantiated Pearson's claim, then took him to a secluded office so he could look at them in private. Because they were in English, Chrétien couldn't read them. He was too proud to admit this, however, and went through the charade of pretending he could understand the documents. Since the minister had been willing to show him the material, he took it as a clear indication that it contained the commitment. Later he came across Douglas Harkness, Diefenbaker's minister of Defence, who assured him that indeed this was the case.

But in changing his position, Chrétien subjected himself to flip-flop allegations in the Quebec media. Instead of dropping the matter, he tried, in a long and convoluted way, to defend himself in his maiden speech. As he did so, derisive comments came at him from across the aisle. In *Le Devoir* he was called a dancing seal. When his father read this and other stories, he chastised his son, telling him what a mess he had made of things.

Mistakes such as this, along with his down-home rural style, his ungrammatical diction, and his lack of pretension, fed the impression in some quarters that he was a fellow with a room-temperature IQ. In a long argument in the House of Commons, Louis-Joseph Pigeon mocked the twenty-nine-year-old for not knowing the rules of order. He continued his assault by openly wondering how Chrétien had been able to pass his bar exams. Chrétien, feeling compelled to defend himself, said he had no trouble with the exams and, in fact, had become a lawyer "when [he] was quite young." As most are called to the bar at a young age, it was puzzling statement that drew more snickers. Pigeon came back condescendingly, remarking that indeed he was still young and, perhaps in a few years, might get around to knowing the rules.

A much more serious confrontation than the one with Pigeon occurred when Chrétien met up with the Tory MP Bob Coates. He was on an elevator in the Centre Block when a spat developed between Coates and the government's minister of Public Works, George McIlraith. The elevator attendant, a French Canadian, had stopped at the second floor, but his car was already too full to allow the many members waiting there to get on. At the third floor he stopped again. One person waited, a page boy, and the attendant allowed him to squeeze in. Coates took great exception to this and berated the attendant in front of the others for letting the boy on after passing by members. He was an incompetent fool, Coates said, who was typical of French Canadians.

In his cabinet position McIlraith was the elevator attendant's boss. "Don't give the guy hell," he started in at Coates. "He's only doing his job." Coates couldn't take the reproach. Once off the elevator he came at McIlraith, grabbing him by the shirt and pushing him back. Chrétien sided with McIlraith. Before the shoving could escalate into a full-scale brawl, he jumped between the two men, seized Coates by the lapels, and rammed him back against the wall. He could barely restrain himself from doing to Coates what he had done to Chartier, Trepannier, and others. The two exchanged deadly stares before moving off in different directions.

Having blundered over his pronouncements during the missile controversy, Chrétien rebounded with a triumph. Triumphs weren't easy to come by for back-benchers on the governing side of the chamber. Their lot, since the exercise of power was primarily a cabinet function, was a trying one. Hourly sessions were reserved for the debate of private members' bills, but these bills, given the variety of measures available to block them, were almost never passed. Back-benchers faithfully trotted off to the sessions, however, because they offered them a chance to be heard, to polish their speaking skills, and to impress whoever happened to be in attendance.

Chrétien wanted to break the losing tradition. He had come across what he considered a great issue for a private member's bill: finding a new name for Canada's airline. The existing appellation, Trans-Canada Airlines, was unwieldy. It didn't translate easily into French and was therefore disliked in Quebec. Moreover, it gave a false impression of the airline being only an internal Canadian service while, in fact, it had international routes. The Liberal Judy LaMarsh had tried, as an opposition MP in the Diefenbaker years, to push through a private members' bill changing the name to Air Canada. This name had the dual advantages of being the same in English and French and sounding less parochial. LaMarsh's bid had failed, but Chrétien wished to revive the matter. He quietly prepared to do so, not letting LaMarsh know of his plans for fear she would claim the issue as her own.

In his first attempt with it, he had failed. But having learned from the experience, he was back with the same measure when it was drawn at the top of the order paper in 1964. This time he was prepared. Usually such bills were defeated by filibuster, with MPs talking them out until the allotted hour was up. The best way to get around this, Chrétien reasoned, was to choose the speakers himself. He lined up MPs who supported the motion from all three parties and had them promise to speak only a few minutes each. He would then follow with a short speech, listing the advantages and citing favourable commentary in the media about the idea.

As the supporting speakers were making their presentations, he noticed Doug Fisher sitting in the chamber and went over to ask his advice on what else might be done. Fisher, who supported the name change, told him there were Tories present who would surely block the bid. But he said he would see what he could do.

Fisher exited, then returned a few minutes later and told the bill's opponents he wished to see them privately. "So the two of them, Rod Webb was one, came out," recalled Fisher, "and we were sitting in the lobby talking behind the curtain, and all of sudden, there's this faint patter of applause. And Webb hears this and says, 'Jesus Christ, what have they done?' He goes and opens the door and looks through the curtain and says, 'Goddamn it. They passed the bill!'"

Well before the hour was up, the speakers had finished. A vote was called, and the measure went through. Chrétien had become one of the few MPs in history to succeed with private members' legislation. That it was a bill of some consequence made the accomplishment all the more significant. The legislation had national unity connotations and was received as such. Furthermore, it was a harbinger of the name formula that would be used for countless government bodies. Transport Canada, Information Canada, Investment Canada would take their cue from it, and there would even be Team Canada for the country's hockey heroes.

The new MP had instantly made a name for himself. A generous letter of congratulations came from Lester Pearson. He gained exposure in the national media and, in his own constituency, the press, most notably *Le Nouvelliste* of Trois-Rivières, was glowing in its praise, predicting a great future for Jean Chrétien. The two previous members for Shawinigan, the short-lived Lamy and the veteran Richard, had been inactive, failing to make an impression. Now the people of Shawinigan saw they had a hustler in Ottawa, someone who could make a difference.

The feat had certainly made Wellie happy. Just as pleasing for the great patriot, who was now entering his seventies, was his son's being part of the Liberal team that secured for Canada its own flag. Colleagues in the House remembered Jean Chrétien on the day the flag motion passed because it was one of the few on which he came out at night and joined them for more than one beer. In Shawinigan, meanwhile, Wellie Chrétien did more than celebrate over a drink. He went out and bought a new Canadian flag for every one of his sons and daughters. Decades later the family members could still recall the moment Wellie presented them with their own Canadian flags. Maurice still has his in a drawer in his Montreal apartment, tucked in neatly with his shirts.

Though Chrétien was receiving good press at home, he had to be ever vigilant. The government in which he served held only tenuous minority status, and the voters in his constituency had shown in the last election how quickly they could change their minds. Moreover, Shawinigan's boom times had ended. Industries were moving out, unemployment was on the rise, and as was so often the case, politicians got the blame.

Aware of the danger, Chrétien sought to bring the riding under his control. He fashioned his Sixties Club core into a domineering machine. Ignoring criticisms that he was forging the same kind of exclusionary and undemocratic dynamic that he had pledged to bring down, Chrétien held St-Maurice–Laflèche in a vise-like grip during his first years as an MP. If in Ottawa he had to be circumspect and mindful of his place, at home he was a different Jean Chrétien. Power politics was the name of the game.

To gain full control, his young supporters had to establish authority over the old provincial machine, which had held sway in the riding since the 1940s. Chrétien had enjoyed warm personal relations with its boss, René Hamel. In Hamel's 1956 provincial campaign, Chrétien did his first heavy electioneering. He then supported Hamel in his leadership bid against Jean Lesage, and it was Hamel whose advice had spurred him to make his own start in politics. But as a minister in the Lesage government, the same Hamel, at least according to the Chrétien team, became aloof and forgetful of campaign promises and a practitioner of old-style patronage politics. He was rumoured to be drinking heavily and was tied to a kickback scandal for which he was later exonerated. Chrétien's campaigners gradually severed ties with Hamel and pushed Chrétien towards a harder line in the relationship. In a test of strength the Chrétien and Hamel camps put up rival candidates for the presidency of the regional Liberal organization in 1964. Chrétien's candidate won. Hamel, finding his local base of support crumbling under him, soon resigned to become a judge. Guy Suzor, Chrétien's campaign manager, said the Chrétien machine had been the catalyst.

Having once pilloried all opposition on Hamel's behalf, saying he represented an end to the Duplessis-era corruption, Chrétien tore the roots from under the same Hamel for becoming the old-style politician he promised not to be. Soon Chrétien would be faced with similar charges himself.

With the provincial organization now eclipsed, the Chrétien group had no opposition. Chrétien was just thirty years old. He and the Sixties Club nucleus now became the politburo of Shawinigan. "We were," Chrétien would say, "the machine." Because he was the new star property, his word was law. When he was known to support a candidate, that candidate became almost unbeatable. The

Chrétien machine could stack the hall of any nominating meeting. Suzor, who was employed by the city as a recreation director, was a key operative. "We elected the aldermen, the mayors, the school councillors. We got everyone elected. When someone wanted to run for city council, if we supported him, he won. We became a very powerful organization."

Infused with a feeling of self-importance that was hardly justified for a young man who had won just one federal election, Chrétien was tempted to turn to provincial politics and take Hamel's seat himself. A man in a hurry, he believed this route would probably get him a cabinet post immediately, whereas in Ottawa he could face a wait of several years. As well, the Quiet Revolution was in full swing. A lot of power could be wielded from Quebec City.

He had come to the notice of René Lévesque, for whom he had stated his admiration. In denouncing the Socreds, Lévesque had helped Chrétien in his election campaign. Now Jean-Paul Gignac went to Lévesque and persuaded him that Chrétien should be the one to replace Hamel. Chrétien was keen to get to know the radical star of Lesage's cabinet. He went to Quebec City, and Lévesque took him out to lunch, entertaining him even before they got to the restaurant, the sumptuous Georges V, with his parking job. There wasn't enough space between two cars for his own, but not to be deterred, the mischievous Lévesque rammed back and forth in between them, as if he were playing bumper cars on a carnival midway, until he had created ample room. Chrétien laughed at the caper. Both men laughed. It was the last time the two of them would ever be on happy terms.

The lunch did not proceed smoothly. Chrétien's main purpose in meeting Lévesque was to ascertain whether he would be assured a cabinet position. For his part, Lévesque tried to explain that there was no sense in planning a career in Ottawa. He made, as Chrétien recalled the conversation, a startling observation. "Jean, you have no future in Ottawa because in five years Ottawa will not exist for us." Chrétien had never presumed Lévesque to be so radical. The remark convinced him that Lévesque was a separatist, and he made the allegation at the table. Lévesque, recalled Chrétien, told him to forget about it, and they changed subjects. Lévesque, in later years, termed Chrétien's account of the conversation as "screwy."

After the lunch Chrétien saw Lesage, who was encouraging but, on the subject of the cabinet, cryptic. When the topic came up, the premier recited a gospel passage. "Behold the fig tree, and all the trees. When they now put forth their buds, you know that summer is near." Chrétien, perhaps reading too much into it, took the words as an indication he would get his wish.

Word of the meeting leaked. Prime Minister Pearson called Chrétien to his office, and Chrétien confirmed that he was thinking of leaving federal politics. Pearson asked him, "Jean, do you believe in Canada?" and told him to go home and think about it for a week. Chrétien's family recommended he stay in Ottawa, but of the nineteen friends he consulted, as many as seventeen told him he should go provincial. The two who disagreed were important, however, for he trusted their advice more than the others. One was Fernand D. Lavergne, the other Marcel Crête, one of Quebec's most respected lawyers. The three had dinner at Crête's home, where Lavergne warned Chrétien that if he went to Quebec, he would never be able to remain clean. In Quebec, Lavergne told him in his inimitable, graphic way, "They want the public man to act like a public woman." This was what happened to Hamel, he asserted. "Hamel was clean enough, but the guys around him were pulling down his pants."

In the end Chrétien decided, as he always would, to play the wider game. He stayed in Ottawa. The decision meant the provincial Liberals still needed a candidate to replace Hamel. The sitting federal member would normally keep some distance from the matter, but since the constituency was now his fiefdom, Chrétien couldn't resist playing the role of kingmaker.

The consensus choice among party regulars for the Liberal nomination was Clive Liddle, a well-respected doctor, an anglophone who spoke French. But in consulting with the provincial Liberals, Chrétien found out Liddle wasn't favoured. Nominating an anglophone would be inappropriate given the political climate, they said. So Chrétien threw his machine against Liddle. The nominating meeting was packed with Chrétien stooges backing another candidate, Sixties Club favourite Jean-Guy Trépanier. He got the nomination but, in an election in which Maurice Chrétien lost almost as much in bets as he had won in his brother's first campaign, went down to defeat.

Chrétien made enemies with his heavy-handedness. Liddle had a lot of friends, and they were disgusted that nothing had changed. The spirit of democracy didn't control the riding—machine politics did. Robert Beaulieu, the organizer Chrétien had sought out when he first decided to run federally, saw how he was placing himself on a pedestal. "He didn't pay any attention to the others," said Beaulieu. "René Hamel used to bring his organizers together at meetings or dinners to motivate them. Jean Chrétien did nothing of the kind. He took them for granted." Workers complained about his lack of gratitude, his flashes of early-morning temper, his rushed decision-making. But many understood it. To get where he wanted to go, said André Grenier, he couldn't always be generous with his time or his smiles. "To succeed in that game, you had to be a bastard."

His dirty-tricks campaign against Liddle extended into the 1965 federal election. Bitter at what Chrétien had done to him, Liddle decided to switch parties. He moved to the NDP and ran against his rival. The NDP was unpopular in the riding, but Liddle thought he might at least siphon some votes away from the Liberal. An all-candidates meeting at which Liddle, facing the machine's packed hall, wasn't even allowed to speak was typical of the Chrétien team's treatment of him. After the meeting, an enraged Beaulieu went up to Chrétien and told him his behaviour was pathetic, reminiscent of some of Quebec's most corrupt politicians. Chrétien smiled in response.

Even Lavergne took exception to the way his good friend was flaunting his power. Chrétien soon came to agree that it was a mistake. "I was making a lot of enemies doing that." He made amends with Liddle, telling him after the election that he had not behaved properly in denying him the provincial nomination. Then he began removing himself from political decisions that did not relate directly to his federal jurisdiction. The machine wasn't dismantled but was diminished in scope.

The allegations of dictatorial practices in Shawinigan were insignificant compared with what Chrétien's party was facing in Ottawa. He passed his first two years as a member of a government that was distressingly crisis torn, lurching from one scandal or pretend-scandal to another. Misdeeds and misdemeanours, mainly by Chrétien's Quebec colleagues, were transformed by the oratorical choreography of John Diefenbaker and henchman Erik Nielsen into screaming national headlines.

Ministers fell one on top of the other. Justice Minister Guy Favreau, a favourite of Chrétien's and an honourable man by most anyone's account, was sidelined over his clumsy handling of allegations of bribery against a government official in the tangled Lucien Rivard drug-smuggling case. The stress was such that it was said to contribute to Favreau's death. Another minister, Yvon Dupuis, resigned over charges he had accepted a bribe as a member of the Quebec government in 1961. He was later acquitted. Yet two more Quebec ministers, René Tremblay and Maurice Lamontagne, were destroyed as a result of minor tie-ins to a Montreal furniture salesman. They had purchased furniture from the dealer on credit shortly before he went bankrupt. As with Favreau, Chrétien thought Lamontagne a man of moral and intellectual integrity. He was distressed over the savagery of politics and concluded, along with his francophone colleagues, that it was not coincidental that the targets of Diefenbaker's attacks were all French Canadians.

The dispiriting introduction to federal politics was nevertheless an educational one. New MPs like Chrétien got a crash course in ethics and skulduggery. If there was a silver lining it was that the greater the numbers the scandals brought down, the greater the number of openings created.

Pearson liked having French Canadians as his parliamentary secretaries. Nineteen sixty-five had begun with Guy Rouleau, an old-guard Quebec member, in the job. Rouleau was heavily implicated in the Lucien Rivard affair, however, having asked the National Parole Board to do a favour for a friend of Rivard's who was serving a twenty-year term. When the RCMP released a report concluding that Rouleau's behaviour was suspect, Pearson fired him. Looking over the list for a successor, he came across a name that he had first noticed one night two years earlier in Shawinigan. It was the night a man at the front of a packed town hall had jumped to his feet with a sign declaring, "Jean Chrétien. Our Future Prime Minister."

CHAPTER TEN

A SHARP IMPACT

F OR A YOUNG MAN devoured by ambition, being appointed Lester Pearson's parliamentary secretary in July 1965 was a heartening development.

It had been hard for the prime minister not to notice Jean Chrétien. He had scored that victory against long odds in the 1963 election campaign; he had accomplished the exceptional feat of winning passage of his private member's bill on Air Canada; he had been hotly pursued by the provincial Liberals in Quebec City. He had taken on an unusual financial committee assignment, asked many questions in the House of Commons, and was unfailingly punctual. There were incidental things as well. Lester Pearson loved baseball. So did Jean Chrétien. It gave them something relaxing to talk about, something to transport the mind from the politics of the day. In a game that pitted members of Parliament against the press, the MP from Shawinigan pitched for the prime minister's team. It was a winning performance.

Three months before his appointment, Chrétien was in the spotlight again, this time as an MP who was called upon to second the speech from the throne. In these, the years that would politically define him, his address set forth, in a rudimentary way, the principal elements of his Liberal creed.

He asked his fellow MPs to look at the plight of his own Quebec riding. Industry was leaving, opportunity was dwindling, the highly educated were uprooting. There and in regions similarly depressed, the federal government had to provide redress. The country was wealthy, Jean Chrétien stated, yet 25 per cent of Canadians lived under conditions "which should not be tolerated in a modern, honest, and generous society." These people had to be helped. A civilized nation could not adopt a laissez-faire attitude. "The days are past when the individual, entirely on his own, without any help and trusting in God alone, had to fight his way to the top. The golden days of the Rockefellers, the Vanderbilts, and the Fords are practically over. . . . No one should hope for the return of that individualistic society."

Mackenzie King, the young MP observed, had fashioned a collectivist nation, and it was the duty of the present governors to nurture it. Economic planning was necessary to bring about full employment across Canada and to develop the most disadvantaged areas. Workers were being displaced by automation. A dynamic program to retrain them to do other work had to be put in place.

His second theme was the impact of the Quiet Revolution. Quebeckers had rightly become preoccupied with their province's profound transformation, he said, but in the process were showing unnecessary contempt towards Ottawa. This approach was misguided because "a full partnership" with the rest of Canada was the only way the fruits of the revolution could be realized. Quebec should join Canada in building a new society, "a country totally different from the United States." Canada had to differ in its mind-set, culture, education, and social-security system. It had to become a country with "much more equality between the rich and the poor. . . ."

Parliament had adjourned when he began as Pearson's assistant, which meant, since his chief function was to help the PM on the Hill, he had little work to do. So he hung around the office, getting to know people and learning how the system functioned. Jim

Coutts, who worked in the Prime Minister's Office at the time, saw Chrétien as someone who had a great desire to learn and who was "a very good student of patrons, of people who took an interest in him." Geoffrey Pearson, the prime minister's son, often saw Chrétien in the presence of the Pearson family and took note of how much his father liked him. He remembered his mother, Maryon Pearson, frequently correcting Chrétien's English, sometimes bluntly. "She gave him lessons in an informal kind of way."

The apprenticeship under Pearson was short-lived. Within a few months of appointing Chrétien, Pearson decided to go to the polls in search of a majority. Chrétien advised against the early call, believing that the standing of the Grits could not be much improved. But the counsel of weightier players prevailed.

Pearson asked the young MP to make some speeches for him in the French section of his riding of Algoma East. Chrétien was proud to do so and did some campaigning in his second language as well. He was pleased with himself for using a new English word he had learned from reading *Time* magazine. He labelled a Tory candidate a "carpetbagger."

In spite of his youth and inexperience, Chrétien was already thought to be merely a step away from a place at Pearson's cabinet table. He had only to listen to the corridor talk of his colleagues or read some of the press notices to be so persuaded. In a shuffle of the cabinet's legal portfolios before the election, he was rumoured to be a candidate. But the post of Solicitor-General went to Larry Pennell and Lucien Cardin took Justice. Until Pearson took him aside in Algoma, however, Chrétien believed that with a Liberal election, there would be another cabinet overhaul and he would likely be involved.

Pearson eased his way into the bad news, asking Chrétien what he thought of the three new figures—Trudeau, Marchand, and Pelletier—who were entering the Liberal fold as election candidates. Chrétien responded diplomatically, saying it was wonderful for the party. "But you know, Jean," the prime minister said, "this

163

might mean that you won't come into the cabinet as quickly as hoped." Chrétien hid his disappointment. If Pearson had better people, he said, he had no choice but to pick them.

In the meantime, Chrétien had his own re-election in St-Maurice–Laflèche to tend to. At his nomination meeting on October 3 he was cocky, asking not just for a victory, but for a rout, a ten thousand-vote majority. His friend and master of ceremonies, the distinguished lawyer Marcel Crête, announced that twenty thousand was a realistic target.

The machine was in place. Chrétien boasted of a good record in Ottawa and declared he was proud of what he had done for the riding, though he was on shakier ground with that claim. "During the 1963 election, some criticized me for being too young," he told the meeting. "But never in the past has the riding of St-Maurice–Laflèche been on the map like it is today." Though he was only a rookie MP, he reminded his listeners, the PM had chosen him as his assistant. Despite harder economic times, he had worked to ensure that the plants kept humming at home. Thanks to him, he claimed, the textile company in Grand'Mère had doubled its personnel, a new post office and paper mill had opened there, and an American tire company he had lobbied was opening a plant in Shawinigan that would create one hundred jobs. Critics countered that his prominence in Ottawa had resulted in virtually no federal largesse for the region. He couldn't even claim the post office, Tory candidate Louis Lizotte said. It was decided on much earlier, under the Conservative government.

A more decisive factor in the outcome was the low quality of the competition he faced. His main opposition, the Social Credit Party, was losing steam. The Tory surge in Quebec under Diefenbaker in the late 1950s was, as expected, ephemeral. The NDP was espousing a new two-nations policy to appeal to Quebec nationalists, but nothing, not even the hard campaigning of the respected Dr. Liddle, could crack Quebec for the party.

Chrétien won, though not with the spread he predicted at his nomination meeting. He defeated his closest rival, the Socred, by 5,615 votes. Liddle finished third, 9,000 votes behind, and later received a visit from Chrétien, who offered his apologies for his heavy-handed behaviour. It was at this time that Chrétien decided to pare down the operation of his authoritarian machine. He found that for every person his team got appointed, there were countless others who were angry at losing. It was a no-win situation. Besides, he'd begun to realize that the machine violated democratic principles. He remembered, as he often would, the advice he had been given on first entering politics. As Chrétien paraphrased it, a friend had told him, "You know, Jean, you cannot fool the public. Those guys in the beer parlours, the factories, and so on, they have a kind of sixth sense, a feeling, and when you're trying to cheat them, they know it. So be careful."

Just like Chrétien had predicted, the Grits failed to win a majority. Pearson then passed on naming either Trudeau or Pelletier, the former editor of *La Presse*, to the cabinet, thus fuelling Chrétien's hopes once again. Again they were dashed. The new Quebecker he did name was Jean-Pierre Goyer, a Montrealer of no great distinction. Chrétien correctly suspected that Guy Favreau, still Pearson's Quebec leader and a man with special ties to Goyer, had arranged the appointment. The highly influential Jack Pickersgill maintained that no slight was intended to Chrétien. In fact, he said, Pearson had wanted a new member from outside the elite to be appointed because there were "too many readers of *Le Devoir* in the cabinet." That left Chrétien in the running, but Goyer had the Favreau card.

After the appointment, Pearson spotted Chrétien outside his office. "Jean, you're mad at me because I named Goyer a minister instead of you." Then he delivered what appeared to be even worse news—Chrétien would no longer be his parliamentary secretary. Trudeau would be his new assistant, and Chrétien was going to Mitchell Sharp, the Finance minister, to perform the same function for him.

Pearson patted him on the back, and recalled Chrétien, "he convinced me—he did not convince me—he *told* me, 'You are going
there, buddy.'" Trying to soften the blow, Pearson added, "You
know, Jean, you were on the Finance committee, you were really
working hard, and since we do not have any francophones knowl-
edgeable in the field, if you were to work very hard [with Sharp]
you might become the first French-Canadian minister of Finance."

Chrétien suspected Pearson was being more kind than sincere.
He had begun the day as a good cabinet bet, but ended it as a de-
moted back-bencher who had lost his place at the prime minister's
table.

Disappointed, Chrétien went off to the Finance minister's office. He did not know Sharp well and could not have been aware
that the appointment would be so rife with consequence for him.
In the unlikely person of Mitchell Sharp, Jean Chrétien would
find the mentor for his public life that Aline Chaîné was for his
private life.

Born in 1911, Mitchell Sharp was raised in the poor back streets of
Winnipeg. He earnestly applied himself, studying history and eco-
nomics at university, working as an economist at the grain trade in
Winnipeg, studying more commerce at the London School of
Economics, and eventually going to work for the Department of
Finance in Ottawa in 1942. He worked his way up through the then
small bureaucracy to become deputy minister to C. D. Howe. In
1963 he entered active politics, and served as minister of Industry,
Trade and Commerce before succeeding Walter Gordon in Finance.

Sharp and the word "technocrat" were synonymous. He had the
reputation of being very smart and very dull. By the time he turned
nineteen, people were already describing him as "avuncular." His
classicist's sense of virtue gave him the air of a brittle prairie
preacher. But he was too learned and too disciplined not to make
career advances. His argumentation was based on documented
and judicious fact. This, combined with his upright manner of

presenting himself, gave his declarations a ring of truth. He would eventually cap a distinguished and honourable career by writing a memoir that bore what some wag described as the dullest title in the history of Canadian publishing. The book was called *Which Reminds Me . . .*

Sharp personally requested Chrétien as his parliamentary secretary. He had first noticed the young MP when he brought forward the Air Canada bill. He liked the way Chrétien applied himself, with such seriousness and dedication and ambition. These were the qualities Sharp wanted in an apprentice. He liked playing the role of teacher and the idea of finding a protégé very much appealed to him. Jean-Luc Pepin served as Sharp's parliamentary secretary right before Chrétien. When he was about to move on, he discussed possible successors with Sharp. Sharp told him of his interest in Chrétien and Pepin passed on the information, telling his friend from Quebec that Sharp made fine use of his assistants. But Chrétien, Pepin recalled, was reluctant. He had bigger things on his mind.

The reluctance didn't last. Under Sharp's wing, Chrétien applied himself with steady devotion. Sharp would never have another student as dedicated and keen, and Chrétien would never have another teacher who looked after him so well.

They were opposites in so many respects. One was a peacemaker, the other, in his own words, a shit-disturber. One had a patrician's air, the other a plebeian's. One, at fifty-five, was nearing the end of his career, the other, at thirty-two, was just beginning.

There were yet more profound differences. They were men of different casts of mind. Sharp was a professorial detail man who liked to intellectualize. Chrétien was a generalist who looked at the big picture. His critics later said he had a mind like Ronald Reagan's. Of the Gipper it was once suggested that "If you walked through his deepest thoughts, you wouldn't get your feet wet."

Chrétien had touched on economics in his Finance committee work, but as Sharp quickly discovered, this didn't mean he was equipped for the discipline. Chrétien was not comfortable with the complexities of economic theory. When discussions around Sharp's desk plunged below the surface into talk of money supply and monetary policy, Chrétien's eyes glazed over.

"Me, I'd take on the economists if they wanted to," said Sharp, recalling his tenure. "Jean wouldn't, couldn't. That's not how his mind works. He likes to get back to the things that are really fundamental to his responsibilities." The only time Chrétien would put forward a complex argument was when it was put down on paper before him and all he had to do was read it. And even reading, noted Sharp, was something "he didn't do very well."

If he wasn't baffled by economic theory, his weak comprehension of English scuppered him. Often it was a combination of the two. Chrétien frequently told the story—the best strategy was to make light of these things—of a meeting with Sharp, the governor of the Bank of Canada, and the financial titans of the nation. Sharp approached him afterwards and asked him not to repeat a word. Chrétien told Sharp that he need not worry: he, Chrétien, hadn't understood a thing anyway.

From his working-class beginnings, Chrétien had come to Ottawa in search of social justice and, while not brazen about it, was an early proponent, as good Liberals of the day were supposed to be, of the economic nationalism advocated by Finance Minister Walter Gordon. In a speech in support of the creation of the Economic Council of Canada, Chrétien said substantial economic planning was necessary to move the Canadian economy from its primitive beginnings as a producer of raw materials to a new, more sophisticated level. He cited the Quebec government's influential policies on its water resources and the development of its steel industry as examples Ottawa might follow. On Canadianization he was clear. "We all know that today this country's economy is impaired by the fact that 60 per cent of the Canadian manufacturing industry is controlled by non-resident corporations. We must hand back to Canadians the ownership and control of their economy."

By party standards Sharp, on the other hand, was an economic conservative who favoured the open investment approach of C. D. Howe and opposed much of the Gordon program. Though he had studied under Harold Laski at the London School of Economics, those socialist teachings had made little impact.

The differences were undoubtedly formidable, but the few things Sharp and Chrétien had in common turned out to mean more. Each man was a worker, deeply believing the adage that you only get out of life what you put into it. Each was pragmatic, meaning philosophical differences could be overcome. Sharp liked to teach, Chrétien liked to learn. Each was a keen believer in government and public service, and most important, each had something to gain in the partnership. Chrétien had a distinguished and influential patron who could advance his career path, while Sharp had a pupil with star potential. As the pedagogue, Sharp could fashion his student into the leader he himself could never quite become.

The Finance minister became convinced that Jean Chrétien was a political phenomenon on the night he brought him to speak in his Toronto constituency. Chrétien said some simple things in terribly accented and raspy half-English about the two cultures and the greatness of Canada. His words somehow prompted his listeners to jump to their feet and clap and cheer and roar their approval—all this for a young Quebecker they had never heard of. The spontaneous reaction astonished Sharp. That the content was pedestrian didn't matter. The speaker was endearingly genuine and blunt and had struck a chord. Roland de Corneille, a friend of Sharp's and a future MP, remembered that night. What Chrétien did, he said, was "hypnotize the crowd with his simplicity." It was clear to the Finance minister that his assistant was a remarkable communicator. From that moment on, Sharp became Jean Chrétien's champion.

As Sharp watched his apprentice in other forums, he came to see that in being, or appearing to be, as unpolished and uninformed as average Canadians, he could speak their language and create a bond with them. "The general public," said Sharp, in an astute observation, "could understand him because he put himself in the position of the general public." In addition to this, Chrétien possessed another endearing quality—absolutely refreshing candour. He impressed Sharp because he knew his shortcomings and never tried to talk about things he didn't understand. "He realized his limitations," observed Sharp. "Sometimes I wish I had."

Chrétien had come to Sharp's riding, so now he brought Sharp to the northern reaches of his. Sharp didn't speak French, but nevertheless awkwardly read a short speech in the language to the locals. Chrétien then took his minister to an old-fashioned bean dinner in the country and plied him with a heavy alcoholic concoction called Caribou. Several shots later, the very staid Mr. Sharp was up on a table, delivering an impromptu second-language stemwinder that had the onlookers laughing so hard that they almost fell over.

Events like this forged a closeness between them, as did Chrétien's being at Sharp's side while the minister experienced a deep personal tragedy. His wife, Daisy Boyd, whom he had met at the University of Manitoba, had always been in the pink of health. She was once the Manitoba junior tennis champion and, according to Sharp, "the best women's hockey player the country had ever seen." Now, in her forties, she was crippled by Alzheimer's. She was going blind, going deaf, losing her mental capacity, and would end up in an institution before she passed away. At the time, Pearson's tenuous minority governments meant that MPs had to be on hand for sudden votes. During long nights in the office with his wife, Sharp tried to provide what comfort he could— and so did the only other person who was present, Jean Chrétien.

He hadn't been Sharp's assistant for long when the debate within the Liberal Party over economic nationalism reached seriously divisive proportions. At a party conference at the Château Laurier in the autumn of 1966, Walter Gordon, using Toronto Rosedale MP Donald Macdonald as an intermediary, sought Sharp's backing for a series of resolutions of pressingly nationalistic intent. Gordon viewed the extent of foreign ownership in Canada as the critical barometer in the measure of the country's independence. In Sharp's analysis, this was an oversimplification. He took the convention floor to argue that the best way to weaken Canadian independence was to follow narrow nationalistic policies in a world of growing interdependence. The robust applause signalled support for his challenge. A vote then defeated the Gordon resolution, though some compromises were later worked out.

Despite his early days as a left-wing Liberal, Chrétien soon swung over to his minister's side. Loyalty, which Jean Chrétien so valued, played a role in this, but Sharp saw more than just loyalty at work. The conservatively inclined minister believed that "Jean was always instinctively on my side." He came naturally to the conclusion, said Sharp, that it was unwise to place heavy controls on investment. They were both convinced that if they were to ask the industrial commissioner of Halifax or Winnipeg or Vancouver whether he would like a new factory in his midst, even one completely controlled by foreigners, the answer would be yes.

To call upon new foreign owners to give as many jobs as possible to Canadians was one thing. But to submit new investments to formal limitations and investigations was quite another. Chrétien, recalled Sharp, made these views clear in cabinet when the opportunity was eventually accorded him. "He was no ideologue, and I think that's what he learned from me more than anything else— that ideology plays a very small part in these matters."

"Sharp had a big intellectual influence on him," said John Rae who, fresh out of Queen's University, had become a special assistant to Chrétien. "He [Chrétien] was very much against the economic nationalism coming out of Toronto. He felt emphasis should be on jobs and employment and investment. Whether it came from outside or inside the country, it should be seen as equal. This reflected his experience in Shawinigan, which had a lot of multinationals."

Given his aversion to being politically labelled, Chrétien tried to obscure any bias he held for one side or the other in the debate. But his transformation under Sharp was noticed, sending a signal that was picked up by party luminaries like Keith Davey. "Beginning in the Pearson years and continuing through the Trudeau years, two divergent political streams subtly developed [in the Liberal Party]," Davey explained. "They were not factions. They were not camps. They were more like two tributaries flowing from the same river. There were the Gordon Liberals, like Larry Pennell, Ben Benson, the Axworthy brothers, Andy Thompson, and the rest; then there were the Sharp Liberals, like Jean Chrétien, the Wright brothers, Bob Nixon, and others. The Gordon people tended to be more liberal, the Sharp people more conservative."

After spending some time around the Finance department, Chrétien began to achieve some economic literacy. He had to acquaint himself with and speak on such complex issues as Sharp's amendments to the Bank of Canada Act, which sought to remove the limits of bank interest and clarify the relationship between the government and the bank. The proposed reforms quickly split the Liberal caucus, and left Chrétien in the difficult position of having to defend a measure of dubious popularity. Walter Gordon, now back in cabinet, went on the attack at a caucus meeting that Sharp did not attend. Chrétien took a pounding but responded well, earning some sympathy for having been left to the lions.

He also had to defend a Finance minister who was delaying the introduction of a prize piece of legislation dear to both Chrétien and his constituency—medicare. Sharp, who had lived through the Depression and so never doubted the need for a strong social-security network, was worried about administrative and deficit problems if the plan was rushed in. With Chrétien's reluctant backing, he sought a long delay but had to content himself with one year owing to intense opposition from the likes of Jean Marchand.

Marchand was a bold new force, the only one of the three newcomers from Quebec immediately to be put in cabinet. Before any top government ministers moved forward with something important, they wanted to know what Marchand thought. Here Chrétien helped Sharp. He had, in his old friend, the union organizer Fernand D. Lavergne, a pipeline to Marchand.

Despite this connection, however, Sharp noticed some distance between Chrétien and Marchand and Quebec's two other bright new lights, Trudeau and Pelletier. He remembered Marchand once telling him that Quebec had to start sending quality people to Parliament, not the low-calibre minds it had been. Sharp didn't think the comment was aimed at Chrétien, but he sensed from the three wise men a reluctance to give him his due.

One story that often made the rounds had Trudeau mocking Chrétien on a plane flight. Trudeau was immersed in a book, while Chrétien twiddled his thumbs and looked for conversation. Eventually, Chrétien noticed some spots on the window. "Looks like it's raining outside," he said. "Well," Trudeau replied, "if it's raining, it must be outside."

Chrétien didn't mingle much with Marchand, Trudeau, or Pelletier. His first significant encounter with Trudeau soured him. In 1966 the Quebec caucus was electing a new chairman. Candidates split into the old guard—those who had come to Ottawa before 1963—and the new—those who had come afterwards. Chrétien and friends of the new order were supporting one of their own, Gérald Laniel. But Trudeau, showing an early flash of the independence that would mark his career, didn't vote with the new guard. He abstained. Laniel lost by the one vote Trudeau could have provided.

Chrétien, who had seen an abstention deny him the presidency at Laval and who had nominated Laniel, went at Trudeau, demanding to know why he hadn't voted for one of their own. With typical insouciance, Trudeau brushed him off, saying that he had abstained because he hadn't been around long enough to know the qualities of either candidate. But didn't he pick up the signal, Chrétien asked, that the new MPs were going with Laniel?

"Pardon me," said Trudeau, "but there is no new guard or old guard for me."

"Gee, Pierre," Chrétien retorted, "you'd better learn something about politics or you won't go very far."

All the new guard members were "angry at this beatnik," Chrétien said of the incident. "The worst part was that in his logic and his objectivity, he was right."

Though the arrival of the Quebec trio set him back a bit in the pecking order, Chrétien continued to carve out his own identity. Trudeau was the quiet thinker and Pelletier the writer. Marchand was closer to the people but had little appeal outside Quebec. Chrétien, "spectacularly unspectacular," in the words of Tory George Hees, was the only one showing a common touch and a wide reach. His qualities were such that some people were already thinking he could go all the way. Solicitor-General Larry Pennell, who described Chrétien as being "clothed in honesty," told his wife, Ann, that Chrétien would one day become the leader of the country. When Ann was introduced to the young MP, she said, "Oh, you're the one my husband thinks will become prime minister." When Chrétien saw Pennell later, he playfully told him what a fine vision of the future his wife possessed.

Chrétien's trip to Mitchell Sharp's riding had showed him he could transcend cultural boundaries. At home, meanwhile, the great veteran political organizer Omer Hill was telling him that his style fit the riding perfectly. "You can be re-elected here for another twenty-five years," Hill said. "He was a guy of the people," explained Hill, "and the guy of the people stays a long time because he takes care of them. If you are too highly cultured as a politician, it's not so good. There are a lot of ordinary things you don't want to tend to because it's too much bother. You don't see them as important."

In his early speeches and in his decision to spurn offers from the Quebec Liberals, Chrétien had clearly demonstrated his federalist bias. In November 1966 he boldly toughened his stance against the new Quebec nationalism with two speeches, one in Cap-de-la-Madeleine, near his home town, the other in Chicoutimi. The speeches struck hard at those who sought special status for the province, asserting that these were the people who were retarding French Canada's economic development by creating a climate of insecurity that deterred outside investors.

"Foreign industrialists and financiers hold doubts and worries concerning Quebec and this translates into a considerable loss of capital. . . . The fact should not be hidden. Even in a period when Quebec has made a leap forward economically, it has fallen back compared with the country as a whole."

In Chicoutimi he declared that "a strike in Quebec is not news in New York, Chicago, Paris, or London, but separatism is." If Quebeckers want foreign capital, he explained, "it is extremely important that the climate be favourable and that we put an end to the sterile discussions, the disruptive statements, the extremist claims."

Chrétien carefully researched these speeches. Taking advantage of the access to expertise his seat next to Sharp gave him, he packed them with statistics showing a decline in investment in Quebec manufacturing while Ontario was prospering. He consulted with four francophone specialists in the Finance department so he would not be accused, as he soon would be anyway, of being a mouthpiece for the anglophone community.

Trudeau, Marchand, and Pepin had all attacked Quebec nationalism, but none made the headlines that Chrétien did. The difference was that Chrétien made the vital link the others did not. He tied nationalism to economic pain.

Many in the Quebec media, impressed by the documentation, gave Chrétien modest editorial support. *La Presse, Le Devoir, Le Nouvelliste,* and Quebec City's *Le Soleil* all came forward with favourable comment. "What counts are economic questions," noted *Le Nouvelliste.* "Without agreeing with his theories completely, it may be he who, in the long run, is right."

Chrétien had already come to the conclusion, one that was to become a mainstay of the Trudeau pitch, that those in English

Canada seeking to provide special status for Quebec were misguided. In Chrétien's view these people would "push French Canadians back onto the Quebec reserve." He openly opposed the idea of holding a constitutional conference aimed at special status. To bolster his case that Quebec could prosper through federalism, he pointed to the big changes in Ottawa since 1960, changes that saw, he claimed, French Canadians in such a position of prominence in the Liberal Party that they held what was tantamount to veto power over government decisions.

In April 1967 the big day came. Lester Pearson granted Jean Chrétien's long-time wish and named him to the cabinet. It was a minor post, minister without portfolio attached to the Department of Finance, but the significance of the occasion could hardly be overlooked. Jean Chrétien was advancing in the game of federal politics faster than any challenger. At thirty-three he was the youngest man to be named to the federal cabinet in the century. Since Confederation, there had been only one younger cabinet minister. In 1888 Charles Hibbert Tupper, also thirty-three, but three months younger than Chrétien, was named by John A. Macdonald. "It was not small potatoes," Chrétien said of the moment. "It was a big deal for me." The appointment meant he would still be at the side of his mentor, Mitchell Sharp, who was already telling Chrétien family members that their brother would one day be Finance minister.

He was one of seven French Canadians in the cabinet, the others being Marchand, Maurice Sauvé, Trudeau, Pepin, Jean-Pierre Côté, and Léo Cadieux. An editorial by Claude Ryan of *Le Devoir*, the pope of Quebec journalism, sized up Chrétien in relation to Trudeau, who was named Justice minister on the same day, and another new cabinet man, John Turner. "Jean Chrétien is in a different class," wrote Ryan. "He has neither the advanced education nor the prestigious background of his two new colleagues. . . . Without being what one calls a man of influence, without always

being sufficiently nuanced in some of his affirmations, he pos-
sesses a practical strength and hunger for action which make him a
logical candidate for the cabinet. A balanced cabinet should include a good balance between intellectuals and specialists on the
one hand and practical men on the other. Mr. Chrétien is a good
practical type, Mr. Trudeau is a pure-bred intellectual, and Mr.
Turner finds himself somewhere between the two."

Chrétien told his new assistant, John Rae, the brother of future
Ontario premier Bob Rae, that he still hadn't seen Western Canada.
Since the national rail service had a private car that cabinet members could use freely, Chrétien put his family and Rae on board and
journeyed all the way to Vancouver and back. Throughout the trip,
he expressed a child-like fascination with the beauty of the land.
He also did a lot of politicking, sizing up Sharp's chances for a possible bid to succeed Pearson and enhancing his own growing list of
contacts. (Unlike many politicians, he never kept a log or record of
the people he met. It was all done by memory.) The trip, noted
Rae, also showed Chrétien how welcome he was in English Canada.
He found anglophones so warm, so friendly, so willing to listen to
him. In Quebec, people were not always so welcoming.

It was on the subject of Quebec that he now stumbled badly.
Just as his first speech as an MP had caused him embarrassment, so
too did his first major effort as a cabinet minister. This time it
wasn't misjudgement that caused the trouble but rather misfortune, the misfortune of one missing word.

His intent was to level another broadside at Quebec nationalists. Because his speech would touch on judicial concerns, he
checked first with the new Justice minister, Pierre Trudeau. In one
of the important lines of the speech, Chrétien wrote that "those
who are in favour of special status are often separatists who don't
want to admit they are separatists." Trudeau agreed with the statement, telling Chrétien that he might be heavily criticized but that
he should go ahead anyway because he was right.

The important qualifying word was "often." It meant, obviously, that some but not all of those who favoured special status for Quebec were secessionists. In the English version of the speech, prepared by Rae for delivery in Toronto, the "often" was present, but in the one that was translated to French, it was accidentally left out. Chrétien was saying, as the Quebec media read it, that anyone who favoured added status for Quebec was a separatist.

Predictably, the reaction was indignation. Chrétien was denounced throughout *la belle province*. *Le Devoir* typified the response, calling his speech a diatribe, "inexcusable and inadmissible." Chrétien had been controversial before but well within the bounds of reason. Now, with a big broad defamatory brush, he had gone overboard. Not only did the intellectuals holler, but mainstream Quebec did as well. So forceful was the criticism that Chrétien thought he might be finished in politics.

He issued a correction, saying that he hadn't meant to lump everyone together, that the word "often" had been accidentally removed, that this big fuss was all due to a clerical error. But after-the-fact explanations don't often stand up and his was no exception. His reputation as a radical federalist hardened to the point that some saw him as a puppet for English-Canadian interests.

Seeking to soften that image, he extended his anti-nationalist argument to English Canadians who spoke negatively about the United States. They were wrong too. Just like Quebec nationalists, he told the Vancouver Board of Trade, these were the people who were scaring off much-needed foreign capital. "In both cases a small elite group seems prepared to make decisions and follow courses of action that would impose costs and sacrifices on the mass of people." Here was another indication that Chrétien, despite his patriotic bent, was no economic nationalist. His was a cultural nationalism. He was, as he had indicated in seconding the 1965 speech from the throne, a fervent supporter of the need to build a society different from that of the United States, but he believed it could be done without erecting economic walls.

Recent world trade negotiations, under the auspices of the General Agreement on Tariffs and Trade, had brought down trade barriers. Canada had to meet the new conditions by looking outward, Chrétien argued, and by becoming more competitive. Canada had fostered an imitative economy, duplicating standard products *en masse*, as opposed to an innovative economy, which was the key to the future.

On the economy and on the Quebec issue, Chrétien was clearly staking his ground. Such was the repetitive nature of the Canadian political dynamic that he was unwittingly setting down policy lines that would carry him forward for decades.

His declarations on Quebec had come in Canada's starlit centennial year. The celebrations were tarnished, however, by the visit of French president Charles de Gaulle, whose brazenly meddlesome declaration "Vive le Québec libre" spurred the sovereignty movement. Chrétien, who was away from Ottawa at the time, rushed back to the capital to argue vociferously—"I was absolutely the strongest of them all"—that de Gaulle be ordered to go home.

The event reverberated throughout the country. Chrétien went to Vancouver. He was answering questions from students at the University of British Columbia's Brock Hall when one of them, a Quebecker named Daniel Latouche, took the microphone. "It is people like you who are preventing French Canadians from building a country," Latouche charged. "You tell the people of French Canada that if they don't elect you, the separatists will take over and they will lose everything. You offer them lollipops and goodies, and they vote for you."

Chrétien looked disconsolate. He listened as Latouche carried on. "It is people like you who use fears to get elected. You know that Quebec has been a colony for three hundred years, first of France, then of England, then of Canada, and now of the United States."

Chrétien finally broke in. "Your kind of independence is just a dream. Do you think you will be free of the United States in a separate Quebec? If we separate, in twenty-five years we will be part of the United States, and it is gone, the French, if we are part of the United States."

He might well have used the example of the French in New Hampshire, the assimilation his father had witnessed. But instead he chose the Italians. "There are now more Italians in the United States than there are French in Quebec. You know that? But there is no Italian society—they are all Americans."

The students, English of course, applauded Chrétien loudly. Latouche, however, was at him again when the meeting adjourned. If Chrétien had any pride, he told the minister, he wouldn't be in English Canada, he would be home in Quebec working to build it.

Chrétien, angrier now, jabbed his forefinger at Latouche. "If you're a separatist, what the hell are you doing in British Columbia?" The people in his own riding of Shawinigan, he told the protestor, didn't want to separate. "They have bellies! They want to eat! They want bread and butter, and they want it for their children."

Later, he spoke to some reporters, describing his dilemma in such situations. If he agreed with the angry young Quebecker, he'd make English Canadians mad. But if he was too hard on him, Quebeckers would say he was cosying up to the English. If it was tough in B.C., he added, it would only be worse back home. He was going to speak at the University of Montreal the following week, where, he predicted, they would probably throw tomatoes at him.

Instead of tomatoes, Chrétien was the target of a stink bomb— that and catcalls and mocking laughter and shouts that he was a sell-out. As soon as he began to talk about having gone to Ottawa to pursue politics, a bearded youth interrupted. "I know why! It's because you've sold out to the English!"

As Chrétien tried to explain himself, saying he was defending Quebec culture at the federal level, another voice cried out, "And in what language do you defend the Quebec fact in Ottawa?" On the defensive now, the young minister admitted that he was forced to do it in English, adding that this had to change.

As the evening progressed, Chrétien was denounced as an imbecile and peppered with other such insults. "At least Marchand and Trudeau, even if they don't share our ideas, are intellectually competent," blasted one audience member. "But you, what is your expertise in matters economic which you talk about all the time?" When Chrétien began his response, a stink bomb landed at his feet, spewing clouds of gas into the air. He waited for it to clear, then continued, gaining a measure of respect from some listeners for his determination. He admitted English Canadians were enjoying a better standard of living than the French but said this would change. It had better, he said, or the country would not survive.

When a student shouted that Quebeckers had been hearing this "bullshit" for a century and nothing had happened, Chrétien fired back that for one hundred years Quebec had been producing nothing but priests and lawyers and teachers. It was about time it started producing economists and engineers and businessmen. It was about time, he said, it joined the real world.

CHAPTER ELEVEN

IN THE CABINET

A S EARLY AS 1967, a prime minister deciding on changes to his cabinet could be assured of a knock on the door or a memorandum from Mitchell Sharp. His message was always the same—Jean Chrétien is the one for the job. Sharp became Chrétien's persistent and painstaking promoter, absolute in his dedication to getting the young Quebecker to the top.

Prime Minister Pearson awarded Chrétien full-portfolio status at the start of 1968, making him minister of National Revenue. Given his professed economic ambitions, the assignment was a good base from which the thirty-three-year-old could build.

Being the country's chief tax collector wasn't exactly enjoyable work. As his top aide John Rae put it, "There are no happy things in taxation." Since the department also had responsibility for customs, the post brought with it an unending string of phone calls from MPs from border ridings pleading for constituents caught smuggling. But no major controversies were there to dog Chrétien. The country, still riding the momentum of the postwar period, was in its seventh straight year of economic growth. Revenues were strong, with a 7 per cent increase forecast for the coming year. The headlines he gathered stemmed more from his provocative declarations on Quebec than any financial concerns.

Chrétien continued to stress the need for Quebec to develop competent economists and businessmen. He asserted that English

Canadians had to become bilingual, or they would go nowhere in federal politics. He decried Quebec nationalists for labelling him a traitor and mocked their infatuation with status. When the Quebec press made big news of a nationalist politician hobnobbing with the French cultural giant André Malraux, Chrétien told working-class Quebeckers, "Yeah, so what does that do for you, when what you're looking for are jobs?"

Before Chrétien could undertake any significant initiatives in his department, Pearson called a leadership convention to choose a successor. Compelled by loyalty as well as admiration, Chrétien decided to support his mentor, Sharp. It wasn't an easy choice. Being a Quebecker, Chrétien was expected to support a candidate from the family. Being of blue-collar stock, he might well have been expected to back a working man's Liberal. Being an avid proponent of bilingualism, he was expected to favour a two-language speaker. Instead, Jean Chrétien was backing a candidate who was the opposite on all counts—the conservative, unilingual anglophone who was a native of Manitoba.

As was his nature, Chrétien campaigned hard for Sharp. He enjoyed politics so much that the hours doing it didn't constitute the burden for him they did for others. The urge was in his blood. Life was a campaign, a race to do well, and there was no better arena for it than politics, where the stakes were so high, the spotlight so shining.

Although he helped line up many delegates for the Finance minister, events conspired against the candidacy. Sharp suffered a defeat in the House of Commons, failing to marshal enough votes on a surtax measure. The set-back almost toppled the government, Pearson was infuriated, and Sharp's standing diminished. He was about to withdraw from the race, but Chrétien convinced him to fight on, making the case that if he dropped out so early, he'd be viewed as a quitter. But Sharp was soon dealt another reversal. Robert Winters, the silver-haired standard-bearer of Bay Street, entered the race, occupying conservative turf that was vital to Sharp's aspirations. Winters, a minister in the St-Laurent government, had promised Sharp he would not be a candidate. His entry angered Chrétien, who labelled him a "Cadillac with a Volkswagen engine." Chrétien, who pictured himself as the opposite, realized after the statement was replayed to Winters that he had erred badly. A Winters triumph, which was distinctly possible, would mean no motor car for Chrétien, only the first bus out of town. His cabinet days would be over.

The Liberal Party had a tradition, albeit an informal one, of alternating the leadership between anglophones and francophones. This time it was a francophone's turn. Chrétien, himself supporting an English Canadian, watched as John Turner, with early-age delusions of grandeur, made a respectable run. Gerald Stoner, who was acting secretary to the cabinet, received a message from Pearson on the Turner candidacy. The PM told Stoner that it was a French Canadian's turn and perhaps Turner shouldn't push too hard against Pierre Trudeau. Stoner caught up with Turner at a lake in the Gatineaus and relayed the message. "They can go stuff that idea," Turner responded. "I'm out to win."

Chrétien, who had not foreseen the spectacular potential of the Trudeau candidacy, was the target of appeals from Jean Marchand and Marc Lalonde to get on board. He resisted but dispatched John Rae to Lalonde to tell him that while still committed to Sharp, he was certainly not unfriendly to a Trudeau candidacy. Lalonde told Rae he was looking for full support, not half measures. As the convention approached and unofficial delegate counts were made, it became clear Sharp had no hope of winning. He withdrew on the convention's eve and, with Chrétien's urging, threw his support to Trudeau. Chrétien phoned Trudeau with the news, significant news because in a tight race it gave him critical momentum at the right time.

The outcome, Trudeau's triumph, was naturally a relief for Chrétien. He had backed the winner. Winters was out. With a Liberal victory in the coming election, he and Sharp would be assured of continued prominence.

On the day Trudeau and his cabinet were sworn in, the mandarin Stoner talked with Chrétien, who was still National Revenue minister, outside Government House. "We both had our morning jackets on. We both came outside looking like a couple of monkeys, and people were staring at us." Chrétien, he noticed, was caught up in the enormity of the occasion. He talked, with a sense of wonder, about the great power the prime minister exercised. It was he and he alone, remarked Chrétien, who would decide whether to send the entire nation to the polls. "You discuss it with your cabinet, but really it's you alone who makes the decision. That's a hell of a responsibility."

Trudeau did call an election, for June 1968. Because this was the beginning of Trudeaumania, lesser Liberals like Chrétien were not essential to the election's outcome. Nevertheless, he campaigned for the Grits clear across the country. In so doing, however, he put himself at risk in his own riding. Because he had won St-Maurice–Laflèche easily in 1965, there seemed to be little reason for concern this time around. He had since become a cabinet minister, one that Shawinigan was surely proud of, and this time was riding the coat-tails of a francophone superstar who was sweeping the province.

But as Chrétien's reputation was growing, so were the economic woes of La Mauricie. The boom times of the 1950s were over. The population was declining, unemployment and insecurity were high. Chrétien's political machine was no longer as strong, given his decision to dilute it, and his belligerent federalist speeches had hardened the opposition of nationalist elements. There was also the presence of Caouette of the Social Credit, a man whose campaigning power was not to be underestimated. Trudeau had provided him with a new weapon. As Justice minister he had displayed a liberal attitude towards divorce and laws governing sexual practices, enraging moralistic firebrands like the Socred leader. Caouette saw Chrétien as an especially vulnerable target because his name means Christian. When he roared into Shawinigan, he had his line all prepared. "Homosexualité! Divorce! Avortement!" he cried. "Ce n'est pas Chrétien!"

The attacks found listeners. The National Revenue minister soon faced voters claiming he approved of homosexuality, which in the 1960s was viewed in a negative light. He had supported Trudeau's thesis—"The state has no business in the bedrooms of the nation"—and found it difficult to back away. Late in the campaign Aline phoned, warning, "You better get back here."

Among the political professionals, the thinking continued to be that Tories and Socreds drew largely from the same voting pool and therefore Chrétien was favoured with a Tory in the race. This time, as fortune would have it, Guy Germain, Chrétien's old school chum from Joliette and Laval, quietly showed up on the Conservative ballot. Le Chien knew that despite the expectations forged by the election of the new Tory leader, Robert Stanfield, he had no chance of winning. But he felt the publicity would be good for his law practice. And if he happened to help his friend Chrétien by drawing votes away from Social Credit, all the better.

Indeed, the latter appeared to be the case. Without Germain, who didn't criticize Chrétien once during the campaign, the Social Credit candidate could well have put an early end to Jean Chrétien's political career.

Many years later, Germain described his campaign effort as nonchalant. "I didn't run against Chrétien," he explained. "I ran for the Conservatives." As for his reason for running against a friend in the first place, Germain said it was "unexplainable in a way. I think I did it as a sport." He granted that it was "quite possible that I helped Chrétien. Quite possible."

Roger Lambert, one of Chrétien's best campaign organizers, recalled a gathering years later when Germain's wife, laughing about the campaign, told Chrétien that she voted for him, not her husband. "I don't know whether the Chrétien camp pushed Germain to run," Lambert said, "but they were two great friends."

The Socred was Alphonse Poulin, the same man Chrétien had decisively beaten in 1965. Poulin had negligible financial resources and never got to confront Chrétien, who was out of the riding most of the time, in a debate. It was a quiet campaign, but when they began counting the ballots, Poulin was doubling his numbers from the previous election. He was running ahead of the National Revenue minister in the rural areas, as well as in Grand'Mère. La Tuque, in the riding's northern reaches, was no longer part of the constituency, owing to a redrawing of the boundaries. It had proven itself to be such a good Socred city. He would have done well there.

Shawinigan and Shawinigan-Sud held firm for a humbled Chrétien. He came away with a narrow victory, earning 13,714 votes to Poulin's 12,023. Germain came in third with 4,559, and Poulin could only wonder how many of those votes would have been his if the Dog hadn't entered the race.

The close result had an important effect on Chrétien, who denied any collusion with Germain. He would never again take his riding for granted. "I visited forty-two ridings and hardly touched my own," he said of the campaign. "The people sure taught me a lesson." The day after the near-defeat he began to become highly preoccupied with his riding, taking a hands-on approach to everything. He had survived two close calls—Trudeau's victory and his own. Had either test turned out the other way, noted his assistant, John Rae, his story might have been very different indeed.

When he named his new cabinet, Trudeau decided to move Chrétien out of National Revenue and off the economic track altogether. He gave him one of the least coveted portfolios of the lot: Indian Affairs and Northern Development. Initially, Chrétien lobbied against the appointment. It was utterly strange territory for him and it had no resonance among his constituents or Quebeckers generally. When he reported his proposed posting to Shawinigan friends, they were unimpressed. "What? You'll be in charge of the savages?" Most had never even heard of Indian Affairs.

He had talked to Trudeau of other possibilities, Public Works being one of them, but the new prime minister was not about to be dissuaded—even by Chrétien's claim that he was entirely ignorant about both natives and the North. On one trip west he had responded to a question about Liberal policies on Indian Affairs by saying, in his winsomely unaffected way, "I don't know a damn thing about it!" Everyone laughed.

He relayed the story to Trudeau, but Trudeau turned the tables, saying it was exactly because he knew nothing that he wanted him for the position. He would come into the job with no preconceived ideas. Furthermore, the PM added, Chrétien was a minority himself, came from a poor family (Trudeau thought he was poorer than was the case), and like most Indians, spoke bad English. In sum, he had the right combination of negatives for the job.

The idea behind the appointment—no knowledge is power—amounted to a radical reworking of an adage. But it wouldn't be the first time Chrétien would profit from it.

After consulting his assistants, John Rae and Jean Fournier, a new young man on the team, and discovering that both had been to the North and were completely enamoured of it, he relented and signed on, becoming the seventh Indian Affairs minister in seven years.

The high turnover was testimony to the disfavour in which this posting was held. It was viewed as a dead-end because there was little a politician could do in the short term to alleviate the bitterness and disillusionment of the people he represented. The department had once been called Northern Affairs and Natural Resources, NANR. "We called it No Action, No Results," said Stu Hodgson, the commissioner of the Northwest Territories. "I mean, it was bad. Everybody up here hated Ottawa."

Hodgson's sense of humour was useful in dealing with Chrétien, a man he came to admire deeply. Hodgson bumped into

Trudeau not too long after Chrétien had begun his work in the new position. "Well, Stu," the prime minister said, "how are you getting along with that new minister I gave you?"

"Oh, great guy!" answered Hodgson. "The only problem, you know, is that I have a little trouble with his English."

"Well," said Trudeau, "you should hear his French."

Indian Affairs had been a relatively anonymous posting, but in the year Jean Chrétien took over, all was changing. These were the most incendiary of the sixties seasons. Civil-rights and black-power movements and anti-poverty crusades were rampant, and Ottawa politicians had begun to fear that the natives in Canada, like the African Americans south of the border, could touch off a wave of civil unrest. The conditions were ripe. There was no doubting—and Canada's centennial year, with its focus on the founding peoples, had drawn attention to it—the degree of destitution. For the 1 per cent of the Canadian population who were Indian, life expectancy was half the national average. The education level of native Canadians was less than half that of other groups, their annual income a fraction, their numbers on national welfare rolls a scandal.

Pierre Trudeau had canoed in Indian bush. He had denounced Canada's maltreatment of aboriginals long before getting into politics and had demonstrated a keen interest in human rights. If the native question was not high on the priority list of other prime ministers, it was on his. In a speech at Queen's University he warned that the potential for native unrest was growing by the month. He wanted, as one of the first priorities of his government, to seek a broad solution to this broad problem. At the same time, he was not prepared to leave the search for that solution up to his new minister. He had his own deeply felt bias, which flowed from a simple philosophical basis point. As with French Canadians and other minorities, he was profoundly against the accordance of special status. Everyone was to be equal under the law. It was, as most things Trudeauvian would be, the intellectually rational course. It was also, for an untested young cabinet minister, a prescription for hard times.

The Indian Act granted special status. It had been around for eighty years and was seen, depending on one's point of view, as generous, paternalistic, discriminatory, or worse, the progenitor of an apartheid system. Native peoples denounced the act, last revised in 1952, as racist, confining them to the reserve system as wards of government. Virginia Summers, a member of the Oneida band, once told Jean Chrétien that the legislation gave the government more power than God over the Indians. As a case in point she cited a section giving politicians the authority to declare a native person's will null and void. "Even in the grave the department runs the affairs of Indians."

Chrétien was also hearing from his nephew Raymond on the subject. Maurice's son was now an External Affairs officer stationed in New York. He informed his uncle, having observed debates in the United Nations, that the federal government's policy on its native peoples was creating a credibility problem for Canada. During a debate on the Soviets' treatment of their Jews, the Russians told the Canadian delegation that they had nothing to say, that they should look at the way they treat their own native peoples.

Chrétien could see that the criticism had merit. In a way, he recalled, the government had put an "apartheid policy" in place. "Trudeau didn't like it, and he asked me to change it. So we spent a lot of time working on that, and he was very much personally interested. Very much. Human rights for Trudeau had always been very important and intellectually it was abnormal to have this system."

Given his bias against special status for any group, Trudeau's preference was to overturn Indian policy entirely. He wanted to find a way to integrate the Indians freely and fully into the Canadian mosaic. He wondered why there should be any different laws or programs or even government department for them. Why not get out of the business of managing Indian Affairs altogether?

Why not give the native peoples total freedom, like other minority groups in Canada?

The PM threw these ideas at Chrétien, and the minister—not being in much of a position to disagree—took the pronouncements to heart. It was a startling development. Two months into a portfolio he knew nothing about, the thirty-four-year-old minister was setting a course towards the most revolutionary change the department had ever seen. The plan, to be fleshed out over months of inquiry and consultation, was to abolish the Indian Act, dismantle the department of Indian Affairs (and hence Chrétien's job), end the reserve system, and give Indians equal status to everyone else.

In 1967, under the previous minister, Arthur Laing, Ottawa had decided to re-examine the Indian Act. A series of eighteen meetings with Indian representatives were set to begin in the spring of 1968, but the election postponed them. Now, in September 1968, they were being struck up again under a new government with a new philosophy. Ostensibly, they were to determine what changes the Indians wanted to the act. But the cat was already among the pigeons. Trudeau knew what he wanted, and Chrétien knew it too.

An approach similar to their own had been tried in the United States, where federal responsibility over the Indians was terminated in the 1950s. The experiment was soon declared a failure. Ottawa's own study of native affairs, the Hawthorn Report of 1965, had rejected an integration strategy of the type Trudeau and Chrétien had in mind. Equal treatment for people without equal competitive capacities, said the report, would be fundamentally unjust. The American experience, which saw sixty-one reservations disbanded, tended to support this conclusion. Even with transitional government aid, American Indians fell on harder times than they had experienced beforehand.

As the consultations got under way, Canadian native activists warned against moving in this direction. "There is an outmoded idea about Indians," said Kahn-Tineta Horn, a respected authority on native rights. "The idea is that Indians are the same as other people and therefore all they need is encouragement, education, and opportunity. This is entirely false. . . . Indians want something else altogether. First is a guarantee of recognition of Indian rights, treaties, protection of our title to our Indian lands forever. Next is honesty and justice in the government, instead of double dealing, treachery, and hypocrisy." She expressed the hope that the new Chrétien ministry would take this course. "But instead," she said, with some degree of prescience, it is "likely to go with an integration-genocide program which will not work."

In the election campaign, under the rubric of Trudeau's Just Society, the Liberals had promoted the idea of participatory democracy. Chrétien's view of participation, as exemplified in the hearings with the native peoples, had a decidedly paternalistic flavour. His attitude, as he stated, was that the government would consult the people, but it alone would make policy. Government was boss. Government knew what was good for the people. The mind-set, recalled Jean Fournier, his assistant, was part and parcel of the perspective of the times. "These were the heady days of government, you must remember. There was this idea, the Kennedy thing and all, that we could change the world, that government was the engineer, the architect, the main engine of social-political change." In considering the history of the Indian Affairs department, he pointed out, it was novel enough that there were consultations of any kind. Before, it had all been top-down.

As well as setting in motion the great sea change on overall policy, Trudeau weighed in heavily on the single most controversial issue on the natives' agenda: land claims. If these claims had existed at one time, Trudeau asserted, they had been effectively extinguished by the occupation of the country by the Europeans. They therefore had no force in law.

If Chrétien could go along with the overall integration initiative, he was less comfortable, noted Judd Buchanan, his parliamentary secretary, with this stance. The position may have had intellectual credibility, but in pragmatic terms it was a burdensome load for the minister to carry. Given the unanimity of the Indians on the issue, it guaranteed hostile relations.

In his first real test as a cabinet minister, Chrétien was being handcuffed by dictates from above. He was inhibited as well by Trudeau's decision to appoint a second minister to assist him. Robert Andras of Thunder Bay was two years an MP and fourteen years Chrétien's senior. Named minister without portfolio assigned to Indian Affairs, he was to sound out the native peoples and recommend policy. Free of bureaucratic constraints, he had time to establish a special rapport with the multifarious Indian groups. He travelled widely, seeing them informally, and becoming, in effect, their ombudsman. Jean Chrétien, who so liked to think of himself as the defender of the forgotten, was being scooped by his junior minister. Andras became the anti-establishment man, the minister without a suitcase, the guy getting the good press. Chrétien, meanwhile, had to keep an eye over his shoulder to his bureaucracy, to the Prime Minister's Office, to the PM himself.

Areas of responsibility between the two men were unclear. It was "an untenable situation," said John Rae, "because among the best politicians in the country were the natives, and when they saw an opportunity to divide the administration, they did it."

Chrétien was peeved, and the situation deteriorated when Andras started speaking out, disagreeing publicly with Chrétien over a reordering of the department that would put Indians and Inuit under the same administrative unit. As Andras saw it, the natives were cool to the idea. He sided with them, but Chrétien went ahead with the reorganization anyway. A power struggle developed, with the head-butting reaching the point that Trudeau finally had to stand up in Parliament and explain that Chrétien was the senior minister.

In the meantime, the consultation sessions with the Indians progressed, with no clear consensus emerging. The native groups weren't used to this. They looked disorganized, "bamboozled" as one writer put it, hardly prepared to discuss the minutiae of clauses in the Indian Act. Andras later acknowledged the farcical nature of some of the proceedings, and if Chrétien wasn't aware of the problem, he had one of his men telling him. Bill Mussell, a native Canadian who worked as an adviser to Chrétien, spoke to the minister about the weaknesses in the process. There was no reciprocity, he told him. "They were ritualistic. It was just a one-way effort by the government of Canada."

Chrétien was in a hurry to bring forward the historic reforms. After a century of disagreement and frustration, he was trying to solve the native problem in the space of months. But even if he'd wanted to go slower, he would have had a difficult time of it. Trudeau was pushing hard.

In December 1969 a twenty-three-year-old Indian woman, Flora Elk, died while hitchhiking back to her reserve in Manitoba from a correctional institution in Saskatchewan. Elk, found dead by a roadside, had been given only two dollars for the trip home. The case attracted national publicity, with Chrétien's department coming under attack for failing to make adequate transportation arrangements for her.

The story hit the prime minister's desk and Trudeau, in pointed terms, demanded an explanation from Chrétien. "I am deeply concerned," he wrote his minister, "with how such a chain of events took place. The data at present available to me leads me to think that this tragedy could have been avoided. . . . I am particularly anxious to know what part the department played in this matter."

While he was on the subject, he addressed some larger concerns. "In view of the growing acuteness of the Indians' problems, it is more than ever imperative to implement an acceptable general policy. . . . I hope shortly to receive your recommendations on the line of action to follow. . . . The government must have, as its frame of reference, a more dynamic policy, a long-term plan for permitting those Indians who wish to do so to become fully integrated into Canadian society."

The tone of the letter, which suggested the department might have been responsible for the Elk tragedy, angered Chrétien. He had gone to Mexico over Christmas to get some rest and had not found the experience entirely pleasant. He and Aline came across Jacques Parizeau, one of Quebec's leading nationalists, and his wife at the airport. The two couples were seated next to one another on the plane. They found themselves in the same Mexican hotel, on the same floor. Chrétien was on vacation for rest, not to dodge men who regarded him as a traitor.

When he returned, he wrote a lengthy letter of defence to Trudeau on the Elk issue, pointing out that it would have been seen as the height of paternalism for the department to ensure that the woman be taken bodily to her home. Elk was in the habit of hitchhiking whenever she was released from jail, he explained, and was not the sort of person who could be directed.

Meanwhile, Chrétien was now ready to march on the overall plan. "The myth," he wrote Trudeau, "that Indians are wards of the government must go if Indians are to feel equal and be regarded as such by other Canadians." He advised the government to move as quickly as possible in transferring responsibility for native Canadians to the provinces. There, "they could be treated with other social problems in a way which would remove the discrimination inherent in the present special federal responsibility."

In February the man of the people put forth a specific policy package. In a cabinet memorandum, extraordinary for its degree of hauteur, he ruled out any possibility of Indian participation in developing his proposals. He stated that no consensus from the hearings had emerged—a curious statement in light of some of his later remarks—and that none was likely to develop. "For this reason, prior discussion on the policy would not lead to a constructive result." The policy, he recommended, should be debated further in the Prime Minister's Office and cabinet and then be delivered to the Indians as a *fait accompli*. The Indians would be highly critical of the proposals, Chrétien predicted, but it was better that they not be told of the contents beforehand, in case they began to undermine the policy before it was even put to Parliament.

Robert Andras, meanwhile, was suggesting a more generous policy. He agreed that the thrust should be towards Indian self-determination, but recommended that the Indians themselves, in partnership with government, work out the route to that goal. Programs to mitigate their poverty and assist their social development would run parallel. For the Andras proposal to gain credibility, however, it required study in cabinet committee. To get to cabinet committee, it required Chrétien's approval. The approval never came.

As the Chrétien policy was being coordinated with the Prime Minister's Office, the last meeting with the Indians took place. Showing a greater degree of unity, native representatives repeated their demands for recognition of treaties and land claims before any changes to the Indian Act were made. Though Chrétien had already committed himself to a quite different set of proposals, the Indians found his remarks at the meeting encouraging. They went away feeling the government was listening to them.

On June 14, 1969, the night before he was to announce his policy paper in the House, Chrétien met with Indian leaders but was vague about what the paper contained. (The government, for obvious reasons, was trying to discourage the use of the term "White Paper.") The announcement the next day revealed reforms of the grand scope Trudeau and Chrétien had outlined months earlier. Initial reaction in most quarters was muted, with some members of Parliament and the media responding favourably. But then the population that counted, the native Canadians, made themselves heard. They were completely opposed. They said their treaty and land claims proposals had been disregarded, the wishes they expressed in the consultations ignored. While the government argued its plan would lead to liberation, the natives predicted a different result: assimilation. The angrier among them accused the government of trying to induce cultural genocide.

They told the minister of Indian Affairs that he had got it all wrong. Indians wanted to be recognized not as Canadians but as Indians, the Ontario Union said. To ask Indians to become Canadians was insulting, because in its genesis Canada was an Indian country. Chrétien had a ready response. "It is the law of the land that people living in this country, from sea to sea, are Canadian citizens."

An old Indian woman asked him, "When did we lose our identity?"

"When you signed treaties," replied Chrétien to murmurs of dissent.

"How can you," asked a grandmother from the Six Nations Reserve, "come here and ask us to become citizens, when we were here long before you?"

Chrétien had no reply.

He was puzzled by the criticisms. He wondered how he could be accused of paternalism when, in fact, he was trying to phase out his own federal department. What minister of any department had ever done that?

Despite the growing storm of protest among the natives, he and Trudeau held firm in their desire to see the proposals implemented. "I urge you," Trudeau told Chrétien in a memo in November 1969, five months after the policy paper's publication, "to mobilize all your possible resources, at the administrative and political levels, in support of the government proposals." The various Indian communities, Trudeau said, were to be given time to develop counterproposals because constructive discussions could be had "only at a price." Since services for the natives would be transferred to the provinces under the new plan, proposals for tripartite discussions among the provinces, Ottawa, and the natives were put forward. Trudeau rejected the idea, saying the Indians would acquire a status "at par with the status of the government," if this were permitted. Therefore, they could remain as only technical advisers to the discussions.

Chrétien came under continued attack. Knowing full well the prominent role the prime minister and his men had played, he was exasperated at having to shoulder all the blame himself. He let his staff know this. During meetings he would frequently launch into a "they hung me out to dry" speech, replaying with gesticulatory passion how they had been so keen to push the policy but ran for cover when the uproar set in. Jean Fournier worried that Chrétien might crack under the strain. "No question a lesser man would have been broken." Others like Judd Buchanan, however, sensed that his skin was thick enough.

Chrétien was not about to take on Trudeau, not at such a junior age. He was cautious and distant with the PM, contacting him only on the most urgent of matters. This was a strategy his deputies thought wise, because Trudeau didn't like being pestered by cabinet members. Chrétien kept an informal score-card on the wide range of issues in his department. He told his aides that if he could keep a high average of good decisions vs. bad ones, he'd keep the PM from his door. At 75 or 80 per cent, he told his cohorts, "we're safe."

Chrétien's policy paper helped spawn a new voice of Indian power in Harold Cardinal of Alberta. Young, articulate, and fearless, Cardinal became the adversary Chrétien most feared. Soon after Chrétien's document was released, Cardinal published a book, *The Unjust Society*, which alleged a Trudeau-Chrétien betrayal for supporting a program that amounted to cultural genocide. He brought forward a Red Paper exactly one year after the Chrétien report. It stated that Ottawa's recognition of treaty and aboriginal rights must be a prelude to a new native-government relationship. The paper demanded that Chrétien's department be split so that one minister handle Indian Affairs only.

Following its publication, Trudeau, with Chrétien at his side, finally laid to rest the integration strategy. In a frank assessment, the PM spoke of the government's miscalculation. "I'm sure that we were very naïve in some of the statements we made in the paper. We had perhaps the prejudices of small 'l' liberals, and white men at that, who thought that equality meant the same law for everybody. . . . But we have learnt in the process that perhaps we were a bit too theoretical, we were a bit too abstract, we were not, as Mr. Cardinal suggests, perhaps pragmatic enough or understanding enough."

It was now time, he said, for the natives to come up with their own solution. The government was listening, he said, and there was no big hurry this time. Trudeau added a few nice words about the effort his minister had made. Despite the public surrender, they made Chrétien feel better.

There were the inevitable calls for his resignation from Opposition MPs and some Indian leaders. But Trudeau, who had moved Andras out, kept him on. He also gave him more freedom to work with the Indians and come up with solutions that would be acceptable to them.

In the final analysis, Chrétien had presided over a deficient consultation process and failed to heed the advice of the constituency he was trying to serve. His memoranda to the prime minister, which recommended pushing ahead without native consent, betrayed a cavalier and unresponsive attitude. A meticulous study on the formulation of Chrétien's policy by the University of Waterloo's Sally Weaver concluded that Chrétien and the PMO had brought forward a rushed and badly flawed document whose chief aim was to bring in solutions that would free the federal government of future criticism and accusations of discrimination. The blame had to be shared, the study's author made clear, by the Prime Minister's Office. But the upshot was that in his first major test as a cabinet minister, Chrétien, at least in the short term, had come up a loser. His revolutionary plan was thrown to the ashes.

In retrospect, he would agree that the policy was probably too intellectually correct. He did not feel, however, that he had failed to heed the consultation process. "In the consultations they were saying, 'You're discriminating against us. . . .' In the White Paper we said, 'Yes, you're right. So we'll abolish the Indian Act, we'll abolish the department of Indian Affairs. . . .' And they said, 'Oh no no, it's going to be a cultural genocide if you do that.' I remember, when I told them, they were in shock. But it's what they had told me for a year. And suddenly they didn't want to be equal. They wanted to have a special status."

He concluded that the natives didn't want to be like the French. "We don't have reserves for francophones. We don't have a department of francophones. . . . A francophone under the law has the same rights as the others."

The way Chrétien saw it, he was beaten either way. Before the paper, the native peoples were saying they were being discriminated against, but after the paper, which recommended abolishing the sources of that discrimination, they said they were being discriminated against again.

Despite his difficulties building a rapport with the natives and despite facing the rejection of the biggest policy initiative his department had ever seen, Chrétien was caught up in the challenge and the people. His early trips to the North, most of which were taken with Aline, enraptured him. For native Canadians, the great underdog population, he developed a special affinity. This became apparent in the summer of 1969, at the very time he was being scorned by so many native leaders.

After Aline lost two children to miscarriages, she gave birth to Hubert. But it was a trying pregnancy, and she was sick for a long period after the child was born. Doctors advised her that it would be too risky to have another. Having planned all along for a large family, the Chrétiens found this hard news, news that made them think about adopting.

One day, they were flying over the Northwest Territories. Aline was seated beside a judge who held court throughout the North. In casual conversation he made the point that it was unfortunate, given the large number of broken native families, that very few Canadians adopted Indian children. His observation prompted Aline to wonder how it would look for the minister of Indian Affairs to adopt a native boy.

Jean was excited by the idea. They made inquiries and, in relative haste, haste they would one day come to regret, made the decision to go ahead. Though he was the Indian Affairs minister, Chrétien didn't think to check into the long history of disappointments and tragedies white families experienced in raising native children. "Nobody told me that there was a big problem to take Indians, that the record was not good," he explained. "We did not even look at that."

That summer his brother Michel happened to be working in Inuvik as a volunteer medical practitioner. He made inquiries for Jean and Aline at the local orphanage, examining the notes the institution had on each child. "There were three Indian babies available for adoption," Aline recalled. "I couldn't look at them because I would have thought forever about the other two. So I let Jean's brother decide." Michel chose a boy who was eighteen months old. He didn't get to meet either of the parents but, with his medical background, made sure the boy was healthy. "I did not put any judgement on it because they had decided to adopt and I think it would have been counterproductive to try to figure out the odds whether this or that might happen."

The other doctor in the family, Maurice, had some thoughts about the odds. He had dealt with adopted children in his medical practice and had seen too many examples of parents adopting without understanding all the implications. He knew it was especially difficult to raise a child from another culture.

Maurice also had concerns about Jean, who had to spend so much time away from home. He had watched Jean raise his son and daughter and knew he was not a tough parent. He was too nice, too soft, in Maurice's opinion. If the newly adopted boy needed rugged discipline, he didn't think his brother was the one to give it. Aline was a little sterner, he said, but not much.

He wished, particularly since he was Aline's physician, that he had been forewarned of their plan. "In this case, the baby was of unknown origin to me and I wasn't consulted about it. The first thing I knew, the baby was at home. I was not too happy about that, but I never said a word."

Perhaps, he theorized, they knew he wouldn't approve of the idea. Though the Chrétien family was close, this didn't mean there wasn't friction. Gabriel, for example, was disappointed Jean didn't do more for him when, in 1965, he tried to become the second Chrétien to make a successful go at politics. He sought the provincial Liberal nomination for the riding of Berthier-Maskinongé but was defeated. Jean did some work and came to the nomination meeting, but he was too busy in Ottawa to do as much as Gabriel had hoped.

For Jean and Aline, the adoption process began on a sour note. They went to Inuvik to pick up the child, but an officious social worker tried to block them. She insisted that the Chrétiens' Ottawa home had to be inspected for suitability. The Indian Affairs minister was insulted. Did they expect rodents, dirt, falling-down walls? He went to his friend, the Territories Commissioner Stu Hodgson. Hodgson called the parties involved, but they insisted on carrying forward with their inspection protocol. Hodgson was incensed. "I'm ordering you to let the baby go!"

A compromise was worked out. The social worker travelled to Ottawa on the plane with the Chrétiens and the baby, whom they had named Michel. She inspected the Chrétiens' home and gave it a pass.

Hodgson couldn't provide the minister with much advice on the adoption. In his opinion, native adoptions were uncommon because Indian families tended to help one another raise their children. "The attitude was that if someone had a bunch of kids and you didn't have any, you'd take one or two of them and help raise them. The tribe was like a big family that way." Chrétien did have a discussion with his native special assistant, Bill Mussell, but Mussell hesitated to say much. He didn't like trying to fit native babies into stereotypes.

The adoption could have served as a big political plus for Chrétien in his relations with the Indians, but he chose to be extremely discreet, avoiding publicity. "He was almost secretive about it," Judd Buchanan recalled.

To begin the new decade, Chrétien's department underwent a shake-up at the top. His deputy minister, the confrontational John MacDonald, was dumped and Basil Robinson, a smooth mandarin from External Affairs, was brought in to calm things down. Robinson had worked with Lester Pearson on the Suez Canal crisis and as an adviser to John Diefenbaker on foreign policy. Chrétien was deferential to him, remembering Mitchell Sharp's advice that he respect and heed his deputy ministers. Robinson found Chrétien conscientious, pressured, serious, and driven. He learned quickly that this minister did not like long memos. A page and a half would do.

It was at this time that Chrétien began to turn things around. In essence, Chrétien started reversing his own native policy and, in so doing, his reputation as head of the department. One of the purposes of the integration plan had been to head off Indian nationalism and so-called Red power. His discarded document had the opposite effect. It mobilized Indians more than ever before, spurring them on to take more matters into their own hands. The policy had "boomeranged," as one of Chrétien's own men put it, but Chrétien was fully prepared to accept that and help the Indians help themselves. He increased funding to native organizations, turned over the management of community development programs to them, and dramatically increased the number of natives employed in his department. A claims commissioner was appointed to help Indians research treaty rights, and money was handed over to the National Indian Brotherhood to research these same issues. Though the policy paper was rejected, it served as the catalyst for change among native groups, who learned to assert themselves and defend their rights. Thus, in the view of John Rae, it served a noble purpose in the long run.

It also taught Jean Chrétien a few lessons about politics. It had been a difficult cabinet baptism, but he had learned how power games were played and he had learned, or so it seemed, that the man of the people must always listen to the people. "Only those solutions which involve Indians in basic decisions," he said, "will have any chance of acceptance and long-term success."

CHAPTER TWELVE

THE LAST EMPEROR IN NORTH AMERICA

H E C O U L D rarely relax. His metabolism wouldn't let him. He had to get a fast walk in almost every day to burn off bottled-up energy. Long vacations were out of the question. "I get restless if I'm away from my desk too long." His prodigious energy level baffled aides just out of college who returned from trips through the tundra half-dead, only to find him yearning for another political mission. While others grew weary of politicking, Chrétien fed off it. Socializing drained most people's batteries. It recharged his.

He was a rare political breed. Clark Clifford, a close adviser to several American presidents, talked of the phenomenon in describing why, despite countless invitations, he never ran for public office. "I simply did not enjoy or need the constant superficial interaction with a myriad of people," he explained. "I knew many politicians who gained a sort of physical strength or energy from such interaction—one thinks of Lyndon Johnson 'pressing the flesh' or Hubert Humphrey joyously revitalizing himself from endless contact with the voters—but I knew I preferred to work with greater deliberateness." As a young politician Chrétien appeared to be cut from the Humphrey politics-of-joy school. The whole business energized him.

It was not only the body that worked in overdrive, but also the mind. It was a fast-food mind. He'd ask for the facts, digest them immediately, and make a decision. The attention span was brief, so memos and meetings had to be short. To take up much of his time was to intrude. On airplane trips with his financial adviser and friend, Robert Matteau, Chrétien frequently read from reports while carrying on other discussions. Matteau found this disconcerting until he realized that despite the double-dipping, Chrétien was absorbing what he said. Matteau was impressed he could do both at the same time. He never doubted Chrétien's smarts, but he worried sometimes about his well-being.

"He only relaxed when Aline told him to," Matteau recalled. "I followed him on a tour across Canada. One night I looked at him at eleven o'clock. I thought, God, he will die this night. He's so exhausted. But then, at seven in the morning, I hear him knocking on the door. 'Matteau! Get up, Matteau. We're out of here!'"

After the failure of Chrétien's Indian paper, he and Matteau went surfing in Hawaii. Matteau thought they were having a good day where they were, but Chrétien wanted to ride higher waves. There were bigger ones a few miles away, and he convinced Matteau they should go. When he saw them, Matteau said, "No, Jean. They're too dangerous."

"Ah! I will try," Chrétien said. "I have to try."

He went out, got up on the wave, and was soon being bounced around like a Ping-Pong ball in a hurricane. The mammoth force of the ocean catapulted him helplessly through the air and up onto the beach, where he crashed like a piece of rubble. Matteau feared he had lost consciousness. When, in short order, he came to, his face bruised and beaten red, Chrétien looked up at his friend. "Jesus, Matteau," he groaned. "This is harder than politics."

Matteau skied with him on occasion and found that all Chrétien cared about was the shortest route to the bottom. Friends called him "the Downhiller." Style on the slopes was for softies, he'd say. He'd break through the doors of the ski chalet and shout, "Matteau! Twenty-four times down that hill and not one fall. How's that, Matteau? Twenty-four times!"

He hated the slalom routes in politics as well. Always the *rassembleur*, he took in points of view from all quarters, put them in his fast-speed blender, and pressed the button that said "pragmatic middle." Free of any intense ideological bias, save ubiquitous Liberalism, Chrétien started from no fixed address and usually ended up there. He was, said his deputy minister, Basil Robinson, "the quintessential pragmatist." He studiously avoided aligning himself with any one group for too long. "Don't try to label me," he advised journalists. "Sometimes I side with the Left, sometimes with the Right."

For all the charging around he did, for all the hundreds of people he met, Chrétien curiously considered himself a man apart, a bit of a loner. Politics left no time to make friends, he said, only acquaintances.

He was perceived as an open book, so candid, a "what you see is what you get" type of person. But he kept a large part of himself in the shadows. In later days, after he had written his memoirs, in which he accorded only a dozen pages to his first twenty-nine years, he would acknowledge having concealed a great deal. "I've been a very private person," he said in a 1990 interview. "In a way, my private life has been very, very private. I made a decision a long time ago that I had to protect my family, and I managed to salvage that."

The interviewer said this was curious because "people feel they know you."

"I know," Chrétien replied. "But they don't know much."

André Grenier, who had purchased the Shawinigan trucking firm with him and worked on some of his campaigns, felt he never even got close to knowing him. "You never get into Jean Chrétien. He's a private man. He is a one-man show."

His early years in Ottawa had alerted him to the dangers of becoming part of the establishment pack. He picked up on this phenomenon—the myopia of groupism—at a relatively early stage. The politicians, bureaucrats, and journalists who formed the ruling class were members of inward-looking cabals. "They all tend to be out of touch," observed Chrétien, "isolated from what other ordinary people are thinking." Wasn't it, he wondered, the average Canadians whom the elite was supposed to represent? That was one of the reasons he felt a need to stay close to the blue-collar worker. "When I open my mouth in cabinet," Chrétien said, "maybe that's him speaking."

Ironically, he was accused in his first big test, the Indian paper, of being too much the inside man, of forming the policy on the basis of bureaucratic opinion as opposed to native Canadian opinion. To succeed in politics, as he would repeatedly discover, he had to be himself.

He had begun to mollify the native groups, allowing them to flex their own political muscle, and was now moving ahead, with more success, in other areas for which his department had responsibility. His duties included policy-making for the entire sweep of lands stretching across the top of the provinces to the North Pole. He was, as he once described it, "the last emperor in North America." Though John Diefenbaker had momentarily stirred the nation in the late 1950s with his thinly defined great vision of the North, Chrétien set more modest goals. "I have no great vision," he said of his plans. "I'm a realist. I don't see cities of a million under plexiglass domes in the next generation." He noted, however, that the North had to be more than just a storehouse of phenomenal natural resources. He wanted development but knew that meant walking a delicate line. On the one hand, native Canadians and environmentalists were fighting for land claims and conservation. On the other, energy consortiums were pushing for pipelines. It was, noted Stu Hodgson, a devilish challenge, "The Stone Age vs. the Jet Age."

Chrétien favoured oil and gas development that would, at the same time, create jobs and economic opportunity for the native population. This was in keeping with his practical side. Chrétien, his colleagues found, was more jobs-oriented than rights-oriented.

He was enthralled by the magnificence of his realm, by its expanse, its spectacular beauty, the warmth of its people, the lakes, the isolation, the utter silence. It was an earthly heaven where even Jean Chrétien could unwind. He ate char, walrus, seal, and bannock. He played hockey on the endless rivers of ice. He bought Inuit art in the local co-ops and began a personal collection. He talked non-stop with the natives of the region, trying to understand what they wanted from the twentieth century. He would say it was these experiences that made him understand the country and develop such a love for it. Indian Affairs and Northern Development had its drawbacks, but no other portfolio could teach a minister as much about Canada. His aide, Eddie Goldenberg, would return to the far North every summer thereafter. "It marks you," he said, "in a way few other things can."

Having surveyed his realm, Chrétien grew excited about the possibility of enshrining major portions of it in national parks. With the environmental movement putting down roots all over the continent, it was a politically perfect idea. Canada had eighteen national parks, but in the previous thirty-five years, only five new ones had been established. Chrétien set his sights on a substantial increase. As a first challenge, he had to crack Quebec. In place there was a long-standing obstacle to any federal plans for such projects—the inviolate principle of territorial integrity. Quebec's land was Quebec's land. For fifty years the province had refused to cede any of it to federal interests.

As he would do so often, Chrétien used his friendship network to gain a vital edge. He had an ally in the Union Nationale government in Tourism Minister Gabriel Loubier. Loubier was his old friend from Laval, the one who sat in his convertible with a bottle of Scotch, watching Chrétien and company pelt the Legislature with tomatoes. Chrétien convinced Loubier of the value of a federal park, and Loubier began to interest Premier Daniel Johnson in the proposal. The three of them sat down and worked out a plan—to the chagrin of those like Intergovernmental Relations Minister Marcel Masse, who opposed the intrusion.

The compromise was designed to save face for Quebec on the territorial integrity issue. A park would be developed at Forillon, on the Gaspé Peninsula, on land leased by Quebec to Ottawa for ninety-nine years. The province would have the right to take back the land after only sixty years, so long as it paid back the initial investment and continued to use the land as a park.

Chrétien wasn't thinking about it during the negotiations, but the breakthrough in the Gaspé presented him with a wonderful possibility: a national park in his own riding. Since Quebec had approved the principle, why not have it extended to his own backyard?

The idea excited him. The park would help him put his own federalist stamp on the riding, and judging by the results of the last election, he could use help of that kind. No one would ever be able to say he did nothing for his constituency. The park would bring jobs, tourists, and publicity and would also serve one of his broader purposes—it would prove to the people of *la belle province* that federalism could work for them.

The imposing beauty of La Mauricie made it a natural candidate for the park. Curiously, although he was the minister responsible, Chrétien didn't think of the idea himself. Allan MacEachen suggested the possibility while the two of them were touring Cape Breton National Park in MacEachen's Maritimes riding. Critics often said that Chrétien never originated ideas, that his skill was in the doing, the execution. In the case of the park, the stereotype fit.

With typical great enthusiasm, he mounted a campaign to gain support for the project. He took guests on flights over the proposed site and boasted that it was the most beautiful place in the world. One day, with Robert Matteau, he trekked up to a peak that he expected would offer the perfect panorama of the area. Some trees had grown up, however, and blocked the view. "We couldn't see anything," recalled Matteau. Chrétien couldn't tolerate this. Unburdening himself of some of his cabinet-rank weight, he told the forest supervisors he wanted the trees chopped down immediately so he could admire his kingdom. The supervisors protested, saying it would spoil the environment. "If you don't cut those trees down," Chrétien told them, "I will go and cut them myself." The managers got the message. The next day, recalled Matteau, the trees were down.

As soon as Chrétien had announced that a proposal for a park in La Mauricie was being studied, local businessmen, led by the Chamber of Commerce president, André Grenier, had thousands of pins manufactured, saying "Je suis pour" (I am for), raising the inevitable question, For what? The campaign was highly effective but simply because the provincial government had approved one park at Forillon didn't mean it would condone another in La Mauricie. Marcel Masse was adamantly opposed. Loubier fought him on Chrétien's behalf, but Masse, with cabinet support, held firm. An angry Chrétien got to display some of his displeasure when the provincial and federal MPs squared off in what was supposed to be a friendly hockey match. Masse wasn't much of a hockey player. At the first opportunity, Chrétien lined him up and crunched him into the boards.

Fortunately, the Union Nationale's mandate was running out and the election offered the possibility of a transfer of power to the Liberals under Robert Bourassa. The Liberals needed the Shawinigan seat, and they knew that Chrétien, with or without his vaunted machine, still wielded considerable power. Bourassa was told that if he wanted to win the riding, he had to agree to the park. Recalled Grenier: "Before he arrived for a speech here, we told his people that if he's not going to promise it, don't even bother having him show up. We'll run him out of town." Bourassa arrived and promised the park. His Liberals won the riding and the election, and they held good on their promise.

In order to show local support for his big initiative, Chrétien piled a dozen Shawinigan businessmen into a plane one night and flew them to the Royal York Hotel in Toronto to attend a black-tie dinner with conservationists. It was nice to be able to do these things, impress the folks back home with a little junket, but this one didn't go off too smoothly. The group was told there would be suites available at the hotel, but when they arrived, there were only two small rooms—and one was for Chrétien and his wife. All the other disgruntled Shawiniganites crammed into the other room to squeeze into their tuxes. Then they went downstairs, ate rubber chicken, and listened to boring speeches from tree-huggers. Miserable, they began the return trip home, only to get caught in a violent storm that forced them to detour to Montreal in the middle of the night and make their way from there.

Misadventures aside, the Chrétien-led campaign was effective. Almost everyone agreed that he was good at mixing on Main Street and mobilizing public opinion. In British Columbia he had mounted an equally successful crusade, generating support for the creation of the Pacific Rim National Park on Vancouver Island.

In his far northern domain he created three new spectacular parklands. For those, no big campaigns to win public support were necessary. He needed, as he put it, only the approval of the minister of Indian Affairs and the minister of Northern Development. He was both, and the arbitrary power was extraordinary. He once flew from Baffin Island to Broughton Island, where he gazed awestruck at the snowcaps, the plunging fiords, the pristine forests. He turned to Aline and announced, "I will make this a park for you." Back at the office, the last emperor of the North took out a map and a felt pen and drew a big circle around two thousand square miles. Another national park was born.

In all, he fashioned ten new ones in his time in the portfolio and collected reams of favourable publicity for doing so, even though the parks didn't live up to their advance billing as job creators or, in some cases, big tourist draws. At Forillon they had talked of one thousand new jobs but only a quarter of that number were created. In La Mauricie, as well, the park would fall short of expectations.

In another time, outfitting his own riding with such an asset might have left him open to charges of crass pork-barrelling. In 1970, however, it wasn't quite the crime. Now Chrétien not only had something positive to point to in future election campaigns, but he also had a fountainhead of jobs with which to reward campaign workers and friends. Requests were numerous. Chrétien not only used the park in his own riding, but also those throughout the country to help meet the demand. His boyhood friend Gilles Argouin, the one Chrétien convinced to lie so he could qualify for his hockey team, asked the minister if he could help with a summer job for his boy. Chrétien got Argouin's son a job in a park in Saskatchewan.

The year 1970, however, was one of events far weightier than tourist-site deliberations. During the October Crisis, the Front de Libération du Québec kidnapped a British diplomat and murdered the Quebec government's minister of Labour, Pierre Laporte. Chrétien's ministry was far removed from the crisis, but he actively participated in the debate that followed. Trudeau favoured enacting the War Measures Act and deploying masses of troops to Quebec. Thinking the prime minister was perhaps exaggerating the threat, Chrétien crossed swords with him in a full meeting of the cabinet. He was firmly rebuked and backed off. Eventually, he agreed that the Boss's strategy in handling the crisis was the correct one.

Despite his junior status, Chrétien was already thinking about making it to the top. No one predicted that Trudeau would stay around for so long, and Chrétien thought an anglophone might take the helm soon. After that, he reasoned, it could be his turn. On the flight home from a conference in Yellowknife, he was seated next to Gerald Stoner, who was now deputy minister of Transport. "Jean and I got onto various things," recalled Stoner, "and he said, 'You know, I'm kind of hoping to hang in there long enough to be prime minister.' He said he thought the next time around it would be Turner. But after that, he didn't think there was much competition among the francophones. So he said, 'I think it's likely I'll get there,' and he was quite determined."

His duties in Northern Development took him on a seventeen-day trip to the Soviet Union, shortly after Pierre and Margaret Trudeau's tour in May 1971. Chrétien visited Moscow, Leningrad, and six northern and Siberian cities to study pipeline construction, Arctic resource development, and assistance to native peoples. The Brezhnev-era Soviets only showed Western visitors their very best, and Chrétien came away quite amazed at the rate of development in the Soviet Union's north. He felt his own country wasn't moving fast enough. The Soviet case showed, he said, that the construction of pipelines didn't spoil the tundra, as Canadian critics back home complained. "All this could be very useful to us," observed Chrétien, "if we had the will it takes to develop our north at an accelerated pace." But he doubted that will was there.

Not an imbiber of any renown, Chrétien was nonetheless cajoled into a drinking bout with his Soviet hosts. The Russian vodka-draining tradition was so ingrained that to refuse to take part was to immeasurably insult the hosts. Luncheon banquets could sometimes feature eighteen courses and two dozen toasts—a toast to the motherland, a toast to Lenin, to Brezhnev, to fathers, to brothers, to relatives, to the war, and to the tyrant himself, Joseph Stalin. Wine toasts—only bottoms-up toasts were allowed in Russia—usually came first. These were followed by servings of pure vodka that were chugged from glasses big enough to hold a pint of beer. Occasionally, hosts provided guests with a special treat—tankards with bells in the bottom. When the beverage was drained, the idea of course was to ring for more. If, by banquet's end, the bells weren't chiming like St. Mary's Cathedral, the fête was a failure.

In Irkutsk, Chrétien met up with a bear-shaped dignitary of Ivan the Terrible mien. He insisted on a bell-ringer of a welcome— a twenty-four-toast salute! Chrétien's assertion that he was an incapable drinker held no merit. As a matter of honour, he had to join in. Having told Stu Hodgson to bar the door to photographers, Chrétien let the toasts begin. Astonishingly, he kept pace, and after a couple of hours, the Russian began to sag. Chrétien was smart enough to sneak in a few shots of water along the way to dilute the force of the heavy stuff. The Russian did nothing of the kind. Finally, by toast number twenty, he had had enough. Dazed and done for, he piloted his woozy bulk over to a corner of the salon, where he collapsed on the carpet. "Never saw a guy so shit-faced in all my life," one of the Canadian spectators later remarked. The Soviet was as brain-dead as Chrétien had been the night he was taken to the forest by brother Guy to sober up under the autumn leaves. Friends back home, having witnessed such shaky drinking performances, could scarcely believe the story of his triumph over the Soviet bear.

He did well too in the Siberian far east, where he was the guest of a Chukchi tribe of caribou herders. Chrétien joined in the caribou chase, lasso in hand, and roped one in on his first try. It wasn't an unusual feat, in that the caribou move slowly enough, but Chrétien was proud of his good luck. That night he sat in a fur-lined tent on the frozen tundra and ate raw fish and washed it back with cold vodka—though in nowhere near the quantities consumed at the Irkutsk banquet.

Early on in the trip, he appeared to be vulnerable to the great gobs of Soviet propaganda. But by tour's end, he was catching on. On the outskirts of Norilsk, the far northern city Trudeau had passed through, Chrétien visited a nickel mine. It was a spectacularly clear morning, but when Chrétien looked back towards the city, he couldn't see anything, so dense was the smoke from the smelters. He turned to the deputy minister, a man named Ganochev, and suggested there might be a bit of a pollution problem. A blank-faced Ganochev replied, "No. There is no pollution in the Soviet Union." But the foul air was clearly evident, Chrétien protested. Didn't the government get criticized for this? "No," replied Ganochev. "There is no criticism in the Soviet Union."

The Soviet trip was one of the few occasions when Chrétien's adopted son, Michel, made the news. While touring a mine in a Siberian city, the minister was shown a treasure the Russians had unearthed, a huge sparkling diamond. It was so spectacular that they asked him to give it a name. Chrétien was on the spot, but Hodgson nudged him and suggested he name it after his new son. It might augur well, offered Hodgson. So the great diamond was called Michel.

During the first two years in the Chrétien household, there was little sparkle in him. Michel worried his new parents because he was terribly uncommunicative. Daughter France, entering her teen years, was a promising student, but Hubert had learning problems. He suffered from dyslexia, which impaired his reading and comprehension capacity. Aline spent long hours with him and Michel, as well as tending to all the household duties without the maid or cook that some cabinet ministers kept. She was adjusting now but had found the first few years as a politician's wife trying. She was sensitive, and "when people criticized Jean, I would cry," she recalled. "He would say, 'You won't last long if you're going to let that bother you.'" The family lived modestly enough, in a middle-class home in Alta Vista in Ottawa South, a ten-minute drive from Parliament Hill. Their home was on Rose Crescent, just down the street from Joe Macaluso, the former Grit MP, who found them to be quiet neighbours who occasionally entertained but preferred, as a general rule, to avoid the dinner-and-cocktail-party circuit.

Chrétien had not had much time to spend on taking care of his children, nor, for that matter, himself. He was no longer the same indefatigable young man he had once been. His time in the port-folio had worn him down. The constant crisis management, the fantastically long travel requirements, the heavy grease diet, the campaigning for Liberals all over the country, the blasts from Quebec nationalists and native groups—all these things were cu-mulatively too much. He was only thirty-eight, but early in 1973 he checked into the hospital, thoroughly depleted. Doctors diag-nosed acute indigestion, exhaustion, and the apparent beginnings of a heart attack.

The days Chrétien spent on his back, tubes sticking out from all over him, gave him time to do something he rarely did—reflect. He had spent ten years in politics, just as he had intended when he entered his first campaign in 1963. He had predicted back then that after a decade he would try another career, perhaps becoming a judge. The possibility tempted him now. He had three children, a mortgage, a small pension, and a fear that he'd leave his family without much if he died early. He went to see Trudeau who, though too proud and independent to implore anyone, said he would like him to stay. But if Chrétien wanted to go, Trudeau said, he would find a place for him on the bench.

The temptation was stronger than many thought. "I always promised my wife I [would] finish as a judge. I wanted to be a judge in Quebec City. . . . It would have been happiness for me." The bench, he noted, was a prestigious way of ending one's career. Dentists remained dentists, accountants died as accountants, but lawyers, he noted, could become something more ennobling.

Chrétien met with family members at his cottage on Lac des Piles, north of Shawinigan. With his shrewd business sense, he had bought land on the lake just before the property shot up in value. Gabriel was there, and the two brothers went on a long walk in the woods. When Jean announced his ten-year plan in 1963, Gabriel had said it was foolish to try to set a definite course. Now, even though Chrétien felt he might be named chief justice of the Quebec Superior Court, Gabriel urged him to stay in politics. "I told him, 'What would you do sitting on the bench? Jean, you're a guy who moves all the time.'"

He got similar advice from others. Even though the dire health warning was just behind him, no one could envisage Jean Chrétien being happy in a state of repose. The blood boiled too hotly in him. He was nothing if not active. So he said to hell with the robes and returned to the fray.

There was no fear of boredom in politics. On those infrequent occasions when controversy over native issues subsided, Chrétien had the developers to contend with. They had been after him since early in his tenure, when he declared at a conference that the government intended to remain a prime player in northern development. Businessmen present at the conference were outraged. "Free enterprise built this country," said Clarence Manning, a Calgary millionaire and utility company director. "That man is a disgrace." The financiers took Chrétien to a hotel room, sat him on a bed, and lectured him till 2:30 in the morning. "He was at a young and convertible age," said one. "We wanted to get to him while he could still be changed."

Like all good Liberals, Chrétien tried to play it down the middle, siding with developers one day, the greens the next. He became incensed when an employee of his department, Dr. Peter Usher, wrote a report accusing him of backing the oil companies exploring on Banks Island at the expense of Inuit trappers. On television Chrétien labelled the report "stupid" and said it was "a shabby piece of research." The Public Service Institute demanded he publicly apologize for remarks that were "opprobrious" and "reprehensible" and that had undermined a public servant's credibility. But Chrétien stood his ground. No apology was forthcoming. He prided himself on having good relations with his bureaucrats and felt Usher should have come to him confidentially instead of going public with his report. "I'm not in the habit of letting myself be attacked without defending myself," he said. "He [Usher] seems like

the typical white man who knows what is best for the Eskimos."
Aides and officials, some of whom felt he overreacted to the Usher
report, found him nettled by the well-publicized spat. He sent directions to his deputy to "get that guy under control."

A policy statement put out by Chrétien in 1972 said, "The government's conviction is that the needs of the people of the North
are more important than resource development and that the main-
tenance of ecological balance is essential." But a few weeks later,
he was telling conservationists that stopping northern development would bring on a "new Dark Age" in Canada's Arctic, creating a welfare economy and forced migration to the south. His
policy set, as his department's priorities, full employment for native peoples, more power for local residents in territorial governments, and liberalization of educational opportunity. He never
reached the jobs target, though he was able to increase native employment through a federal policy stipulating that 75 per cent of
all public jobs go to local inhabitants. With pressure from his department, responsible government was brought to the Northwest
Territories. Council members, formerly appointed, now had to be
elected.

Chrétien had been counting on a planned pipeline down the
Mackenzie River valley that would transport Alaskan natural gas
from Prudhoe Bay to American markets. He expected the pipeline
project to bring development that would benefit the natives, while
still allowing them to maintain the integrity of their settlements.
But his plan backfired. On his recommendation, the government
chose Justice Thomas Berger to lead an inquiry into the pipeline,
consulting native groups and environmentalists. Chrétien thought
Berger's mandate was to tell the government how to build the
pipeline. Instead, he told it how not to build the pipeline, recom-
mending postponement for at least ten years. Chrétien, who believed construction of the pipeline would have meant greater
leverage on land claims, as well as more employment opportunities for natives, was discouraged.

Always on the alert for ways to discredit Quebec separatists, he envisaged great oil and gas deposits in the North, right in Quebec's backyard. But Quebeckers, he warned, would be deprived of these riches by choosing a separatist route. "You will be the laughing-stock of the world if you separate today and we find a couple of Prudhoe Bays in the North." If they then turned around and asked for a share of the wealth, Chrétien said that other Canadians would tell them to go to hell.

When he fired such shots at the nationalists, he usually got ones back, and they hurt him. Ever since he took a leading federalist role in the mid-sixties, he had been accused of lacking the intellectual weight to be taken seriously. Few things bothered him more than this. "I'm from rural Quebec," Chrétien later observed, "and I've always had a chip on my shoulder about Montreal, the intellectuals, and everything. Even though I've been a cabinet minister all these years, with all the experience and success, I still feel that way—as if they're superior, as if they're looking down on me." He was an unusually resilient person, noted his assistant Jean Fournier, but in the face of scornful treatment by Quebec intellectuals, the resilience sometimes crumbled. He grew dark, brooding, depressed, Fournier recalled. They had wounded his pride.

Chrétien knew that some of that same snobbery existed around the cabinet table where he sat. Gérard Pelletier, Marc Lalonde, Trudeau, and Jean-Luc Pepin, among others, considered themselves intellectually superior to him. Health Minister John Munro, who worked closely with Chrétien because their portfolios overlapped on many matters, was offended by the "belittling way" some of them looked upon Chrétien. "His mannerisms, the way he talked, his slang, this mortally offended the bourgeois of Quebec," recalled Munro. Lalonde, he noted, was particularly condescending. "It must have been terribly embarrassing for Jean, this questioning his intellectual capacities and things. It must have been extremely painful for Jean." Chrétien acknowledged occasionally feeling the scorn, "but I realized very rapidly, in the debate on Indian Affairs for example, that around the table with Trudeau and others, I could hold my ground intellectually, so they stopped considering me too much a regular guy."

He wasn't in the inner cabinet, so he didn't have the access to Trudeau that the elite circle did. Gerald Stoner, who served as deputy minister under Chrétien and Jean Marchand, noted the differences. "Marchand had an office right below Trudeau and when he got excited about something he'd say, 'I'll go up and see the prime minister.' And he'd just walk right up and right in and almost regarded the PM as his nephew. He'd say, for example, 'We've got to get Pierre to stiffen his back with that fellow Bobby Bourassa,' and go tell him." Of course, recalled Stoner, there was none of this access for Chrétien. "Chrétien was quite respectful, quite distant with Trudeau. I think they didn't have much in common because Trudeau could sit with you for an hour and say very little and make it kind of awkward, and I suspect that Jean, who has a certain *bonhomie* with people, found that a little difficult."

Following the 1972 election, Chrétien spent another year and eight months in the Indian Affairs portfolio. The eternal frustration of it, he recalled, was the lack of consensus among the people he tried to serve. "I don't think you would ever have the natives in positive agreement on something." Nonetheless, he continued to make up for his sullied debut. Robert Bourassa presented him with a particular challenge when he announced what was grandiosely termed "Quebec's project of the century"—a $6 billion hydroelectric power project at James Bay. The operation would mean the occupation of the lands the Cree and Inuit of northern Quebec inhabited. The Cree and Inuit feared, as they calamitously put it, "extermination." In keeping with his preference for helping Indians organize and do battle for themselves, Chrétien readily backed their cause, funding their legal fight to receive fair compensation for their lands. In so doing, Chrétien was making a hard choice. He was challenging the big dreams of a leading Quebec federalist.

On the broad issue of Indian land claims, Trudeau had been reluctant to cede an inch. But a court ruling on claims by the Nishga Indians of northwest British Columbia, a sophisticated and well-organized band, changed his mind. The Nishga pushed their comprehensive claims case all the way to the Supreme Court. There they lost by one vote, but it was from a justice who ruled against them on a technicality. Trudeau decided that if the Supreme Court was that close to being persuaded, he should be less intransigent. Ottawa subsequently announced it would look at claims from Indian groups in regions where no treaty had been signed. The PM's change of attitude made Chrétien's job easier.

On James Bay, Chrétien weighed in heavily on the native side, telling Quebec to "go to hell" when it tried to insist that the federal government should only be allowed to observe talks between the conflicting parties. The natives won a tremendous initial victory when their lawyer, James O'Reilly, got an injunction that halted Quebec's construction on the project until the lands question was settled. Chrétien was ecstatic. He told the House of Commons the order gave him "one of the few moments of satisfaction" during his five and a half years as a minister.

Bourassa soon announced an appeal of the injunction, and Chrétien, donning his legal garb, advised a strategy for the Indians. He felt they should suspend the injunction while talks on compensation for the lands continued. That way they could hold the threat of reinstating the injunction over the head of Bourassa like the sword of Damocles—until he came up with a generous offer. But Chrétien's counsel was rejected. O'Reilly and the natives then lost their case in appeal.

In a sometimes incendiary climate, negotiations dragged on and on until a settlement—the first large native lands settlement with a province—was reached. The fight showed Chrétien as a crafty go-between, alternating his allegiances, blowing hot and cold, angling for victory. A piece of sly manoeuvring provided him with a key ally in the Quebec government. Bourassa had been looking for strong election candidates, so Chrétien offered him his assistant deputy minister, John Ciaccia, on the condition Ciaccia be given an important post. When Ciaccia was subsequently elected and Bourassa then needed a chief negotiator to deal with the natives on James Bay, Chrétien was on the phone. "Ciaccia's your man. He knows the issues, he knows the people." Ciaccia got the job. Though the Quebec government was Chrétien's adversary in the dispute, putting the case for the adversary was a Chrétien friend.

Bourassa and Ciaccia eventually came up with what Chrétien considered a good settlement offer, but the Indians balked. Chrétien got on the phone to offer Chief Billy Diamond, who was in far-away Val d'Or, a bit of advice. "I'm telling you, Billy, it's the best offer any Indian in Canada ever got." Diamond wouldn't budge. Chrétien told him he was on his way up. He sat down with Diamond and the Cree, but they soon insisted on going out for lunch. Demanding that talks continue, Chrétien told them he would order lunch and pay for it. He sent for barrels of chicken. Everyone ate, everyone negotiated, but nothing was settled. Chrétien threw his hands in the air and left without paying for the chicken, saying the Indians could take care of it. They sent the bill back to Ottawa.

It was time for harder tactics. The minister threatened to cut off all financial aid to the natives in their fight if they didn't accept the Quebec offer as a basis for negotiation. He was attacked from all quarters for these blackmail measures and backed off. But the ploy helped push the Indians towards a compromise. They decided that going it alone, without Chrétien, would have been too tough.

The James Bay deal, which was signed after Chrétien left the portfolio, proved over time to be a good model for allowing the natives to advance their rights and their autonomy. In the end, with this being another example, Chrétien could argue that his strong support for native organizations helped them make some important progress. In a way his legacy was to set in motion the very nationalism he and Trudeau initially tried to avoid.

Harold Cardinal, a man never known for the generosity of his evaluations, came to the lasting opinion that Chrétien was a puppet in the hands of bureaucrats, a likeable well-meaning guy who was out of touch with native aspirations. "He was a professional who did his work well. I don't think he ever knew what we were talking about, but at least he made life interesting." Other native leaders spoke more charitably. Like many others who dealt with him, they found Chrétien about as honest as politics allowed white men to be. When Trudeau had faced pressure to shift him out of Indian Affairs, telegrams poured in from native leaders, Chrétien proudly noted, convincing the PM to keep him in place.

In other areas of responsibility, he had acquitted himself well, creating parks and helping bring a more responsible form of government to the territories. On development issues he had, whenever possible, run the middle course, balancing the competing objectives of capitalism and conservation.

In what was considered a dead-end portfolio, he had skirted disaster and, by most accounts, fought back to leave with a good record. In the end, after six and a half years, Chrétien was able to say, "I'm quite happy. I still have my scalp."

CHAPTER THIRTEEN

DOCTOR NO

T HE FIRST DECADE in Ottawa, while adding a smattering
of diplomacy to the Chrétien persona, had done little to
suppress his instinctive combativeness. At base he was still
belligerent.

A tendency to resort to duplicity or aggression when cornered
had been with him since the beginning. It had shown up in his re-
cruitment of the over-age hockey player; his staging of the appendicitis sham; his deceiving his father into believing he'd completed
his year at college; his physical assaults on fellow students and,
later, a law colleague; and his dirty tricks campaigns against Clive
Liddle.

While some of his underhandedness could be attributed to
the excesses of youth, there were too many examples from post-
adolescence for the tendency to be dismissed as no more than that.
If winning sometimes required deceitful tactics, Jean Chrétien
wouldn't hesitate to use them. If more evidence was needed, the
election campaigns of 1972 and 1974 provided it.

He had been frightened by his near defeat in the 1968 election
and, as his bright young assistant John Rae noted, became highly
preoccupied with sealing his support. As the country headed into
the 1972 campaign, the enthusiasm for Trudeau's Liberals was on
the wane. But in Quebec the prime minister was still a potent
force, which had to be seen as a plus for Chrétien. So too did the

state of the other parties. They weren't strong. The best days of the Créditistes were already behind them. The Conservatives had a new Quebec leader in Claude Wagner, who was also a native of Shawinigan, but the party was still a long way from making a big breakthrough. The outlook was promising but, in Jean Chrétien's analysis, by no means promising enough. He could use a little help from his friends.

He had an ally in Grand'Mère, Antonio Genest, whom he had met after graduating from Laval. Genest, a parochial man, was the owner of a small hotel, the Hotel Windsor. Chrétien went to him and asked, as a favour, that he run against him in the election. The idea was that Genest would come forward with what seemed to be the best intentions, capture a party's nomination, then proceed to run a pitiful campaign, playing right into Chrétien's hands. Genest agreed to do it, no strings attached.

He got the Conservative nomination and the fix was on. "I stayed in the hotel without going out once for the whole campaign," Genest admitted many years later, when pressed about what had happened. "I did it as a service to him." He was reluctant to talk about the episode, saying only that Chrétien was a friend he wanted to help and that in the end "it made a prime minister."

In addition to the counterfeit candidacy of Genest, Chrétien's old friend Guy Germain, who may have saved Chrétien's political life by appearing as a Conservative candidate in the 1968 campaign, was back—this time in different party colours. Le Chien had always been a conservative, first as a Union Nationale partisan, then at the federal level with the Tories. Robert Stanfield's party and the Créditistes of Caouette didn't have a whole lot in common, but this time the Shawinigan lawyer curiously decided to run under the Socred banner.

He won the nomination, which meant Chrétien was outfitted with a stacked deck. Genest didn't put on any campaign at all, while the Dog limped along, not wishing to criticize his good friend Jean.

In the case of Genest, Chrétien conceded, when asked many years later, "I asked him to run." He talked of the deceit in a tone that suggested it was a routine development. But it was not routine, not even in the Duplessis years.

Chrétien maintained that he never asked Germain to run. Party insiders didn't think he would have needed much asking anyway. They thought it more likely that Germain entered, as in 1968, to help publicize his law practice. If in so doing he could help Chrétien, all the better. Many lawyers in town, noted the political organizer Omer Hill, used politics as a pathway to the bench or other patronage rewards. Germain eventually got his. In the 1990s, Chrétien named him to the National Parole Board.

The noteworthy irony of the 1972 campaign was that it featured the so-called candy-man controversy, right in Chrétien's backyard. During a stopover in Shawinigan, Trudeau remarked that he had goodies for the voters. "We have, as they say, some candy to offer you." He was referring to a Chrétien plan to create a scenic route of parks and heritage trails stretching from Quebec City to Toronto. The press jumped on his choice of words, labelling him "the candy man" who was trying to buy votes.

Chrétien was a bit nonplussed by the PM's remark. "He certainly didn't help by saying that." But of course, he already had the sweetest candy man any candidate could possibly hope for! A bogus opponent, in effect, working on his behalf. Chrétien won easily, by 8,400 votes over Germain and by a whopping 17,000 over Genest. Given that the election knocked the Liberals into minority-government status, his margin of victory was impressive.

Despite Genest's duplicitous and dismal showing, he did not go away quietly. In the next campaign, which followed quickly in 1974, he again came forward on behalf of Jean Chrétien. He had the gall to seek the Tory nomination once more, but he was promptly defeated. So, following the precedent set by Germain, Genest played his own game of musical chairs. The Socreds were having trouble fielding a candidate. Genest pursued that party's nomination, won it, and proceeded, to Chrétien's obvious delight, to put up a performance equal to that of 1972. He might even have set a record of sorts—as the only candidate of a major party to fail to deliver a single speech in the course of an entire campaign. "I didn't make a speech anywhere," Genest said. "I never left the hotel."

Richard Durand, the Grand'Mère restaurant owner who won the Tory nomination, had thought he had a chance to score well. Until Genest's last-minute entry, Durand was the only candidate on the Right. With the combined Socred-Tory vote, he believed he could make a challenge. "What happened was a surprise for us," he recalled, "because I already beat Genest at our nomination meeting." He had no way of knowing for certain if any Chrétien-Genest deal existed, but he began to suspect something. "Genest did nothing. He was simply a name on the ballot. We have an expression for it. *C'est une putain politique.* [He's a political whore.]"

Stanfield embraced unpopular wage-and-price controls during the campaign, further dampening Durand's hopes. The resulting Chrétien victory was of a scope never before seen in St-Maurice. (Chrétien had the riding's name changed from St-Maurice–Laflèche to simply St-Maurice.) He crushed Genest by 15,000 votes and Durand by 17,000. Genest had managed to diminish, by more than 50 per cent, the level of support the Créditistes earned in 1968. The candidate from that election, Alphonse Poulin, watched from the sidelines. "It was dishonourable, but what could we do? He, Genest, won the nomination."

The Tory, Durand, was unusual in that although he tended to side with the federalists in La Mauricie, he was never a Chrétien man. His unflattering opinion of the Liberal candidate was not enhanced by the campaign. When asked if he thought Chrétien was an honest man, Durand said, "That's a question I wouldn't like to answer." The problem with any politician who built a political machine like Chrétien's, he noted, was that they had to do things to keep it well oiled and effective. That, in turn, led to the type of politics Durand could not countenance.

Even Chrétien's own supporters had difficulty defending his use of Genest. Guy Suzor, one of his lead campaigners and closest friends, agreed that it was the 1968 campaign that led Chrétien to more severe tactics. The use of a counterfeit candidate, said Suzor, was not the type of thing that was done often, even in Quebec. André Grenier, however, was not surprised it happened. "Chrétien is a little bit like everybody in this province," he said, in reference to Quebec's unscrupulous political heritage. "He's a victim of the system."

Chrétien suffered no repercussions from the foul play because the Genest affair never came to light. But his passion for protecting his home turf would put him in the national headlines before too long.

In March 1976, the *Globe and Mail* reporter Richard Cleroux revealed that Chrétien had telephoned a judge to try to find out when a decision would be coming down. The phone call was part of Chrétien's bid to restart Malibou Fabrics, a Grand'Mère textile company that had closed down in 1971, putting four hundred people out of work. As a hands-on MP who would be facing another election soon, Chrétien wanted to find new buyers for the abandoned plant and get the jobs back. He located several interested parties, but they told him their decision could not be made until bankruptcy proceedings involving Malibou were settled by the courts. Chrétien called Justice Harry Aronovitch of the Quebec Superior Court. He asked, as he recalled, "When are you going to make up your mind? I've got four hundred guys out of work. I don't care what you decide, just decide something so these guys can get back to work."

Chrétien was one of three Trudeau cabinet ministers cited by Justice Kenneth Mackay in Cleroux's article as "trying to interfere in the judicial process." Mackay termed the interference "appalling."

The revelation devastated Chrétien. He had earned a good

measure of popularity from his perceived ethical standards, standards that were now being called into question. His deputy minister, Gordon Osbaldeston, walked into his office one day and found him drenched in despair.

Chrétien was quick to counter-attack, however. He contacted Aronovitch and asked him to issue a statement about the phone call. Aronovitch wasn't prepared to clear him. Chrétien, he said, should have known better. But, importantly, he did issue a statement saying he did not consider the call to be interference, as Mackay had alleged. In a situation that was open to interpretation, Chrétien was fortunate that the judge chose to give it this positive spin. The call was clearly meant to push Aronovitch into moving quickly on the case. As a former lawyer and a current cabinet minister, Chrétien should have been expected to realize the inadvisability of such an act. Telling a judge to hurry could still be characterized as a form of interference. Aronovitch decided not to interpret it as such.

Chrétien now had the stick to beat back the critics with. He sent a copy of Aronovitch's letter to Mackay, who retreated from his initial allegation. Chrétien then moved on to the *Globe and Mail,* insisting it had been negligent in not printing his version of the story as he stated it in the House of Commons. While on the phone to a *Globe* editor, Chrétien suggested he might sue. "Is that a threat?" the editor asked. "No," said Chrétien, "it's a promise." He kept his promise, bringing suit and eventually winning damages of three thousand dollars. Aline bought a piano with the money. Chrétien thereafter called it his *"Globe and Mail* piano."

The year of "the judges' affair," as it was labelled, was also a year of triumph for the separatist Parti Québécois. The unanticipated development brought more distress for Jean Chrétien than for other federalists. It meant that one of the dark forces in Chrétien's life, his political arch-enemy, was now at large. In the nation's capital, indeed in all of English Canada, Yves Duhaime was unknown. But in the sheltered world of Shawinigan, where he was elected for the PQ, he was a force to be reckoned with. No one got under Chrétien's skin like Duhaime. He brought out the worst in him—which was saying a lot.

They began as friends. Duhaime was once a good Liberal and a Chrétien supporter. He attended the University of Montreal law school in the early 1960s and worked for a few weeks as a summer student in Chrétien's firm. Upon graduating, he applied for a job there. Chrétien had only just filled a vacancy, but he wanted to help Duhaime, so he set him up with a position in the prestige firm in town, the one run by Chrétien's close friend Marcel Crête. Duhaime was also interested in politics, and Chrétien helped him become head of the riding's provincial Liberal association.

The town's Liberals predicted big things for Yves Duhaime. The businessmen's group, the Pic Club, which was controlled by the Grits, gave him a six-thousand-dollar loan and sent him off for three years' study in Paris. During that time he was wooed by Lévesque's separatist movement, and when he returned from France, prior to Quebec's 1970 election, he had a difficult decision to face. He chose, to the absolute consternation of the local Liberals, to change trains.

"Everybody wanted to kill him," said Chrétien of the decision. Duhaime had benefited so much from his Liberal contacts, and now he had turned his back on them. From that moment forward, Chrétien threw all his resources against Duhaime, and the Péquiste responded in kind. Duhaime was not only a PQ traitor, in Chrétien's estimation, but also, particularly since his time in Paris, a man with the air of a pretentious intellectual. Thus, in matters of both philosophy and style, the two men were at loggerheads. The Duhaime mix—separatist and snob—was something, as a Chrétien friend colourfully put it, that "drove him apeshit."

Chrétien didn't think Duhaime had a chance of winning St-Maurice. After all, these were the same voters who re-elected him, the leading federalist, with huge majorities. "He told me I was wasting my time," said Duhaime. "When I won, oh Christ, was he mad. He said Quebeckers must have been drunk."

Duhaime was quickly named to the Lévesque cabinet. But when he and Chrétien attended a public function soon after, Chrétien dropped him a rank, referring to him as "Monsieur le député provincial [the provincial member]." When Duhaime got up, he returned the slight, referring to Chrétien as "Monsieur le député fédéral." The gloves were off. Both men were cabinet members, both had the responsibility and the means for developing the same riding, and both, most of all, were eager to claim the credit.

Chrétien had fought many battles with Quebec over the question of who took the bows for gifts to the riding. When the federal government built a home for the aged, Chrétien was furious to see that at the official opening the governing Union Nationale had draped the building only in provincial flags. "We have given you a grant for a half a million dollars," he complained. "You can't find five bucks to buy one Canadian flag?" When another Ottawa-funded old-folks' home was opened, this time with the Péquistes in power, Chrétien wasn't even invited. So he invited himself. At the official sod-turning, after watching the Péquiste take his scoop of dirt, Chrétien grabbed the shovel and took several dips for the federal side. "Just to show that Ottawa had given more."

But these were minor incidents compared to the hostilities that, though shielded from the public, would flow from his feud with Duhaime. One of the first came over the issue of provincial and federal funding for an extension to Shawinigan's cultural centre. Normally each man would show up—Duhaime in a limousine, Chrétien in a Honda—for official openings. But, sensitive to the ongoing ego war between them, Henry Blanchard, the director of the cultural centre, thought better of bringing the two men together on the same evening. He scheduled separate take-your-bow nights, one for each. For Ottawa's turn Chrétien, who couldn't make it himself, sent along his beloved riding representative, Rachel Bournival. The evening went fine. A month or so later it was Duhaime's night, and he turned up personally. But to the consternation of Blanchard, so did Chrétien.

When Blanchard saw him, he tried to explain that there was no room on the program for him. He had had his chance. Chrétien, however, insisted that he be allowed to speak. As they debated the problem outside Blanchard's office, Duhaime came into view. Shouts, insults, and cheap shots ensued, with Chrétien the aggressor. Blanchard, fearing a hallway brawl, came between them. "You're both mature people!" he shouted. "We've got eight hundred people in this building and the press is all over the place." Did they want to be seen on the front page of the papers the next day shaking hands or beating the hell out of one another? His mediation restored order. He got them to come into his office, then he called in the photographers and had the two rivals shake hands. It was a rare photo.

But Chrétien was still incensed. Though it was seldom apparent in Ottawa, he could be haughty and authoritarian on his home turf or fiefdom, as he sometimes treated it. His riding organizers had an unwritten rule: "Steer clear of him in the early mornings." He was at his most rancorous then.

While Duhaime made his speech, Chrétien paced back and forth like an animal in a cage. Blanchard, who thought he had gone home after the photo session, suddenly found the cabinet minister in his face, throwing a tantrum. Blanchard, Chrétien charged, was ungrateful! Stupid! Ignorant! Didn't he realize what Chrétien had done for him? Blanchard, trying to explain himself once more, almost had to physically block Chrétien from going on-stage.

At evening's end the director went home so angry with Chrétien's "spoiled brat" behaviour that he vowed to see the minister the next morning and give him a piece of his mind. "Fortunately for both of us, Chrétien wasn't there." He told Rachel Bournival what had happened. Bournival, who provided outstanding service for Chrétien in the riding, usually gave the impression that she thought the world of her boss. Blanchard was surprised when she complained of how foul-mouthed and egotistical he could be when he didn't get his way.

Until this incident Blanchard had enjoyed a reasonably good relationship with Chrétien and his wife. Now those relations noticeably soured. Despite the confrontation, however, he continued to regard Chrétien as a cut above the average politician. "He got things done." He was like a tornado, said Blanchard, all nervous energy. Constituents, he explained, would line up, see him for a moment, and action was taken. "He could size up a situation very quickly and come to a good decision." The sessions were always intense. "I was present in his office once when he was screaming at the guy at the other end of the telephone line. It happened all the time. They'd start yelling at one another. That's how he got his message across. I've met a lot of politicians who were nice guys. They'd take you out to lunch but never do anything about your projects. It's action that you want and that's what Chrétien was all about."

Chrétien's differences with Duhaime and the nationalist crowd, already irreconcilable, only grew worse when he began giving his "pea-souper" speeches. "I am a goddamn pea-souper," Chrétien would bellow at English-Canadian audiences, "and I am proud of it." Sometimes he used the word "frog." Sometimes he stuck only to the soup. The English audiences, especially in right-wing provinces like Alberta where they perceived favouritism from Ottawa towards Quebec, loved it.

He meant it as a joke, he later explained, just as people joked about "Pollacks" and "Newfies." But the French press isolated the remark, and in their efforts to "drag down" any federalist, Chrétien charged, made it appear as if he were purposely trying to demean Quebeckers. Had any of those journalists had the energy to actually cover the speeches, Chrétien continued, they would have been able to hear the remark in its proper context. Some press reports did indicate that his "pea-souper" quote was meant to be taken lightly. In June 1977 he used the line in a speech to the Liberal riding association in Ottawa. The *Ottawa Citizen's* account read, "Rather than being a melting pot, [Chrétien said], 'Canada is a country which permits every one of us to be what we are and still be good Canadians. . . . I'm a goddamn pea-souper and proud of it,' he quipped, joking about his heavily accented English."

In the opinion of the Quebec establishment, however, Chrétien was committing the most vile of sins. By playing up the lowly caricature and perpetuating the basest stereotype, he was diminishing all Quebeckers. Claude Rompré, a Shawinigan teacher and nationalist politician who ran against Chrétien in several elections, had admired the man. Then he read that in a speech in London, Ontario, Chrétien said all Quebeckers want "is our beer, our Ski-Doos, and our hockey games." Rompré was ashamed to be presented this way. "It wasn't honest. I began to hate not the man, but the politician behind the man. He said this sort of thing several times in English Canada, and I realized that this man was preparing his future political career by riding on the back of his fellow citizens in Quebec." It was pure politics, Rompré believed, a springboard to his ultimate ambition—becoming prime minister of Canada.

Other intellectuals decried what they called Chrétien's Uncle Tom act. While less vocal, even some of his Ottawa colleagues took exception. One was Jean-Luc Pepin. What Chrétien was saying was "massively demeaning," Pepin said. But he chose to see it as a mistake by a politician who didn't make many, who normally displayed great common sense and judgement. He could put it aside. Others, both in and out of Quebec, were not so forgiving. Though the controversy passed, the words were not easily forgotten, and Chrétien would come to rue the day he ever uttered them.

After his crushing victory in the 1974 election, an election in which Trudeau earned a majority, Chrétien was put back on the economic track with a cabinet promotion to president of the Treasury Board. At forty, after spending so many years in Indian

Affairs, he found the change welcome. He had long had his eye on the Treasury Board post. Money was power and the Treasury Board controlled the money flow. The Finance minister set the budget, but the Treasury Board executed it.

Chrétien had sat on the board when he was minister of Indian Affairs, eventually replacing Eric Kierans as its vice-chairman. The long meetings under C. M. "Bud" Drury, the patrician board president, tested Chrétien's patience, but he usually stayed around until the very end. It was then, when Drury was weary, that Chrétien felt he could slip in added requests for funding for his department.

Ever ambitious, he had anxiously awaited Trudeau's decision on a new post, nervously pacing the floor in his office. While Indian Affairs had put him on the outside, Treasury Board put him at the nerve-centre. The appointment pleased him so much that he was quickly on the phone to a friend back home, a businessman named Roger Caron who had been predicting great things for him since the 1950s. Chrétien told him of his new position. "Not bad for a little guy from Shawinigan, eh?"

He came into the job just as expenditures by the federal government were in spectacular ascendance, increasing by roughly 25 per cent annually. The circumstances called for restraint and discipline. Chrétien, a disciple of Mitchell Sharp's, was ready.

He had come to Ottawa as the anti-establishment man, the street fighter ready to do battle with the ruling class. Then he had moved Right, becoming a spear-carrier for Sharp in the fight against economic nationalism. Taking over Indian Affairs, he was again on the side of the downtrodden, giving native bands the resources and moral support they needed to organize against the entrenched prejudices of the government.

But now, as Treasury Board president, Jean Chrétien was speeding across the spectrum again, leaping from the social-activist Left to the economic Right. He wielded what was considered at the time to be a budget axe. He didn't try to reduce federal spending from one year to the next, but slowing down the precipitous rate of increase was enough to be seen as conservative. Chrétien, in fact, was considered so tough that he was dubbed Doctor No, a name he liked.

Under the circumstances, any minister would likely have undertaken similar, though perhaps more modest, measures. In the mid-seventies the government's attitude towards spending was changing. A realization had set in that the programs of the Pearson era, in particular medicare and the Canada Assistance Plan, involved expenditures whose scope was not really understood. Finance Minister John Turner, who had budgeted the great increases, was suggesting a cut of $500 million for his 1975 budget, a sizeable decrease for the time. He and Chrétien met with Trudeau, and Chrétien upped the ante. Politically, he said, it wouldn't be much worse to go for $1 billion. Trudeau agreed.

The cut-backs were part of the government's anti-inflation drive, which moved into higher gear with the imposition of something Trudeau had defiantly promised not to impose—wage-and-price controls. But the cuts only stemmed the tide. Despite Chrétien's spadework, spending still went up a portly 15 per cent. These were the years, most experts concluded, that set in motion the spectacular debt build-up, which led in turn to the 1990s retrenchment, threatening the integrity of the welfare state.

As Treasury Board president, Chrétien worked from an office that was spartan compared with those of some of his colleagues. His trappings cost only two thousand dollars, some others as much as fifty thousand. He dressed in ready-to-wear clothes, stayed away from limos and Guccis, and looked, as Dalton Camp described him, much like "the driver of the getaway car." He was handsome in these years, with a tough-guy charm reminiscent of Jean-Paul Belmondo.

His style was brusque and to the point. He'd go to his fellow ministers with a target in mind for budget cuts. If the minister was obstinate, Chrétien would threaten to ask cabinet for double the cut. He had no patience for air bags. He boasted that compared with Trudeau, who tended to let ministers ramble, especially if they managed to insert his favourite word—"planning"—into their discourse, he stopped them in their tracks. "Gino, my friend," Chrétien would say to Agriculture Minister Eugene Whelan, "we heard that a few times already. You got anything new to add?" Then he'd go back to his Treasury Board office and announce, "We got through in an hour and a half today because I told Gino to stop talking."

Some, like his cabinet colleague John Roberts, thought Chrétien's tough image was entirely calculated. Roberts, the secretary of state, sat on the Treasury Board with Chrétien. "He labelled himself Doctor No," said Roberts. "This was for public consumption." The image, including his insistence on speaking English with such a heavy French accent, was "a construct." Noted Roberts, "It's like Maurice Chevalier. He kept his French accent long after he could speak English."

Roberts did admire Chrétien's style around the Treasury Board and cabinet table. He thought he was immensely smart and shrewd. But he also saw him as a process politician. While thinkers like Marc Lalonde "were leading their departments instead of acting as their spokesmen," Chrétien "stuck very closely to his civil servant's brief." He used his political judgement in selling or amending it, but "he didn't have a strong blueprint of what he wanted to build for the future."

For Chrétien, cutting government expenditures included slowing the growth of the nation's biggest employer, the public service. It had been multiplying at a rate of 7 per cent a year. Chrétien cut the rate to 3 per cent in his first year and 1.5 per cent in the second. The squeeze meant killing off Information Canada and Opportunities for Youth, disbanding the Company of Young Canadians, ending financial assistance for the heavily indebted Montreal Olympics, and dealing harshly with public servants who were demanding huge wage increases to keep pace with inflation.

Areas left untouched included those Chrétien knew to be favoured by the prime minister: the arts and foreign aid. The bilingualism program was another sacred cow, precious to Chrétien as well as Trudeau. This program, which was Chrétien's responsibility, fit his core belief in equal opportunity for all. He went so far as to state that students should not be admitted to university anywhere in Canada without being bilingual.

Besides trimming the growth in the number of public servants, Chrétien also wanted to disperse them throughout the country. The idea took shape when the Department of National Revenue ran short of space for its taxation processing centres. Chrétien and his officials began to wonder why only Ottawa benefited from the abundance of federal government jobs. In a substantial decentralizing initiative, he moved ten thousand federal jobs out of the capital to far-away places like Matane, Quebec. Chrétien was hoping to counter the migration to the big cities. In his own riding he had seen two pulp-and-paper research laboratories move to Montreal, taking two hundred jobs with them. The company managers informed an angry Chrétien that they wanted to be closer to the universities, the cultural links, and other scientists. Chrétien believed the real reason for the move was that the laboratories' director wanted to be in the corporate headquarters in Montreal, where he could stay in touch with the big bosses and schmooze his way to a promotion.

Gordon Osbaldeston, Chrétien's deputy minister, and Eddie Goldenberg, a new assistant he had brought in near the end of his term in Indian Affairs, described their boss as deadly serious about getting the good jobs out to the smaller towns. "I think it went back to how he grew up, the idea of equality. Those kinds of jobs didn't belong to Ottawa, they belonged to everyone," explained Osbaldeston.

Chrétien regarded this decentralization as one of his major accomplishments in the portfolio. He was also proud that building on his experience as a labour lawyer, he had established warm relations with the public-service unions. But it was his Doctor No act that was the palpable media hit. Within a year of entering the Treasury Board post, Chrétien was being talked about in a context he could most appreciate. His dream of becoming the nation's first francophone Finance minister was not so far-fetched any more. When John Turner left the job and politics in the fall of 1975, Chrétien was written about as a possible successor. While he joked that the media were only trying to lead him to the gallows, Sharp was lobbying for him backstage. He got him on a short list along with Donald Macdonald and Otto Lang, but Trudeau turned to Macdonald.

Given the wonderful headlines he was harvesting, more time at the Treasury Board could do Chrétien no harm. In a cabinet that was perceived to have too many profligate, quiche-eating softies, here was a tough guy who talked straight. He was the man of the people—the little guy from Shawinigan, as he was now referred to in the press. Editorials in the *Globe and Mail* lauded him as a man of candour, a man of action, a man of charm. The Southam columnist Charles Lynch wrote: "To me, Jean Chrétien is the most appealing minister in the Trudeau cabinet." The syndicated columnist Doug Fisher, no longer an MP, argued that Chrétien was possibly the most effective French-Canadian cabinet minister in twenty years. Peter Thomson of the *Montreal Star* began a column, "So far as the Parliamentary Press Gallery is concerned, Treasury Board President Jean Chrétien wins hands down as everyone's most popular cabinet minister."

The scribes were dazzled, for example, at how easily he shrugged off a scathing analysis of the bilingualism program. The Bibeau report, which he had commissioned, called the program political, wasteful, impractical, an appeasement of Quebec—everything but a fraud. At a press conference Chrétien turned this doom-and-gloom story into a light-hearted one, humouring the media with mispronounced words and one-liners. No one expected bilingual perfection, Chrétien said. The idea was only to be able to communicate, to be understood. With his "hack-cent," as he put it, Chrétien was the perfect example. If he could become bilingual, he joked, anyone could.

He made people happy. He could make cuts in the budget and still come across to the outside world as a folksy, feel-good minister. Out of the public eye, however, the politics of joy were far less in evidence. He was "straight, straight, straight," said John Rae. He became, noted Gordon Osbaldeston, very absorbed in what he was doing. "He saw life as a serious process, a serious endeavour, and his conversation therefore was always about serious problems and how they could be mended. He wasn't negative or depressed about it, just seriously in search of solutions. There therefore could be no mulling about. It was always, 'What do we do next?'"

He spent two years at the Treasury Board, confident on his departure that he had put the nation's finances in order. As Doctor No, he had increased spending by 16 per cent in his first year (down from 28 per cent) and forecast a similar jump for his second. "The federal government," Chrétien told the Metro Toronto Board of Trade in the spring of 1976, "has had, and continues to have, effective control over its programs and bureaucracy." Any trends that might be considered alarming, he added, could be reversed. A spending bulge that had started appearing in 1973 would, he acknowledged, be disturbing if it became a trend. But there were good reasons, Chrétien incorrectly predicted, "to consider this bulge as a temporary and reversible phenomenon." He pointed to irregular developments in the economy—the recession and the fantastically swollen social-security outlays due to it and to inflation. He pointed to the four-fold increase in energy costs because of the OPEC crisis, which prompted $2 billion in oil subsidies. In difficult times, he argued, the government had come to the rescue. If it hadn't, he said, think of the suffering that would have resulted.

When the *Globe and Mail*'s publisher, Richard Malone, printed a full-page tirade against Liberal spending policies, labelling them "a case of tragic mismanagement," Chrétien fired off a full-page repudiation. The *Globe* held off printing it, so Chrétien had it sent to Claude Ryan at *Le Devoir*. Ryan ran it under the headline "A letter the *Globe and Mail* delays publishing." The *Globe* printed it the next day.

Malone was not alone in his criticism. The Conservatives charged that Chrétien's cuts were purely cosmetic. "Well," countered Chrétien, "you can buy a hell of a lot of lipstick and face powder with a billion and a half [*sic*] dollars!"

In the context of the time, his restraint was noteworthy. Over the long haul, however, it looked meagre. The Liberals, Sharp analysed, had made a crippling mistake in agreeing to Opposition Leader Robert Stanfield's plan to stop indexing income taxes to the inflation rate. "That had enormous consequences." Government pay-outs on expenditures such as family allowances, old-age pensions, and medicare were still tied to the swiftly increasing inflation rate. But with the tax measure, government revenues were not increasing at the same pace. "And so you had these two things operating in opposite ways," explained Sharp, "and it was one of the reasons why deficits began to accumulate just about this time."

However it would look in the long term, in the short Jean Chrétien's term in Treasury was a career booster. Not only was he back in the middle of the political spectrum, but he was also now a friend of business, a constituency any Liberal ultimately needed.

Chrétien never appeared to think much of businessmen. To him, they had no range, no overview, only a "very limited, specialized knowledge, which often gives them a narrow view." That was why, he felt, they didn't make good politicians. At the same time, however, he wanted to be on their side, and that meant staying away from the left wing of the party. "They think we're pink," he said of the business view of the Grits not long after Trudeau had joined in song with the Cuban dictator, Fidel Castro. "The Boss goes to Cuba and shouts *Viva!* And they think we're pink!"

(left) Maurice Duplessis held Quebec in his iron grip for more than two decades, ushering in a period of unprecedented corruption and favouritism. Despite his distaste for Duplessis's politics, Chrétien was impressed by his personal charm. [CBC/Public Archives of Canada/C-19522]

(below) Four prime ministers. This 1967 photo shows the men who would would lead Canada for most of the next thirty years: Pierre Elliott Trudeau, John Turner, Lester Pearson, and Jean Chrétien. [Canapress]

Trudeau chose Chrétien to lead his Indian Affairs ministry in 1968 because Chrétien professed to know nothing about the department and so would have no preconceived ideas about how things should be done. [Courtesy of the Chrétien family]

Chrétien and Quebec Liberal leader Claude Ryan struggled throughout the 1980 Quebec referendum to keep a lid on their personal differences. As a final insult, the intransigent Ryan refused to allow Chrétien to speak at the massive rally held to celebrate the federalist victory. [Canapress/Doug Ball]

Eddie Goldenberg, first hired when Chrétien was Indian Affairs minister, became his life-long friend as well as his top aide. Chrétien once described him as his "pocket computer. . . . If you talk with Eddie, he will say what Chrétien will say." [Carisse Photo]

Chrétien acknowledges the applause of Prime Minister Pierre Trudeau (left), Indian
Affairs Minister John Munro (right), and the other Liberal members as he opens
debate on the constitution in the House of Commons in 1981. [Canapress/Mitchell]

As Attorney-General, Jean Chrétien was asked to sign the constitutional proclamation
alongside Queen Elizabeth and Prime Minister Trudeau. Ironically, Chrétien, the
one minister who never showed much interest in constitutional issues,
played a lead role in bringing the document home. [Canapress]

When Chrétien lost the Liberal leadership to John Turner on June 15, 1984, it was the most bitter defeat of his life. Not even his beloved wife, Aline, could stave off the deep depression that followed. [Canapress]

(left) During the leadership campaign, Chrétien felt he was betrayed by those he thought he could trust, and he reserved his deepest disdain for André Ouellet. Although the two had once been good friends, their relationship suffered severe harm. Chrétien had vowed never to forgive Ouellet, but he eventually reconsidered. [Canapress/Bregg]

(below) Chrétien had planned to stay on and serve beside John Turner, even though relations between them had soured. But he found he just couldn't countenance being second-in-command to the man. In this photo, taken just a few months after Turner won the party leadership, the two appear to be enjoying one of their few happy moments. [Canapress]

(above) On the surface, it seemed that Chrétien had little in common with the patrician Mitchell Sharp. But being named Sharp's parliamentary assistant in 1967 proved to be a turning point in Chrétien's life. The few things they did share turned out to be more important than the vast differences separating them, and Sharp quickly became Chrétien's mentor. [J. M. Carisse Photo]

(left) "Some people wanted blood on the floor," said Chrétien on the 1985 publication of his memoirs, *Straight from the Heart*, "but I'm not vindictive." He thought nobody would show up to his first book signing but arrived to find a line-up stretching around the block. [J. M. Carisse Photo]

Chrétien's popularity is enduring. Scenes like this, where he is being mobbed by young admirers, demonstrate the extent of his appeal. [J. M. Carisse Photo]

After Treasury Board, he moved to another portfolio that would enhance his business ties—Industry, Trade and Commerce. It wasn't a promotion, and he was enjoying the Treasury Board so much that he was reluctant to take the job, but Finance had gone to Donald Macdonald and Trudeau wanted a good salesman in Trade. By this time, the prime minister had initiated the so-called third option, an effort to lessen Canada's economic dependence on the United States by expanding trade elsewhere. Mitchell Sharp, the same man who had opposed the economic nationalism of the 1960s, was the architect of the option.

Chrétien agreed to take the ITC post as long as Gordon Osbaldeston joined him. The pairing was eventually arranged, but initially Chrétien served alongside Gerald Stoner, the same mandarin Chrétien had confessed his prime ministerial dreams to during a plane trip in 1970. "He was the young idealist back on that plane," recalled Stoner, "but seven or eight years later, he'd become a bit mystified as to what Trudeau would do next." Stoner had been serving in ITC under Don Jamieson. Right away he noticed a change in style with Chrétien. "At the end of the day with Jamieson you would go in there at 6:30 or so to clear up a couple of things and you were sure he was going to put his feet up and have a belt or two." He'd ruminate, reflect, chew the fat, and sometimes stall. "I don't believe in everything the British do," he'd tell Stoner, "but this problem might go away if we leave it long enough. So let's try that." Stoner saw a man "looking beyond immediate problems. He really wanted to know where it would all come out fifteen or twenty years down the line."

But there was no feet up and Scotch on the rocks with Chrétien. "He was inclined to get the discussion over with and out of there. He hated problems to hang around. He thought the worst thing you could do was let a problem hang around." Decisions from Chrétien came at breakneck speed. During his first week in the job he went to Venezuela to help a Canadian firm bid on a transit system. He wanted to sell. He talked of Canadians being boy scouts abroad and said it was time to get aggressive. He praised Pearson's profound commitment to internationalism, peacekeeping, and NATO and all the world's other august institutions, but added that this had to be complemented by an internationalist approach to economics and the markets. He came across, explained Gordon Osbaldeston, as neither a nationalist nor a continentalist, but as an assertively Canadian internationalist.

The Trade portfolio forced Chrétien to deal with many technical matters that were not to his liking. He was compelled to master a new range of English-language phrases on things like textile quotas. It reached the point where, in preparing for press conferences, the Quebecker sometimes had to ask his aides for the equivalent words in French.

All his decisions were carefully tied to the political agenda. His assistants would sometimes lay out a seemingly obvious course of action, only to have Chrétien say, "That makes perfect sense from the point of view of logic, but it's no good. You've forgotten the politics." In public he operated with an ad hoc abandon, but behind closed doors his political antennae were sharp. Labour Minister John Munro considered Chrétien an expert at sniffing the winds. It didn't really matter whether Chrétien thought your viewpoint had merit, said Munro. "If he detected with his political astuteness that your position wasn't going to go anywhere, well then, he'd step aside and let you go down by yourself. But if he thought you had something going for you, he'd come in and give you a hand."

In the Trade portfolio the highly valued Canadian dollar, which stood at a princely $1.02 U.S., hampered Chrétien's more aggressive efforts at boosting exports. The headlines he garnered stemmed mainly from his actions surrounding the Foreign Investment Review Agency (FIRA). In the late 1960s he had sided with Sharp against Walter Gordon's economic nationalism. Now he was following the same line, in several instances turning the review agency into a welcome mat and earning the admonition of FIRA promoter Herb Gray, who accused him of dereliction of responsibility.

At the same time, however, Chrétien would come across as a great patriot, delivering pro-Canada barn burners across the land. "He believed what he was saying so passionately," recalled Jim Bennett, one of his special assistants, "that no matter how many times you heard it, it still made the hair stand up on the back of your neck." Some of his decisions did have a nationalist flavour. In order to protect Canadian manufacturers, for example, he continued to impose quotas on imported textiles and clothing. He tied his continued defence to a plan that saw the domestic industry improving productivity and keeping price increases below the rate of inflation. One of his more controversial decisions involved throwing enormous sums of money into the development of Canada's aircraft, the Challenger. This marked one of the few occasions when Chrétien went against the advice of his deputy minister. The previous minister, Don Jamieson, had balked on the project, feeling that given concern over the government spending surge, the aircraft subsidies were too much. Deputy Minister Stoner took the same line, warning Chrétien, correctly as it turned out, that the aircraft would not be ready in time to meet the contract specifications of the American company waiting for the plane, Federal Express, and that Ottawa would have to pay a big penalty. But in this instance, the minister so often portrayed as simply following the briefs of his deputy ministers turned down departmental advice. He went ahead with the aircraft subsidies, and Canadair eventually became a success story in Montreal.

When Stoner left the department, he sent Chrétien a report card. It noted that Canada's trade balance had improved under Chrétien's stewardship, that some progress had been made on new trade links with Europe and Japan, and that controversy had been generally avoided. It cautioned Chrétien, however, not to let his staff, particularly Eddie Goldenberg, get too arrogant in speaking for him. In summing up, the deputy minister spoke of the qualities he admired in Chrétien. "You are blessed with innate good judgement and a healthy sense of caution, as well as a capacity to be decisive," the deputy minister wrote.

As the summer of 1977 approached, and Chrétien closed out his time in ITC, the pressure was mounting for him to leave federal politics and fight the separatists as leader of the Quebec Liberals. He believed that Quebeckers, in choosing René Lévesque in the 1976 provincial election, had voted more for a change from the failed policies of Robert Bourassa than for an independence ticket. Nonetheless, he feared that under the wily Lévesque, a man for whom he had no admiration, the separatist movement could gain momentum.

Going to Quebec was an option he had faced before. But another, more tantalizing prospect was in the winds. Donald Macdonald, it appeared, was leaving Finance. Chrétien was next in line. "Don't do it," advised Gordon Osbaldeston, who had established close ties with Chrétien. "It's a political graveyard."

CHAPTER FOURTEEN

FALL IN
FINANCE

A S HIS CAREER took shape in the capital, back home the times got tougher. Shawinigan's industrial decline continued. From its rank as one of the top Canadian cities in per capita income, it had fallen far below the national average. Its population dropped by 6 per cent between 1971 and 1976. The jobless rate stood at 13 per cent.

Chrétien had tried to forestall the worst of it. When Shawinigan Carbide, a major employer, threatened on several occasions to close down, Chrétien was there with government money to save it. When an industrial park was needed to attract business, Chrétien pushed the Department of Regional and Economic Expansion to put up $1.5 million of the costs. When 350 jobs were threatened by Gulf Oil's plan to close its chemicals plant, Ottawa came forward with grants of $2.2 million to keep it going. Being Doctor No, a liberal in the Sharp wing of the party, still involved a lot of "Yes" work. Chrétien looked to the most successful and socially equitable countries in the world—the Scandinavian countries, the wealthier European states, and the best of the lot, his very own Canada—and could see that they all had one thing in common: a very large public-sector role in the economy.

Occasionally, he stepped beyond the more conventional forms of assistance so as to help his riding. He made the ill-fated phone call to Judge Aronovitch. As Northern Development minister he had expanded Canada's parks network, which in turn led to a grand park for his own riding. There was also, though it involved some aggravation, the big gift he awarded to his riding while at Treasury Board. His decision to shift government jobs out of Ottawa to smaller communities got him thinking about his home town. Revenue Canada was moving tax data offices to the region. It occurred to Chrétien that a large $20 million data-processing centre for Shawinigan would do nicely.

The plan proceeded smoothly until Yves Duhaime became involved. By chance, the land in Shawinigan-Sud where Chrétien wanted to locate the tax centre belonged to Duhaime's mother-in-law. She asked Duhaime to look into the situation. Readily agreeing, he decided that the federal offer was far from adequate and said as much to the president of the Treasury Board. Chrétien, in turn, threatened to expropriate. Duhaime, in turn, threatened to challenge the expropriation bid in the courts.

The two antagonists came together at a meeting of the regional bar association at the Shawinigan Golf Club, and it wasn't long before they were into a highly unpleasant exchange. Just what did Duhaime think he was doing trying to block a project that would bring so many dividends to the community, Chrétien demanded. "You're trying to destroy everything I want to do and everything I want to build."

Duhaime tried to explain that he only wanted fair recompense for his mother-in-law's property. Then he goaded Chrétien. "Don't go around believing you can have everything for nothing just because your name is Chrétien!"

Their spat had by this time drawn the attention of the others in the room. Bob Lajoie, the honest lawyer from Trois-Rivières who was one of many to witness Chrétien's attack on Chartier at one of these same meetings, had visions of another punch-up. "Uh-oh," he said. "It looks like the old Chrétien is back in town."

Chrétien, made livid by Duhaime's rejoinder, glared at the

Péquiste and decided he would let him in on his plans. "I think I'm going to punch you in the f——g mouth!"

Duhaime, a bespectacled, stockily built man who moved with a bit of a Napoleonic strut, thought that the days when politicians settled scores by combat had ended in a previous century. He could scarcely believe that the president of the Treasury Board of Canada was preparing to enter into a slugfest in public view. "If you ever try that," he barked at Chrétien, "good luck!"

At this point, other lawyers came between them to restore calm. As Chrétien remembered the event, there was no need for this intervention because Duhaime was staging a pusillanimous retreat. "He walked away. He ran away." This wasn't the way Duhaime recalled it. "If he had raised an arm," the Péquiste said, "he would have had a good and solid reply from me because I was not afraid of him."

While aware of Chrétien's bellicose past, Duhaime had assumed the years around the cabinet table had matured him, instilling perhaps a measure of polish. Disappointed, he went home that night and said to his wife, "I thought he had changed. But I can tell you, dear, he hasn't changed." He had never come across such a fierce politician. Chrétien's body, he noted, reacted in the same impetuous way as his mind. Everything was black and white. "He is not," said Duhaime, "a sophisticated man."

In the Péquiste's opinion, there were things to admire in Chrétien—his frankness, his appetite for hard work—but he saw a man driven only by the realization of power. Chrétien cared much less for the average Canadian than people imagined, charged Duhaime. If he seemed to be standing four-square behind them, it was only because he saw it as the best strategy for reaching the top.

Eventually, the two rivals reached a deal on the land for the taxation centre. A truce was called. But like most of their cease-fires, it wouldn't remain in place very long.

Chrétien did well by the taxation centre. It became one of the riding's major employers, providing work—though much of it seasonal—for eight hundred people and serving as a symbol of what Chrétien and his cherished federalism could do for the area. If it was only an example of raw ambition at work, the hundreds with the jobs were thankful for Chrétien's appetite for power. Jim Coutts, watching from his perch next to the Prime Minister's Office, saw the pulsating Chrétien ambition at work as he surely saw his own. But he did not share Duhaime's understandably pejorative interpretation. Chrétien's drive, said Coutts, had its basis in a genuine desire to help average people. "He looked at things as ordinary people do. It wasn't an act. I think Jean never took on the veneer of elitism that hurts so many politicians."

One of the qualities Coutts liked most in Chrétien was his faith in government. Chrétien was a Pearsonian Liberal, and one with at least some sense of fiscal discipline. Because of his Shawinigan background, "he understood where government had stepped in to make the balance wheel work and how it had been of enormous support." At the same time, having been an eyewitness to the corruption of the Duplessis era, he knew when people were taking advantage of the system.

These were all words the little guy from Shawinigan would have liked to hear. But notwithstanding his favourable view of Jean Chrétien, Jim Coutts was soon to be one of the trigger men in a shocking piece of PMO brinkmanship that came close to toppling him.

The bad times for Chrétien began with Trudeau's decision to offer him the Finance post in September 1977. Although the PM knew of Chrétien's experience with economic portfolios, he still had his doubts, as did many of those who surrounded him, about Chrétien's capacity to handle the complexities of the job. Finance was a post traditionally reserved for the silver-haired set, not the blue-collar MPs like Chrétien. Because he lacked any academic or technical background in economics, he was not an obvious choice. These considerations, however, were set aside. The professional economists in the department could handle the theory, reasoned Trudeau. The important point was that Chrétien could take a policy and sell it. If anyone had the potential to make a bad economy look good, it was he.

Chrétien had amassed so much political capital, so much goodwill with the public, the bureaucrats, colleagues, the media, the business community, labour, that he could not be overlooked. He was the most popular man in the cabinet and, though only forty-three, one of the most experienced. Only House Leader Allan MacEachen had more years at the cabinet table. Furthermore, in his fierce opposition to Quebec nationalism Chrétien had a tie with Trudeau that other MPs, like Jean-Luc Pepin (who favoured a more pliant federalism), didn't have. Given the election of the Parti Québécois, Trudeau needed a Finance minister who could sell Quebeckers on the advantages of Confederation. Chrétien had been doing that anyway, but the Finance portfolio would be a potent platform from which to fire his missiles. Donald Macdonald, whose French was laborious, had not carried much weight in *la belle province.*

Thus, having meticulously examined, as was his habit, the cabinet possibilities, Pierre Trudeau chose Joseph-Jacques Jean Chrétien for the job. Aware of Mitchell Sharp's keen interest, the prime minister wrote him a note. "Dear Mitchell, you'll be happy to know I have named Jean as minister of Finance." Sharp, who didn't feel an academic understanding of the fiscal and monetary issues were a prerequisite for the position, had envisioned this possibility a decade earlier. His elation was surpassed only by that of Chrétien. In 1967 he had become the youngest man in the cabinet in the century. In 1977 he had achieved his ambition of becoming the first French-Canadian minister of Finance. So much for all the doubters. He was soon on the phone again to Roger Caron, his friend back home. "Hey, Roger! I've just been named minister of Finance. Not bad for a little guy from Shawinigan, eh?"

Support for the appointment came from all quarters. Both

business and labour cheered, which was testimony to the breadth of appeal Chrétien had engendered. Words of congratulations were on everyone's lips, except those of Chrétien's father. From Wellie, Jean was still awaiting his first compliment.

On September 16, the day he took over the portfolio, the economic indicators did not augur well. The unemployment rate was 8.3 per cent, a postwar high. After almost two years of wage-and-price controls, the inflation rate still stood at an unacceptable 8.4 per cent. The dollar, weighing in only a few years earlier at $1.02 American, had plunged to 93¢. The budget deficit was predicted to be $8 billion. The rate of economic growth was a modest 2 per cent.

As a lifelong adherent—though not in as fulsome a way as the leftists in his party—of the Keynesian school of economics, Chrétien got off the mark with an appropriate assertion. "My preoccupation is with unemployment. It is my main problem." At this time, however, many economists were experiencing a profound shift in their thinking. For a large number of them, inflation had become public enemy number one. The Organization of Petroleum Exporting Countries' (OPEC) four-fold increase of oil prices in 1973 caused a surge in inflation that contributed to a discrediting of Keynesianism. Monetarism—a competing doctrine that promoted vigorous control of the money supply—argued that to get unemployment under control, inflation had to be brought to heel. Previous conventional wisdom had suggested a trade-off. When one was high, the other tended to be low and vice versa. Though some evidence of a trade-off would in fact remain in place, with inflation grinding to a near-halt in the ensuing decade and a half while unemployment remained unusually high, the monetarists nonetheless held sway.

In Finance, Chrétien came under the influence of Gerald Bouey, who held the immensely powerful position of governor of the Bank of Canada. Bouey, a former Keynesian, had switched sides. In a speech lauded by the conservative guru Milton Friedman as "marvellous," Bouey said, "For more than twenty years almost every country in the Western world has given rapid growth and high employment much higher priorities in its policies than the preservation of the value of money. This approach worked well for quite a while, but it won't work well any longer."

The competing theories were symptomatic of the conundrum the Finance department faced. Controlling inflation and the debt required one set of policies, while combating unemployment required quite another. Chrétien was being asked to hit the brakes and accelerate at the same time.

As if to remind everyone that he was the first francophone in the portfolio, as if to tell Quebeckers that they had someone with their interests in mind, Chrétien quickly made headlines by choosing to speak exclusively in French to the annual Washington gathering of the International Monetary Fund and the World Bank. It was rare for a Canadian politician to speak only French in the United States. At the turn of the century Wilfrid Laurier, one of Chrétien's heroes, had done so. He went to Chicago and, to a sea of raised eyebrows, restricted himself to the foreign tongue. He wanted to demonstrate the distinctive nature of Canada and, as no one understood his oration, certainly achieved his goal. For Chrétien's speech there was a simultaneous translation, but reporters, led by the CBC's Washington correspondent, Don Newman, pointed out that the tradition was to use both official languages in speeches to international gatherings. Chrétien didn't see why the newsmen were "uptight about it." He didn't have to apologize to francophones when he spoke in English. Why should he apologize now? French was his native tongue, he said, and French was an official Canadian language.

On the same visit, the new Finance minister provoked his Quebec counterpart, Jacques Parizeau, by stating that at the rate investors were ignoring Quebec since the election of the sovereigntists, the province risked becoming "another New Brunswick."

Parizeau hit back where it hurt Chrétien the most—on the question of grey matter. Chrétien was showing himself to be an amateur who didn't understand elementary economics, charged Parizeau. It was Ottawa's discriminatory policies towards Quebec that were creating the miserable economic situation. There was nothing new about this. Before the 1976 election, Parizeau said, the same investment problems existed. Chrétien accused Parizeau of intellectual arrogance, saying that unlike him, "we didn't have rich fathers to send us to English universities."

One month into the job Chrétien brought in a mini-budget. He announced the gradual lifting of wage-and-price controls, a tax reduction of $100 for low-income earners, a $150-million investment in works projects, and a tightening of government expenditures in other areas. In announcing the changes, which received moderately good reviews, he was only putting forward what the department had brought before the Priorities and Planning Committee shortly before he was named minister. He was not yet in a position to originate something of his own. These first few months were devoted primarily to on-the-job training, with deputy minister Tommy Shoyama as teacher and Mitchell Sharp, retired from the cabinet, as back-up. Chrétien was a little awestruck. One day, early in the new posting, he told Shoyama, "You know, this has to be the most wonderful country. Here I am, a little guy from a working-class home who speaks fractured English, and I can become Finance minister of the country. And here you are, a Japanese Canadian accused of disloyalty in the war, and you can become deputy minister of Finance. Where else in the world could something like this happen?"

Optimism infused his rhetoric. When an interviewer catalogued all the depressing economic statistics, Chrétien told him these were still the good years. If people didn't realize it now, he said, someday they would. "In ten years the people will say, 'Oh, gee, 1977, it was great.'" Unlike almost every other country in the Organization for Economic Cooperation and Development

(OECD), Chrétien pointed out, employment and gross domestic product had increased in Canada every year in the 1970s under the Liberals. With the fantastic wage increases to keep ahead of inflation, per capita income had grown an amazing 45 per cent since 1970, compared with only 18 per cent in the United States.

Yet his optimism was often misplaced. He incorrectly forecast a strong economic recovery for 1978. He followed that up with a claim that the country was entering a period of new prosperity, which would extend right through the 1980s. In fact, the postwar era of ever-increasing wealth was drawing to a close as he spoke. Throughout the 1980s and into the 1990s, after-tax incomes would level off and, for great numbers, decline.

He journeyed to Quebec City, where he spoke to a predominantly federalist audience at the Chamber of Commerce. After a long discourse on the costs of separation, he threw away his dry script and launched into a patriotic tirade, a performance so bursting with Canadian pride that he left half his audience in tears. The main headline in the next day's *Le Devoir* blared, "The Little Guy from Shawinigan Electrifies the Chamber of Commerce."

His *cri de coeur* spoke of his own experience as a unilingual French kid from a modest home going all the way to the top. He talked passionately of the golden wheat of Alberta, the deep green forests of Quebec, the potash of Saskatchewan, the riches of Ontario's golden horseshoe, the abundant fish of the Maritime waters. He spoke of the beauty, the wealth, the people joined together. Then he cried, "No! No! No!" He would not let this glorious heritage be torn apart by "a corporal's guard of separatists wearing medals from the last campaign of France."

As 1977 drew to a close, his credibility level was high. As NDP Finance critic Max Saltsman noted, he was a politician who could get away with a lot. Because of his folksy charm, the media rarely imposed the harsh criteria they reserved for others. Statements that from others might be judged as blunt or rash or dumb were often treated as an example of refreshing candour from Chrétien.

In answering questions on the plunging dollar, for example, about all he would say was that "a floating dollar means it floats." The remark was perhaps not quite of the same rank as Calvin Coolidge's celebrated definition of unemployment: "When people are out of work," the president declared, "unemployment results." Nonetheless, Chrétien's words might have brought ridicule from a press less favourably disposed to him.

One MP who tried to deride Chrétien for his unconventional style and manner of speaking was the Ontario member for Durham-Northumberland, Conservative Allan Lawrence. He went so far as to distort his face and imitate Chrétien's accent in the House of Commons. No one thought it was funny. Chrétien said the next day that he hoped the honourable member was "sober last night when he made his foolish speech."

He appeared at the Liberal Party's annual convention early in 1978 and was clearly the team's Most Valuable Player, surrounded by cheers and applause wherever he moved. Although cracking jokes is difficult in a second language, Chrétien's raspy cadence worked. "We've got the best goddamn health system in the world," he said in a rousing address. "I had a friend who went to Florida, where he had a heart attack. When he saw his hospital bill, he had another one."

A troubling development saw the Sun Life Assurance Company announce plans to shift its headquarters from Montreal to Toronto because of the unstable political climate created by the Parti Québécois. Chrétien urged company executives to reconsider but was quickly rebuffed. He was angered by this move, which he saw as further evidence of the selfish and unpatriotic attitude of big business. Ottawa's investment laws, he noted, had saved Sun Life from a potential American take-over. He was amazed that ungrateful executives could then turn around and tell him the government had no business getting involved in the headquarters transfer. To Chrétien, it reeked of hypocrisy.

He couldn't help, on occasion, displaying his resentment towards the attitude of businessmen in general. He once spent an afternoon with some Vancouver financiers who were "bitching" about everything in sight. Looking out the window, Chrétien spotted their yachts bobbing in the harbour. "Must have been tough for those guys, eh?" he said, recalling the incident. "Paying for gas for those things."

The spurning by Sun Life was but a minor example of what was in store for him in 1978. The dollar began to skid so much that Ottawa had to prop it up by borrowing on foreign markets for the first time in a decade. Chrétien then had to announce that in the coming year the federal deficit would jump by an egregious 25 per cent, to a record $11 billion, reaching double digits for the first time. The increased spending was required, he explained, to avoid hardship in less advantaged regions of the country.

In April 1978 he brought forward his first full budget, the centre-piece of which was a reduction of 3 per cent in provincial sales taxes for a six-month period. Ottawa would reimburse the provinces for two-thirds of the amount. The measure, which amounted to a tax cut of $1.1 billion, was designed to stimulate an economy in which unemployment numbered over a million. It was also the fourth year of the Liberals' five-year mandate. They needed a tax break to take to the people.

Initially, the sales-tax initiative met a fine reception. It was an unusual example of federal-provincial cooperation in budget-making. Chrétien had carefully negotiated with all the provinces, taking advantage of the goodwill his personal style generated. Following the budget announcement, he attended a luncheon with economic journalists. After he had fielded questions for an hour, the journalists applauded him. Though it was considered inappropriate for the press to show such admiration for politicians, Chrétien had moved them to do so.

The sales-tax idea wasn't his. It had come from the formidable Ontario treasurer, Darcy McKeough. Because of the importance of budget secrecy, negotiations with the provinces had to be conducted on the sly and in hypothetical terms. In a "what if" way,

Chrétien spelled out what he wanted to do and won general agreement. But this was the Achilles' heel of the deal. It gave rivals like Parizeau of Quebec an escape clause. With nothing in writing, anything that was said was a matter of conjecture.

In initial talks with Chrétien, the Quebec Finance minister was a master of obfuscation, refusing to commit one way or the other. Chrétien and McKeough later dined with Parizeau, however, and came away certain that he had agreed to the sales-tax proposal. But a couple of days before the budget was to be tabled, he began sounding noncommittal again, telling federal officials, "I can't give you an answer." Chrétien pushed ahead anyway. He was aware, said Tommy Shoyama, that he was playing high-stakes poker. "We debated that question, whether it was worth the political risk. Mr. Chrétien was convinced very much he could carry the political heat in Quebec." Chrétien believed he had a strong hand. He was offering Quebec what was tantamount to $226 million in tax cuts. How could the PQ refuse? If they did, they would look foolish.

In the days immediately following the budget, the Quebec position was made clear. Parizeau refused to go along with the terms set out by Ottawa. He was prepared to trim the Quebec sales tax on certain items, but not across the board as the deal required. At the same time, he demanded financial compensation identical to that which all the other provinces were receiving.

Now Chrétien was trapped. If he accepted Parizeau's terms, it would look to the other provinces as if he was according Quebec special treatment. If he stuck to his own terms, it would look as if he was trying to dictate to Quebec how it should run its economy.

Made bitter by what he saw as a double-cross, Chrétien resolved not to compromise with Parizeau. His decision sparked outrage in Quebec. Even the Opposition Liberals, now led by Claude Ryan, supported the PQ, as did the Union Nationale and the Quebec media. In Trudeau's cabinet, members argued that Chrétien should be more conciliatory. He faced a torrent of criticism the likes of which he'd never seen before. His policy paper in

Indian Affairs had prompted bitter censure, but nothing as widespread as this.

The controversy dragged on, with interested parties putting forward a myriad of possible compromises. Chrétien finally decided that Quebec would get the same amount of money as the other provinces, but that it wouldn't be channelled through the Quebec government. He would do it himself. The Finance department would send a separate cheque for eighty-five dollars to every Quebec taxpayer. What other Canadians were receiving via sales-tax cuts, Quebeckers would receive via direct payment.

The plan failed to assuage the critics. Even the federalist voices of the Montreal *Gazette* were outraged. An "immense blunder," ranted columnist Gretta Chambers. If Chrétien is kept on as minister of Finance, Quebeckers will be "horrified." Trudeau and Chrétien, she said, were acting like dictators, going over the head of the premier and giving to individual taxpayers what rightly belonged to the provincial government.

Premier Lévesque brought forward a motion denouncing the measure. Desk-thumping was heard from all Quebec parties. To defend himself, Chrétien appeared on CTV's *Question Period*. The show had hardly started when a journalist told him, "You got suckered by Mr. Parizeau." Chrétien stammered that Parizeau had acted in bad faith, that the federal government had put its trust in him and been betrayed. But most observers concluded Chrétien was naïve to have accorded a separatist minister such trust without a written commitment. In his first big confrontation with the sovereigntists, he had come out on the losing end.

The Quebec media wouldn't let him forget it. Jean's brother Maurice, who often went on long walks with him in Ottawa, said Jean was bothered by repeated references to his being knocked out by Parizeau. He could barely tolerate it, recalled Maurice.

Years later, asked why he had trusted Parizeau, Chrétien replied, "Because I had a witness." When, in 1984, he began to write his memoirs, Chrétien was determined to set the record straight. He phoned that witness, Darcy McKeough, and told him he was going to use his name in the book and write about their dinner with Parizeau. McKeough balked, saying he didn't want to get mixed up with it. But Chrétien wasn't going to let it pass. He issued a threat. "Fine," he said. "Would you like me to write a chapter on you too? You were there!" McKeough eventually backed down, agreeing to let his name be used.

It was hurtful enough to be undermined by a Parti Québécois minister of Finance. To be undermined in the same year by his own prime minister was yet more grievous. That summer Trudeau went to Bonn, West Germany, with Chrétien for the economic summit of the seven leading industrial countries. In the months preceding the summit, the prime minister's cabinet had been debating deep cuts in expenditures. After talks in Bonn with West German chancellor Helmut Schmidt, Trudeau was encouraged to move ahead with them. He then holidayed in Morocco and returned home on Sunday, July 30, to disturbing news.

In a meeting at Sussex Drive, his advisers told him that new polls showed support for the Grits was plummeting. A planned election call would have to be put off. Since the state of economy was the voters' chief worry, the prime minister and his men decided that it was time to signal a bold, prompt change in economic direction.

By Tuesday, without providing any notice of intent to the Finance minister, Trudeau's advisers had prepared what was tantamount to a mini-budget. Trudeau went on national television that night and announced the changes: a $2 billion shake-up in expenditures, including large budget cuts; a major tax reduction; and a freeze in the public service. Chrétien was at his cottage, north of Shawinigan on Lac des Piles. When he heard the news, he was dumbfounded, humiliated. His role as the country's senior financial officer had been usurped. To be excluded from the formulation of budgetary policy was a shocking affront. To not even be notified of the policy until it was announced was astonishing. In relations between a prime minister and his minister of Finance, it was a snub the likes of which the country had never seen. Many thought Chrétien had no choice but to resign.

The Guns of August, as some termed the fiasco, had its origins in a number of factors, one of which was the nature of this particular Finance minister. As a member of the cabinet's lunch-bucket brigade, Chrétien, at least in the opinion of the power players in the Prime Minister's Office, lacked *gravitas* in Finance. He had been put in the job less to originate policy than to be a mouthpiece for it. In other departments, where less technical knowledge was required, a minister could get by on one-page memos and broad strokes. Chrétien had been able to pass by the huge briefing books, pick up the gist in oral sessions, and wing it from there. Finance, however, required, at least in some measure, the skills Chrétien never had—patience, an appreciation of nuance, an in-depth understanding of complex and delicately intertwined issues. He could talk all he wanted about his experience in financial portfolios, but almost everyone knew he possessed only a surface knowledge of the discipline. For those who didn't know it, it had quickly become apparent in the ten months preceding the prime minister's speech.

"The general impression of Mr. Chrétien," said his deputy minister, Tommy Shoyama, "was one that he himself carefully cultivated—the little guy. What does he know other than what he learns on the job?" Shoyama soon discovered that the minister was "not a great student of written documents." Moreover, he said, if Chrétien didn't understand something he was sometimes hesitant to ask Shoyama for an explanation. What he would often do, recalled his deputy, was go to his old friend Mitchell Sharp, who was no longer in the cabinet. Sharp would provide him with some explanations, then play Chopin and Mozart on the piano to ease his concerns. Despite the briefings, it was still apparent that he did not have a strong command of all the issues at play. Gerald Bouey, who personally admired Chrétien, found him somewhat uncomfortable in the portfolio. Other ministries, he said, were more suited to his skills.

There were times in the House of Commons when, in response to technical questions, Chrétien appeared to be caught short. Finance department officials would rush out afterwards to issue clarifications. His brother Maurice offered a frank assessment: "He was unable to understand things at times." When complex issues were raised on the floor, "he didn't know what to do and what to say about them. And by the time he consulted his experts and advisers, well, sometimes he was too late to give an answer." His wife, Aline, wasn't happy about the situation at all, Maurice recalled. Usually, she felt confident that Jean had the information at his fingertips. Not so in Finance.

In the months before the Bonn summit, Shoyama and Chrétien had been advocating some of the cuts Trudeau eventually announced in his August speech. It was Shoyama's opinion, however, that the Finance minister did not carry enough weight with his cabinet colleagues to get the recommendations passed. "Being new on the job, he was not necessarily in a powerful position to insist that this be done."

Trudeau had observed the difficulties, said Shoyama. When he came back from Bonn, he found it "a convenient stratagem" to go over everyone's heads and say, "Okay, I'll take care of this now and zap it right on them." Shoyama saw this as an appropriate strategy, and since the budget cuts were consistent with the policy-line Shoyama had favoured, he welcomed it. Like everyone else, however, he said he didn't countenance isolating the minister of Finance. No one, in fact, sought to defend the actions of the PMO. While Chrétien may have created some of his own problems, nothing could excuse the treatment he was subsequently accorded.

Before his address to the nation, Trudeau met with Michael Pitfield, the clerk of the Privy Council, and Jim Coutts, his principal secretary. Pitfield had prepared a speech that contained no specific economic measures. He wanted the PM to lay out some broad general principles indicating the new direction that economic policy should take. Coutts, however, felt Trudeau had to show command, he had to convince the country that real change was in the offing. His speech therefore needed punch and hard numbers. A big, round figure, say $2 billion, would have that impact.

Pitfield's pitch was rejected, Coutts's position won the day. He then helped draw up a new speech, with much of the material coming from the Treasury Board, whose new president was Robert Andras, Chrétien's rival from Indian Affairs.

Had Pitfield's strategy succeeded, Chrétien would not have had any problems to face. A speech on the general economic state of the union was entirely within the PM's prerogative. Trudeau and Chrétien had discussed the need for restraint in Bonn, and Chrétien was under the impression that Trudeau might talk about it in broad terms.

Given his decision to draw up a specific plan full of actual numbers, Trudeau might well have been expected to get on the phone to Chrétien himself. He later told Chrétien that Coutts was supposed to have called. Coutts, however, maintained that as principal secretary, he did not have this responsibility and therefore he did not call. He assumed Shoyama, the deputy, would brief the Finance minister. Shoyama, Coutts recalled, was at the crucial meeting with Pitfield and Trudeau. For his part, Shoyama could not remember being there or knowing in advance of Trudeau's plans to give the speech.

When Chrétien saw the televised address, he immediately telephoned Trudeau's office. The PM returned the call the next morning, defending himself with the claim that he had talked to Chrétien about some of these things in Bonn. Chrétien snapped back that they didn't talk about numbers. "I gave him hell."

Trudeau apologized, acknowledging that he should have kept him informed. Chrétien asked, "Where the hell is the $2 billion supposed to come from? It's very nice to say we're cutting $2 billion, but what the hell! We have to know where it's coming from. I'm the minister of Finance."

In the course of the conversation, Chrétien said he was thinking of resigning. Trudeau went into his "Oh, come on now" mode, suggesting there was no need to overreact. In fact, Chrétien didn't ponder the possibility for long. He had spent fifteen years building a career in Ottawa and wasn't about to ditch it because of a PMO power play. He was overlooking the lake when he spoke to Trudeau. No, he told the prime minister, he wasn't about to throw himself in.

But the call did nothing to ease his humiliation. "Trudeau embarrassed me severely," he said of the speech, still rankled by the memory of it seventeen years later. The PMO was "doing stupid things. Two billion dollars without consulting anybody? It was stupid to do." He thought Shoyama was at fault too, because he knew about it and didn't tell him. But most of all, he blamed Coutts, one of those people in the PMO "who wanted to have their fingers in every pie." Coutts was the $2-billion man. As far as Chrétien could tell, he'd just pulled the number out of a hat. "I knew we had to cut, but there was no agreement by anybody and no one had looked at any goddamn paper."

Chrétien confronted Coutts and a row ensued, with Chrétien blasting him with words he didn't want to repeat. At another meeting, with most of the cabinet present, Coutts suggested that Chrétien would be able to find the $2 billion in budget cuts. Chrétien lashed out, saying that if Coutts was so smart, why didn't he just do the whole goddamn thing himself? Coutts grew flustered and speechless, turning beet-red with embarrassment.

NDP Leader Ed Broadbent was the first to make public how Chrétien had been hung out to dry, saying what had happened was both stunning and unprecedented. But the media had not thoroughly focused on this aspect of the story, and Chrétien could have saved himself from public humiliation had he been able to convincingly handle a press conference called to explain the new numbers.

The press encounter turned into a disaster. Chrétien and Shoyama didn't have their figures straight and disagreed in front of the cameras. Chrétien appeared to suggest that the government would have to pay out more when, in fact, major spending reductions were supposed to be taking place. He was peppered with questions he had difficulty answering. He was in a sweat. Reporters grew frustrated, one throwing up his hands and declaring, "This is the most ludicrous thing I ever heard of. Nobody knows what's going on."

Members of the PMO and Finance department looked on in embarrassment. "Let me put it this way," Shoyama said, recalling the moment. "I don't think that by this time Mr. Chrétien had enough grasp of priorities for spending cuts." Coutts was more blunt. It appeared, he recalled, "that he didn't understand what he was talking about. That would have been a very painful moment for any minister."

In the media, Chrétien was lashed and lamented. The *Financial Post* said his performance had to be viewed with immense sorrow. He was "grievously unprepared, sadly unable to answer questions, and cruelly laughed at." What had been mere speculation to this point—the suggestion that Chrétien had been intentionally left in the dark by the prime minister—was now highly credible.

It was therefore natural for Chrétien and his advisers, recalled Coutts, to try to shift all the blame to the PMO. After such an embarrassment, almost any politician would seek to cover himself. "I think, if the truth is known," said Coutts, "that in the scurrying after the press conference, probably Jean's staff was anxious not to take the rap and for their minister not to take the rap, and if the PM's office could be made to, that would be fine."

Chrétien later maintained that he was prepared for the press conference, but when he and Shoyama disagreed, the press jumped all over him. "If you have, in front of the press, a disagreement between Jean Chrétien and Tommy Shoyama, they will say that Shoyama is right and not Chrétien."

Because he was such a proud man, he bristled, as he always did, at suggestions that he wasn't in sufficient command of detail to handle Finance. "That is nonsense," he insisted. "You cannot be minister of Finance and president of the Treasury Board and minister of Industry, Trade and Commerce, all the success I had as a politician, not reading anything." Of his aversion to anything longer than two pages, he explained that any official who can't summarize the problem in that length lacks focus and shouldn't be where he or she is. He didn't read all the documents, he said. Having been in government so long, he didn't have to. He understood the issues.

When the controversy hit, Chrétien was just coming off the flogging he took in the uproar over the sales tax. He had also considered resigning over that. The Bonn episode led many ministers to believe he was finished. Others, even those not directly involved, thought it was a shoddy enough affair that they themselves should consider leaving. What were they needed for if the PMO was in such control? "At least three others considered stepping down," said Secretary of State John Roberts.

Few could imagine another Finance minister, John Turner or Donald Macdonald or Edgar Benson, staying on after being struck down as Chrétien was by the Guns of August. His official reason for remaining was that with an election around the corner, resigning would have been a disaster for the party. The more likely explanation was that it would have been a disaster for him. Nothing moved him as much as politics. A resignation would have served no purpose but to terminate the career he loved and was born to pursue.

He was in a hurry to recoup his losses. If there was anything he didn't need, it was sniper fire from a former Finance minister. In a series of newsletters that were leaked to the media, John Turner, who shortly before leaving Ottawa had described Chrétien as one of the best ministers anywhere, now said he was suffering from a "credibility gap." He also suggested that Chrétien wanted to leave Finance for External Affairs. "Turner knows damn well," Chrétien said in response, "that my personal ambition is not to be minister of External Affairs. . . . I want to stay here." The heavily publicized newsletters marked the beginning of a downward turn in the Chrétien-Turner relationship, which would have enormous consequences for the Liberal Party.

Ed Lumley was Chrétien's parliamentary secretary in Finance. He was a friend of Turner's but was furious at his actions. "To be undercut by a predecessor, especially one on your own side, was just outrageous." Chrétien didn't take the matter up with Turner directly, but Lumley did, phoning him and saying, "John, this is unforgivable what you are doing to him."

In addition to this series of controversies, Chrétien was being buffeted by the harshness of the economic times. His first year in the portfolio ended with unemployment higher than when he took the job, inflation slightly higher, the debt rising frantically, and the dollar on a tumble. Because of his faith in and reliance on the word of his bureaucrats, Chrétien had clung stubbornly to the Finance department's initial estimate of 5 per cent growth. He came increasingly under fire until finally, after everyone else knew the goal was unreachable, he admitted it was wrong.

In preparing his new budget, he was given the *carte blanche* he requested of Trudeau. But the economy's dismal mix of problems left him with few options other than to tinker at the margins. With the unemployment rate high and an election coming, he was under pressure to provide a budget with a good measure of economic stimulus. One proposal was to adopt mortgage tax deductibility as they had in the United States. Although it was a policy recommended by Joe Clark's Tories, it was favoured by many in Chrétien's own party, who felt it would have magnificent pre-election appeal. Chrétien, however, decided to take the high road. He reasoned that such a policy would be prohibitively expensive, given the deficit and the debt.

After a long series of private-sector consultations, he chose a cautionary approach. He introduced a federal sales-tax reduction, but only to offset provincial taxes, which were returning to their old level following the spring budget agreement. Modest income-tax relief and small incentives for business were added to the package. But by and large, it was a hold-the-line budget, conservative in its orientation, supported by the business community. Anyone who had doubted that Chrétien was a Mitchell Sharp Liberal had those doubts wiped away. The left wing of the party was stung. It soon wanted a new Finance minister.

Quite apart from the content of this budget, what was important for Chrétien was his performance in bringing it in. He had to demonstrate that he was in control, that he knew the material, that he hadn't been trotted out by his department to read numbers he didn't understand. To this end, he rehearsed in his living room in front of son Hubert every night for a week. Reading the speech over and over, memorizing passages, and citing background documents it was like studying for an exam in law school.

By budget night he felt comfortable. He delivered the budget with authority and answered questions by providing sound statistical backing. The performance was enough to convince some of the sceptics that he was not quite the lightweight they had imagined.

The budget wasn't out long before Turner followed with another newsletter criticizing the government's continued inability to put its fiscal house in order. It was a fitting end to 1978, the worst year in Chrétien's political career. Early in 1979 Trudeau called the election and Chrétien's tenure in Finance, only a year and seven months of it, was mercifully over.

These were times when no Finance minister anywhere was looking good. The new disease called stagflation continued to baffle everyone, including Chrétien. Though unemployment dipped a bit in his term of office, inflation was up marginally and the public debt was sky-rocketing. It rose 41 per cent under Chrétien, to $64 billion.

But if no Finance minister could have looked effective under these circumstances, Chrétien looked worse than he might have. On the one innovative measure he tried, the sales-tax cut, he gambled on Quebec and lost. Though the Guns of August were not of his making, they might not have been fired at all had he shown himself to be formidable in the job.

Chrétien came out of Finance diminished but alive. He survived because he had so much political capital in the bank to begin with that he was in a position to expend a great deal and still have some left. His long-time drive to become Finance minister had been founded not on any wish to bring something new to the job, but on ambition. He wanted to be the first francophone to have it. When he achieved his dream, he had little idea what to do with it. In the end, said the writer Ron Graham, "he became a prisoner of his own creation, his public image. He had worked so hard to seem ordinary that no one could believe he wasn't."

CHAPTER FIFTEEN

TRUDEAU'S FIREFIGHTER

A FTER the hard rain that fell on him in Finance, Chrétien was compelled to defend his record throughout the 1979 election campaign. He could talk of Canada having been the only recession-free economy among the big industrialized countries for the previous five years and of job-creation numbers better than all other OECD nations, but the combination of stagflation and mounting debt was a heavy cross to bear. The people had grown tired of the Grits, and if confirmation of the growing gulf was needed, it could be found in Trudeau's illogical decision to focus the campaign on constitutional issues. Not even Jean Marchand's teasing—his line about a labourer coming in from the fields, shaking his head sadly, and saying, "Couldn't get much done today, was worried too much about the constitution"—could register the point. The Liberals went down to defeat everywhere but in French Canada. For the first time in his sixteen-year political career, Chrétien found himself on the Opposition benches. In his own riding he was re-elected by a smashing twenty-thousand-vote margin. Almost all the Liberals who ran in Quebec—sixty-seven of seventy-five—were winners, but the size of Chrétien's victory was gratifying. It secured his power base at home and his position in the party hierarchy. It showed his rough ride as Finance minister hadn't diminished his popularity.

The Tories under Joe Clark won only a minority, thus leaving Chrétien some hope of returning to the governing councils before too long. In the meantime, though, a referendum on the future of Quebec was drawing near, and as an Opposition MP, he was without a major platform from which to fight for the federal side. That task was evidently falling to Joe Clark, William Jarvis, John Crosbie, and the like. How, Chrétien wondered, could these well-meaning anglophones mount a credible, formidable campaign in Quebec?

It might have been clear to him, as it was to many, that English Canada had not produced a Chrétien equivalent. No English-Canadian politician could go to Rimouski as Chrétien could go to Medicine Hat and speak from the gut in his second tongue and be heard and felt and cheered. No anglo politician could bestride the two cultures as Jean Chrétien could.

On appointing his shadow cabinet, Pierre Trudeau asked Chrétien his preference. He had no hesitation in stating it; he wanted to fight the separatists. It was difficult to worry about the inflation rate, he said, "if you don't have any goddamn country." Accordingly, Trudeau named him his federal-provincial relations critic, and Chrétien set about lambasting Clark for hesitating to plunge into the Quebec maelstrom. There would come a day when, in the early run-up to a referendum, Chrétien too would hold back when faced with a similar situation. But at this time he thought differently. The fight was on, cried Chrétien, and the prime minister's head was in the sand. "Can you imagine if President Carter said to the people of the United States if Texas wanted to separate, 'I can't go there, I can't talk to them, I come from Georgia.'"

He was worried that René Lévesque would hoodwink the Quebec population with an ambiguous question that tried to camouflage the sorcerer's intent. The real meaning of sovereignty-association had to be made clear. "What they say is that there won't be a piece of legislation from any other government that will apply on the territory of Quebec. That means separation. The rest is bullshit!"

The referendum issue fired Chrétien's blood like no other. He'd been fighting a class struggle against the sovereigntists much of his life. These were the "snobs" who sneered at his intelligence, who mocked his use of language, who were phoney intellectuals. In his own riding there was now Duhaime, that "bastard" in the three-piece suit. Chrétien had had another run-in with him. This time the Péquiste had paraded his supposedly superior intelligence right in his face. It came at a meeting where they had to address a Chrétien bid to increase the land mass of La Mauricie National Park. Since Duhaime was Quebec's minister of Tourism, Chrétien had to negotiate with him. At Shawinigan's Hôtel des Chutes, Chrétien took out a map and began randomly marking the boundaries that the expanded park would extend to. He'd compensate the province for the land.

Duhaime was astonished. "Do you know who you remind me of?" he indignantly demanded. "You remind me of Czar Alexander at the Congress of Vienna." At the congress following the Napoleonic wars, the czar had taken out a pair of scissors and set about cutting up a map of Europe to his liking. As Duhaime expected, the reference left Chrétien totally in the dark, wondering what was the Congress of Vienna and who in hell was Alexander? No deal on the park was reached.

Duhaime also trumped him on a highway extension for the twenty-mile stretch from Trois-Rivières to Shawinigan. The costs were divvied up by Quebec City and Ottawa, but for the grand opening, Duhaime told his colleagues, "We don't need the feds. We'll open it ourselves." The formalities were held without Chrétien even being notified. Duhaime got all the press. "I plead guilty on that one," Duhaime recalled with a broad smile years later. "Christ, was he mad!"

In the months preceding the referendum, they met again at the funeral of the mayor of Shawinigan-Sud. Relations between them had soured so much that even for this solemn occasion, they could not remain civil. With the dignitaries looking on, they started haranguing each other in the funeral cortège.

As well as the Quebec controversy, other issues preoccupied Chrétien in Opposition. As federal-provincial relations critic, he displayed his bias for a strong central government by vigorously opposing Joe Clark's "community of communities" vision of Canada. The equality of peoples and the equality of regions was central to Chrétien's philosophy, and it was obvious to him that only the federal government could ensure such standards and values. Ottawa was the great equalizer, he believed, the redistributor of wealth from rich to poor. Expenditures on redistribution, he noted, accounted for roughly half of all federal spending. If the power was left to the provinces, the country would further polarize into haves and have-nots.

The resource-rich provinces, particularly those with oil and gas reserves, were getting too much of the pie, Chrétien charged. He found it "cruelly ironic" that the federal government was running up big deficits to prevent a recession while provinces like Alberta were building big surpluses during the same time of need. The Tories, he complained, were giving away offshore oil rights to the provinces, surrendering the resources of the North, and dismantling the one Crown corporation that gave Ottawa some clout in the business, Petro-Canada. In bending over backwards to appease the duchies, Clark had become, said Chrétien, "the Neville Chamberlain of Canada." In the hyperbole sweepstakes he was outdoing Trudeau, who had labelled Clark the "head waiter to the provinces."

Being in Opposition allowed Chrétien time to enjoy a more relaxed lifestyle than the one he was accustomed to. But the calm was not to last. After eleven years as Liberal leader, Pierre Trudeau resigned. In what began as a leadership campaign, John Turner was the favourite, followed by another former Finance minister who had chosen to leave the government, Donald Macdonald. Though it wasn't a francophone's turn, Chrétien prepared to make a bid himself. He told top aide Eddie Goldenberg that "if you don't run, you never win." It was the same advice he had given Joe Clark when the Albertan was contemplating a long-shot try for the Tory crown in 1976.

He began phoning his friends in the party and putting an organization in place. When Turner decided to forgo a bid, the Chrétien prospects brightened. But before he officially entered, the Clark government, barely seven months in power, self-destructed, losing a vote on a non-confidence motion over a budgetary matter. An election was called and the Liberals, caught without a leader, turned again to the Northern Magus. Chrétien put his leadership ambitions back on the shelf. In the campaign, with his own riding secure, he concentrated again on the national effort. The Liberals led the polls by a wide margin going in and, without much effort, were able to soft-shoe their way back to power. Jean Chrétien was elected for a seventh straight term in St-Maurice, this time by the remarkable margin of twenty-five thousand votes.

As Trudeau put together his new cabinet, Chrétien surprisingly—some thought shockingly—made a bid for a return to Finance. He believed that he had yet to prove himself there and that given another opportunity could do so. Trudeau much preferred having him fight the referendum campaign, however, and was also under pressure to name a Finance minister from outside the Sharp wing of the party. "The Left of the party," recalled Chrétien, "wanted to have MacEachen." Chrétien went to MacEachen and warned, "You won't like it, I have been there." But he promised to support him if MacEachen took on the job.

Chrétien's second choice was the prestigious External Affairs post. It would elevate his image, taking him away from the dirt and grind of the home front. Trudeau was perplexed. The previous spring Chrétien had clearly wanted to fight the sovereigntists. Now, with Trudeau offering him a chance to do so as minister of

Justice, Chrétien was backing off. "I don't understand you, Jean," Trudeau told him. "Home is burning and you want to be in Paris, London, Tokyo, and Washington."

Trudeau wasn't normally unyielding when dealing with such a senior minister, but on this one he dug in because he thought Chrétien was the ideal choice for the position. He and Trudeau had been the foremost advocates of rigorous federalism. Their impact on the Canadian polity could not be underestimated. They had been architects of what was nothing less than a cultural revolution. When they arrived in the capital, Ottawa was primarily an English-speaking city where power was exercised by an anglo elite. Quebec politicians had been happy to look after their own and leave the rest of the nation's business to the English. The revolution, for which some of the groundwork was laid by Pearson, saw the ascendancy of a new French-Canadian power elite who set about transforming the Canada of two solitudes into a bicultural entity. To this end, Quebeckers were given powerful positions throughout the ruling hierarchy, and a comprehensive bilingualism program aimed at making the government and the nation functional in both languages was implemented.

No one other than the prime minister himself had played a more central role than Jean Chrétien in bringing about the transformation. He was the great advocate of opening Quebec to the rest of Canada and opening the rest of Canada to Quebec. In occupying so many prominent cabinet positions and acting as a chief proponent of bilingualism, he was a leading example of francophone power on a national scale. No other French Canadian was as welcome in English Canada as Chrétien.

By 1980 this, his role in the cultural revolution, was his most vital contribution to Canadian public life. His cabinet work had unquestionably brought some other important results. He had raised the profile of native Canadians and helped empower them; he had, as Doctor No, slowed down federal spending; and he had served as an effective salesman of Liberal and federalist values. But none of the accomplishments, outside of his changing of the cultural dynamic, was of unusual significance. Now his work in this area was at risk of being nullified by forces bent on severing Quebec's relationship with Canada and isolating the province as a separate, sovereign unit.

Canada, as Trudeau told him, was burning, yet Chrétien wanted to be elsewhere. One reason for his hesitation was that he had never been enamoured of the Justice portfolio. It was a traditional post for Quebeckers, usually awarded to charter members of the province's legal establishment. But there were other explanations. Eddie Goldenberg detected an unusual degree of nervousness in Chrétien over the referendum question. He worried about losing. He worried about his relationship with Quebec Liberal leader Claude Ryan, under whom he would have to work. Trudeau, meanwhile, was throwing him all kinds of carrots. Besides the Justice portfolio, he was offering him the posts of Attorney-General and minister of state for Social Development. But still he hesitated.

The Justice position, with its focus on the referendum campaign, was one others in the Quebec wing of the cabinet were climbing the walls for. Jean-Luc Pepin, for one, felt he was more qualified. He had co-authored the Pepin-Robarts unity report, which gave him a deep understanding of the sensitivities, the nuances, and the politics of the dossier. "I should have been the one," he said, "that Trudeau asked to lead the referendum fight."

Pepin had long been perplexed, if not bitter, at Chrétien's rise through the Liberal ranks. He had quickly realized on meeting Chrétien that he, Pepin, had more breadth, intellect, and understanding. And while he liked Chrétien personally and recognized that intellect wasn't the pivotal criterion for political success, it still gnawed at him that the less enlightened man was winning out. Mitchell Sharp could sense the hard feelings. "It puzzled Jean-Luc," said Sharp, "that Chrétien was so successful. . . . He found it very difficult to take." Unlike Chrétien, "Pepin could deal with the most difficult questions on any subject." Other Quebec caucus members, Sharp noted, were also resentful. But they too should have realized why Trudeau was turning to Chrétien, he said. It was because he was "infinitely the better politician."

Chrétien once told Pepin why he was coming up short. The problem, he said, was that Pepin was getting too bogged down in detail. He read all his briefing books and all his correspondence and signed it all and wrote explanations. It was no good, Chrétien told him. He had to learn when to cut and run.

As his unity report revealed, Pepin favoured a greater flexibility on the Quebec issue than Trudeau and Chrétien. When Pepin and Robarts went to discuss their report with the prime minister, Trudeau had held it in his hand for a moment and then said, "You will understand there are things in here with which I disagree." With that, he put it on the shelf behind him. On the day the PM handed out the cabinet assignments, Pepin was still hopeful. But he got a strong hint of what was to come when the PM said, "I've been thinking about a job for you that will keep you very busy." The implicit suggestion was to stay as far away from the unity debate as possible. Trudeau gave him Transport.

Chrétien got the job, Pepin concluded, because he was willing to be Trudeau's yes-man. "Chrétien took it as essentially a job to do for Trudeau. He was a good soldier. He said and did what Trudeau wanted." When he finally made up his mind to accept Trudeau's offer, Chrétien wouldn't dispute this. He would later say of the role, "I became Trudeau's firefighter."

Claude Ryan took the news of Chrétien's appointment gracelessly. They had had an unfortunate misunderstanding. When the Liberals were choosing a successor to Robert Bourassa, Chrétien, who was thinking of seeking the position, visited Ryan to get his opinion. Ryan told him there were three potential candidates: Claude Castonguay, Chrétien, and himself, Ryan. Chrétien, deaf in one ear, missed the third name. He then talked on and on about his own possible candidacy and that of Castonguay. After the meeting, Goldenberg told Chrétien he had battered the eminent editor's ego. Then, instead of rushing to make amends, Chrétien dug himself in deeper. The next day he saw Ryan again, but rather than talk about what a fine candidate the editor might make, he told him exactly what was on his mind: good newspaper editors don't make good politicians.

Before being appointed by Trudeau, Chrétien had attended an organizational meeting of the referendum's "No" side. At the gathering he was snubbed by Ryan, snubbed so blatantly that Marc Lalonde and André Ouellet, who had been looking on, later told him he should never have taken such abuse. When he was officially named, he travelled to Montreal to show Ryan some poll results and discuss strategy. Ryan was not ready to see him, so the minister of Justice waited outside his office. Fifteen minutes went by, a half-hour, forty-five minutes. Still no Ryan. Chrétien was fuming, but when Ryan finally opened his door after an hour had passed, Chrétien was able to hold his temper in check. He remained calm and polite. Ryan, who was purposely trying to stake out his territory as the paramount leader of the "No" forces, maintained his posture of vainglorious condescension. On hearing the latest poll results from Chrétien, the former newspaper giant dismissed them. He didn't need polls, he said. He and his party were so close to the people that they could sense how things were going. To prove it, he took Chrétien on a walk from his home to Liberal Party headquarters. Along the way Ryan stopped passers-by, shook their hands, and chatted with them at length, all the while ignoring his federal companion.

Ryan often missed scheduled conferences with Chrétien or cancelled them at the last minute. Meetings of the combined federal and provincial teams had an almost surreal quality to them, with Ryan adopting an air of papal supremacy and transcendence, and treating Chrétien's side like minions. "Chrétien was acting on behalf of the federal government and Mr. Trudeau," Ryan later recalled. "And I was a bit suspicious."

Chrétien still maintained a steady calm, however, never rising to the bait. Years later, it was bluntly put to him that given the type of treatment he faced, he must have felt like doing what he did in the good old days—punching his adversary in the mouth. Chrétien paused for a moment, then replied, "If I talked about all the temptations I have had in life to kick people around, you would have a long list between the temptation and the doing it."

When the referendum campaign officially opened, he had to hurry home from California, where he had been resting up for the big fight. His family members worried about poll results that were not encouraging. But Guy Chrétien sensed an inner confidence in his brother. "Don't worry," Jean told him. "We're going to win."

Soon after the start of the campaign, he ran into Duhaime and managed to keep the conversation on a civilized level. They bet a bottle of Scotch on the outcome, an outcome Duhaime was starting to feel increasingly positive about. The first federal rally was dismal. Organizers half filled an arena in Chicoutimi and didn't bother to cover all the ice. The audience froze. No fewer than twenty speakers droned on and on with repetitive messages. By the time it was Chrétien's turn, people were streaming out, bored to death. Cold and irritated, Chrétien delivered a choppy, uninspiring speech and went home mad. Lévesque, meanwhile, faced a small hall jammed with supporters and steaming with emotion.

At the University of Montreal, where Chrétien had been booed and stink-bombed in the past, he again met with hostile students. When he referred to the Péquiste star Claude Charron by his last name only, he was stopped by a clamour in the hall. "We say, 'Monsieur Charron'!" someone yelled. The meeting had been organized by Chrétien's own side, but his opponents turned out in greater numbers than his supporters. One student demanded to know what had happened to the Pepin-Robarts study and the suggestions for reform contained therein. Chrétien began his response with, "To answer that, we studied it—" But before he could continue, howls of derisive laughter stopped him. One student mocked the way federal and provincial Liberals communicated with one another. Hadn't Trudeau called Bourassa "a hot-dog eater," he shouted. For the most part, however, Chrétien held his ground. For an important question suggesting that a "No" vote was simply a "Yes" to the status quo, he was ready. The opposite was the case, Chrétien declared, "because a 'Yes' will lead to an impasse. Neither the provinces nor Ottawa will agree to negotiate on the basis of the separation of Quebec."

Because of the way the federal campaign was organized, Ryan and Chrétien appeared on the same podium most nights. Ryan, as the Chrétien people realized, had some different issues to worry about. He had a provincial election coming soon and didn't want to take as hard a line as Chrétien. He had prepared a broad constitutional platform, the Beige Paper, as an alternative to the sovereigntist route. But Chrétien wanted no meddling in the constitution, no compromise.

Ryan, who had at least agreed not to talk about his Beige Paper in the campaign, spoke late and long and well into the night at the "No" rallies, often missing newspaper deadlines. It was a development that struck Chrétien and the media as bizarre. The Liberal leader, who had spent decades in the newspaper business, was breaking one of its first commandments—meet your deadlines. His long, cerebral speeches were also heavily laden with dry economic statistics. A similar performance during the referendum debate in the Quebec National Assembly saw him crushed by the PQ.

Ryan's slogan for the referendum campaign—"Mon non est québécois"—was representative of what Chrétien saw as his inability to focus on the basics. Chrétien hated it. He had buttons made up saying, "La séparation—Non, merci." Eventually a compromise—"Non, merci"—was settled on.

Chrétien was acutely aware of the dangers of speaking over the heads of the people, of spending too much time in a bubble and feeding only off elite opinion. He had articulated this problem before and understood it more fully than others did. The effective politician, he knew, spoke from the point of view of the people on the street. Bourassa and the Quebec Liberals had lost in 1976, Chrétien thought, in large part because of this failure to understand his audience. He had talked as if the voters were academics.

What would work best in the referendum campaign, Chrétien was convinced, was a gut-level emotional appeal. He told organizers, "We've got to sell Canada. Quebeckers are proud Canadians. There's an attachment to Canada." He wanted a straight-out street fight, in which he'd take the virtues of Canada into the ring and score a knockout. Polls commissioned by the Canadian Unity Information Office, which was set up in the PMO for the campaign, confirmed that this approach would work.

Long after the referendum was over, Ryan acknowledged, in an unequivocal manner, that it was Chrétien who was right. If he, Ryan, had had more experience, he said, he would have done things differently. Unlike Chrétien, "I did not have a full grasp of the importance of symbolism in politics at that time." He was also impressed by Chrétien's loyalty to Trudeau. The PM's strategy was being called into question by Quebec Liberals at several meetings Chrétien attended. Though the temptation was obviously there, said Ryan, not once did Chrétien speak out against him.

As planned, Chrétien, who was chosen for the job because he was the best salesman the party had, campaigned with a brash, intensively patriotic fervour. This was the land of freedom, the land of opportunity, he declared, where little guys from Shawinigan like himself could look upon the Prairies and the Rocky Mountains and Vancouver as part of their birthright. The Rockies, he said time and again, were his Rockies. His mother had regaled her children with descriptions of the magnificence of these mountains. She had gone on for hours, and now her son remembered. He listed the names of the French discoverers of the great lands— Radisson, Des Groseilliers, and La Vérendrye. They were Quebec's lands and they were his. "I want them for my children and grand-children!"

This patriotic spiel, which he delivered with great effect in the campaign, had been perfected over the preceding few years. In the many economic portfolios he had held, he got bored reading out dry, dull texts that left audiences numb. So he often decided to fire things up with what he called his "Rockies speech."

"Very often I would come to a speech, a technical speech as minister of Finance, and I would always be very bad at reading—I'm better now, but I hate to read—so I would say to the press, 'You guys, I will make a deal with you tonight. I have a speech written by my bureaucrats. You have a copy in the back of the room. You read it. It has all the boring stuff. It's boring but important. But now let me talk to you.'" So he would speak from the heart, giving voice to views that from others would sound hackneyed and trite. But Chrétien's accent and fractured prose and primitive passion worked well. "Always I would make the people feel good."

He told Canadians to stop complaining because, although they had problems, they weren't nearly so badly off as other nations. Trudeau didn't like this. He once told Chrétien he wished he would stop talking in such a way. But since, as part of his larger rant, it was so popular, Chrétien decided to carry on. He had stopped making his "pea-souper" and "frog" speeches, but the Rockies sermon would stay.

At many campaign stops, he went beyond the patriotic blasts to pillory the Péquistes as a bourgeois breed bent on attaining statehood simply so they could bathe their egos in the adornments of power. He would compare the cost of gasoline in Canada to the price in France, where it was about three times as much, invoking the obvious gamble a turn towards independence would mean. Chrétien always referred to a "tank du gaz." The Péquistes, he unfailingly noted, called it a "réservoir d'essence." They thought themselves so far above the common man that only such pompous words would do.

Canada was fantastically rich in oil and gas reserves, Chrétien explained, but would these fields be accessible to an independent Quebec? What possible benefit, he asked in mocking terms, could come from going the independence route? So that a paragon of arrogance like Claude Morin could become the ambassador of Quebec in some far-away country, gliding through the streets "dans un gros Cadillac avec le flag de la province sur le hood?"

For many Quebeckers his portrayal of the separatists as ego-driven elitists had resonance. But the charge was off the mark when applied to the head of the movement. Lévesque looked like an unmade bed covered in a cloud of cigarette smoke. He was as comfortable carrying a lunch bucket as Chrétien, and less arrogant than Trudeau.

No one had ever seen Chrétien—"I lost fifteen pounds and I never was a fat guy"—so tense, so pressured, so determined as he was in this campaign. He hadn't faced stakes this high before. The Finance portfolio, as he told Goldenberg, had been hard. Make a big mistake there and you could bring down the government. But in this job, he said, the stakes were even higher. Make a big mistake and you could bring down a country. After a meeting with Ryan, during which some depressing poll results were revealed, Chrétien emerged with a deathly look, as gloomy as Goldenberg had ever seen him. "Now you know how serious this is," he told his adviser. "We're in this deep. We have to win."

Below the surface tension, however, an inner confidence remained. One morning he arrived in Shawinigan at dawn from a trip into the Gaspé. He called Guy, who was getting ready to go to work at his pharmacy, and asked him to bring over a razor so he could shave and get back on the road. When Guy arrived, he saw the deep bags under his brother's eyes, the sallow skin, the long, frail diminished body. This was Chrétien's third campaign in the space of a year. In each of the general elections he had visited fifty ridings and given three times that many speeches and press conferences. Now he was doing it again, under even greater strain. Yet that morning he had the same message for Guy he had had at the outset. There would be victory.

He was accompanied by Aline throughout the campaign. The journalist Robert Sheppard followed them on a tour of small-town church basements. "Sometimes they'd do six, seven in a row," he recalled. "It was something you couldn't imagine Trudeau or Lalonde being able to do. The energy, the stamina, was remarkable. They'd be taken by volunteer drivers from one town to the next, and Chrétien would be briefed on the local issues and always make sure he wove them into his speech." Aline was always there, said Sheppard, "like a secret-service agent of an American president, watching from behind his back." With so many political wives, the look on their faces was a giveaway—just another ordeal they had to endure. But Aline seemed to be enjoying it all the time. "They'd come into a hall and they'd work the room for ten or fifteen minutes and then they'd meet in the middle of the room and join hands. Chrétien would get up and speak and she would smile genuinely and laugh at his jokes. Then they were gone to the next church basement."

Trudeau was disappointed by the lack of progress early in the campaign, once questioning whether the federalist forces were demonstrating sufficient pride. "The prime minister reads the newspapers," responded Chrétien, disagreeing. "Me, I'm on the ground. Sometimes there's a difference." Trudeau's advisers warned the prime minister that Chrétien could be going overboard with his pointed attacks on the enemy, driving the stakes higher than they already were. Less apocalyptic pictures had to be drawn, they thought, so that in the event of a PQ victory, Trudeau could say this was just the first battle. After all, the question on the ballot concerned sovereignty-association. It was far from end-game.

This complaint got to Chrétien, but he continued to smite the enemy the way he knew best—with a two-by-four. It was becoming his show. With Trudeau in the background, the Pied Piper of Confederation held centre stage. Members of the Liberal cabinet in Ottawa, as well as members of the caucus, grew terribly anxious that reinforcements were needed, that Trudeau should be in Quebec, fighting on a daily basis. Chrétien argued that it was more effective to use the prime minister sparingly. Continual exposure, he pointed out, would only debase the coinage.

While Chrétien was getting a lot of attention in English Canada, thereby boosting the morale of the federalist forces, the coverage of him in the Quebec press was muted. A sour relationship had long existed between him and the sovereigntist-leaning media in Quebec, particularly in the period following the election of the PQ. Chrétien grew bitter about the lack of coverage, once rising in the House of Commons to blast the CBC French network for allegedly boycotting his national unity speeches.

Three weeks before the May 20 vote, he became more confident. He noticed that his message—a "Yes" vote means separation—was getting through. He noticed a different mood. "The campaign has changed tones and now people are talking tremendously about Canada." He noticed that the serenity evident in René Lévesque at the beginning of the campaign was leaving him.

With the sizeable federal resources at his disposal, Chrétien, who was going back and forth to Ottawa, coordinating all aspects of the federal effort with the provincial side, bombarded Quebec with advertising and with documents and statistics refuting PQ claims of Quebec having got a bad deal in Confederation. Because Ryan was hyper-sensitive about any strategy that came from the federal offices, Chrétien's team had to work a little subterfuge. Happily, Ryan's assistants, like Pierre Bibeau, got along well with Chrétien's. Campaign ideas and materials they got from the federal offices were presented to Ryan as their own.

But the fight was far from being all Chrétien's. The "No" campaign received a major psychological boost from the "Yvette" phenomenon. A PQ minister, Lise Payette, accused Claude Ryan of being the type of man who wanted all Quebec women to stick to their traditional roles—making the porridge, sweeping the floors, and serving the husband. He wanted, she said, a Quebec full of these servile "Yvettes." Why, even his wife's name was Yvette, she pointed out. The remarks sparked a controversy that could not be contained. Mrs. Ryan was a sophisticated woman who had served in a number of important public-service roles. Quebec women who saw themselves as far more advanced than the Yvette stereotype rallied in huge numbers behind the "No" banner. Fifteen thousand turned up for a demonstration at the Montreal Forum.

Late in the campaign, before Trudeau took part, internal polls by the Quebec Liberals showed a major shift in momentum to the "No" side. Trudeau then gave three dramatic speeches, making that momentum unstoppable. The Quebec provincial Liberal machine successfully organized the "No" vote, with provincial premiers coming forward to lend a hand and anglophone-led citizens' groups playing an important part.

But even though his role was negated somewhat by the Quebec media, Chrétien had been vital. He had provided the federal effort with much of its strategy and its emotional force. He had turned the morale of the federal campaign around when, in the early going, it was flagging. He had staved off a potential disastrous rift between the federal and provincial sides by turning the other cheek to the disdainful patronizing of Claude Ryan.

On the night of the triumph he was with friends and advisers at the Hotel Bonaventure, but when the results began to come in, he went off to a separate room to watch by himself. Despite the clear-cut victory, sixty per cent of the vote for the "No" side, he showed little emotion when he returned to the others. Someone suggested they crack open a bottle of champagne to celebrate, but Chrétien responded with a categorical no. He felt some relief, but no joy. It was hard to feel happy at the thought, as he put it, of destroying someone else's dream. It was, after all, the dream of a great many of his own people.

He went to the Radio-Canada headquarters for an interview and was snubbed by everyone in the building except the security guard. Then he went to the Verdun arena for the victory rally. There, for Chrétien's moment of triumph, with the whole nation looking in, Claude Ryan imposed his final insult. He wouldn't let the Justice minister speak.

On his way to the arena, Ryan had heard Trudeau on the radio, commenting on the results. There had been no prior arrangement for this, "no permission from me," Ryan recalled. So he decided that the federal government had made its response and that would be all. At the arena, he told his aides, "I'm going to speak and Mr. Chrétien will not speak."

Accepting the news with apparent equanimity, showing again a subtle, diplomatic side people didn't think he had, Chrétien stopped himself from telling Ryan what he really wanted to say.

Recalled Chrétien, "Ryan felt I had stolen enough of the show already."

CHAPTER SIXTEEN

FATHER OF
RE-CONFEDERATION

T HE MORNING after the triumph, Chrétien made the te-
dious two-hour drive from Montreal to Ottawa and
stopped in to see the Boss. Having just completed his third
long campaign in a year, the minister of Justice was planning to
board a plane with Aline and, though it was a splendid Canadian
spring, head to Florida for some rest. The prime minister, however,
interrupted his plans. He had another assignment for him.
Chrétien was to fly to every province and, capitalizing on the momentum of the "No" vote, sound out the premiers on moving
ahead with constitutional reform. Trudeau had pledged to
Quebeckers that their referendum vote was not a vote for the status quo, that there would be a new deal for them. "We have to
strike while the iron is hot," Trudeau told Chrétien. "A plane is
ready. You're leaving at four o'clock."

Chrétien ordered a fresh batch of shirts from his home. With
them came a message from Aline: "Tell him if he doesn't start
spending some time at home, he's the one who's going to get the
sovereignty-association!"

She well knew, however, as did Jean-Luc Pepin and others, that
when the Boss spoke, Jean Chrétien listened. That Trudeau had
hung him out to dry a few times—with the Indian paper, with his
mini-budget—didn't matter. He was the faithful soldier. Trudeau

could wind him up, send him out, rewind him, and send him out again. He was the doer, the fixer. Once, Chrétien's old friend Jean Pelletier, who had become mayor of Quebec City, came to Trudeau with a big problem on his mind. Who in the government, he wondered, should he see about it? "See Chrétien," Trudeau instantly responded. "He's the one who gets things done around here."

Chrétien's attitude was passed down from Maurice and Wellie and Grandfather François. There's a job to do, you do it, you do it well, you move on. He was always ready for more and was always more enthusiastic than others. He went about things "with such goddamn fervour," explained one of the men who worked alongside him at the mill. "It was kind of unreal." There was a relentlessness about him. His lean, hungry frame combined all the elements. He was earth, wind, rain, and fire.

He loved a challenge. Get me to the big waves, he'd cried to his surfing friend Robert Matteau on the beaches of Hawaii. Let me at the downhill, he'd barked at skiing companions. Slaloms were for cowards. Once, when he was just a kid, someone had dared him to swim all the way across the lake at Maurice's cottage. He wasn't a strong swimmer, but he was Chrétien, so he had to accept the dare. He got out in the deep water and almost drowned.

In Ottawa they said that Trudeau was the mind of the party, Chrétien the heart. Chrétien preferred the gridiron analogy. Trudeau was the quarterback and he was the best damn fullback ever to put on the pads. Just point him in the direction of the end zone. He'd pound his way through the enemy line, gaining more yardage than anyone else. And, as he let everyone know, with his "hack-cent" at full throttle, he'd never fumble the ball. "Trudeau give me da ball," he'd shout. "Den everybody pile on me. But when dey get off, who still got the ball? Da little guy from Sha-win-i-GAN!"

He'd scored in the referendum fight, but a bigger battle—the drive for a new constitution—was just beginning. The referendum campaign lasted but a few weeks. The fight for the constitution—getting the document home from Britain, finding a method of amending it, reaching agreement with the provinces on the Charter of Rights and Freedoms—would be a different test, a marathon of two years' duration.

Opposing the quarterback and the star running back were a mix of formidable adversaries: the provinces, Opposition parties, British MPs, and a half century of precedence.

The cross-country tour ordered by the prime minister was a senselessly hasty affair. One day saw Chrétien at breakfast in Winnipeg, lunch in Regina, afternoon tea in Edmonton, and dinner in Victoria. The following morning he flew five thousand miles east to tour the Maritimes before being deposited, a heap of exhaustion, back in Ottawa. He immediately picked up Aline and they flew to Miami. They arrived at 11:00 p.m., then waited for a rental car. He finally got the car, drove it for a half-hour, and then it went dead. Standing with Aline at the edge of a dark highway somewhere between Miami and Boca Raton, the minister of Justice, who had no money in his pocket, just a credit card, started hitchhiking. After twenty-five sleepless hours, he reached his hotel.

The blitz of the provinces only confirmed what could have been discovered in a few minutes on the phone with each premier—that there was a willingness to give constitutional renewal another try. The next phase was a set of summer negotiations involving Chrétien, the Justice ministers from all provinces, and their staffs. Their goal was to try to find common ground on the wide range of thorny constitutional issues.

Chrétien had never pictured himself in this role. Though he had a law degree, constitutional chatter was alien territory, boring him just as it did most of the rest of the population. It was hardly the stuff the workers talked about in the taverns of Shawinigan. In his seventeen years in the Commons, in his hundreds of speeches, remarks, and interviews, Chrétien had mentioned the constitution but once. In his years in Indian Affairs, he displayed no interest in enshrining constitutional securities for the natives. In his statements on Quebec, he expressed doubt that a unity solution could be found by re-arranging words on a piece of parchment that only intellectuals cared about. Despite his total disinterest, however, Chrétien would soon be holding forth on the urgency of it all—of the dire need, after fifty-five years of bitter and fruitless struggle, to find a way out of the constitutional impasse and save the country.

He'd come into the Justice portfolio, as he had come into others, with a vast deficit of expertise. His deputy minister was Roger Tassé, the same man who taught Chrétien and Pepin the law course in 1963. Tassé quickly noticed that Chrétien "wasn't greatly interested in the legal system and how it works." What concerned him was the politics. His orders to his deputy were brusque. He told Tassé he wasn't going to spend time reading incoming correspondence—or even the outgoing letters written in his name. "You're responsible for this department," he told him. "There are a lot of letters that will be going out, and you better make sure these letters are appropriate for me to sign because I'm telling you in advance I won't be reading them. If there is something wrong and there is a comeback on some of them, you are responsible. I don't want any comebacks."

Chrétien worked almost exclusively on the upfront political issue, at times ignoring other important social matters. There was, as Tassé saw it, a pressing need for a liberalization of the divorce laws. The process had to be speeded up. Tassé put the case to the minister but was quickly rebuffed. "I don't want to touch that," Chrétien dismissively replied. The changes to the divorce laws were later brought in by the Tory Justice minister, John Crosbie.

Another Justice official brought forward a matter that had been bandied about in the press for some time: the need for a Freedom of Information Act. The official began laying out in detail what he thought had to be done, but he soon noticed Chrétien's eyes glazing over. That was the telltale sign. The official took his cue and left the room. Freedom of Information was put on the shelf.

Chrétien began the constitutional negotiations with the provinces with few firmly held biases, save his faith in a strong central government. Canada was already one of the most decentralized

jurisdictions in the world, he argued. "By trying hard to decentralize at any price, we could very well find ourselves inadvertently
without a country."

His bias paralleled that of Trudeau and of the clerk of the Privy
Council, Michael Pitfield. But Chrétien soon found himself listening to the arguments in the provincial capitals with increasing sympathy. His hard line softened, and in his reports to Trudeau and
Pitfield he'd say, "You know, maybe they have a point here." When
they inevitably shook their heads in response, Chrétien suggested
they might try standing before the provincial representatives for a
week at a time as he had and listening to their explanations. Maybe
then they wouldn't feel that way.

Chrétien was "caught in the middle," said Tassé, "and he was
trying to keep his mind." Sometimes Pitfield's learned references,
like Duhaime's on Czar Alexander, got on his nerves. Once, when
the clerk began tracing the evolution of participatory democracy in
the United States, peppering his lecture with references to
Alexander Hamilton and Thomas Jefferson, the little guy from
Shawinigan couldn't take it anymore. "Tell me, Michael," Chrétien
snapped, "what baseball teams do these guys play for?"

The summer hearings put the main players together for four full
weeks. With not much to do in the evenings, they got to know one
another over a good Canadian beer. Chrétien's likeability, always
one of his strongest political assets, saw him fashion some important friendships, particularly with Roy McMurtry and Roy
Romanow, the Attorneys-General for Ontario and Saskatchewan
respectively.

He opened negotiations with a call for a provincial free-trade
pact, but since the proposal would mean more economic powers
for Ottawa, the provinces turned up their noses at it. The reaction
didn't surprise the federal representatives. Their proposal was largely
tactical. Chrétien, under orders from Trudeau, had to show that the
federal side was going to play it tough and make demands of its own.

The negotiations heightened his visibility. Only the Ayatollah Khomeini was taking up more space on the front pages that summer. But not much progress was made on the raft of divisive issues, and at the conclusion of the hearings, the mood was fouled by the leak of a cold-blooded federal strategy paper asserting that, failing provincial cooperation, Ottawa was prepared to move ahead unilaterally on its constitutional goals. The provincial premiers felt as if they had been pushed into a corner and viciously snapped back. A conference with the prime minister in September, which was designed to advance the work of the summer, degenerated into rancour and calumny. No consensus was possible. While no one blamed Chrétien personally, the failure of the talks didn't reflect well on him since the summer sessions were supposed to bring to the table something the first ministers could agree on.

It was a tough month. That same September, Jean's father, Wellie Chrétien, died at age ninety-two. His moral fibre, self-discipline, and strong will were among the qualities his children inherited from him. His youngest son, Michel, had travelled to China the previous year and brought back a statue of Confucius. "This is for you, Dad," he said, presenting it to his father, "because it symbolizes what you are—the best philosopher I know."

That philosophy had made a famous medical researcher of Michel, who had wanted, until Wellie stepped in, to become a hockey player; it had made a lawyer and a famous politician of Jean, who had wanted, until Wellie stepped in, to go to a technical college; and it had made great Canadians of them all. "We're Canadians first," said Guy Chrétien. "The attitude came from our father, and it's a family attitude."

Without Wellie's severe discipline, young Jean, who had shown many signs of waywardness, might never have found his way onto the right track. If he realized this, however, he wasn't inclined to say it. He had respect for his father, but no great fondness.

Though Jean had done well in life, seemingly fulfilling his dad's dreams, he rarely got a kind word from him. It would have made a difference had Wellie just taken him aside a couple of times and said, "Well done, son." But he never told him he was proud of him, and it left a wound.

"He was a pusher, he was demanding," Jean said, looking back. "He never had a compliment for me until he was about to die. You know . . . it was never good enough."

Jean recalled being "afraid of him." He remembered the fear that he faced because of his problems at school. He wondered if his dad—"not a very jovial guy"—had ever really enjoyed himself. At Wellie's funeral, Jean was quiet, not wishing, Maurice recalled, to dwell on memories of his father. "Before me, he never said a word about him." Maurice attributed Jean's resentment to his father's being rigid with him. In the Chrétien household, the mother was the one who gave out the compliments. "Father's attitude was 'That's all right, but what's next?' He was that type of man." Too many compliments could lead a man to rest on his laurels. Jean could tend to forget, Maurice noted, some of the things his father did for him. When Jean became a lawyer, Wellie lent him money to buy his first car. And though it was true that Wellie didn't have time to enjoy himself, Chrétien family members noted that Jean himself became quite the social loner, very preoccupied with Aline and with his work.

Jean was pleased that Wellie had lived long enough to see the federalist triumph in the referendum campaign. Although he was ill during it, Wellie received a visit from Jean in the hospital. "You can't go now, Dad," he said. "We need you for the 'No' vote." For someone like Wellie Chrétien, who cared so deeply about the country, the federalist victory was a happy send-off.

More trouble on the family front had surfaced. Jean's nephew Paul, the son of his brother Gabriel, had been jailed in Peru two and a half years earlier for alleged drug-trafficking. The incarceration was never publicized at the time. But in 1980 the story leaked, generating headlines—"Chrétien's Nephew Jailed"—and the like.

Paul Chrétien, talented and bright, had gone off to South

America with his girlfriend, just three months before he was to graduate from college. His mother, Françoise, pleaded with him to finish school, to get his degree, but to no avail. She'd always thought her Paul was so much like Jean. But Jean had grown up a generation earlier, when "it wasn't in style to be against everything," and Aline had come along just in time to tame his rebellious instincts.

Owing to the vagaries of the Peruvian judicial system, Paul Chrétien still had not come to trial by 1980. As Finance minister and then Justice minister, Jean Chrétien was in a delicate situation. If he tried to help, he would face conflict-of-interest allegations. Françoise was highly sensitive to his predicament and understood there was little he could do. But "he called us many times. He phoned once to say that if I wanted to go to Peru, he would arrange everything for me."

Eventually, the Justice department reached an agreement with Peru, allowing Canadians to return to their homeland to serve the rest of their sentences on the condition that they not appeal the verdicts. Chrétien, then twenty-nine, finally came to trial in Peru a few months after the news had come to light in Canada. He was sentenced to three years for trafficking. The reciprocity agreement allowed him to return home shortly thereafter, and because he had already served almost three years, he was free when he landed. To shield the family and the Justice minister from further media coverage, diplomats saw to it that Paul was spirited into Canada quietly.

After the failed conference between Trudeau and the first ministers, Ottawa, as threatened, pushed ahead unilaterally on the constitution. A plan to patriate it, amend it, and insert a Charter of Rights and Freedoms was put forward. Chrétien, acutely aware of the sensitivities of the provinces, argued privately against such one-sided action while publicly endorsing the plan. The premiers announced they would fight the bid in the courts. In the meantime, a joint parliamentary committee began televised hearings on the proposed charter.

The charter had the potential, legal specialists counselled, to become a seminal document. It could change the very nature of Canadian society, setting it on a more individualist track. Chrétien, however, showed virtually no interest in the charter. At the beginning of the summer Trudeau had told him he wanted one, so Chrétien took the matter up. But as senior Justice department officials like Roger Tassé and Barry Strayer saw time and again, Chrétien didn't really worry about what was in it, as long as he got one. Because he was the Justice minister, he of course had the prerogative to weigh in heavily. Instead, he willingly ceded his territory to other ministers and experts. He didn't, for instance, push for an aboriginal-rights clause in the charter at this stage. The only measure he was insistent on having was one on minority-language rights.

The draft charter put together in the wake of the failed September conference was purposely weak so as not to scare off those provinces who felt their powers threatened. The government also realized that the public-hearings process would significantly change the charter's content. In fact, the hearings, refereed by Chrétien, overhauled it completely. Civil-liberties groups, women's groups, Japanese Canadians, native Canadians, handicapped Canadians all trashed the charter. An astounding 124 amendments were put forward, more than half of which were accepted in the committee's final report. In January 1981 Chrétien announced the details of a completely revamped document. It pleased many but not everyone. The Conservative MP John Fraser accused Chrétien of being gutless for refusing to impose institutionalized bilingualism on the Ontario government. Chrétien was infuriated. "The people of Canada know that I have guts," he countered. "If John Fraser had any guts, he would go to Toronto tomorrow . . . and put his fist under Davis's nose. Then I will say, 'You have guts!'"

The protracted hearings process often showed Chrétien, as he had been in Finance, somewhat out of his depth. As Justice minister, he was frequently called upon to discuss fine points of constitutional law and detailed legal possibilities. Departmental officials supplied him with copious briefing materials so he would be able to handle the tough questioning. But they sometimes found that he hadn't read or digested them and, as a result, was often caught short. Some days he was nervous. Some days he repeated simplistic answers over and over again, frustrating his questioners. Some days he was overly reliant on corrections or elaborations from Strayer or Tassé.

Justice ministers were expected to know their briefs, but compared with his predecessors, Chrétien did not know his well. His performance in the portfolio raised eyebrows among the well informed, as it had in Finance. His inattention to detail was vaguely reminiscent of a neighbouring politician, President Ronald Reagan. Reagan was renowned for his generally hazy ways. Once, prior to a G-7 summit that Reagan was hosting, his chief of staff, James Baker, found he hadn't even taken the wrapper off his briefing books. With the summit about to start, Baker gingerly asked the president what had happened. "Well, Jim," the Gipper replied, "*The Sound of Music* was on last night."

Chrétien was a far more alert politician than Reagan. But while he detested being categorized by Quebec intellectuals and others as an unlettered man, his performance in the hearings tended to reinforce that image. They offered additional evidence that he was indeed a generalist, a man without a finely textured mind that could absorb a rich quantity of information, contemplate it, and recall it in an articulate, thoughtful, or imaginative way.

A combination of stress and indigestion put Chrétien in the hospital during the hearings. His condition was not as serious as it had been a decade earlier, when he was admitted to hospital with suspicions of a heart attack, but he was nevertheless sidelined for a week.

As green as he was in the Justice portfolio, he was relieved just to get through the hearing process without committing an enormous gaffe. He would profess, to the surprise of the well informed, to be happy with his performance. Ironically, the beating the charter took in the hearings proved to be a boon to the entire constitutional-reform process. The general population had no great interest in the constitution, and the push to bring it home could well have aborted owing to widespread indifference. But the hearings galvanized public opinion, giving the major players the impetus to move ahead.

Chrétien's close alliance with Trudeau, which survived despite the treatment he had received in Finance, wasn't going unnoticed. The *Globe and Mail,* which had praised Chrétien through much of his career, pummelled him with an editorial entitled "He Was a Good Man." The newspaper made a point that other observers were picking up on: Quebec had been promised renewed federalism in the referendum campaign. Now, as Claude Ryan was pointing out, Ottawa was moving ahead without Quebec and the other provinces to impose a unilateral solution that would not enhance Quebec's status. Promises were being broken. With his own prime ministerial ambitions the likely cause, said the newspaper, Chrétien was afraid to stand up to the Boss. "There were Trudeau ministers— John Turner, Donald Macdonald, and others—who had convictions of their own and departed rather than give them up. But Mr. Chrétien adjusts and remains."

Chrétien's back-room conversations with colleagues like Tassé were in fact spiced with references to plans to succeed Trudeau. As for Claude Ryan, ignored by Chrétien in the hunt for the constitution and bitter about it, he could hardly have expected anything more. He had been condescending to Chrétien during the referendum campaign. Now it was payback time.

The constitutional question was soon in the provincial courts. Manitoba and Quebec ruled Ottawa could act on its own, while Newfoundland's justices said no. The ultimate ruling, however, that of the Supreme Court, was still some months away. In the meantime, opposing premiers aligned themselves into the so-called Gang of Eight. It consisted of everyone but Ontario's wily and wise Bill Davis, whom Chrétien admired, and the colourful and exotic Dick Hatfield, the New Brunswick premier whom an unkind writer once described as a "prancing buffoon." The upstart Gang of Eight signed its own accord, which rejected a charter entirely and agreed to patriation with a different amending formula than Trudeau's. René Lévesque, fresh from a majority victory in the Quebec election, joined the gang, giving up his province's long-time claim to the right to veto any proposed amendment.

In September 1981 the Supreme Court ruled that unilateral action was technically legal but odious in spirit. Such action, the court said, would run contrary to the tradition of seeking provincial consent on matters of constitutional change. Chrétien, pronouncing the decision a clear victory, cared little about the spirit. He compared the situation to a federal election. Law required one every five years, though traditionally they were held every four. What mattered, he argued, was not the convention but the reality. A five-year wait was perfectly legal and so was Ottawa's decision to act alone on the constitution. After a press conference, Chrétien enjoyed a celebratory beer with some MPs. "It would have been too bourgeois to have had champagne," he said.

Despite the ruling, he pressed the prime minister to try again to reach consensus with the premiers. Going it alone, though legal, would leave an enduring bitterness. Moreover, without provincial assent it would be tougher to get approval for the historic change from the Thatcher government in London.

The first ministers convened again at the Conference Centre in Ottawa in November. During the first two days of meetings, Chrétien scrambled about in a bid to find common ground. Few premiers were forthcoming, however, and the last-chance conference appeared on the edge of collapse. Trudeau was now considering going over the heads of the provinces and directly to the people. He'd hold two referenda, one on the question of an amending formula and another on the Charter of Rights. Chrétien opposed holding another referendum, but he could see that mere talk of it was working to the federal side's advantage. The solidarity of the Gang of Eight was dissolving. Lévesque, for one, liked the

Trudeau proposal. It pricked his democratic spirit. Other premiers, however, were not keen to fight the popularity of the charter in their own provinces, and Chrétien exploited their doubts. He told them he didn't want a referendum, but if one was held he'd come in and clobber them, saying they were opposed to religious rights, women's rights, minority rights, and so on. By scaring them with the referendum proposal, he knew he was making them more willing to compromise on other issues.

Having played the role of go-between for a year and half, working his personal charm on all parties and demonstrating a more conciliatory attitude to provincial concerns, Chrétien had become both the most credible and the most popular politician at the table. He was the one figure on the federal side whom the provincial representatives could look to without suspicion. There was trust and *bonhomie*, particularly with Romanow and McMurtry. If a deal was possible, the politician who was positioned to fashion it was Chrétien.

Chrétien and Romanow had sketched out possible compromise positions on a piece of yellow paper. As the situation became more desperate, they decided that the best chance for success lay in a proposal featuring a trade-off: the provinces would accept the charter in exchange for Trudeau's accepting the provinces' amending formula. This was not a new idea, though in his memoirs Chrétien would leave the impression that it was. Ontario premier Davis and others had previously talked of similar compromises. Almost everyone knew that if a compromise could be found, it would be in a mix of this sort.

Romanow circulated the proposal and found some support. He and Chrétien then moved off to a quiet kitchen pantry at the conference centre, called in McMurtry, and worked out some final details. With approval from some provinces likely, the next step was to convince Trudeau of the merits of the proposal. Chrétien gave his pitch while the PM listened expressionlessly. Chrétien then suggested they try it out on a couple of MPs. In fact, he had already sold the deal to the MPs he had in mind. Serge Joyal and Jim Peterson were trotted in to tell the Boss that it was a fine compromise. Chrétien then convinced Trudeau to extend the conference another day.

The prime minister hosted a dinner at 24 Sussex that night for leading cabinet members. The majority appeared to side with the Trudeau plan for a referendum, but Chrétien argued strongly against such a venture. When Trudeau left the room to take a call from Bill Davis, Chrétien employed the exact opposite tack he had taken with the premiers. He had told them he would crush them in a referendum, but now he told his cabinet colleagues that if they opted for that route, he wouldn't campaign. "I won't be putting on my running shoes again for you. I've had enough of villages divided, French against English. A national referendum will be worse."

Chrétien would write that his work at the dinner was significant because it sucked away some of the momentum for a referendum and focused the cabinet on the compromise being worked out in the wings.

Others who attended the dinner, like John Roberts, saw it differently. Roberts didn't really think Trudeau was prepared to go ahead with the referendum. At any rate, he said, those in the room had already made up their minds, one way or the other. "While Chrétien spoke strongly and very effectively, as he always did, he was speaking to the converted."

At the end of the dinner, "there was a sense that Jean should go off and see what he could do," remembered Roberts. "But we really didn't believe he would come back with an agreement that was acceptable." Trudeau took Chrétien aside before he left and said he might be willing to consider the compromise proposal if it was clear that enough provinces were in favour of it. "Let me sleep on it," said the PM.

While Trudeau slept, the final pieces fell into place. Chrétien's compromise proposal was finding enough backers. B.C.'s minister of Intergovernmental Affairs, Garde Gardom, told Chrétien that his province was aboard and that there was enough support for the necessary majority. Before going to bed, Chrétien, confident that Trudeau would now come around, told Aline that Canada had a new constitution.

Chrétien didn't sleep that night. After further checks in the morning, he was able to inform the prime minister that the required numbers were there. He went to the PM's residence, where they reviewed the plan in detail. While they drove together to the conference centre, Trudeau complimented Chrétien's work and scoffed at those like Lévesque and Morin who had the nerve to think he wasn't sufficiently educated.

During the day, the compromise was cobbled together. The provinces all signed on, with the grand exception of Quebec. Lévesque couldn't accept the proposal, which didn't surprise Chrétien. He had suspected all along that there was no chance a separatist could accept a unity package. But though he understood this, Chrétien would call Quebec's decision and its isolation one of the saddest moments of his political career. Whether he was really as sad as that was debatable. He had been fighting these people throughout his political life.

But "Chrétien knew a big problem remained," his deputy minister, Roger Tassé, recalled. "The problem of political legitimacy." Tassé, a francophone, felt it acutely the evening after the package was finalized. He went home and told his daughter the deal was done. "Yes, but Quebec?" his daughter responded. "What about Quebec?" She was fifteen years old.

Any regret on Chrétien's part about Quebec's refusal to sign was tempered by the thought that Canada now had its constitution and a Charter of Rights, and that he was a principal architect. No one doubted the crucial role he had played in bringing a deal together. They could criticize him for his lack of depth, but in the end it wasn't depth that counted. What counted was the pragmatism of a generalist, of a politician who could see the big picture, who wasn't emotionally tied to a given position, and who had built alliances in competing camps.

"He was able to contemplate compromises that Trudeau wouldn't have been able to," said Barry Strayer, one of those who had witnessed Chrétien's limitations but now clearly saw his worth. "Everybody saw him as an honest broker. Without him you could argue it would not have happened."

The story was full of ironies. Chrétien, the politician who hadn't cared a whit about the constitution and who had known so little about its complexities, was the one who brought it home. "My sense," recalled a cabinet minister close to the proceedings, "is that Jean never had a strong view as to what should or should not be there, that any deal that was acceptable was acceptable to him." This was the key, he said, to "bringing about a result that no one was very happy with, but that almost everybody was prepared to accept." Roy McMurtry saw Chrétien as the Liberal with wide wings. "He was able to bridge the gulf that existed between Eastern and Western Canada in an effective and good-humoured manner."

During his years in the cabinet, Chrétien had played a central role in Canada's cultural revolution, making the country a bicultural one. This was a somewhat abstract accomplishment, made more tenuous by Quebec's failure to sign the new deal. Now, however, Chrétien had two big prizes to mark him. The referendum and the constitutional accord had given him a place in history, no matter what was to follow. Of the two, sealing the constitutional package was his more important achievement. The referendum, given the large margin of victory, could well have been won without him. But without the cohesive energy he brought to the constitutional process, it was difficult to see how those negotiations could have been saved. There were no other potential mediators. Jean Chrétien became, in the final days, the father of re-Confederation.

The question that remained, however, was what kind of re-Confederation had he forged. It was one without Quebec. It was one with a charter that the master cobbler had shown little passion for or interest in. He had had a job to do, he did it, he was moving on.

CHAPTER SEVENTEEN

FAMILY MATTERS

WELL HIDDEN from the drama of Jean Chrétien's public world was the private pain he was going through in these years because of his adopted son. It wasn't long after little Michel was selected from the orphanage in Inuvik and brought to the home of the most popular politician in the land that it became clear that something was not right with him.

At times he was uncommunicative, sullenly sealed off in whatever world he had created for himself. He didn't smile or laugh as much as other children. Uncle Gabriel visited a few weeks after the new member of the family arrived. He rearranged his hat and made funny faces, and Michel responded with a giggle. This delighted Jean and Aline because it was the first time, they told Gabriel, they had seen Michel smile. Gabriel thought he was a good kid that day. "But things turned bad."

Although Michel had been taken from the orphanage when he was too young to know his Indian world, it was obvious that he felt strange in his new non-native environment. He could be cute at times, but he was remarkably stubborn. If he didn't want to put on his shoes, it would be hours before they could get him to put on his shoes. Guy Chrétien, the pharmacist, tried to be friendly but got no reaction from him. "He didn't want to speak. Even though he was adopted so young, it was clear there was this mistrust that was in him."

He had a robust physique and showed some inclination for sports. The Chrétiens outfitted him in a new football uniform, and Guy, who was a great fan of Canadian football, went to see him play. Michel joined in the action for a few minutes but then shied away to the sidelines, not a mark on his new uniform.

At school he was a disaster. Jean and Aline had so hoped that the school environment would acclimatize him, ending his reclusive ways. But he was a very slow learner and was terribly undisciplined. Unable to accept the regimentation, he frequently skipped classes. Some days he would show up on time, then leave when the mood struck him. The Chrétiens tried him in a variety of schools, including boarding-schools, but he detested them even more than Jean had.

His new parents employed several tutors; they brought in doctors, psychologists, and psychiatrists; they took him to the Northwest Territories for visits. Maurice Chrétien estimated that Jean and Aline spent hundreds of thousands of dollars trying to get him the best care possible. Nothing seemed to work. Michel would be fine for a period—especially at the big Chrétien family gatherings, where he was always very friendly—but then he would shut himself off again.

"He was like a bird in cage," said Maurice, who dearly wished Jean or Aline had checked with him before going ahead with the adoption. As a teenager, Michel would lock himself in his room for long stretches, and sit in the dark and drink beer. A family friend reported that once he had stayed locked away for twenty hours, drinking and staring at the darkness. Sometimes he ran away from home. A close relative said this happened frequently, not because he didn't like his new parents, but because he had to get out of the cage. His disappearances frightened the Chrétiens, adding untold stress to a father already burdened down with cabinet responsibilities.

They had made a quick decision about adopting him, not knowing of the sorry record on white couples taking native children. They were prepared to have him live long periods of time in Inuvik. But Michel, said one of the relatives, wanted the best of both worlds. He liked the Chrétiens and the comforts they could provide. He wanted the good clothes they bought him, the spending money, the well-being.

For Jean's brother Michel, the situation was so depressing. He had handpicked the boy from the orphanage. "It was extremely difficult. I felt sad about it and I still feel sad about it because of my role in choosing him. But there is absolutely nothing that could have given us some hints about the results." Although Michel was "disturbed by the character problems that the boy had," he felt advice on how to handle him should come from experts, not himself.

Maurice also hesitated to give his personal views, but he did consult a doctor for whom he had enormous respect. The doctor said the only thing the parents could do in such a case was impose very strong doses of discipline. Maurice knew it was not in character for Jean to be that way with his children. The widely held view in the family was that he was too soft and kind with them.

The Chrétiens had moved from Alta Vista to a more exclusive home on Bower Avenue, overlooking the Ottawa Canal. Formerly owned by Defence Minister Barney Danson, the home was a cubed bungalow with big windows, similar in style to but more upscale than their first home in Shawinigan. Chrétien maintained his straight, disciplined lifestyle, trying to get home for dinner most nights, even if he had to return to the office afterwards. But given his frantic schedule, it was impossible to spend the amount of time with Michel that a normal working father would.

Occasionally Chrétien pondered, as he had in the early 1970s, the possibility of leaving politics altogether so he could devote more time to his children. But he concluded once again that he was "too hyperactive a guy" to settle into a quiet lifestyle. Politics was too much a part of him, too much in his blood to leave behind. There was the well-being of not only his family but also an entire country to keep in mind.

He and Aline remained stoic about their adopted son, never complaining to other family members. Eventually they became guarded, talking less and less about him.

To the traumas of Michel were added the misfortunes of Hubert, who suffered from dyslexia and asthma. Despite his health problems, Hubert was an ambitious teenager. He wanted to become a lawyer and a politician, just like his father. But one day he sat down with his dad to talk about these dreams—and got the wind knocked out of his sails.

Jean Chrétien was not enthusiastic about Hubert's plans. "It will always be very tough on you," he told him. "You will always be compared with your father. And it is very public and it will be unfair to you. I have been very lucky. Perhaps you will not be so lucky."

As a young man, Jean had to be pushed into law by his father. Now he had his own son, one who didn't need any pushing, who was eager to charge ahead himself. But rather than encourage him, his famous father was applying the brakes. Still, if Hubert was dead serious about it, he said he would help him. Hubert, a tall boy with straight fair hair and glasses, went away and thought about it. When he came back, he told his father he was dropping the idea.

From that moment forward, Hubert, who worked part-time on office jobs for Trade Minister Ed Lumley, distanced himself from his father's work and from politics generally. He found that much like his father, he had a knack for science and mathematics. He pursued that option, learning a lot about car servicing and working at various dealerships. Friends said he came to hate politics. He would never be seen at one of his father's functions.

After the dramatic eleventh-hour agreement on the constitution, it was time to put the icing on the cake. Chrétien's role was to take a copy of the resolution adopted by Parliament to the Queen. It was a welcome assignment for him. He was riding a wave of popularity and he knew Her Majesty well. His first encounter with her, when, as Indian Affairs minister, he and Aline had escorted the Queen on a visit to the Northwest Territories, had become the source of infamous Chrétien folklore. In Fort Providence, Chrétien unveiled a plaque in honour of Alexander Mackenzie, the explorer who had charted the Mackenzie River. The dignitary assigned to lead everyone in a healthy chorus of the national anthem begged off. His voice, he told Chrétien, was so delinquent of timbre that he couldn't possibly endure the humiliation.

Chrétien's voice was no better. At the best of times he sounded like a cement-mixer. But he reluctantly volunteered to lead the way, forgetting for an instant another problem: he didn't know the words in English and was in part of the country where French was as foreign as Swahili.

As soon as he started the Québécois rendition, Chrétien realized no one would be joining in. For the entire anthem, he had to drone alone. At the opening of each verse, he sounded like a stalled car. The mortified onlookers—royals, natives, journalists alike— lowered their heads, waiting helplessly for the final bars. At the end, the collective sigh of relief was so pronounced that the limp flags were said to waver. Aline later confessed to have never been so embarrassed in all her life.

Long after the incident, Chrétien met Prince Charles. He was surprised that the prince instantly recognized him. "How could I possibly forget?" Charles put in. "Your rendering of the Canadian anthem has become legend!"

This time around, Chrétien's visit to the Queen brought flattering media exposure. The two of them sat down for twice their allotted time, and the Queen delighted Chrétien by speaking mostly in French. What an excellent example, he told reporters, for Canadians so reluctant to take up the second language.

As he made the rounds of London officialdom, reporters queried him about his schedule. He'd had a few meetings, he said, one with "Lord I-forget-his-name," and another with "a fellow named Luce—you know, like that guy from *Time* magazine." He didn't take in much theatre, he said, because "my English isn't good enough to follow those English plays." But he did catch *The Sound of Music.*

At forty-seven, he was in his prime, at the top of his game. To the British media, inquiring about Quebec, he said poor Lévesque had tried high-stakes poker and been buried. For the British MPs, who sought to delay passage of the patriation package, he had a blunt message: keep your noses out of it. Having been lobbied by Canadian native groups, some British members alleged that Ottawa was countenancing a system of apartheid. Given his history in Indian Affairs, Chrétien fumed at such talk. "It's a Canadian problem that we'll solve in Canada."

The Queen signed the official proclamation of the new Constitution in Ottawa in April 1982. Chrétien now had little incentive for staying in the Justice portfolio and anxiously awaited a cabinet shuffle. In the interim, however, controversies dogged him.

The quality he probably valued most in public life was integrity. "There is only one thing that matters [in politics]," he said in October 1979. "To be honest with the public. That's all I ask of the government." In eighteen years of high-powered public life, he was proud that there had been so few challenges to this aspect of his reputation. In response to accusations that it was dictatorial, he had scaled back his political machine. When he was called to account for his actions in the judges' affair in 1976, he had been able to explain them away as an inadvertent miscue. Some practices, such as his lining up an opposition candidate in his own riding, had remained undisclosed.

The controversy that arose now involved a dispute over Newfoundland's offshore resource jurisdiction and the timing of Ottawa's decision to refer the matter to the Supreme Court. On a Tuesday afternoon in May, Chrétien told the House of Commons that the cabinet had not yet decided to turn the dispute over to the court. In fact, that very morning the cabinet had given the go-ahead, subject to some conditions, which were expected to be met. Chrétien flew to Newfoundland that Tuesday evening and, the conditions being satisfied, made the announcement the next day. That same next day, Trudeau revealed in the House that the cabinet had in fact given the conditional go-ahead in the morning.

The prime minister's statement touched off a furious row because it appeared that Chrétien had lied to the House, or at least used a technicality to mislead it. MPs wondered why he had not just said that the conditional go-ahead had been given? Instead he had stated that "there has been no decision made by the government at this time on that question."

John Crosbie, the Newfoundland Tory, flatly accused Chrétien of lying. Opposition parties demanded his resignation. Chrétien, testy and hurt, called the furore a "tempest in a teapot." "I said the truth," he asserted, his voice harsh with emotion. "I said what was in my mind, just the plain truth. There was no intent to mislead the House." Crosbie threw Shakespeare at him, quoting a line from *Macbeth* about "the fiend that lies like truth." There was no such thing as a half decision, Crosbie said. "You can't be half-pregnant. . . . You're either pregnant or not."

When the affair finally blew over, Chrétien was involved in an imbroglio over his efforts to change the Criminal Code to outlaw child pornography. The House's Justice Committee, as well as countless editorialists, criticized his recommendations as being poorly prepared and unconvincing. Where was the evidence of the extent of the problem, he was asked at a committee hearing? An angry Chrétien said he didn't have to see a truckload of child porn to know it existed. "You don't want to deal with it," he shouted. "If you want to have child pornography in every bloody store in the country, you vote for it." His fit of pique ended with his storming out of the committee chamber.

As Trudeau prepared to shuffle his cabinet, Chrétien hoped he might retake the reins at Finance or, failing that, move to External

Affairs. But Allan MacEachen was shifted from his recessionary budgets in Finance to External, and Marc Lalonde, sinking as fast in the Energy portfolio as the world oil prices, moved into Finance. That left a slew of lesser jobs, and after much to-ing and fro-ing, Chrétien reluctantly opted for the factious Energy post. This was a department that, in the view of the Alberta newspaper publisher Patrick O'Callaghan, "had ruthlessly wiped out a decade of Western progress." His was a widely held opinion. Chrétien, no stranger to controversy, had gone from Finance to the referendum to the constitution. Now he was putting on his fireman's suit again.

Westerners, deeply antagonistic towards Lalonde, expressed relief at Chrétien's appointment. He might not do much more than change a few lightbulbs, they reasoned, but he was more pro-business and easier to deal with than Canada's Cardinal Richelieu.

The western provinces had been through intense battles with Ottawa on energy pricing. Then came Lalonde's bolt of nationalist thunder, the National Energy Program (NEP), with its aim of increasing Canadians' control of their energy resources. The plan was conceived on the widely held premise that world oil prices would rise to eighty dollars a barrel. Instead they tumbled to thirty dollars. Investment dried up, and Albertans were left with deep holes in their pockets. The NEP's Canadianization measures took much of the blame.

Chrétien had been getting an earful on the NEP from his western friends and conservative cabinet colleagues. When he took the job, he told one of them, Ed Lumley, of his alarm over the growing animosity in the West. "We've got to back off on the NEP without destroying our credibility," Chrétien said.

Since he was viewed with suspicion by those on the Left of the party, Chrétien spread fears with his appointment that he was about to do his tough-guy act and scuttle the whole energy program. His first meeting with departmental bureaucrats, the people who had formulated the NEP and had a stake in maintaining it, did little to ease their concerns. His pointed questions made them feel like villains for ever having thought it up.

At this point in his career, Chrétien was feeling, as Eddie Goldenberg put it, "very comfortable" in the Sharp wing of the Liberal Party. Unlike the leftists, he felt the Sharp wing was realistic. On questions of nationalism, as in the case of the NEP, Chrétien drew a fine line. He saw himself as a great patriot but not a nationalist. Some saw no difference between the two, but Chrétien saw a significant one. Patriotism meant loving your own, he said; nationalism meant opposing others. It was a convenient comparison to draw because it allowed him to be neither Left nor Right, but hug the big Liberal middle. As a patriot, he could say he favoured the NEP's Canadianization goals. As a non-nationalist, as a supporter of open markets, he could oppose its protectionist elements.

Like those of most politicians, Chrétien's actions were dictated in large measure by the circumstances in which he found himself. By a coincidence of timing, he had stepped into cabinet positions throughout his career just when the circumstances demanded a conservative policy approach. He had come into the Treasury Board portfolio at the very time federal spending was going through the roof. He had come into Industry, Trade and Commerce when FIRA was under sustained attack and the pressure was to streamline it. In Finance, any desire he might have had to throw money at the nation's problems was circumscribed by the conditions of the time— growing debt and inflation. And now, with his arrival in Energy, the NEP was being vilified and a recessionary economy needed all the outside investment it could draw.

In all the circumstances he faced, bleeding-heart liberalism was never a viable option. But nor did Chrétien, the great middle man of Canadian politics, swing too far in the other direction.

Any possibility of a radical scaling-down of the NEP (it had already been cut back during Lalonde's term) was diminished by the broader political dynamic. Chrétien's department was solidly behind the program; its architect, Marc Lalonde, who now held the purse-strings in Finance, was prepared to fight for it; and the prime minister, while wishing to see some changes, did not want to back off too much.

Chrétien was but two weeks into his stewardship when, despite what he had said to Lumley, he announced that no substantial changes were necessary. The NEP "provides an excellent framework for the achievement of energy security." In modest gestures to oil companies, he promised to streamline the administration of the plan and to introduce longer-term export licences for Canadian natural gas in order to boost sales.

His first major initiative in Energy involved bailing out the oil-and-gas giant, Dome Petroleum Ltd. Dome had made many ill-timed investments, most when oil prices began to dive and interest rates started to rise. Chrétien was hesitant about stepping in. The West was already screaming over excessive government involvement in the resource sector. But Chrétien decided that if the giant were left to fall, the losses entailed—losses to subcontractors, to financial institutions, to Canada's presence in the industry—would be too severe to abide. At the same time, however, hundreds upon hundreds of small Canadian businesses were going bankrupt without any hope of assistance from Ottawa. Despite protests from more conservative ministers like Lumley, who for the first time disagreed with a major government policy at the cabinet table, Chrétien came forward with the bail-out gold.

He sided as well with the nationalist forces in maintaining an element of the NEP that was vociferously opposed by the Reagan administration. This was the notorious back-in provision, which allowed Ottawa to expropriate 25 per cent of producing fields on frontier lands. When the petro magnates, the heads of Sun Oil and Standard and Mobil, descended on Ottawa to protest the provision, they were sent packing. As an independent country, Chrétien told them, Canada had a right to make its own rules, rules in this instance he considered as fair as those anywhere else in the world. With Trudeau and Lalonde in the room, Chrétien would have been ill advised to take any other position. But he felt secure in stating the case strongly because of his experience in Indian Affairs and Northern Development. He was responsible for Crown lands in the North in those days, days when Ottawa had a much higher claim on producing fields than they would under the provisions of the NEP. Back then, Ottawa could take up to half of any oil or gas field without having to pay any compensation. Chrétien had been willing to work out a better arrangement for the oil industry in the 1970s, but no deal could be reached. In the 1980s, Chrétien reasoned, the 25 per cent figure was fair.

If he wasn't doing much to change actual energy policy in the early going, he was putting on his always effective charm offensive. With his change of style, he made the industry feel better. He didn't threaten westerners with intellectual superiority, he made fun of himself and others, and he showed a rough-and-tumble unaffectedness that was endearing. As the Calgary political scientist Roger Gibbons put it, Chrétien was the type of man who came across as a 1950s Quebec hockey player doing an interview with his teeth knocked out. Westerners loved those guys.

In the spring of 1983, he journeyed to the heart of ten-gallon-hat Tory country, Calgary, and drew a record 1,650 people to a chamber of commerce luncheon. He announced a policy change, a small decrease in the export price of gas, which in the eyes of industry experts was not nearly enough. But then he talked about his Alberta grandparents and trotted out his "Rockies" homilies and joked about Brian Mulroney's chin and Joe Clark's lack of one and as usual won big applause and warm reviews.

In the always contentious debate over oil pricing, he was able to thrash out a compromise. Alberta favoured matching the higher world tariff while other provinces, led by Ontario, naturally favoured a lower rate. Ottawa had maintained the price at about 75 per cent of the world mark, but as the world rate dipped through the early 1980s, Canada's, by definition, became proportionately higher. It got to 84 per cent of the world mark. Ottawa wanted to give consumers a break and roll it back to the 75 per cent level, but Alberta argued that existing agreements prohibited such a reduction. Chrétien authored a compromise wherein the possible roll-back was dropped in return for Alberta's pledge to forgo planned price hikes on natural gas. In case anyone in the East wanted to complain too loudly, Chrétien had his rebuttal ready. Didn't Canadians realize how lucky they were? Over the previous decade, because of government policies allowing Canadians to pay far less than the rest of the world for energy, they had saved no less than an astronomical $46 billion.

It was becoming customary for Chrétien, any time he felt public moaning was getting out of hand, to trot out his "Would you rather be in Chad?" speech. Canada, as he harshly put it, was a "society of bitchers" who didn't appreciate being number one in the world. Once, as he spoke in Ottawa to oil executives complaining about government policies, his sarcasm was undisguised. "I know it's getting tougher for a guy to make his third million," he told them. But "there are millions of people who would give the shirt off their backs to come to this country."

He railed against the attitude of western premiers who, in moping about sharing their resource bounty with the East, were always, as he saw it, putting the interests of their little corner of the country over the national interests. Where was the perspective, Chrétien wondered? What about the times when Ottawa had come to the aid of a crippled Alberta, such as during the Great Depression? Or when the Liberal Party had risked its neck and lost it in 1957 after pushing to build a natural-gas pipeline from the West to generate prosperity for the Prairies? Where was the love of country that his mother and father had shown? "We've not yet developed a sense of patriotism in Canada."

Coming as it did when unemployment was into double digits, when bankruptcies and plant closures were soaring, as were interest rates and the federal deficit, Chrétien's attack on the complainers was not greeted kindly. Editorialists tore into him. Chrétien shouldn't worry so much about the national air of gloom, har-rumphed the *Victoria Times-Colonist*. "He must realize that our grumpy condition isn't permanent, that a change of government would serve as a wonderful tonic."

His success in working out a pricing deal with Alberta couldn't be duplicated in the case of Newfoundland and offshore oil rights. One of the causes of the failure lay within Chrétien's own depart-ment. For the first time in his political career, he was having ongo-ing difficulties with his bureaucrats. Fifteen years earlier, Mitchell Sharp, who now headed the Northern Pipeline Agency and was in frequent contact with Chrétien on energy-related matters, had un-derlined the importance of building a close relationship with the deputies on down. Chrétien had followed the advice to the letter. But in Energy he came up against two deputy ministers, Mickey Cohen and Paul Tellier, who had deep stakes in the NEP, having both worked on its development, and who were wary of his plans for the program. Though some were moved out, several Lalonde loyalists remained in the department. Chrétien didn't help win them over by being quoted as saying that the department was in a mess when he took it over. When the Newfoundland matter came up, factions within Chrétien's department disagreed with his offer on the offshore resources. News of their dissent made its way to St. John's, imperilling the negotiations. Newfoundland, Chrétien complained, "used our disagreement as an excuse to walk away from the table, claiming that I wouldn't be able to deliver what I was promising." Though Chrétien would deny there was a major rift in the portfolio, relations with Lalonde soured through this period, hurting Chrétien's chances of gaining the backing of a major player in the Liberal leadership test to come.

Relations also soured, though in this case by choice, with the new leader of the Opposition, Brian Mulroney. The Tory leader harshly condemned the NEP, calling it a tax grab Ottawa was using to pay off its deficits. The retroactive clauses had led investors to lose faith in Canada, Mulroney said. He would end the discrimination against American and other foreign oil interests. Chrétien lashed back. If the government was profiteering, why was the Canadian industry share of energy revenues up since the pre-NEP days? "All Mr. Mulroney is trying to do is please his American friends in the big multinationals. I cannot help but think that the [former] president of Iron Ore was so happy to take his orders from Cleveland that as prime minister he would be happy taking his orders from Washington."

Mulroney gained entry to the Commons through a by-election in Nova Scotia. While mocking him for not running in his Quebec home, Chrétien suggested that next time, "who knows . . . he might be running in Florida." Unaware that there would come a day when he too would look to the Maritimes for a seat, Chrétien boasted that Canadians would never see him doing that. "The little guy from Shawinigan—he will run in Shawinigan!"

In Energy, Chrétien found himself having to do some of the government's dirty work. One of Ottawa's reasons for increasing the tax burden on outside investors under the NEP was to use the revenues to enlarge Canadian control of the energy sector. Unbeknownst to the public, however, the Trudeauites decided to funnel the money elsewhere. Chrétien was opposed to the double-dealing and, at a cabinet meeting, let his colleagues know how he felt about having to carry the load. Eugene Whelan, speaking a language that everyone could understand, blasted the policy. "Chrétien, this is shit! Everybody knows it's shit, and you know it's shit!"

With an equal degree of scatological fervour, Chrétien replied, "Yeah, it's shit. I know it's shit. And you know what happens when there's shit. They say, 'Hey, Jean, here's the shovel.'"

His activities in the Energy portfolio were often overshadowed by speculation over his leadership ambitions. Some of his thoughts were inadvertently made public in January 1983, when he met with a group of American politicians in Ottawa. It was a behind-closed-

doors session, but one of the doors was accidentally left open. A
Canadian Press reporter happened to be close by, tape recorder
rolling. Chrétien was heard asserting that the tradition of alternating French and English leaders in the Liberal Party was no tradition at all. It was more the "luck of history" than formal design.
But it would hurt him. "I'm born on the wrong side of the river. If
my name was John Christian and I was born in Ontario, I'd have a
chance." John Turner, he insisted, would have his own problems.
He'd been so long on the sidelines that Liberals would surely say,
"When we needed him, he was not there."

By late 1983, speculation over Trudeau's departure and the leadership battle to follow had become intense. Chrétien was being
urged once again to lead the Quebec Liberals, who were looking
for a replacement for Claude Ryan. He attacked Robert Bourassa,
who was making a comeback from the self-imposed exile that had
followed his 1976 defeat, for being wishy-washy on federalism.
"Personally, I don't like fence-sitters," he said. But he had no hesitation in spurning the provincial overtures. His sights were clearly
set on the bigger prize, one for which he was actively lining up
support. He became so busy behind the scenes that an irritated
Trudeau finally took him aside, telling him, "Jean, be careful." In
October, Ron Irwin, an Ontario MP, announced that he had lined
up forty-seven MPs in support of a Chrétien bid. Louis Duclos, an
MP in the Turner camp, said that he had a similar number supporting his candidate.

The early line from media pundits didn't augur well. They were
already writing that Jean Chrétien was number one in their hearts,
but number two in the leadership race. He had maintained positive
relations with the anglophone journalists throughout the years.
Among the Liberal flock, they considered him the most honest, the
most experienced, the most liked, the best salesman, the hardest
worker. But they didn't think he could win. Allan Fotheringham
was bluntly prescient: "Jean Chrétien has no chance of succeeding
Pierre Trudeau as leader of the Liberal Party." Hugh Segal, a Tory

strategist, applauded Chrétien in the *Toronto Star*, describing him as a conciliatory, honest, experienced man with true Liberal values. But the Tories need not worry, Segal predicted, because the Grits will "go to a candidate with little or no heart and less humanity. If today's Liberals had the courage to make the right choice, they would not be today's Liberals. They would be the kind of Liberals for whom cooperative federalism, regional conciliation, and social conscience once again meant something."

Despite Chrétien's popularity, his experience, and his good record, early opinion polls showed John Turner the preferred choice by a healthy margin. Even in Chrétien's home province, Turner had a good lead. Chrétien would need Quebec, but it was here that his long warring history with the sovereigntists and the establishment could come back to haunt him. These leadership tests were still, in large measure, ruled by the elite, and the elite of Quebec did not like Jean Chrétien.

If he needed evidence of the latter, he had only to compare the press he received in his home province with that of the rest of the country. If his fractured English and fractured French played well with anglophones, helping him look genuine, inside Quebec it often had the opposite effect. Lise Bissonnette, the editor of *Le Devoir*, summed up the attitude of many in the province. "English Canada likes him because that's how it wants to see us," she said. "Mr. Chrétien's very language, this deliberate *franglais*, which isn't even *joual*, indicates clearly to his compatriots the extent of the contempt he feels for them, how he would like to see them forever confined to the past. . . . He has, with stupefying success, been parading around English Canada doing this number of the ill-spoken vulgar Quebecker, the happy slave who asks his master for more punishment."

Bissonnette was joined in her analysis by Lysiane Gagnon, the outstanding columnist for *La Presse*. She bristled at his inarticulateness and intellectual vapidity. Compared with Trudeau, Chrétien was, in her opinion, almost devoid of depth and therefore totally uninteresting. She leaned to the view that worthiness as a political leader required erudition and articulation. She also thought it fraudulent that Chrétien passed himself off as "the little guy," while at the same time maintaining cosy connections with the Power Corporation and living an upper-class lifestyle.

Through the years, Gagnon would be so persistent and repetitive in her attacks that some of her English-Canadian colleagues would become disappointed with this obsessive aspect of her work. Chrétien traced his problems with her to a personal confrontation that occurred at an editorial board meeting of her newspaper when he was Energy minister. Chrétien told friends that during the meeting, Gagnon had the nerve to ask him, "Do you really think you have the class to be prime minister?" Infuriated, Chrétien held his fire until after the meeting. Then he went at her, telling her that she was "nothing but a goddamn snob from Outremont." Gagnon denied the incident ever happened. She recalled an editorial board session and an interview with him, but she said he was always civil. Besides, she said, "I've never lived in Outremont."

Claude Ryan observed that in Quebec there was "a certain arrogance of the metropolitan media, a false intellectualism at times." He knew that Chrétien was highly sensitive on the subject but, while sympathetic, thought he provoked, to some degree, the treatment he received. The speeches in English Canada portraying Quebeckers as pea-soupers, said Ryan, "were a bit hard to swallow, and he has had to take the brunt for that." With Ryan, as with many others, Chrétien was anxious to show he was no lightweight. Chrétien had once phoned him after he noticed that Ryan had said some kind words about Ottawa's most recent judicial appointments. He thanked Ryan and reminded him that two of the three new judges were from his own region of La Mauricie. He added that it was he, Chrétien, who had put the names forward and lobbied for them. Then came the real point of the phone call. "Not so bad," said Chrétien, "for a man who's supposedly not very bright."

Bissonnette and Gagnon wielded substantial influence over public opinion in Quebec. Chrétien was stung by their criticisms, as were family members and friends, one of whom labelled them "the snob sisters." Especially aggravating for his supporters was the frequency of the attacks. They agreed, however, that his French was often deplorable. They had been after Jean for decades about this, warning him that he had better be more careful. His written French was grammatically perfect, and they sensed he could speak much better if he tried harder. "But you know Jean," said Françoise Chrétien, Gabriel's wife. "Whether we love him or not, he's a stronghead. If he thinks he's right and he likes it, you won't change him one bit. He found he was liked by the people the way he was and he said, 'Why should I change myself?' It was like a show he was putting on. He knew he wasn't expressing himself well, but he would keep on doing it. Then he got more popular and said, 'Well, there's more people liking my style than criticizing it.' He almost took pleasure in being criticized for it, then winning in the end."

Chrétien defended his style, once saying that politics is "the art of communications, and I make myself understood. I'm a populist." The guys in the taverns weren't fools; nor, he said, was he a fool for communicating with them. By maintaining his factory style of speaking, he was able to stay close to his roots. "I could have become a snob and talked *à la française*," said Chrétien. "I didn't want to. I wanted to remain what I am. You know, I'm not faking with anybody. My tactic is not to fake. It's easy to put some mascara over the body. But I want the people to know who I am."

The interesting thing about Quebec, Chrétien observed, is that "there is a big, big gap between the intellectuals and the people. The intellectuals live in an unreal world, and I am very happy they don't consider me as one of their friends."

For the coming leadership convention, however, he would have been happy to have a few friends in that group.

CHAPTER EIGHTEEN

A MAN
BETRAYED

N o one had to tell Jean Chrétien what a vicious game
politics could be. He'd had a couple of decades to learn
that. He had seen a lot. Still, he never realized there were
so many snakes in the grass until he made his bid for the leadership
of the party in 1984.

He said once that you never make friends in politics, only acquaintances. It was a game of alliance building. Sometimes a rapport could be built over a number of years and have the look of
something enduring. But then the reality of the "whole goddamn
cheap game," as one of his friends put it, would hit like a hurricane, smashing whatever had been built to rubble.

Jean Chrétien and John Turner had gotten along so well. There
was mutual respect. In 1974 Turner had travelled to Cornwall,
Ontario, to meet the incessantly cheerful mayor of that smelly
town on the St. Lawrence, Ed Lumley. Turner wanted to convince
Lumley to run for the Grits in the next election. In the course of
their conversation, he mentioned what a great, hard-nosed cabinet
minister the Liberals had in Jean Chrétien.

When Turner quit politics little more than a year later, Chrétien
was one of those who stood behind his decision. Not long after
that, Chrétien read a quote from Turner saying Chrétien was one
of the best ministers anywhere. The relationship remained solid

until the fall of 1978, when the hurricane hit, when Turner released the newsletters criticizing Chrétien's performance as minister of Finance. Lumley, by then Chrétien's parliamentary secretary, saw him after he got the news. He was burning with anger.

Early in 1979, the Liberals brought together all their former Finance ministers to attend a speech by Chrétien in Ottawa. Hoping to use this as a forum for reconciliation, Lumley got Turner to meet with Chrétien in a hotel room afterwards. During their talk, Lumley sensed that Turner was apologetic, but Chrétien never got that feeling. Besides, any private expressions of regret couldn't make up for the public damage. Chrétien's resentment simmered, and by the time the leadership convention began, he looked on Turner with an attitude approaching disdain. The repercussions of the downturn in the relationship, for both Chrétien's own peace of mind and that of his party, were grave.

In laying the groundwork to succeed Trudeau, Chrétien was naturally trying to gather all the support he could. One minister he was certain he could rely on was Lumley. Good old back-slapping Ed was angry at Turner and had come to be a good friend of Chrétien's. He enjoyed working for him in Finance because Chrétien involved him in everything—just as Sharp had once done for an ambitious MP from Shawinigan.

Out of the office, they played golf. On a couple of occasions they had teamed up with two men from the Power Corporation: John Rae, who after leaving Indian Affairs had become a fixture there, and Paul Martin Jr., who was a rising star on many fronts, though not on the fairways. By this time, Lumley learned, Chrétien's connections with Power were thick. Rae was still a close confidant; France, Chrétien's daughter, would soon marry André Desmarais, the son of Power's chief executive; and Chrétien's own friendship with the chief, Paul Desmarais, was growing. They had met in the late 1960s through a mutual acquaintance, the lawyer Pierre Genest. Genest had worked for Mitchell Sharp on several political campaigns and subsequently did legal work for Chrétien. Chrétien loved the man and so did Desmarais, a former school friend.

The golfing outings were rushed affairs. Chrétien rarely had time for post-game drinks or dinner. He'd finish the round, rush off for a visit to his ailing father, and eat in the car on the way back to Ottawa. He and Lumley barely survived the return trip once. They were speeding down the highway when a car, which was in their lane, came at them at a screaming speed. Chrétien and Lumley thought it was over. The car missed them by a fraction.

When Chrétien first prepared to make a leadership bid in 1979, Lumley signed up as one of his campaign directors. When Lumley became a cabinet minister under Trudeau, he hired Chrétien's son Hubert to work in his office. When talk of another leadership race began, Lumley helped plot strategy with Goldenberg and Chrétien.

It was assumed, it was a given, that when an official race began, Lumley would be at the head of the line, waving the Chrétien banner. Nothing had prepared Chrétien for what followed, for the day good old back-slapping Ed appeared at his door with some interesting news. He had decided, he told his friend, to support John Turner. He had decided, he explained, that the country wasn't ready for another francophone leader.

Chrétien was staggered. He was a politician who cherished loyalty. Lumley, who had seen him cut down so many times in Finance, knew this. He tried to soften the blow by saying that he wasn't going to work hard for Turner, that he would just support him quietly. Chrétien couldn't abide that. "For Christ's sake," he said, "if you're going to support the guy, work hard for him. Don't double-cross him like you've double-crossed me!" Their meeting lasted a wretched three hours. Lumley felt "guilty" when he told Chrétien of his decision, he felt guilty throughout the campaign, and he felt guilty thereafter. "It was a mistake."

Although Lumley was important in that he would have helped bolster Chrétien's support from the business community, he was not a critical loss. It was a desertion Chrétien could survive, especially if he held on to his other expected supporters. But the shocks weren't over; Lumley was merely a sign of what was to come. Chrétien soon found out that the town was full of Ed Lumleys, men he had worked hard for, men who had watched him sell the party the way no other Grit could, men who were now turning their backs and fleeing. Chrétien's leadership campaign became a story straight out of Shakespeare's book, one tableau of grief and wormwood following on another until it was too late.

Labour minister André Ouellet, a powerful Liberal who was forever lurking in the shadows of power, had been a good friend to Chrétien over the years. Their wives also shared a close relationship. The four often dined together and were present at each other's important family occasions. Ouellet was a critical force in the leadership campaign because he, along with Marc Lalonde, controlled the party machine in Quebec. Because of this, because challenging Ouellet's wishes meant severing profitable Liberal ties, Ouellet was capable of influencing literally hundreds of Quebec's 850 voting delegates. Chrétien needed a big block of Quebec delegates, maybe three-quarters of them, to win. He needed Ouellet.

As well as being close friends with the Labour minister, Chrétien was also the only francophone in the race, another plus. But what really mattered was that Chrétien had Ouellet's word. In January, only a month before Trudeau's resignation, the two of them went skiing together. Ouellet told Chrétien that he didn't think he had too much chance of winning. But he advised him not to worry. "I will be with you."

A few weeks later, just before John Turner officially declared his candidacy, Ouellet appeared at Chrétien's door. He told Chrétien that he didn't think he should enter the race. He would only be hurt. He added, watching as the blood drained from Chrétien's face, that he would be supporting John Turner.

The other Quebec kingpin was Lalonde. Chrétien had crossed swords with him while in the Energy portfolio. But Chrétien also knew that Lalonde did not have a high opinion of John Turner. In a choice between him and Turner, he was confident the Iceman would come to him. If not, he expected him to stay neutral.

The confidence lasted until the day Lalonde declared that this wasn't the time for another francophone leader of the Liberal Party. Newspapers quoted him as saying that given two equal candidates, delegates should choose the anglophone. His remarks, which he claimed were exaggerated by the media, were seen as a wholehearted endorsement of *alternance*—and of John Turner.

Chrétien was so discouraged that he was ready to disavow his intention to run. Mitchell Sharp was advising him that if the Quebec establishment wasn't with him, it was no use. Chrétien met with Trudeau and told the prime minister he had been shafted and would not enter the race. Trudeau told him to hold off; he had something to say. He then went to a caucus meeting, where he declared, "If alternation is everything, then I don't belong here as prime minister. I thought I was selected because I was good, not because I was French."

Yet another friend appeared at Chrétien's door, another person he had counted on having in his corner. He was Judd Buchanan, his parliamentary secretary for four years in Indian Affairs. Buchanan was no longer in the caucus but was still an executive in the party. "I'm sorry, Jean," Buchanan told Chrétien. "I really feel that if we are going to rebuild the Liberal Party in western Canada, John Turner can make a more effective contribution in that regard." Buchanan had witnessed and been amazed by Chrétien's ability to bring western audiences to their feet—even the businessmen of the oil patch—but he too was caught up in the Turner mystique. Chrétien told him that he was wrong, that he was the man to build the party in the West, but Buchanan had made up his mind. In short order, he would determine that he too had made a terrible mistake. But having committed to Turner, he felt he couldn't change boats halfway across the river.

Chrétien, who had been in cabinet for sixteen years, was unable to get one senior minister to support him. Of the entire cabinet, only three unknowns came his way—Pierre Buissères, Charles Lapointe, Pierre DeBané.

"I had collected some IOUs," Chrétien explained, but when "I went to collect, they were not there. These are people who told me, 'Jean, when you need me, I'll be there.'" Their decisions had nothing to do with believing Turner was the better candidate, thought Chrétien. It was simply a matter of them spotting the winner and scurrying, like rats up a drain pipe, to be with him. "You know what it is?" said Chrétien. "They're saving their own asses. They don't love the man [Turner]. They love power."

Chrétien was starting the race with a huge disadvantage. The way the cabinet turned was always a signal for the way the party establishment turned. The delegates to the convention would include close to one thousand members of this party establishment, delegates not elected in ridings but there by virtue of their ties to the party. They represented almost a third of all the delegates who would elect the new Liberal leader.

Everything was turning against the Chrétien candidacy. On the day in February that Trudeau resigned, the CBC's *The National* and its newsmagazine, *The Journal*, correctly anticipated huge audience numbers. The shows would be viewed by almost every important Liberal in the country. The news hour included a retrospective on Trudeau, with Chrétien sitting in on a panel discussion and providing his reminiscences. Having put away the old leader, "The Journal," with its thumping, portentous air, then followed with what had the look of a coronation of the new one—the prince-in-waiting, John Napier Turner. The segment on him was laudatory, anticipatory. The message was unmistakable. He was the front runner, he was the odds-on favourite, the crown was his to claim. Hugh Winsor, the seasoned veteran who prepared the piece, maintained, on good grounds, that he was only reflecting the reality of the situation. But it wasn't so much the content of the report as its immediacy and its timing that was important. Had the producers waited for Trudeau to be put to rest, and then given equal time to Chrétien and Turner, Chrétien backers felt that it would have made a difference. But aired as it was, the show hurt Chrétien badly. Watching the piece progress, he envisaged delegates reaching for Turner. At show's end, he had his proof. "I saw the effect immediately when one MP who was on the panel with me declared for Turner as soon as he saw the documentary."

As the dice rolled against him, as kingmakers and friends turned their backs, Chrétien felt alone. Even his trusted lieutenant, Eddie Goldenberg, told him a victory was probably not in the cards. John Rae, slated to be his campaign manager, launched a ten-day survey to see if a credible campaign could even be mounted. He reported back that even though he was up against a juggernaut, he could make a strong run. Chrétien's decision to enter was ultimately made easier because he believed that he deserved the leadership, that he had done more for the party than Turner, that he was the better man. He also thought that this could be his last chance. He was only fifty, but Liberal Party leaders did not come and go quickly. The great ones—Laurier, King, Trudeau—stayed, on average, more than two decades each.

By this time, Trudeau had fallen into considerable disfavour. The predominant feeling among Liberals was that not only a new face but also a new direction was needed if the party was to have any chance in the next election. As Trudeau's long-time workhorse, Chrétien was tied to the old face and the old direction. His style was different from Trudeau's, but his beliefs were much the same. He was the continuity candidate.

His campaign team debated at length the wisdom of distancing him from the prime minister. But Chrétien was not prepared to part with the old Liberalism. "He made a calculated gamble," recalled Goldenberg. Chrétien told Goldenberg and others, "I cannot say I've been with Mr. Trudeau for sixteen years and disagree with what he did. It would make no sense. Nobody would believe it. They would say, 'What type of person are you?' Not only that, but I agree with what I've been associated with."

With no fresh agenda, Chrétien had nothing to run on except the gutsy stuff that got him there—plain talk and patriotism and raw force. "Hang on to your seatbelts," he told his allies. "We're in for a hell of a ride."

He got some help from Turner, who was error-prone and robotic. Having tripped up at the beginning of the campaign on the question of minority-language rights, suggesting they were a provincial responsibility, Turner had to issue several statements of clarification. In the House of Commons, Chrétien seized the opportunity. Asked for his reaction to another remark by Turner, he paused, then asserted, "I will wait for the clarification." Trudeau, quietly hoping for a Chrétien victory, was sitting beside him. He buckled over with laughter.

Turner wanted, perhaps wisely so, to slash the budget deficit. But Chrétien replied that as long as there was high unemployment and little growth, "We have to use the deficit to keep the dignity of our people." A swing to the Right would be disastrous for the party, he said. It needed a leader "who reflects Main Street, not Bay Street." For years, Turner had lunched at Winston's, a stuffy businessmen's restaurant in Toronto. Chrétien mocked him for it. "You know," he said, "Toronto has changed a lot. When I came the first time, Winston's was a cigarette. Eventually, it became a restaurant. Now it is a riding without delegates." As the lunch-bucket candidate—even though the friendly Power Corporation was contributing to his campaign—he enjoyed painting Turner as part of the beau monde. "I'm not an elitist," said Chrétien. "I don't use the word 'new' every second phrase like one candidate. You know, he's still wearing garter belts."

Turner played right into his hands by appearing to be out of touch. After laying out in detail his deficit-cutting package in Quebec, he came to Ottawa and snapped at demanding reporters. "I spent fifteen minutes in Quebec City with the national media describing exactly what I had in mind, and I'm not able to shorten that to two minutes." But in the sound-bite world of shortened attention spans, what couldn't be reduced to two minutes? Chrétien was bowled over by the comment. Two minutes was all he ever took.

He had once been impressed by Turner, much as he had been impressed and intellectually intimidated by Lalonde, Trudeau, MacEachen, and the rest. As a small-town lawyer, he accorded them due respect. But with his successes, his feeling of inferiority had gradually disappeared. He realized he was as good as anyone else. As the campaign wore on and he gathered support, his self-esteem grew. In most of the all-candidates' debates, he clearly out-performed Turner. Polls showed him gaining ground. The media began to portray him as the people's choice and very likely the best choice. Yet, to Chrétien's dismay, despite all the momentum coming from the party's grass roots, the party establishment still held out. It still clung to the mystique of John Turner.

Although he was gaining on his opponent, Chrétien was making his own mistakes. One came when he confirmed, as opposed to just leaving the question in the realm of the hypothetical, that he would be prepared to serve in a Turner government. He later tried to back-pedal on the remark, but he couldn't get all the way back and left himself open for a deft and, in Chrétien's view, devastating Turner ploy that would come on the day of the convention.

Another mistake was his failure to present any new ideas. He was not endorsed by the Quebec elite partly because of a perception that he lacked depth and a capacity for innovation. Although he had spent sixteen years in the cabinet, serving successfully in so many portfolios, the perception wouldn't go away. Nor would Chrétien do much to dispel it. The journalist Richard Gwyn detected throughout Chrétien's career an absence of original thought. Gwyn badgered him in an interview to name just one new policy or program or administrative process he, as leader, would change from the Trudeau years. Chrétien was unable to come up with one.

All he had was old stuff. Some could well wonder if all those years, in all those portfolios, wrestling down all those crises had left him any time to think for himself; if, in fact, he had anything to offer besides boilerplate.

Years after the madness of his cabinet days and his campaigning days were over, Chrétien bumped into Judd Buchanan. Despite the rift that had developed between them during the leadership campaign, they maintained good relations. They chatted briefly, then Chrétien said, "Buchanan, I feel better now. I'm not hurling myself all around the country like I used to. As you know, I would speak at every damn fund-raising dinner for everybody. Now you don't see those big black rings under my eyes any more. I sit now and I think about things more—and think things through."

For the purposes of his campaign, root Canadian values were enough. He'd win it on those and on spirit. He'd win it on the politics of joy. "A leader," Chrétien said, "is someone who gets the people to go with him on a mission to do better for their country. I think I am the man to do that."

As the convention neared, he clung to the hope that he would receive an eleventh-hour lift, as Trudeau had in 1968 when Mitchell Sharp joined him. Chrétien eyed Allan MacEachen, who had ostensibly remained neutral. MacEachen was sphinxlike to begin with. Few knew what lurked in that Cape Breton soul. Chrétien had been tracking him since day one through a special link, Patrick Lavelle. Lavelle had been the executive assistant to MacEachen in the 1960s and had worked on his forlorn leadership bid in 1968. Lavelle was surprised at how difficult it had been for MacEachen to absorb that defeat. It was as if he hadn't seen it coming, as if it hadn't been screamingly obvious well before the vote. The experience made Lavelle worry about what leadership races did to people.

Lavelle became a good friend to Chrétien. When he was president of the Automotive Parts Manufacturing Association in the mid-seventies, he wrote Chrétien a letter saying he should become the leader of the Liberal Party. He was one of the first to push him on this idea; it endeared him to Chrétien and they stayed in close touch thereafter. When Chrétien was Finance minister, Lavelle peppered him with memos full of gratuitous advice. As the representative of the Ontario government in Paris, Lavelle hosted Chrétien on several trips to France. They enjoyed good wines and good food and pointed political talk. Lavelle, like many others who knew him well, found Chrétien a detached man. Although he liked being close to people, he was independent of them. He had hundreds of friends, but he wasn't a conscious alliance-builder, a schmoozer who systematically went about securing support.

During the leadership campaign, Lavelle became Chrétien's Ontario campaign manager. But Chrétien always greeted him with the same question: "What's going on with MacEachen?" Lavelle spent fruitless hours with the Grits' Maritimes dean trying to find the answer. In the days before the convention, Chrétien dispatched him to MacEachen's home. As if that weren't enough, he went a step further, phoning Lavelle while he was there to give him negotiating instructions.

Lavelle came out of that meeting puzzled but sensing that MacEachen was preparing to go the other way, that he believed, whether it was an accident of history or not, in *alternance*. He tried to tell Chrétien to prepare for the worst, but Chrétien didn't appear to believe him.

Then, in the glare of the convention, when the big moment came, when MacEachen got up and moved to Turner in a very public way, Lavelle felt a chill come over him. He looked over at his candidate's box, where he could see Chrétien's dim grey eyes, fixed in a cold and ghastly stare, aimed right at him. Chrétien held the stare for the longest time. It was the most withering look Lavelle had ever received from anyone.

When the convention was over, Lavelle got the first plane out of town. Knowing what these events did to people, he had planned his escape in advance and was happy he did. But the image of that horrible gaze would come back to him time and again. He could escape town, but he could never escape the stare.

When the day before the vote arrived, the day of the speeches, Chrétien's momentum had unfortunately prompted him into believing he could win. He had prided himself on being a realist, on keeping one eye outside Ottawa. If there was a politician capable of seeing beyond the hype, it was probably Chrétien. But such are the extraordinary dynamics of leadership races that even he was now losing perspective. The hard facts of the situation still had Turner well in front, but the hard facts weren't clear to the little guy from Shawinigan. They were buried under a heap of emotion and hype and past history that told him that he, the underdog, always triumphed.

He was desperately hoping to show Ouellet and the other turncoats that he could win without them. He was asked late in the race if he would have a place for people like Ouellet in his cabinet. He didn't answer directly but, of those who abandoned him, said, "I'm in the process of proving that I don't need them. They perhaps thought that they were bigger than they really are."

Only the keynote speeches remained. Thought to be the better speaker, Chrétien was expected to gather important support among the undecideds. John Rae, knowing an old-fashioned Chrétien stemwinder might pay off handsomely, had been urging him to speak without a text. At the convention policy sessions, Chrétien's extemporizing was a hit. He told youth delegates to "Raise hell and shake up the world. If you're not a radical at twenty, you're a Tory at twenty-five." Everyone assumed he would go without a text. Everyone, Chrétien most of all, knew he was better without one. With a script in his hand, he sometimes missed words entirely, or mispronounced them, or stopped and had to focus for a few seconds to get it right.

There was an explanation for this. Chrétien had a special problem that he never talked about and that explained, at least in part, the inarticulateness for which he was so often derided. Dyslexia, a handicap that inhibits comprehension, ran in the Chrétien family. Hubert had it, as did one of Gabriel's grandsons. Jean's brother Michel had a problem related to dyslexia, and it was clear to family members and some friends that Jean had a form of it as well. In his case and that of Michel, the affliction, as diagnosed by Maurice, was dyslalia. While dyslexia applied to problems of comprehension, dyslalia was the term for unusual difficulties in articulating certain sounds. "This is why Jean has trouble," said Maurice. "He can't control a few things. Sometimes he will hesitate on a long word. He won't be able to pronounce the whole word. Sometimes he'll say a word twice, and twice he won't be right. This is part of dyslalia."

Jean didn't dispute having an unusual problem. "Sometimes I stumble on a word," he acknowledged. The senator Philippe Gigantes drew his attention to the problem once, he recalled, but he never considered it serious enough to seek medical assistance or undergo therapy.

Having discussed the convention speech repeatedly with Chrétien in walks along the Ottawa Canal, John Rae thought they had an understanding. Chrétien would speak from the gut. The day before the speech, however, Rae went into Chrétien's office and saw him reading from a prepared text. "I thought we were going to do it differently," Rae said.

"I know the way I want to do it," Chrétien responded.

Instead of a grammar-murdering, endearingly earthy stem-winder, Chrétien gave a restrained conventional performance, a no-risk effort at a time when every risk had to be taken.

Rae returned to his hotel, got in the elevator, and there stood the great Grit, the dean of election campaigns, Keith Davey. Davey, having made a decision he would come to regret, was supporting Turner. For the moment, though, he was a happy man. "John," he said, "why did you put that text in his hand?"

The next morning, voting day, Chrétien arrived at the Ottawa Civic Centre to be greeted by signs and literature put out by the

Turner people. "Buy one, get one free" they said. The message was that by voting Turner, the delegates got Chrétien too. He had confirmed that he would stay on to serve in a Turner government. Turner, on the other hand, would be lost to the party if Chrétien won. Chrétien's heart sank when he saw the signs. His seasoned political instincts told him it was over. He sadly passed on his feelings to Aline.

The Turner camp had set the worry barrier at 1,250 votes. If Chrétien got that many, then picked up support from other candidates, he might make up enough ground to win. Chrétien's team had a similar estimate. But the 1,067 votes Chrétien eventually received, 526 behind Turner, was 183 short of the magic number. Three of the other candidates, Eugene Whelan, John Munro, and John Roberts, dropped out after the first ballot and streamed to Chrétien. But Turner was too close. The fight was over. Party president Iona Campagnolo issued the memorable declaration that Jean Chrétien was number one "in our hearts." But it was little solace for the candidate. The hearts had lost.

He sat in the stands, surrounded by the clan, thirty or so brothers, sisters, relatives. They were always a unified group, free of rivalries or petty jealousies towards Jean and very much glued to his cause. From their ranks now poured torrents of emotion, some like Jean's sister Giselle and brother Guy unable to hold back the tears. The clan had mobilized for this campaign unlike any other, knocking on the doors of seven hundred Quebec delegates.

Crestfallen, the losing candidate turned to his wife and hugged her. But not even the gallant Aline, his wellspring of resolve, could forestall the spiral of descent into which he now plunged. A long period of sustained bitterness and gloom awaited him, a period that few would have thought possible. He had been a resilient man.

The defeat was a combination of *alternance*, of the media's early anointment of Turner, of Chrétien's being viewed as the candidate of continuity when voters wanted change, and of his rejection by the party's Quebec establishment.

This last was what pained Chrétien the most, in particular because of what he saw as the traitorous behaviour of the one man he felt was most responsible for it. Chrétien had won the outside fight, the fight for elected delegates across the country, but he had badly lost the inside fight, the fight for the votes of the party's ruling class. In a sense, the leadership race had been a class struggle, and the underclass had lost. John Rae, a cautious and conservative man in his pronouncements, did some tabulations when it was over and concluded that if Chrétien had had only a fraction of the party establishment behind him, he would have won.

The loss of Ouellet and Lalonde was of great significance. Chrétien and Turner had a rough split of the Quebec delegates, but because it was his home ground, Chrétien needed more than a split. The two hundred extra votes that he needed on the first ballot (a swing of one hundred from Turner to Chrétien would have made up that number) were in the hands of André Ouellet. The support of Ouellet alone at the beginning of the campaign would have moved more than that amount into his camp.

If the outcome could be put down to one man, if one man could be said to have changed the political course of the nation, it was Chrétien's friend Ouellet. Chrétien could understand, although with some difficulty, that many in the party's ruling echelon, men like Lalonde, Pepin, and Francis Fox, did not want to come his way. But he couldn't countenance desertion by a friend. For Ouellet, he reserved his deepest disdain.

No one was proud of the way Jean Chrétien behaved after the convention. With everyone coming to him, pouring out their sympathies, saying he deserved to win, he became convinced that a grave injustice had been perpetrated. His supporters thought he should have returned home, left the scene of the crime, instead of sitting around the capital sulking and waiting for calls from Turner. But Chrétien didn't want to leave. He had a score to settle with the conspirators—the Quebec party machine. Ironically, in the mid-seventies Trudeau had given him the opportunity to become boss of it himself. Had he accepted, his leadership bid might have been easier. But he turned the position down because his own experiences in Shawinigan had given him a distaste for that side of politics, the world of sinecures and spoils and pork-barrelling.

Having been beaten up by the machine once, he now wanted to control it so it wouldn't happen again. Turner was prepared to give him any cabinet position he wanted, as well as the post of deputy prime minister. But Chrétien made more extravagant demands. He also wanted to become party boss in Quebec and he wanted safe havens—cabinet appointments or other sinecures—for his key supporters in the campaign. Turner was put in an extremely delicate position. Ouellet and Lalonde had been invaluable to his victory. He could not turn around and say to them that now that you have knocked off Jean Chrétien for me, I am going to wrest control of the machine from you and put Chrétien in charge. On the other hand, he could not be seen to deny the extremely popular Chrétien his wishes. As polls confirmed, he was the most popular Liberal in Quebec, if not the entire country.

Negotiations between the two men continued over several difficult meetings. The situation had not been helped when, the day after the convention, Turner's office had called to say that the new Liberal leader wished to speak to Mr. Chrétien. Chrétien got on the line and then had to wait twenty minutes before Turner came on. If it was unintentional, as was likely the case, it was an indication of Turner's organizational folly, which would be painfully evident during the election campaign and for the better part of his besieged stewardship of the party.

Throughout the negotiations, Chrétien was blunt. "You owe me Quebec," he told Turner. "I can't be number two in Canada and number three [behind Ouellet and Lalonde] in Quebec." A compromise was ultimately worked out. Chrétien would become minister of External Affairs, deputy prime minister, and general overseer of a three-man group, including Ouellet and Charles Lapointe, in control of Quebec. The arrangement satisfied him temporarily and he made plans to get away. In conjunction with his new duties in External Affairs, he would travel to Southeast Asia, where he would try to get his mind off the biggest set-back of his life.

In some respects, the failed campaign had been good for Chrétien. His popularity and standing throughout the country had increased. He had reaffirmed his populism. He had won what many were describing as a moral victory. Had he not entered the race, he could well have come to be viewed as a relic of the Trudeau era, much like MacEachen, Lalonde, Pepin, and others. Instead, he had become the pre-eminent Quebecker in the party, as well as the presumed leader-in-waiting.

Despite all this, the pain of defeat would not wear off. His friends reported never having seen Chrétien so distraught, so bitter, so anguished. One night the family got together over dinner to do a post-mortem. Maurice, now in his mid-seventies, was there. He was the one who had shaken some sense into Jean when he was a boy; he had got him reinstated in school and had set an example for him. Probably the toughest of the Chrétiens, Maurice had a backbone of iron. But Jean's loss shook him badly. During the dinner, asking how it could have happened, he covered his face with both hands.

Jean was at the dinner. He had come to Shawinigan briefly in the middle of his negotiations with the Turner people. He and Aline drove into Belgoville and stopped at the home of his old neighbour and close boyhood companion, Yvon Boisvert. As teenagers, Jean and Yvon had gone to Trois-Rivières to watch the great orators speak, and Jean had dreamed of being able to move crowds the way they did.

Boisvert was the only one of Jean's old rue Biermans gang who still lived there. The others had gone on to become factory workers, private contractors, or bus drivers. It was just as Wellie Chrétien had predicted. Without the classical college education that he had forced on Jean, the road was narrow.

Boisvert knew from experience how losing affected Jean. He knew that with Chrétien, "you had to win." But he still wasn't prepared for the "pain in the extreme" that he saw in the face of his old friend when he came through the door with Aline.

Chrétien sat on Boisvert's couch and told him what had happened, how unfair it all had been. He prided himself on being tough in the hardest of times. Commandants were supposed to be resolute. But it wasn't long after he sat down in Boisvert's modest living room that the tears welled up in his eyes.

"Listen closely, Jean," Boisvert told him. "It was not your turn this time. The tradition is *alternance*. It was Turner's time. Next time it will be yours."

Aline interrupted. She was inconsolable, as heartsick as her husband. "But Jean is the best," she kept saying. "Jean is the best."

CHAPTER NINETEEN

STRATEGIC
RETREAT

W HEN THE WARRING between the two men temporarily subsided and an election loomed, Chrétien
weighed in against the majority opinion. His instincts
told him that Turner should put off going to the polls until the
spring of 1985. He felt that the new leader had to provide evidence
of a new direction. Patience would improve his chances. Turner
listened attentively, but conventional wisdom suggested his momentum coming out of the convention could hold.

The election call came while Chrétien was on his official tour
of Southeast Asia. He returned, beaten down by thirty-six straight
hours of sleepless travel and suffering from the disease of the local
water. He put off some scheduled appearances and rested a few
days at his cottage, drinking beer to put some weight back on.
Then he was back into the fray, campaigning for a leader he hoped
would lose. A drubbing of Turner would vindicate Chrétien, proving that the party establishment had been so wrong, proving that it
had made, in the words of Jeffrey Simpson, a "monumental miscalculation."

Chrétien could campaign vigorously, knowing that he wouldn't
make much difference, that what really counted in these elections
was the leader's platform and performance. He was one of the few
bright spots in what even Turner supporters conceded was one of

the worst campaigns—if not the very worst campaign—in the history of the federal Liberal Party. Chrétien sometimes put in fuller days than Turner, whom he privately called lazy. He was once again the marathon man, jumping over hedges, reaching for hands, and with his rasp at its coarsest, intoning, "The name is Chrétien . . . from Shawinigan." He fed off the contact, as all ego-politicians do. "I feel it," he said, "and I love it."

In Toronto, Chrétien was mobbed by Portuguese, Italians, Irishmen. "Deep inside of me, I don't understand the popularity of Chrétien," said Alex Lampropoulos. "What is it? Do you know? I don't. I only know I feel it." Guiseppe Lombardi was watching Chrétien work the crowd. "I can't think his days are over," he explained. "When you see something like this, you have to think his days are just beginning." They were seeing Chrétien when he was at his height as a campaigner, when, with the exception of Diefenbaker, he was perhaps the best campaigner postwar Canada had ever seen.

Supporters appeared with pins, badges, and signs from his leadership campaign. The message was always the same: "You should be the leader, Jean. You deserved to win, Jean. You're the better man, Jean." The outpouring moved Chrétien and his wife, but there were occasions when, with all the voices shouting out what might have been, it became too much for them. They left early, sadly, knowing it was rightly theirs.

Because he was always greeted so enthusiastically, he professed not to understand why the campaign was going so badly. One of the many reasons was the infamous spate of patronage appointments that Trudeau had handed over to Turner. Turner drank fully from the cup, occasioning a media-inspired outcry that lasted the duration of the campaign. Chrétien defended the appointments, arguing that by naming so many sitting MPs to the patronage posts, Trudeau had saved the taxpayers money. Instead of drawing big pensions, the appointees would only earn their new salaries. If outsiders were named, the government would have to pay their salaries in addition to the pensions for the retiring Grits. Moreover,

Chrétien added, with the possible exception of Bryce Mackasey being made ambassador to Portugal, Trudeau had chosen qualified people. "So there was one out of nineteen," he told a Montreal crowd. "If the Expos had won eighteen out of nineteen, you'd be pretty happy." Privately, however, he told friends that had he been in Turner's place, he would have rejected many of the postings.

Since he was constantly reminded of his leadership defeat, Chrétien couldn't help talking about the people who had turned their backs on him. "When it's your friends, it's hard," he explained at one stop. "They feel a little uneasy when they are around me now. . . . I can look them in the eye, but they are self-conscious." He saw many of his so-called friends in a lesser light. "I'm turning the page," he said, "but I have a good memory."

Asked if he still hoped to become leader of the party, he'd say maybe in about sixteen years, when the job was open again. But he realized that the situation was much more promising than that. If Turner was resoundingly defeated, as polls were beginning to predict, and if he lost his own riding, he would likely have to resign. The leadership would be Chrétien's.

He watched the election results in Shawinigan, where he had made only four stops during the campaign. That wasn't many given the inroads Mulroney was making in the province. But sitting on a 25,000-vote majority, Chrétien didn't have to be concerned, even as evidence of a Tory sweep mounted. In fact, the Conservatives won a record 211 of 281 seats, while the Liberals were reduced to a humiliating 40. Chrétien bucked the trend, holding on to St-Maurice easily enough, though his 8,000-vote victory represented a huge decline from the last campaign.

He appeared at his victory party at the Hôtel des Chutes, but he didn't stay long. He was more interested in the results coming in from western Canada. He didn't want to be disturbed watching those, so returned to his campaign headquarters in a run-down appliance dealership on Fifth Street.

He sat there alone, in a stiff-backed chair, watching the returns.

It was a humid night, so the door was propped open, and the only sounds that interrupted the news of the Liberal catastrophe were the squealing tires of the high-backed cars of local greasers. As he watched, Chrétien remained silent, but the journalist Roy MacGregor, who happened by, detected in him a deep satisfaction as the slaughter unfolded. There was a sense of vindication. The contentment was mixed, MacGregor noted, with a growing tension, betrayed by a twitching nerve in his face. The twitch worsened as the clock moved towards the hour when the results from Turner's riding, Vancouver-Quadra, were due.

Occasionally, the election commentators talked about how much wiser the Grits would have been to go with the little guy. Samplings of opinion had shown all along that Chrétien would have done far better in Quebec and that his populism would have held off the sizeable NDP vote, which was cutting into Grit support. And the mistakes—surely Chrétien wouldn't have made the flood of mistakes that Turner had.

As the pundits made their observations, as the tires squealed, as campaign organizers gave away free beer by the gallon up the street at the victory party, Chrétien remained glued to his hard-backed chair, waiting for Vancouver. If the national trend held, Turner would fall. Chrétien's ordeal would be over. He could return to claim the crown unfairly denied him.

When the announcement came, when the anchorman said that John Napier Turner had moved well in front in Quadra, Chrétien got abruptly to his feet. His face frozen but for the twitching nerve, he moved wordlessly to the exit door. He paused there, stabbed a hand in his suit pocket, and said, "I might be back."

He returned to the hotel—and to a victory party where there was nothing for him to celebrate.

As expected, John Turner decided to stay on as leader. The Liberal Party now faced a situation not unlike that of 1958. Lester Pearson had defeated Paul Martin in a leadership convention in January of that year, then chose to go quickly to the polls, only to be destroyed by Diefenbaker in the March general election. The Tories won 208 seats, the Liberals just 49. Paul Martin thought he would have done better as leader, but for the next few years, while sometimes away from the Commons practicing law, he performed ably and loyally under Pearson. No challenge to his leadership was mounted, and helped by the chaos and folly into which the Tories descended under the Chief, Pearson was able to bring the party back.

There were important differences between 1958 and 1984, however. Unlike Chrétien, Martin was a distant second to Pearson in the leadership race. Unlike Chrétien, he wasn't number one in Liberal hearts. Moreover, John Turner didn't have Pearson's public stature.

Chrétien didn't think he could have won the 1984 election. He told friends, Judd Buchanan among them, that although he would have done much better, winning probably eighty or ninety seats, the conditions for victory were not there. Watching Turner lose the way he did, however, was clear confirmation for him of what he had known all along—the convention chose the wrong man.

Unlike Paul Martin, Chrétien wasn't prepared to bide his time peaceably. The party now entered into the type of internecine quarrelling for which the Conservatives had become notorious. The forty-member Liberal caucus, which included about fifteen Chrétien loyalists, was a lugubrious, sharply divided group. The first big meeting, in Montebello, Quebec, as recalled by the caucus chairman, Doug Frith, turned into a horror show. The party had done an internal poll to assess its popularity and that of its leader. Frith assumed the results would be kept under wraps. Instead, the pollster Angus Reid spilled them out in front of everyone. "I couldn't believe he did it," recalled Frith. "I mean, Turner was in single digits. It was brutal."

Turner brooded through the fall, licking his wounds. Chrétien did the same. He had assumed, after his post-election discussions with Turner, that he was still the Quebec boss of the party. But when he attempted to assemble the leading Quebec members, a party official told him only Turner would be calling such meetings. The tension between the two men was palpable. Chrétien's conviction that he was the better man, recalled the caucus member and Chrétien supporter Roland de Corneille, was eating away at him. All politicians had big egos, the MP noted, but Chrétien was a special case. "He was gifted with enough for an entire Parliament." As he wallowed in his sorrows, Chrétien frequently talked of those who had done him in. He vowed to de Corneille and others that there was one man he would never forgive: André Ouellet.

Chrétien was appointed External Affairs critic in the Turner shadow cabinet. He also joined the Toronto law firm of Lang Michener, taking an office in its Bay Street headquarters, where he planned to work one day a week. As a cabinet minister, he had been earning $110,900. As an Opposition MP, his salary dropped to $52,815, with an additional $17,640 for expenses. The legal work was to help make up the shortfall. Having just come off a leadership campaign in which he impugned his opponent as the candidate of Bay Street, Chrétien was now walking down that same avenue, briefcase in hand. He thus became the target of some pointed *badinage*. Brian Mulroney was quick to pick up on the irony, tagging him, "The Honourable Member from Shawinigan and Bay Street."

A rather lacklustre External Affairs critic, Chrétien focused his attacks on the Mulroney government's new American policy. Too cosy, he said, too sycophantic. When Mulroney moved to dismantle the Foreign Investment Review Agency, Chrétien declared, "The only policy [the Conservatives] have is to get on their knees and ask the Americans to come and invest in this country." When Mulroney held his sing-along summit with President Reagan in Quebec City in 1985, he was showing once again "his ambition of becoming governor of America's fifty-first state." When Mulroney started sending positive signals about free trade, it was but another example of his continentalism. Although he was not alone in his denunciations, Chrétien was picking up on an issue that would define the Mulroney years. Shortly before he became prime minister, Mulroney visited Reagan in Washington. White House records of their meeting show that after telling Reagan how much he personally admired him, Mulroney went so far as to tell the president that "one line" had got him elected leader of the Tories— his declaration that his first policy would be to greatly improve Canada's relations with the United States.

In taking his positions, Chrétien was once again following the lead of his mentor, Mitchell Sharp. Although he had helped undermine Walter Gordon's nationalist economic policies, Sharp had also authored Trudeau's third option, which promoted decreased dependence on the United States. He was now opposing free trade, which prompted Mulroney to relieve him of his job as head of the Northern Pipeline Agency.

Chrétien, meanwhile, continued to speak out on other issues, including the constitution. Given the record size of Mulroney's majority, Chrétien saw a splendid opportunity for the new prime minister to make progress on bringing Quebec into the fold. In an interview in December 1984, with the Quebec City newspaper *Le Soleil*, Chrétien said it would be very difficult, but that Mulroney had a historic opportunity to return to Quebec its right of veto and get it to sign the constitutional agreement of November 5, 1981. His remarks were significant in light of the criticisms Mulroney would later face from the Grits for having dared reopen the constitutional file at all.

Despite the headlines he was making, the party and the press were starting to take note of his disinterest, his absence from party functions, his time spent on non-parliamentary work. Chrétien felt trapped. If he worked hard for the party and was too visible, people would think he was overly ambitious and trying to upstage Turner. On the other hand, if he stayed in the background, he would be accused of sulking and not pulling his weight.

He hired a new aide, an eager young man from Montreal named Jean Carle, who had supported John Turner in the leadership campaign. That fact would normally have eliminated Carle from any consideration for employment. But Chrétien saw something in the young Carle that he was missing. An adopted son had gone astray. Another son had soured on politics. In his embrace of Carle, there was the suggestion that he needed someone to fill the void.

Carle had been an active member of the Quebec Liberal youth wing and had worked as an aide to Francis Fox. When the leadership campaign began and Fox moved to Turner, Carle, twenty-one, got a call inviting him to head up the Young Liberals for Turner. Fresh out of the University of Montreal, keen, and ambitious, Carle was flattered by the offer and couldn't turn it down, even though his parents much preferred Chrétien. Carle wasn't in the post long before his father started getting phone calls from Chrétien. "Do something about your son," he said. "He's with the wrong guy." Having committed, however, the young man felt he couldn't make the change.

Soon after the convention, Carle concluded he had made a terrible mistake. He was still working for the Liberals, organizing a fund-raiser for which he wanted the party's number-one draw, Jean Chrétien. Having arranged an appointment, he went to Chrétien's Ottawa office. Chrétien kept him waiting a long time before greeting him coldly. Carle then nervously began making his pitch about why the Liberals needed Chrétien for the dinner. He stumbled on for about ten minutes, with Chrétien not saying a word, only staring inhospitably. Finally, when Carle had finished, the lips of the famous Liberal moved. He had but one hostile question to ask: "Why didn't you support me?"

The student started fighting for words. He explained that he was young and naïve, that he couldn't turn the Turner people down, that he had made a grave error. As Carle stammered on, Chrétien's mood quickly began to change. He took Carle to a side chamber, where he pulled out some pages of a book he was working on. He read from them and asked for the young man's thoughts. He seemed impressed by Carle's presence of mind and his intelligence, and they talked at length. Then Chrétien stunned his visitor by asking, "Would you come and work for me?"

Minutes earlier, Carle had been on Chrétien's blacklist. Now he was being asked to become his right-hand man. Carle responded that while he hadn't come looking for a job, he was interested. They talked some more and Chrétien sent him to John Rae for further discussions. Carle moved to Ottawa and began work soon after. With little money and no place to stay, he was then invited by Chrétien to live in the basement of his home. Carle couldn't resist the offer. He moved in, took the room opposite Hubert's, and soon found himself at his master's side for the better part of each day. It wasn't long before people started referring to him as the third son.

Chrétien campaigned enthusiastically for David Peterson's Liberals in the 1985 Ontario provincial election. It didn't escape the notice of party professionals that he had barely won a vote from that province's Liberal caucus in the leadership race and had some shoring-up to do in that area.

He held a meeting of all his key campaign supporters in February 1985 at his Ottawa home. The reunion was ostensibly to thank them for their efforts, but as could be expected, the talk turned to his future and what plans he should make. The party's constitution required a leadership review, regardless of the leader's performance. It was scheduled for the fall of 1986. As 1985 began, few believed that Turner could be toppled at such a review, but it wasn't beyond the realm of possibility. It had happened to Joe Clark.

The book Chrétien had begun writing was a memoir of his life in politics. The timing was peculiar. There generally wasn't much of a market for books on second-place finishers in leadership campaigns. Few could imagine a volume by Robert Winters after his loss to Trudeau in 1968 or one by Paul Martin after his defeat by

Pearson in 1958. Chrétien had just lost the fight of his life. More-over, as the journalist Peter Worthington told his publisher, Anna Porter, "This guy doesn't read books. How do you expect him to write one?"

Porter thought differently. She had a feeling that the wide-spread admiration and sympathy for Chrétien would translate into book buyers. His non-literary image was not an issue because Ron Graham would write the book with him. Graham was then lighting up the firmament of Canadian political journalism with some of the most eloquent and insightful pieces *Saturday Night* magazine had ever printed.

The book, *Straight from the Heart*, became a torrid best-seller. The first printing of twenty-seven thousand copies disappeared within days. Still, when Chrétien went to his first book signing in Ottawa, he was sheepishly nervous. What if no one showed up? When he arrived, he found a line-up extending around the block. For the book launch in Montreal, Trudeau and Turner attended, piquing the interest of the press. Like two ships passing in the night, they managed to avoid each other. Chrétien saw Turner, however, and signed a book for him. "Thank you for having won the convention," he wrote, "because if you had not won, I wouldn't have had the time to write this book."

He steered a cautious course in writing about Turner in the vol-ume, coming nowhere close to revealing his true feelings about the man. Nor was he mean-spirited towards others. "Some people wanted blood on the floor," he said, "but I'm not vindictive."

Any politician hoping that the best is still to come could hardly afford to be vindictive or, for that matter, entirely candid. In *Straight from the Heart*, Chrétien was neither. Although he did make some pointed gibes at Quebec nationalists and those who bolted on him in the leadership race, Chrétien for the most part produced a safe, entertaining, and as is to be expected when politi-cians write about themselves, self-promotional work.

The text was about as candid as most books of the genre, but for someone who takes great pride in honesty and who chose the title *Straight from the Heart*, Chrétien took many detours.

The more noteworthy omissions included his using a counterfeit candidate as an election opponent; his execution of the great appendicitis deception; his rivalry with his political arch-enemy, Yves Duhaime; his assault on Marcel Chartier; and the traumas of his adopted son, Michel. Not surprisingly, the common thread in most of the overlooked stories was that they reflected poorly on the author.

The appendicitis episode was dealt with deceitfully in *Straight from the Heart*. The one-line reference to the story implied that he missed a year of school because of illness. Chrétien acknowledged years later, when the truth was put to him, that he had not been ill at all. "Absolutely true," he said. "I'm not very proud of it, but they really operated on me and I was not really sick.... I faked it."

While other controversial incidents from his youth could add to the Chrétien lore, this was considered by the family to have stretched the bounds. They hoped it wouldn't come to light. Michel Chrétien, the most protective of Jean's brothers, was still trying to keep the story hidden in 1994. He said in an interview that Jean left Joliette because he was ill with appendicitis, then corrected himself later when questioned more closely.

The impression Chrétien left of his family life was one of harmony. But given the difficulties with Michel and Hubert, it was hardly that. France's marriage to André Desmarais was mentioned, but "the little guy" apparently thought better of making note of the warm friendship he had developed with Power Corporation chairman Paul Desmarais—even though there was no suggestion of anything untoward about the connection. While he might have been expected to put his own positive spin on the controversies of his political career, the one-sidedness of his analysis of such matters as his period as Finance minister was glaring.

Whatever its faults, the book was a wonderful tonic for Chrétien's then-flagging ego. "He was just like a kid when he came to my office," remembered Eddie Goldenberg. "He had just got a copy and he was proud, happy to call himself an author."

With the publication of *Straight from the Heart*, he was once again the darling of the media. Reviews were almost uniformly positive. The book's warm reception and magnificent sales were yet more evidence that Chrétien possessed a magic touch rare among politicians. Chrétien, wrote Dalton Camp, "remains one of a very few public men who are endearing."

If the book thrust him again into the national spotlight, it also served to further divide a party that Turner was trying to knit together. Before the book, the threat from a sulking Chrétien seemed remote. Now the leader could no longer relax. Now, with Chrétien's fantastic popularity on display, the outcome of the approaching leadership review was suddenly in doubt. Now Liberals were saying it again—"We made the wrong choice."

"I can't stop the press from writing about my ambition," Chrétien said of his leadership aspirations. "But the job is not open." Yet, in the same breath, he added, "It is not for me to decide. It is not for John to decide. The delegates will address that situation." For many Liberals, it was clear that he was vying to usurp the throne. "It's suicidal what Jean is doing," said the president of the Quebec Liberal caucus, Raymond Garneau, who had turned to federal politics at Turner's invitation. "I didn't leave everything that I had to come here and fight with other Liberals. If Chrétien tries to stir trouble, I'll be after him." For his part, Turner vowed an all-out campaign to protect his position. He came to the party's annual meeting in Halifax, just as *Straight from the Heart* was grabbing headlines, and turned in a popular performance. All the while Chrétien was being besieged by book buyers in a local store.

The tension in the party increased as 1986 began. Because he was working for Chrétien, Jean Carle was treated as a leper. "They wouldn't even say hello to me. You're just a young kid. It's tough. They were paranoid." Chrétien, who had occupied a record number of cabinet posts, soon found himself unable to ask a question in the House without writing it out in advance and having it vet-ted by a Turner acolyte. "I have to get permission from a third-rank guy just to ask a question." He went on vacation to Hawaii and missed a Quebec caucus meeting, prompting charges that he wasn't working hard enough. His performance in Opposition was savaged by Michel Roy, the editor of *La Presse*. Roy argued that Turner was now performing well, and that Chrétien should either shape up or ship out. Chrétien called Roy in anger to rebut his points.

The media kept the focus on the party split. Turner emerged from the Quebec caucus meeting all set to discuss the policies that had been debated, but the first five questions put by reporters were on Chrétien's threat to his leadership. Efforts to bring Chrétien and Turner together for a reconciliation had failed, but another at-tempt was made February 4 over a dinner at Stornoway, the Oppo-sition leader's residence. Some expected Turner to extend an olive branch by offering to reinstate Chrétien as his Quebec lieutenant. That didn't happen, but they did discuss the question of the party presidency in Quebec and Chrétien's push to have Francis Fox in the job. After a long meal followed by cognac and cigars, Chrétien felt he had won Turner's agreement on the posting. He felt better when he left Stornoway. The dinner seemed to have cleared away a few layers of animosity between the two. Chrétien had no sense as he drove away that this was the last supper.

Turner subsequently contacted Fox and asked him to drop out of the race in favour of Paul Routhier, a Quebec City lawyer. Fox agreed, leaving the way clear for the acclamation of Turner's choice. Chrétien felt double-crossed and said as much publicly. There was a malaise in the party, he said. People were acting undemocratically. Why, he wondered, didn't Turner inform him of his plans at din-ner? "We spent three hours together, and he never told me that he was going to ask him to withdraw. Perhaps he forgot."

Marc Lalonde sided with Chrétien on the Fox dispute, as did many in the caucus. But Chrétien, criticized for making the matter

355

public, soon faced headlines labelling him an ingrate. "Chrétien Should Work with Turner or Get Out" blared one. "Chrétien Spoiled Brat" cried another. When he rose to speak in the House of Commons, he was mocked by Tories who laughed and applauded and cried in mocking tones, "Leader! Leader!"

The Fox episode triggered a decision Chrétien had been contemplating for months. On the evening of February 26, 1986, he huddled with his staff. On the morning of twenty-seventh, he went to Turner's office by a side route to escape the press, and waited to see him in the office of Senator Bud Olson. With him was Jean Carle. He had told Carle of his decision a week earlier. But as they waited, Carle couldn't contain himself. Caught up in the emotion of the moment, he broke down and began crying like a baby. Chrétien came over and patted him on the shoulder. "Don't worry," he said. "There's worse things in life than this."

Chrétien told Turner he had made his contribution to Canada and that now, after twenty-three years in politics, it was time to leave the public stage. Describing the moment as a shock, Turner told reporters the Liberal Party needed Jean Chrétien. Managing to keep a straight face, he added, "And I certainly did in personal terms." More credible was his other assertion: "There can be only one leader."

Though the media responded as if it was the end of an era, it became clear within a short period that this was not so much a retirement as a strategic retreat. Some analysts saw the resignation as a boon for Turner, but many in the leader's camp reasoned that Chrétien was now in a mightier position than ever to mount a challenge. When he was inside the caucus, his every move could be monitored and picked over, but now he would have more room to manoeuvre. Leaderships were often more easily won from the outside.

On the day of his resignation, Chrétien returned home to Shawinigan to inform his long-time supporters of his decision. The CBC reporter Jason Moscovitz went to Chrétien's home, where he found the dignified Aline packing his bags. Aline began talking to Moscovitz, telling him how badly the party had been treating her husband. As she spoke, her temperature noticeably began to rise. Finally, she exploded. "He doesn't have to take that shit!"

Arriving at the Hôtel des Chutes, Chrétien wore a big Inuit parka he had received while minister of Indian Affairs and Northern Development. He looked back on that period, 1968–1974, when he had helped the native peoples organize themselves, as his most memorable years in government. His proudest moments, however, as he told his fellow Shawiniganites, had been his role in the federalist triumph in the Quebec referendum fight, in bringing home a new constitution, and in creating a national park in his home riding. Being out of politics wouldn't be so bad or, as some suggested, so boring. Gesturing towards Aline, he asked, "How can you be bored with a lady like that?" A reporter suggested that he hadn't willingly retired but had been pushed out. "That is a very funny question," Chrétien fired back. "Have you ever tried to push out Jean Chrétien? Don't try!"

The premature obituaries were kind. Although the denouement had been tawdry, Chrétien's record of achievement was undisputed. Chrétien, more than any politician of his generation, wrote Hubert Bauch in the Montreal *Gazette*, "exemplified the spirit behind the somewhat elusive concept of French power in Ottawa." It was he who had demonstrated that any Québécois with drive and dexterity could occupy some of the highest positions in the land. Tom Axworthy, the former principal secretary to Pierre Trudeau, made the compelling observation that the Liberal Party had done great things "for" the common man but had never been "of" the common man until the true populist, Jean Chrétien, came along. "He offered a new way of doing things. Policy by feel, not by flow chart."

It was soon apparent, however, that referring to Chrétien in the past tense was inappropriate. As he told reporters in Shawinigan, "You never tell the fountain you will never drink its water again." Within a week of his so-called retirement, he announced that he would campaign for the Manitoba Liberal leader, Sharon Carstairs.

He had long before made plans to do so, but on the very day he announced his retirement, he called Carstairs to confirm he would be there. When he arrived in the province, he was in peak form, barging into restaurant kitchens to banter with the sweaty cooks, cajoling a woman out of a clothing-store change room to shake hands. "I will always be a politician," he told reporters. "I love politics."

As Turner backers watched with increasing alarm, Chrétien visited Alberta premier Don Getty to discuss energy prices, campaigned for Liberal leader Nick Taylor in the Alberta election, and on Parliament Hill, personally intervened to end Senator Jacques Hebert's twenty-one-day hunger strike to protest the Tory government's decision to cancel Katimavik, a community works program for young people. Chrétien, who helped set up a non-profit corporation to solicit funds for Katimavik's continuation, stood at Hebert's side, under the full media spotlight, as the senator ended his fast.

Polls showed that the party would be doing considerably better under Chrétien's leadership than Turner's. Such polls traditionally favoured outsiders over incumbents, and were to be seen in that light, but they nevertheless provided the Chrétien forces with ammunition. So did polls in Quebec that showed him, despite the negative press he frequently received there, getting a 65 per cent approval rating—higher than that of Trudeau, Mulroney, Turner, and several others on the list.

Chrétien hadn't yet organized a formal anti-Turner movement, but Eddie Goldenberg, who was contacting riding executives who had supported Chrétien in the leadership campaign, saw nothing inappropriate in doing some planning himself. Wisely or unwisely, the party's constitution stipulated a leadership-review process. Therefore, Goldenberg reasoned, it was one's democratic right to favour the leader or someone else. "I felt it should not be considered almost subversive to take a side."

The pro-review forces were dubbed "the contras." They included Goldenberg and other strong Chrétien loyalists like Jacques Corriveau in Quebec, George Young in Ontario, the ebullient

Toronto businessman Dennis Mills, and the Alberta party president Ken Munro. But many, not comfortable with the review process, sat this one out, including John Rae, Patrick Lavelle, Roland de Corneille, and others. Because they considered it too unseemly to mount a visible, formal campaign, Chrétien's contras never emerged as a powerful team. Their potential was also hindered by divisions in the pro-review ranks. Chrétien represented old-guard Liberalism, but the roaring eighties were the years of Reagan and Thatcher and Mulroney, of neoconservatism and big business. Many of the Liberals who wanted a new leader wanted one who was seen as more in touch with the new times. Mills, one of the best organizers in the country, sampled a lot of opinion and came away wondering whether it was even a good idea to attach the Chrétien name to the contra movement. Many people were looking to Paul Martin Jr., a successful businessman who was smart, forward looking, and rich in Liberal tradition. But Martin wasn't ready yet. His supporters concluded that the toppling of Turner would be counterproductive at this stage. If he fell, they knew Chrétien would be the likely successor.

Despite the contras' problems, they were still a strong enough threat to leave Turner seething in suspicion and self-doubt. His wife, Geills, was away a good part of the time, and rumours spread that he was looking increasingly to his decanter of Scotch to buttress himself. Chrétien was not usually one to tear people down behind their backs, but the Liberal leader became the exception to his rule. He told friends of Turner's laziness and occasional heavy boozing.

In the family struggle there were potential traitors in every house. The executive director of the Liberal Party was David Collenette. Collenette was a Chrétien supporter, but those who worked for him, including Mark Resnick, who was hired by Turner as policy director, saw no evidence of any bias. Nonetheless, Turner suspected sabotage. He even imagined, Doug Frith recalled, that the ballots would be tampered with to give Chrétien a victory. Resnick had prepared a series of resolutions for the convention, including one on the constitutional issue. In the typing and printing, an error slipped in, changing the meaning. To his utter surprise, Resnick was accused of being a fifth columnist, secretly working for Collenette to depose the boss. Resnick had been new to politics. Overnight he was old.

The pro-Turner group, many of them young men who saw in victory a chance to win personal power and put their own stamp on the party, convinced the leader that only an all-out effort, an assault using every tactic available, could prevent an overthrow. Having been given the green light from Turner, they stacked delegate-selection meetings with instant Liberals, attacked pro-review forces as saboteurs, and created a huge secret slush fund to pay the expenses of youth delegates and stuff the pockets of any Turner supporters in need. Unbeknownst to the party executive, the fund was put together by the Bay Street car dealer John Addison. Senator Leo Kolber, the Grits' upright long-time bagman, was one of the many who were kept in the dark and was outraged because of it. One Turner organizer told the journalist Greg Weston he had re-ceived a gift-wrapped shoe box of $20,000 in $100 bills. Weston was working on a book chronicling the failings of Turner's leader-ship. He was wined and dined by Tories eager for a preview of what it would contain. Since it was coming out before the convention, the Chrétien camp hoped it would provide momentum for their cause. The book, *Reign of Error*, edited by Hubert Bauch, was a powerful indictment. Critics, deriding it as a hatchet job, failed to produce any examples of serious inaccuracies. The Turner forces successfully performed their own hatchet job, however, convincing the media it was an unworthy enterprise. Another Chrétien oppor-tunity was lost.

Chrétien stayed silent, refusing to grant interviews through much of the run-up to the vote. Behind the scenes, though, he sounded out many MPs and senators about their intentions. Two weeks before the convention, Marc Lalonde, who had backed Turner in the leadership campaign, released a letter that, in the precise logic that became him, put the case for the removal of Turner. He cited the party's debt, the habitually low popularity ratings of Turner, and the threat of being overtaken as Canada's second major political party by the rising NDP. Shortly before writing the letter, Lalonde had dined with Turner at 24 Sussex Drive. They talked pleasantly about a variety of subjects. Then Turner walked Lalonde to a waiting taxi and, when he was in it, stuck his head in the window and said, "So, Marc, I guess I can count on your support at the convention, eh?"

"I'll have to think about it," Lalonde replied.

Senator Keith Davey, who had taken over the Turner campaign midway through the disastrous 1984 federal election, had already declared himself in favour of review. Davey's increasing disenchantment with Turner had reached the point that he concluded he had made an unforgivable error in not supporting Chrétien in the leadership campaign. Davey had derided those, like Roland de Corneille, who supported Chrétien. One day he came across de Corneille in the VIP lounge of the Toronto airport. In an emotional outpouring, Davey told him that he was right. "The one big mistake in my political career," said the Rainmaker, "was to support John Turner."

But what counted in politics, as Jean Chrétien had once noted, was not logic but mood. This was a party tired of rule by the old guard. Young Liberals had been making that point for years. To them, the manoeuvrings of Davey and Lalonde looked like a ganging-up by the heirarchy. Instead of helping Chrétien, they inadvertently kindled sympathy for Turner, moving undecideds into his column. Turner had been trying hard to rebuild the party, many delegates reasoned, and indeed, although thanks largely to the scandals tearing through the Tory ranks, the party had risen in the polls under his leadership. Prominent caucus members, such as Lloyd Axworthy, Herb Gray, Bob Kaplan, Brian Tobin, and Sheila Copps, were sticking with Turner. Many of them were closer ideologically to Chrétien, but that didn't sway them.

As the convention began, the Turner forces were uncertain of the outcome. Chrétien reasoned that the vote would either be about 60 per cent for Turner, which would necessitate a new leadership campaign, or 75 per cent for Turner, giving him a clear-cut victory. Chrétien's only planned appearance, to register as delegate, resulted in bedlam. About three hundred delegates and members of the media had jammed the lobby of the Westin Hotel next to the Ottawa Convention Centre. As Chrétien tried to get through the tangle of bodies, shoving matches turned to fist fights, leaving four people injured. Contras cheered Chrétien on while Turner loyalists hooted him down. A distressed Chrétien said he should have stayed home.

On the day of the vote, he took several long walks and drove up and down the canal to kill time. For the third time in two and a half years, he was facing the possibility of becoming leader of the Liberal Party. He had thought the dream was near at the 1984 convention, then again during the long night in Shawinigan waiting for the election results to come in from Quadra. Now the prize was at his fingertips once more, and once more it slipped away.

He watched the results at his home with Aline, their daughter, France, and her husband, André Desmarais. The outcome was a crushing disappointment. "I've been waiting a long time to say this to you, John," Convention Chairman Doug Frith announced. "Now you are first in our hearts." Turner won a 76.3 per cent endorsement, well exceeding expectations. It was a triumph.

With a shower of congratulations falling on Turner, Eddie Goldenberg made his way forward to pass on the best wishes of the Chrétien camp. Goldenberg reached the Liberal leader, proffered his hand, but got only dagger-eyes in return. "I know where you're coming from," Turner spat. Then he moved off.

Although his victory was celebrated as a personal triumph, the Turner forces could be under no illusions. They had won not because of any great admiration for the leader, they realized, but because of strong-arm tactics. "Let's face it," said Terence Popowich, one of Turner's campaign managers, "what we did was stack the place." There was the stacking and, noted Frith, there were the interventions of Lalonde and Davey. For Chrétien, the sad irony was that he had lost in 1984 in large part because the party establishment had deserted him, and he had lost in 1986 in part because it had joined him.

After the results were announced, Chrétien spoke to reporters. "The delegates made a decision that is clear and that will make life easy for everybody." He told them he would be back at work at his law office at 9:00 a.m. the next morning. "I find private life agreeable, but you know, I got out of politics and I'm still trying to get the politics out of me." Had the vote given Turner one last chance, a reporter asked. "We'll see after the next election," Chrétien responded. "If that election is a great success, then it's obviously not his last chance. But if it's a problem, then it would be his last chance."

He couldn't resist speaking of others who, like himself, had been considered down and out. Trudeau quit in 1979 and came back, and Bourassa and Turner, Chrétien noted, did the same.

And of course there was Richard Nixon.

"Nixon said they wouldn't have him to kick around anymore," the little guy from Shawinigan reminded reporters. "And he came back."

CHAPTER TWENTY

POISED
FOR POWER

E HAD FREQUENTLY SAID that he didn't believe in destiny, that he was never one of those young men who went around telling people he would be prime minister of Canada someday. But many of those who knew him well had seen a relentless ambition at work since the early days of his youth. They'd been close enough to Jean Chrétien to hear the clock ticking within.

His only hope now was that John Turner would again stumble badly, plunging the once-proud Grits into another season of despair and another election drubbing.

After the party's reanointment of him at the leadership review, this scenario seemed unlikely. It seemed as if the trembling man of the previous few years would be able to relax now and, riding the momentum of the review, move the party forward. But although it was not apparent from the media coverage, the review victory was a packaged triumph, and the momentum was largely a mirage. Divisions over the big issues—free trade, Meech Lake, cruise-missile testing—still tore at the party's inner soul, as did personal conflicts over past loyalties. Turner's intense and insecure nature left him unsuited to play the role of healer. Soon his poll ratings were tumbling again, soon the party's morale was plummeting, and soon the conspirators were at the door.

In the two years between his review victory and the 1988 election, while Jean Chrétien looked on contentedly, Turner faced no less than three coup attempts. The first, in August 1987, had thirteen of the forty Liberal caucus members signing letters asking for his resignation. For the second, in April 1988, the number was up to twenty-two, a majority. The third bid came—astonishingly—during the 1988 election campaign. With the party trailing the NDP in the polls and Turner's popularity ranking horribly low, party chieftains reasoned that even an eleventh-hour switch of leaders would be better than facing election day with him. But Turner once again fended off the insurrection.

Then, in a brief shining moment during the leaders' debate, he reversed his party's fortunes. His vehement attack on Mulroney, alleging that the PM had sold out the country on free trade, struck like a knockout punch. The Grits rallied to take the lead over a startled Tory machine. But as quickly as the Liberals surged, they receded. In the final days of the campaign, Turner was back to dismal popularity ratings of 12 to 14 per cent, and Mulroney had swept back in front. The Tories won another majority government. The Liberals won eighty seats.

Papers quoted Chrétien as telling fellow Grits that he wanted "a stake through Turner's heart." The election result didn't amount to that. Turner's performance in the debate had pulled the party back from the near-oblivion to which he had led it. The eighty seats, while still a resounding defeat, doubled the 1984 result. What mattered most, however, was that John Turner was no longer in a position to continue as leader of the Liberal Party.

For the two years between the leadership review and the election, Jean Chrétien had been far from idle. Watching from the sidelines, he became everything that little guys were never supposed to be— a millionaire and an establishment man.

His father, Wellie, once told the story of the time he and three other working-class men appeared as the guests of honour at a banquet held by the insurance company they worked for. They were being singled out for their long-time service and so were seated on a raised podium that stretched narrowly across the front of the hotel banquet hall. The podium had only enough space for the long table and the chairs. When Wellie Chrétien and the others, not used to being up there, were introduced, they pushed their chairs back and promptly tumbled onto the floor behind them.

Though it looked like a scene straight out of a slapstick comedy, Wellie Chrétien found a moral to the story. "Nous ne sommes pas faits pour les hauteurs," he said. "We aren't made for the high places."

The lesson was hardly applicable to son Jean. Fresh out of politics, he was right into money. In short order, he was bringing in $500,000 a year while working at a pace not half as hectic as political life demanded. He held two official positions, one at Lang Michener, the other at a big brokerage house, Gordon Capital, where he was a special adviser. In addition, he collected tidy sums from investments, from sitting on corporate boards, from giving speeches, and from royalties on his book. These many incomes supplemented an already handsome government pension of $55,000 to $60,000.

Having been a politician almost all his life, he had often wondered how he would fare out in the real world. Now he had his answer. Comparing himself with other ex-politicians, he announced happily, "I think I'm beating them all, including Trudeau." He chastised the Tories, then being undermined by one finance-related scandal after another. "Those guys thought politics was a way to get rich. I never saw many get rich in my twenty-three years." It wasn't in the halls of power that the money was made. It was in the wake of it. Much of his income simply came from spinning knowledge off the top of his head. "Judgement and experience," he said, when asked what assets he had to sell to clients. "I have seen so much in government, Trudeau got me involved in so many areas, that I know what is necessary for them to do."

With the tension and trauma of the leadership review out of the way, his life grew calm. He kept his home in Ottawa, opening a branch office of Lang Michener with Eddie Goldenberg and Roger Tassé. He commuted to Gordon Capital in Montreal a couple of days a week and on weekends often drove up to the cottage he loved on Lac des Piles. He occasionally contacted former political colleagues but spent more time with his business friends and family. Always comfortable without company, he sometimes attended a movie by himself or ate alone in the restaurant at the foot of his Ottawa office tower.

He sharpened his golf game and took steps to make sure he never lacked for a tee-off time. As a young man in Shawinigan, he had chafed at the discrimination exercised by the Grand'Mère Country Club, which denied access to many francophones like himself. Now, with his new-found wealth, he settled that old score. He bought the golf course.

He and two associates paid $1.25 million to buy it from Consolidated Bathurst, which also owned the Belgo mill where he and his father had laboured. When he was working summers on the hot floors, Jean Chrétien was not always happy answering to his anglo bosses. But now he could wave that bad memory goodbye as well. He took a seat on Consolidated's board of directors.

More good news arrived. One day, while playing a round on his golf course, always sitting in the golf cart's passenger seat so he could hear his partner with his one good ear, he got word that Viceroy Resources, a mining company in which he held many shares, had made a major gold strike in California. Chrétien was so delighted that he bought everyone hot dogs after the round. Members talked about that rare event—the hot dogs, not the gold strike—for days.

As a director of the Vancouver-based Viceroy, which was owned by his good friend Ross Fitzpatrick, Chrétien had an option on fifty thousand shares. He sat on its board, as well as those of Consolidated Bathurst, the Toronto Dominion Bank, the Brick

Warehouse Corporation, and others. He no longer drove cheap cars but instead had a luxury model Saab, the 9000. He hung around, golfing, skiing, and socializing, with men worth millions—Paul Desmarais, the Bronfmans, Fitzpatrick, and many others. His position at Gordon Capital, where he handled major negotiations for giants like the Power Corporation, lengthened his list of chief executive contacts.

With it all, the boardroom positions, the wealth, the upper-crust friends, Chrétien could hardly be considered an anti-establishment man. By 1989 the little guy from Shawinigan was a millionaire. He'd gone from blue collar to blue chipper, and friends worried, particularly because of his tight personal and professional relations with the Power Corporation, that he would lose his sensitivity for society's less privileged.

If, in politics, he had sold himself as the man of the people, out of politics, his detractors would say, he was showing his truer colours. His wealth and comforts seemed to confirm what they had suspected all along: that, as the columnist Lysiane Gagnon put it, the little-guy stuff was just a big act. "It's outrageous," she said, describing how the Power Corporation nestled him. "It's such demagoguery. . . . Just think about his wealth and lifestyle."

Critics presupposed that being the little guy meant excluding oneself from riches, millionaire friends, and upscale living. Chrétien saw it differently. He was determined to have it both ways. Just as in politics, where he swung randomly from Left to Right, so too could he scoot across the social spectrum. He could spend a weekend at Paul Desmarais's fishing lodge in La Malbaie, then go home to Shawinigan and show his other side. One day, while visiting his old factory floor at the Belgo Mill, he found some workers who were just ending their shift and heading to the showers. Chrétien's politicking didn't end with the handshakes and small talk. He stripped off his cabinet minister's suit and went into the showers with them.

John Rae, who worked next door to Desmarais at the Power

Corporation, discovered that Desmarais and Chrétien were very close friends. But while Chrétien was comfortable with him and with the business elite, there was a big difference, argued Rae, between him and politicians like Brian Mulroney. One was a charter member of the club. The other was an occasional guest.

Those like Chrétien who start life low on the economic ladder face many changes on the way up. Thoughts change, living standards change, friends change, environments change. Instincts, however, tend to remain the same. Chrétien's instincts didn't appear to have changed much. A working-man's edge still governed his value system. The big lights impressed him, but he was never blinded by those lights. Mulroney could make the leap from his mill-town roots and become one with the monied class, losing touch with not only his roots but also the majority of Canadians. Chrétien, by contrast, took on some of the trappings of the ruling class, but his sense of self remained drawn from the street he grew up on.

He liked, said Ross Fitzpatrick, to associate with successful people, whether in business or in politics, because he found them stimulating. "But I don't think you'll ever see him budge from his basic values. And I don't see him as one who is entranced by big business people. I don't think he's entranced by anybody. He deals with them as they are. He's independent."

Chrétien's new life was comfortable, but he missed the rush, the day-to-day pulse, the power of politics. In the law office, Tassé always found the conversation reverting back to speculation over what was going on two blocks up the street in those grand Gothic buildings. Most legal issues held little interest for him. He'd interrupt discussions on client files with comments like "Hey, that guy's for Meech." He couldn't escape his instincts. A few months after he lost the leadership review, Chrétien bumped into Palle Kiar, a Shawiniganite he didn't know well, on the terrace at the Royal Ottawa Golf Club. When Kiar approached, Chrétien recognized him as the big basketball player from Shawinigan High School.

Kiar mentioned that his high-school class would be holding its fortieth reunion in a village near Shawinigan. Passing on the date, he invited Chrétien to drop in. Realistically, he realized there was no good reason for him to come. He didn't know many in the class, he was out of politics and, noted Kiar, there wouldn't be many votes there anyway, mainly Quebec anglophones. "But he showed up with Aline and spent the whole afternoon there and just delighted everybody. He told me the English from Quebec always supported him."

Although he finally had time to develop other interests, Jean Chrétien, at age fifty-five, was not about to start immersing himself in Tolstoy and Voltaire. If it wasn't politics or golf that occupied his leisure time, it was baseball. He'd sit for hours watching baseball games with Jean Carle. "To me, it was obvious," said Tassé. "He was looking for the opportunity to get back into politics."

For the two issues dominating the political agenda in 1987 and 1988, free trade and the Meech Lake constitutional renegotiation, Chrétien staked out his positions. Building on his opposition to free trade, he argued that the proposed agreement would see Canada surrender its rights to its natural resources and get drawn into an ever-narrowing economic corridor. Canadians would eventually have to seek representation where the real power lay—the American Congress. "And then Canada as a country would disappear." There might be economic advantages to free trade, but there was more to life than the bottom line. "I know," said Chrétien, "that Canadians are willing to pay a price to be Canadian."

From the outset, he opposed Meech Lake, the 1987 federal-provincial accord that recognized Quebec as a distinct society and was designed to make the province a signatory to the constitution. Tassé, who had helped draw up the agreement and felt that Mulroney had done splendid work on it, was the first to take the accord to Chrétien and explain it to him. But his reaction was sharply negative. He believed the Meech Lake Accord threatened to override sections of the Charter of Rights and Freedoms.

371

Moreover, it would bring on greater decentralization, putting too much power in the hands of the provinces. Lumping together the free-trade pact and the Meech agreement, the twin pillars of Mulroney's new Canadian edifice, Chrétien came up with a potent oversimplification. "Mulroney," he said, "gave half the country away to the provinces and the rest to the United States."

He had naturally watched with keen interest as the plots to overthrow Turner unfolded. A few days before the second coup attempt, he sought to add impetus, declaring that "people want to vote for the Liberals, but they don't want to vote for Turner." Most of the letters demanding Turner's resignation were from MPs outside Chrétien's camp, so Chrétien could not easily be accused of scheming.

Repeatedly, hypothetical polls showed that with Chrétien as leader, the Grits would have won the 1988 election. Free trade would have been defeated, history rewritten. The surveys strengthened Chrétien's view that the party had made a dreadful error in 1984. Now, with the Liberal defeat and Turner's fall, he had an opportunity to remedy it all. Less than a day after the election results came in, he announced his availability. He had wanted a stake through Turner's heart; now he wanted a quick leadership convention. But a long and frustrating delay was in store. The party, persuaded by supporters of Paul Martin Jr., decided to push back the convention to June 1990.

Martin, a formidable opponent for Chrétien, was the answer for those Liberals looking for a new face, a new image, a new dynamic, a way to the future. Chrétien had vulnerabilities. Many looked on him as a leftover from the Trudeau era, a man of old ideas and worn-out thoughts. They asked of him as they had of Walter Mondale when he sought the Democratic Party nomination in the United States: "Where's the beef?"

Chrétien held a few aces, however. This time it was a francophone's turn. This time he had the party caucus and establishment behind him. This time the party knew it owed him one. Preliminary surveys by John Rae showed that 95 per cent of the delegates who had supported Chrétien in 1984 were still behind him. About half those who supported Turner were now ready to come to him.

Many Liberals who had turned up their noses at Chrétien in 1984 were now asking forgiveness. He had once vowed that some of these "bastards," most notably André Ouellet, would never be forgiven. But the lure of power was not to be underestimated. It could change people's minds.

Many of those who had dealt with Chrétien over the years took note of his long memory. He could hold grudges forever. There were exceptions to the rule, however. If the party in question was indispensable to him, he could forgive. Ouellet was more responsible than anyone else for putting Chrétien through the nearest thing to torture he'd ever experienced in his life. But Ouellet was also a politician whose support was vital to any candidate wanting to carry Quebec.

A friend of Ouellet's called Chrétien and asked him to lunch. Shortly before the lunch, he called back to ask if he could bring Ouellet along. Chrétien agreed. The lunch was extremely difficult at the start. It was as if the tension had sucked the air right out of the room. But then Ouellet came forward with the apologia, the one Chrétien had been hearing so often from old "friends" since 1984—the "I made a terrible mistake" confession.

Chrétien then broke the anxiety of the moment by telling a joke, a joke with a pointed edge. He waited to see if this dark prince, this politician who was as cunning as they come, would take it the right way. He did, and they both laughed. The man Chrétien said he could never pardon was pardoned.

As Chrétien was now poised for power, other people came to him. His closest friends, both politically and personally, had remained the very serious grouping of Mitchell Sharp, who was more than two decades older, and Eddie Goldenberg and John Rae, each more than a decade younger. Goldenberg was, in Chrétien's words, his "pocket computer." The two were extremely comfortable with each other. "He knows how I will react very well. If you talk with Eddie, he will say what Chrétien will say."

Remarkably, Goldenberg, Sharp, and others wanted to change Chrétien. Having decided that one of his problems in 1984 was that he was considered too shallow, too bereft of ideas, they wanted to overhaul his image. "We have been talking to Jean about his image problem," said Mitchell Sharp as the leadership battle got under way, "and I think he is aware that some people view him as superficial." Sharp, having been Chrétien's mentor, his coach, his pedagogue since 1965, was now saying he wasn't ready. After holding ten cabinet posts and spending two decades at the top, he needed work on the "content."

Chrétien, who had almost always followed Sharp's line on major policy initiatives, the latest example being the Meech Lake Accord, had bristled at accusations that he did no reading or was thin on content. But now he willingly underwent education sessions. Sharp brought together panels of experts on foreign policy, economic policy, trade policy, and other areas. He simply wanted his fifty-five-year-old pupil to listen. Chrétien obliged, letting the experts ramble on for hours, not saying much himself, just asking the occasional question. Mel Hurtig, the fervent Canadian nationalist, was invited to a panel to offer his anti–free-trade spiel. After listening to Hurtig's excoriation of the agreement, Chrétien had just one question. Hurtig found it rather a curious one. "Yes, Mel," he asked, "but how do I tell this to my friends in business?"

Addressing Chrétien's lack of depth wasn't deemed to be enough. His handlers decided that he needed a Madison Avenue makeover as well. He needed sophistication, class. He had to appear more prime ministerial. Chrétien had once spoken so derisively of those who tried to disguise their true selves, of those, he said, who tried to put mascara over the body. But now that power beckoned, he was willing to compromise again.

So they brought in the plastic surgeons, including an "image coach," and the grammar murderer got lessons on language; the driver of the getaway car learned how to read from a Teleprompter; and the little guy from Shawinigan, the natural politician, was taught to be someone else.

As time would tell, the image transplant was an ill-conceived enterprise. Much of Jean Chrétien's appeal lay in the people's belief that he was genuine. His handlers, if they did not already know this, would soon find it out. They would find that it made no sense to mess around with pure Canadian rock. They would find that in Jean Chrétien they had a political phenomenon the likes of which the country had rarely seen; that by letting him be his own handler, all would be well indeed.

Some compared him to the strong-willed Harry Truman, but Chrétien's special appeal was more akin to that of Ronald Reagan. Chrétien was to Canada what Reagan was to the United States. He embodied Canadian values in much the same way the Gipper embodied American ones. They each possessed a rare ability to communicate great truths in homey phrases. They were each imbued with a stellar patriotism that encouraged their fellow citizens to feel good about themselves and their country. They were both uncomplicated, non-intellectual men who could see things in black-and-white terms and transmit clear pictures. Reagan was exceptional in that his appeal ran from the upper classes to the lowest common denominator. But Chrétien crossed traditional political boundaries in even more spectacular fashion. As the 1990s began, he had come to occupy that unique station in Canadian politics: He was both a populist and an establishment man.

Being a populist, as he surely was with his lack of intellectual pretence, his bargain-basement persona, his scorn for pomp, was unusual enough at the summit of Canadian politics. John Diefenbaker was perhaps the only other leader from the two great federal political parties who merited such a description. But unlike Diefenbaker, who was loathed on Bay Street, Chrétien was accepted by the business class and by many on the conservative side of the political spectrum. He had held four economic portfolios, had worked on Bay Street, had avoided the nationalist label, and had the wealthiest of friends.

If the trick of the game of politics was to be all things to all people, Chrétien had positioned himself brilliantly. As the party of the centre, the Liberals attempted to be universal in their appeal. Chrétien had become the most universal Liberal of them all. As such, his potential for political endurance was vast, so vast that it brought to mind the other great master of the middle in Canadian politics, Mackenzie King.

In rearing this *homme de terrain*, this man with the crooked grin and the chain-saw voice, the party had fashioned a product unique in many respects. No Canadian on the threshold of top office had ever accumulated such a breadth of experience in Ottawa. Probably none had met or spoken with so many Canadians. Probably none had explored the regions and its peoples as much as Chrétien. Very few had the reputation of being so genuine. Despite having spent so much time in politics, Chrétien had remained remarkably untouched by scandal. His roaring ego and ambition had led him to be deceitful on too many occasions. But in relative terms, in the context of an enterprise so bloodied as politics, he was noticeably clean. That so many would rush off to purchase a politician's memoirs titled *Straight from the Heart* was due testimony. Those who spent a lot of time with this politician noticed something very strange about him. He found it difficult to lie.

He had many flaws, some of which would always be with him. He was inordinately power hungry and, as he had shown time and again, would go to unseemly lengths to attain and maintain that power; he was not an articulate or profound man; he had a terrible impatience for detail; and he showed few signs of being able to understand, as perhaps the greatest of leaders must, the great currents of change, both the dismal and the grand, sweeping the world around him.

He never did see the world in terms of blueprints. But if he wasn't a man of vision, what carried him on a steady course were his values: integrity, equality of people, equality of opportunity, dedication to country. With Chrétien, the values were the vision.

Intellect doesn't make a good leader, nor does it make a good country. Values do. As Jean Chrétien prepared to take the reins of the Liberal Party, Canadians seemed to find comfort in his values. They were old-fashioned values, and for a time, he would be derided for representing a bygone era. But in a global-village world, increasingly given over to super-technologies, currency speculators, and transnational corporations, the more stable world of yesterday was beginning to look better that the uncertain world of tomorrow.

As the twentieth century was drawing to a close, Canada consistently topped the rankings of all the world's nations in quality-of-life studies. Perhaps Laurier's famous prophecy—the twentieth century will belong to Canada—had merit after all. Canada had enjoyed so many of the remarkable features of its great neighbour to the south, while escaping its dark underside, its wars, its violence, its racism, its glaring disparity between the rich and the poor.

Poised for power, Jean Chrétien was a man steeped in the values that had made his country exceptional. He was a man who never left the street that he lived on. He had passed such a large part of his life in the hellstorm of politics, but he was still able to look at things as average people do. Therein lay his basic appeal. Therein lay the reason he came to occupy such a singular place in the governing pantheon. Therein—with the realization that he was probably the best ordinary Canadian the country's politics had ever produced—lay the people's hopes.

NOTES

Unless otherwise indicated, all interviews referred to in these notes were done by the author specifically for this book. The interviews cited herein all took place between November 1993 and July 1995.

Chapter One: Survival of the Fittest

1 Gros Jean's death was related to the author during interviews with Gabriel and Maurice Chrétien.

3 The "make me grow" scene was recounted in detail by Maurice. Jean could not remember the specific visit to the doctor but didn't doubt that it had happened. Other family members corroborated Maurice's account.

4 Mrs. Chrétien's habits were described by daughter Giselle in an interview. Jean Chrétien also recalled her high-minded manner.

4 Philippe Boisvert was remembered in interviews with several members of the Chrétien family.

7 The account of the atmosphere of Shawinigan and La Baie Shawinigan came from interviews with the Chrétiens, Palle Kiar, Ole Kiar, Marcel Bérard, and André Grenier. See also Fabien LaRochelle, *Shawinigan depuis 75 ans* (Shawinigan: Imprimerie Publicité Paquet, 1976); Claude Bellevance, Normand Brouillette, and Pierre Lanthier, "Financement et industrie en La Mauricie, 1900–1950," *Revue d'histoire de l'Amérique française* 40 (1986); and "Stratégie industrielle et développement régional: le cas de La Mauricie au vingtième siècle." *RHAF* 37 (1983).

10 Chrétien has always maintained that he and other francophones were barred from playing at the Grand'Mère golf course. Others who lived in Shawinigan said the club had no such discriminatory policy.

11 In his attitude towards anglo dominance, Jean was somewhat less compliant than his brothers. He noted in an interview, however, that the reality—the English were the providers of the jobs—was not something one could be dismissive about.

11 The description of François Chrétien was drawn primarily from interviews with grandson Maurice, with additional input from Guy and Gabriel Chrétien.

14 For Roosevelt letters to King, see Lawrence Martin, *The Presidents and the Prime Ministers: Washington and Ottawa Face to Face* (Toronto: Doubleday, 1982).

14　The memories of Wellie Chrétien were from an interview with Émilienne Godin.

Chapter Two: The Little Guy

17　The anecdotes about Giselle's coat and Jean as a rabble-rouser came from Giselle and the Chrétien brothers.

18　Jean's role as the commandant was recalled in interviews with Yvon Boisvert and Gilles Marchand.

19　Jean's days at the Jardin de l'Enfance were remembered in an interview with classmate Marcel Bérard.

20　The description of Jean's behavioural problems at Sacré-Coeur came from interviews with Normand Déry and Gilles Argouin.

21　The accident at Amateau Creek was described by Guy Chrétien.

22　The story of the over-age hockey player came from interviews with Jean Chrétien and Gilles Argouin. They differ on some of the details.

24　The description of angry young Chrétien being forced to play goal was from an interview with Jean Harnois.

25　Fernand D. Lavergne, a close friend of the Chrétien family, said in an interview that Wellie was rumoured to be informing on draft dodgers.

26　For the extent of patronage under Duplessis, see Jeffrey Simpson, *Spoils of Power: The Politics of Patronage* (Toronto: W. Collins & Sons, 1988), p. 207. "The UN's long fingers coiled around individuals and whole communities; and an enormous war-chest served to tighten its grip." Simpson argues persuasively, however, that the system was more inherited than originated.

28　Information on Maurice's background came from interviews with him. Other members of the family testified to his importance as a role model.

Chapter Three: The Joliette Years

31　Giselle's wedding day was described by Jean, Giselle, and Juliette Chrétien.

32　Jean's response to taunts from other children was recalled in an interview with Robert Lamothe.

33　In rating the seminary colleges, Pierre Garceau and several other of Chrétien's friends gave Ste-Anne-de-la-Pocatière the nod as the toughest of the lot.

34　Guy Chrétien described his run-in with Father Galarneau in an interview. Galarneau himself had some memory of the Chrétien boys, particularly Jean, whose unruly behaviour made him the easiest to remember.

34　The "Take the door!" incident was related during an interview with Françoise Chrétien, wife of Gabriel. The story, she said, was typical of the attitude Jean displayed in those years.

35　The two ear-pulling incidents were described in interviews with Fathers Lanoue and Galarneau.

36　During interviews with Jean, Michel, and Guy Chrétien, all three recalled the broken nose Jean earned in his boxing match with Michel.

37　The appendicitis scam came from interviews with Jean, Michel, Guy, and Maurice Chrétien. Although Jean Chrétien gave a misleading impression of what had happened in his memoirs, *Straight from the Heart* (Toronto: Key Porter Books, 1985, 1994), he was forthright and candid when the author raised the issue with him, providing even more details than requested. Maurice and Guy were also very open, although Maurice asked if the incident could be kept off the public record, saying, "Maybe this story can be put aside." Of all the Chrétien brothers, Michel sought to protect Jean the most. Interviews with him were generally less reliable than those with the others.

40 The line about missing a year of school because of illness is in *Straight from the Heart*, p. 21. The full quotation reads, "A large part of the problem was that I had missed a year of school because of sickness, and so I was in the same class as my smart younger brother."

41 In describing his relations with Maurice, Jean Chrétien added that he called him an s.o.b. for trying to push him around. Given the big age difference between the two and the type of man Maurice was, it's unlikely Jean got away with too many comments of that nature.

43 Robert Lamothe described his friendship with Chrétien in an interview.

45 Chrétien's performance at Séminaire Ste-Marie was related during interviews with Raymond Langevin, Gabriel Houle, Réginald Savard, Jean Chrétien, and several other classmates. Chrétien attributed his lacklustre performance entirely to the fact that he was repeating the year. He stayed on reasonably good terms with Langevin, the director of the school. When he first prepared to run for public office, he asked Langevin's advice.

46 August Choquette and Jean Chrétien both remembered denouncing the Union Nationale in front of Father Galarneau's office at Joliette.

Chapter Four: Aline

49 Marcel Chartier and Jean Chrétien described the passing on of the master-key during interviews.

50 The story of Chrétien pummelling a fellow student during his first days at Trois-Rivières came from interviews with other students, his brothers, and Jean Chrétien.

51 Chrétien's fight with Georges Trepannier was described in interviews with Gabriel Chrétien and Jean Chrétien.

52 During an interview, Raymond Chrétien recounted Jean's reluctance to perform menial chores at Maurice's cottage on Lac des Piles.

54 Details on Aline's background were partially drawn from an excellent profile of her by E. Kaye Fulton in *Maclean's*, April 18, 1994. This is one of the few in-depth interviews Aline Chrétien has granted.

54 Jean's meeting with Aline was described by Claudette Germain, Ghiselaine Marchand, and Guy Chrétien.

55 Robert Lamothe stated that his sister had had the first deep romantic involvement with Jean Chrétien. Chrétien did not seem to remember it that way, greeting the question with a look of surprise.

55 The comment about Jean not being interested in girls until he met Aline came from an interview with Jean Chrétien.

55 During an interview, Chrétien briefly talked about the issue of sexually abusive priests. One of his close friends said that at Trois-Rivières, it was a problem that was often discussed by the students, including those in the Chrétien group.

56 Memories of life at the seminary college are from the student journal, *Les Finissants*, and from interviews with John Maloney, Pierre Garceau, André Bureau, Laurent Déry, Jean Pelletier, Marcel Chartier, Robert Bilodeau, Henry Boudreau, and Claude Rainville.

58 Chrétien's first encounter with Duplessis was described in interviews with Chrétien and Jean Pelletier, and was also related in *Straight from the Heart*, p. 12.

59 Gérard Dufresne related the story of Chrétien's victory in the public-speaking contest. Chrétien himself had only a very vague memory of the event.

60 Chrétien could only dimly recall his aggression towards Robert Bilodeau, but Bilodeau remembered it clearly.

62 Chrétien described his black-market chocolate bar business during an interview. Classmate John Maloney claimed that he and Chrétien began this practice when they were attending Séminaire Ste-Marie. Chrétien maintained that it was only done at Trois-Rivières.

64 The warm relationship between Aline and Marie Chrétien was described by Jean Chrétien. He also talked at length about the positive impact Aline had on his life.

65 Chrétien's new, responsible attitude was related in an interview with Laurent Déry.

66 Some of Chrétien's grades were supplied to the author by the college at Trois-Rivières. Chrétien, however, turned down a request to have the school release a full transcript.

68 Chrétien's progress in English was given differing appraisals. It was safe to say, however, as Henry Boudreau pointed out, that he knew a lot more than he claimed to on arriving in Ottawa.

Chapter Five: Jean Fidèle

69 The description of the death of Marie Chrétien was drawn from the memories of all family members.

73 Jean-Claude Ladouceur's reputation was described in interviews with Ladouceur, Jean Chrétien, and other students.

76 During interviews, Chrétien and Pierre Garceau both recalled their visit to Duplessis.

79 Guy Germain described his confrontation with Chrétien that night at Chez Houde.

81 For a description of the influence of political patronage on Quebec life, see *Straight from the Heart*, p. 13.

82 Duplessis's comment about the "Saint" in St-Laurent's name came from an interview with Ladouceur.

82 The student protests in favour of reforming the system for financial aid were reported in the Laval student newspaper, *Le Carabin*.

83 André Bureau described Aline's influence on Jean's life.

84 Jean's days at the paper mill were remembered by Marcel Samson, Maurice Poirier, Laurent Lachome, Roland Corriveau, Ole Kiar, and Guy Chrétien.

85 For an account of Jean crossing the picket line, see a profile of him by Lewis Harris, "Chrétien pea-souper but at the top of the pot," *Ottawa Citizen*, October 5, 1982.

86 In interviews, Gilles Marchand and Gabriel Chrétien said Jean was behaving like a wind-up attack dog. For his part, Jean Chrétien maintained that none of the charges he made in his speeches were unfounded.

Chapter Six: The Sixties Club

87 Aline's comment about Jean—"I never thought of another man, ever"—came from an interview she did with Joan Sutton, *Toronto Sun*, June 12, 1994.

88 This description of Aline's background was drawn in part from Fulton's profile in *Maclean's*.

89 Jean and Aline's wedding was remembered during interviews with Jean, Gabriel, and Guy Chrétien, Pierre Garceau, Guy Suzor, and Jean-Pierre Plante.

89 Fernand D. Lavergne, Gabriel Chrétien, Marcel Chartier, and Jean Chrétien all described Father Auger's behaviour during interviews.

91 The account of the Bardot caper was based on interviews with Chrétien, Pierre Garceau, André Bureau, and Jean Pelletier.

92 August Choquette denied that he was the voice behind the phoney Senate appointment. Others involved said it was him.

93 The atmosphere of the 1958 Liberal leadership convention was drawn from interviews with Louis Batshaw, Chrétien, Pierre Garceau, and Jim Coutts.

94 Jim Coutts described seeing Chrétien for the first time.

95 The election for student president of the law faculty was related in interviews with Bernard Flynn, Chrétien, Pierre Garceau, and Jean-Claude Ladouceur.

97 The formation of the Sixties Club was remembered by Jean-Pierre Plante, Guy Suzor, Marcel Bérard, and Chrétien. Explanations for the origin of the club name vary. Chrétien claimed it was chosen with a view to the coming decade. Marcel Bérard, however, distinctly recalled a meeting where they were all trying unsuccessfully to come up with names. Finally it was decided that since they wanted about sixty members, they would call it the Sixties Club. No one was too happy with the name, but it stuck.

98 The description of early Sixties Club speakers and activities came from a booklet commemorating the club's fifth anniversary in 1963.

99 During an interview, Georges Cossette recounted his prediction that Jean Chrétien would become prime minister of Canada one day.

Chapter Seven: The Young Lawyer

103 Chrétien's admission to the bar was described in *Les Chutes de Shawinigan*, July 1, 1959.

103 In an interview, Chrétien remembered his chance meeting with Louis St-Laurent.

104 Guy Germain related during an interview the story of Wellie Chrétien trying to buy Jean's graduation gown.

104 The job offer from Lafond, Gélinas was described by Jean Lafond, Jean Chrétien, and Raymond Landry.

105 The expropriation case was recounted in an interview with Jean Chrétien.

106 Maurice Chrétien described some of Jean's work habits.

107 The account of the Gilles Huard murder case was based on interviews with Chrétien, Pierre Garceau, Fernand D. Lavergne, and Gérard Dufresne.

109 The spartan office atmosphere at Lafond, Gélinas was discussed by Raymond Landry.

112 Chrétien's assault on Marcel Chartier was described by Chartier, Chrétien, and Raymond Landry. The comment by Marcel Chrétien came from the Lewis Harris profile in the *Ottawa Citizen*.

114 The description of the relationship between Pierre Trudeau and Fernand D. Lavergne was based on an interview with Lavergne.

115 For Chrétien's remarks on fighting religious domination in Quebec, see *Straight from the Heart*, p. 13.

117 Gabriel Buisson described his visit to René Hamel.

118 In an interview, Ole Kiar explained how impressed he had been with Chrétien during their trip to Quebec City.

118 Jean-Paul Gignac and André Grenier both outlined the decline of Shawinigan in separate interviews.

Chapter Eight: The Will to Win

122 Guy Lebrun, Chrétien, and Pierre Garceau remembered Lebrun lecturing Chrétien.

124 Chrétien related Hamel's advice that he should run in the 1963 election, despite the long odds.

125 Chrétien's first meeting with Claude Ryan was described by Ryan in an interview.

125 The initial encounter between Chrétien and Robert Beaulieu was recounted by Beaulieu in an interview.

126 The banner declaring Jean Chrétien to be "Our Future Prime Minister" was remembered by Claude Lacoursière and several other Chrétien supporters.

127 Auger's ploy during Chrétien's debut appearance in La Baie Shawinigan was related by most of the Chrétien brothers, although Jean himself had no specific memory of it.

131 The advertisement in the *Shawinigan Standard* appeared on March 27, 1963.

131 Chrétien's comment that "it's not the time to send buffoons to the House of Commons to represent French Canadians" was reported in several newspaper accounts of his speech.

133 Georges Cossette, Guy Suzor, and Gilles Marchand all mentioned Chrétien's dictatorial style of running his first campaign. When asked about this, Chrétien said, "I ran a show."

133 During an interview, Gérard Lamy described his own lacklustre performance in the campaign. Despite the tough tactics Chrétien used against him, Lamy noted that he eventually came to respect the man and still does to this day.

134 The Trois-Rivières daily newspaper, *Le Nouvelliste*, recounted Chrétien's admiration for René Lévesque in its reports on the election campaign. Lévesque appeared in Chrétien's riding during the race to denounce the Créditistes as "loudmouths who didn't know what they were saying."

135 The description of the all-candidates debate in Grand'Mère is based on local media reports, as well as interviews with Chrétien, Gérard Lamy, and Marcel Bérard.

136 Not everyone could agree on the size of the big bet that came at the end of the campaign. Maurice Chrétien put the amount at five thousand dollars.

Chapter Nine: The Wider Game

139 In an interview, Chrétien described his feelings when he arrived in Ottawa. See also, *Straight from the Heart*, p. 25.

140 Chrétien's "I can make it here" remark came during an interview with the author.

141 Brian Mulroney and Chrétien, several years apart in age, never attended the same schools at the same time, but Bernard Ducharme's wide-ranging educational experience managed to land him in classes with each one of them.

142 August Choquette clearly remembered the picture of John and Robert Kennedy that Chrétien hung on his office wall. Chrétien himself couldn't recall it, but his efforts to have a building named after the president point to the extent of his interest.

144 Doug Fisher recounted his first meeting with Chrétien. As an MP and a journalist, Fisher was one of the first to spot Chrétien's potential. In assessing Chrétien's performance in the 1960s, Fisher noted two key developments. The first was Chrétien's desire to play the wider game. The second was his attempt to stake out federalist turf with speeches delineating the economic costs of Quebec nationalism.

145 Jean Chrétien made the remark that learning English wasn't important to him during an interview with the author.

146 The story involving the Shawinigan Transport Company was related by Chrétien and André Grenier.

147 Jean-Paul Gignac described his limousine rides to Montreal with Chrétien during an interview.

150 For Chrétien's altercation with Bob Coates, see *Straight from the Heart*, p. 30.

152 The account of the passing of the Air Canada bill was based on interviews with Doug Fisher, Chrétien, Joe Macaluso, August Choquette, and John Munro. While Fisher suggested that his own role was integral to the outcome, Chrétien was not so certain of its significance.

153 The story of Wellie proudly presenting the new Canadian flag to his children came from an interview with Maurice Chrétien.

153 Guy Suzor, Marcel Bérard, Chrétien, Robert Beaulieu, Fernand D. Lavergne, André Grenier, and Omer Hill all described the far-reaching power of the Chrétien machine in interviews.

155 For René Lévesque's remark that Chrétien had no future in Ottawa, see *Straight from the Heart*, p. 32.

156 Fernand D. Lavergne recounted the dinner he and Chrétien had at Marcel Crête's.

Chapter Ten: A Sharp Impact

164 Pearson's remarks on the coming cabinet changes were related in an interview with Jean Chrétien. See also his account in *Straight from the Heart*, pp. 47–48.

164 Chrétien's accomplishments for his riding were the subject of an article—"Never in the Past Have You Seen the Riding on the Map Like it Is Now"—in *Le Nouvelliste*, October 26, 1965.

165 Jack Pickersgill revealed during an interview how close Chrétien came to being named to the cabinet in 1965.

167 The description of Mitchell Sharp's background was drawn from an interview with Sharp and from his memoirs, *Which Reminds Me . . .* (Toronto: University of Toronto Press, 1994).

167 Jean-Luc Pepin remembered mulling over with Sharp possible successors for his position and telling Chrétien of Sharp's interest in him.

168 Sharp made the comment that he'd willingly take on the economists during an interview with the author.

170 Sharp and Roland de Corneille both recounted Chrétien's successful appearance in Sharp's Toronto constituency.

171 Sharp's relations with the economic nationalists were recalled in interviews with Sharp, Larry Pennell, Chrétien, Joe Macaluso, John Munro, Roland de Corneille, and John Rae.

172 For the two streams in the Liberal Party, see Keith Davey, *The Rainmaker: A Passion for Politics* (Toronto: Stoddart, 1986), pp. 322–323.

173 Chrétien's relations with Jean Marchand were described during interviews with Fernand D. Lavergne and Mitchell Sharp.

173 For Chrétien's relationship with Trudeau, see Stephen Clarkson and Christina McCall, *Trudeau and Our Times*, vol. 1, *The Magnificent Obsession* (Toronto: McClelland and Stewart, 1990).

174 For Chrétien's remark that many MPs were "angry at this beatnik," see *Straight from the Heart*, p. 52.

174 Larry Pennell recounted his prediction that Chrétien would be prime minister one day during an interview.

174 Omer Hill remembered telling Chrétien that he could be re-elected in St-Maurice–LaFlèche for twenty-five years.

176 Chrétien described the importance of his first cabinet appointment during an interview with the author.

176 Claude Ryan's editorial appeared in *Le Devoir* on April 5, 1967.

177 The train tour that Chrétien and his family made of Western Canada was related in an interview with John Rae.

178 *Le Devoir's* reaction to Chrétien's attack on Quebec nationalists came in an editorial on June 1, 1967.

179 The description of Chrétien taking a hard line on Charles de Gaulle came from an interview with Chrétien.

179 Chrétien's confrontation with Daniel Latouche was reported in the *Vancouver Sun*, October 18, 1967.

180 The stink-bomb attack was reported in the *Montreal Gazette*, October 27, 1967.

Chapter Eleven: In the Cabinet

183 Mitchell Sharp described himself as Chrétien's tireless promoter during an interview. He said the two most important things he did for Chrétien were to act as a lobbyist on his behalf and to teach him how the system works. He could have added another. In a great many instances, he was Chrétien's policy guru. On major issues, Jean Chrétien rarely departed from the Sharp script.

183 Chrétien's period as National Revenue minister was described by John Rae in an interview.

184 Chrétien's assertion that English Canadians had to become bilingual came from a Canadian Press report in the *Montreal Star*, January 22, 1968.

184 The counter-attacks Chrétien launched on those who were denouncing him as a traitor were reported in *La Presse*, May 15, 1968, "Jean Chrétien est 'écouré' se faire traiter de 'traître'."

185 During an interview, John Rae remembered Chrétien calling Robert Winters a "Cadillac with a Volkswagen engine."

185 Pearson's suggestion that John Turner not press too hard in the leadership race

against Pierre Trudeau was related to the author by Gerald Stoner.

186 Stoner recounted his conversation with Chrétien outside Government House.

187 Guy Germain supplied details of his nonchalant campaign performance.

187 Roger Lambert speculated in an interview about Chrétien's relationship with Germain.

188 Chrétien's changed attitude towards St-Maurice–LaFlèche was described in an interview with John Rae.

189 For Chrétien's remark that he didn't know anything about Liberal policies on Indian Affairs, see *Straight from the Heart*, p. 62.

189 During an interview, Stu Hodgson revealed that people in the North used to call the department No Action, No Results.

190 Trudeau's remark that Chrétien's French was even worse than his English was recounted by Hodgson during an interview.

191 Virginia Summers's indictment of the government's policy on native peoples was reported in the *Toronto Daily Star*, September 21, 1968, under the headline "Chrétien promises angry Indians new act by spring."

191 The comment from the Russian delegation to the United Nations about Canada's poor treatment of its native peoples was remembered by Raymond Chrétien during an interview.

192 Trudeau's thoughts on the native question are contained in memoranda exchanged between him and Chrétien, which were obtained under the Access to Information Act.

193 Chrétien's contention that he and the federal government knew what was best for the people was discussed in an article entitled "Jean Chrétien à la hâte de régler la question," *La Presse*, July 11, 1968. This same mind-set was described in an interview with Jean Fournier.

194 Chrétien's conflict with Robert Andras was recalled by John Rae. See also Anthony Westell, "A new deal outlined for Indians," *Montreal Star*, February 20, 1969.

195 Bill Mussell's comment that the consultation sessions with natives were "ritualistic" was made during an interview with the author.

195 The explanation of the Elk affair came from Chrétien. These and other memos and letters cited in the rest of this chapter were obtained under the Access to Information Act.

197 Native criticisms of the new reforms were reported in *La Presse*, July 5, 1969, under the headline "Les Indiens sont en beau fusil!" and in the *Toronto Telegram*, July 5, 1969, under "Ontario Indians blast Chrétien"

199 Jean Fournier and Judd Buchanan both remembered the toll the continued criticisms of Chrétien's native policy took on him.

200 For an excellent analysis of the making and breaking of the Indian paper, see Sally Weaver, *Making Canadian Indian Policy: The Hidden Agenda, 1968–1970* (Toronto: University of Toronto Press, 1981).

201 Chrétien's impassioned defense of his White Paper came during an interview with the author.

202 The story of Michel's adoption was drawn from interviews with Jean, Maurice, Michel, Guy, and Gabriel Chrétien, Stu Hodgson, Judd Buchanan, John Rae, Bill Mussell, and Diane Comeau.

204 The remark that the policy had "boomeranged" came during an interview with Jean Fournier. He and John Rae both outlined the positive results of the policy during separate interviews.

Chapter Twelve: The Last Emperor in North America

207 Jean Fournier made the remark that socializing seemed to recharge Chrétien's battery.

207 For Clifford's analysis, see Clark Clifford, with Richard Holbrooke, *Counsel to the President: A Memoir* (New York: Random House, 1991), p. 238.

208 Chrétien's surfing trip in Hawaii was described in an interview by Robert Matteau.

209 For Chrétien's remark that he is "a very private person," see Linda Diebel, "Man of Contradictions," *Toronto Star*, June 24, 1990. This mammoth profile of Chrétien is the most thorough and revealing piece of journalism done on him.

210 For Chrétien's remark that the ruling class is out of touch, see Peter Thomson, "Don't Try to Label Me," *Montreal Star*, August 3, 1974.

210 For Chrétien's explanation that he hoped to be the voice of the blue-collar worker, see an interview he did with George Radwanski, *Montreal Gazette*, September 5, 1974.

210 His contention that he had no great vision came from an article entitled "Understand North, Chrétien Urges," *Toronto Telegram*, January 20, 1969.

210 Stu Hodgson's "Stone Age vs. Jet Age" remark was made during an interview with the author.

211 The importance of Chrétien's term in Northern Development in developing his love and understanding of the country was emphasized in interviews with Eddie Goldenberg, Jean Fournier, John Rae, and others.

213 Chrétien's insistence that the forest supervisors cut down several trees was recounted by Robert Matteau.

213 The "Je suis pour" campaign was described by André Grenier.

214 Chrétien's ill-fated Toronto junket was remembered in an interview with Guy Tremblay.

215 Chrétien's feelings about Trudeau's response to the October Crisis were expressed by Chrétien during an interview.

216 Details of Chrétien's Soviet tour were gathered from interviews with Stu Hodgson, Jean Fournier, and 1971 press reports.

217 For a description of Soviet drinking habits, see Lawrence Martin, *Breaking with History: The Gorbachev Revolution* (Toronto: Doubleday, 1989).

219 In an interview, Chrétien described the great temptation he felt when Trudeau offered to make him a judge.

220 For Clarence Manning's comments on Chrétien, see Douglas Sagi, "Angry businessmen take Chrétien aside after Yukon speech," *Globe and Mail*, April 14, 1969.

220 The description of the Usher affair was drawn from interviews with Basil Robinson, Jean Fournier, and John Rae.

223 During an interview with the author, Chrétien made the comment that the natives were never in agreement.

224 For a discussion of the native position on the James Bay project, see Roy MacGregor, *Chief: The Fearless Vision of Billy Diamond* (Toronto: Viking, 1989).

Chapter Thirteen: Doctor No

228 The account of the counterfeit candidate came from interviews with Antonio Genest, Jean Chrétien, Guy Germain, Richard Durand, Guy Suzor, André Grenier, and Omer Hill.

231 The judges' affair was described in interviews by Gordon Osbaldeston and Richard Cleroux.

233 Chrétien's relations with Yves Duhaime were described during interviews with Chrétien, Duhaime, Raymond Roy, André Grenier, Guy Suzor, Dominique Grenier, and Henry Blanchard.

234 The cultural centre confrontation was related by Blanchard. Chrétien had only a vague recollection of the incident.

236 Chrétien maintained during an interview that the "pea-souper" speech was simply a joke. The June 16, 1977, *Ottawa Citizen* report was written by Donna Balkan.

237 Claude Rompré's remarks were made during an interview with the author.

238 Chrétien's excited phone call to Roger Caron was recounted by Caron during an interview.

240 John Roberts expressed the view during an interview that Chrétien labelled himself Doctor No.

244 Mitchell Sharp's comments about the critical mistake the government made in de-indexing income taxes from inflation came during an author interview.

244 For Chrétien's comments on the big business view of the party, see Stephen Duncan, "Chrétien: 'I'm a practical guy,'" *Financial Post*, September 20, 1976. In 1976 he told the *Financial Times*, "I've never been much of a nationalist." As Trade minister he had emphasized the need for a vigorous private sector, which, he said, would succeed or fail on the basis of its ability to compete in international markets.

Chapter Fourteen: Fall in Finance

249 For a discussion of the government's role in helping Shawinigan, see Sheldon Gordon, "Plenty of problems in Shawinigan—but having two ministers is a great asset," *Financial Post*, March 11, 1978.

250 Both Yves Duhaime and Chrétien gave their versions of their confrontation at the Shawinigan Golf Club.

252 Jim Coutts's remark that Chrétien saw things as ordinary people do came during an author interview.

253 Mitchell Sharp described the note he got from Trudeau announcing that he'd named Chrétien minister of Finance.

255 For Wilfrid Laurier's Chicago speech, see Martin, *The Presidents and the Prime Ministers*, p. 16.

256 Chrétien's observation that Canada was the only place where he and Tommy Shoyama could have risen to such heights was recounted in an interview with Shoyama.

257 For an account of Chrétien's performance at the Quebec City Chamber of Commerce, see Michel Vastel, "The Little Guy from Shawinigan Electrifies the Chamber of Commerce," *Le Devoir*, November 14, 1977.

259 The description of the sales-tax controversy is based on comments from Tommy Shoyama and Chrétien, as well as on English- and French-language press reports. See also Graham Fraser, *PQ: René Lévesque and the Parti Québécois in Power* (Toronto: Macmillan, 1984), pp. 154–166.

263 Shoyama made the observation during an interview that Chrétien was "not a great student of written documents."

264 In an interview, Gerald Bouey described Chrétien as being uncomfortable in the portfolio.

264 Maurice Chrétien was typically candid in talking about his brother's troubles in Finance.

264 In an interview, Shoyama expressed the belief that Trudeau's move to go over everyone's heads was "a convenient stratagem."

265 The account of Coutts's position winning out over Pitfield's is based on the memories of Ian Stewart, the PMO economic guru, with input from Jim Coutts, Tommy Shoyama, and Chrétien.

265 Trudeau wrote in his memoirs that he telephoned Chrétien shortly before going on the air to deliver his speech, but in an interview Chrétien made no reference to any such call. He said he heard the speech was coming shortly before its delivery, then tried to reach Trudeau immediately after it.

266 During a 1995 interview, Chrétien became quite agitated when the subject of Coutts came up. He spoke of bitterly confronting him but wouldn't repeat what he said to him.

267 Jim Coutts outlined his take on the disastrous press conference during an interview with the author.

268 In an interview, Chrétien displayed his great sensitivity to questions concerning his depth. When the subject of him not reading briefing documents was gently raised, he responded testily, "Nobody knows what I read, sir!"

268 John Roberts revealed in an interview that at least three cabinet members considered stepping down.

269 Ed Lumley termed John Turner's newsletters "outrageous" during an interview.

271 For a discussion of Chrétien in Finance and other portfolios, see Ron Graham, *One-Eyed Kings: Promise and Illusion in Canadian Politics* (Toronto: W. Collins & Sons, 1986), p. 227.

Chapter Fifteen: Trudeau's Firefighter

275 Yves Duhaime told the anecdote about Czar Alexander and the Congress of Vienna with relish in an interview.

276 The story of Duhaime and Chrétien haranguing each other in the funeral cortège came from an interview with Dominique Grenier, the former mayor of Shawinigan. Duhaime said he couldn't recall the incident.

277 Former aides confirmed Chrétien's peculiar desire to return to the Finance portfolio. Goldenberg explained that although he, Chrétien, and his assistants were so new to the job the first time around, they all found Finance an energizing and challenging place to be.

278 The term "cultural revolution" took on a particularly negative connotation after Mao's version of it in China in the 1960s. As a result, it is not a term usually applied to developments under Trudeau, but it is nonetheless appropriate. The first use of the term in the Canadian context was in the July 1969 edition of the *Monetary Times*, which featured an excellent, un-bylined article on the subject.

278 It is Eddie Goldenberg's view and that of others that until the referendum, Chrétien's "contribution to Canadian life" was good but not terribly noteworthy. Had he left public life then, he would have been remembered, Goldenberg said, as simply a good cabinet minister.

279 Jean-Luc Pepin's remark that he should have been the one Trudeau chose to lead the referendum fight was made during an interview.

280 Chrétien's assessment of Pepin's shortcomings was passed to Pepin through his wife, to whom Chrétien made the comments.

281 The story of Chrétien waiting for an hour outside Claude Ryan's office was related by Eddie Goldenberg during an interview. Ryan admitted that his attitude towards Chrétien was frosty, but he claimed not to remember this moment. In an interview, Ryan acknowledged that Chrétien's approach to the referendum was the right one, and he was conspicuously complimentary towards Chrétien not only for the way he handled the federalist strategy, but also for his professionalism in dealing with people.

282 In an interview, Chrétien made the comment that he had to resist the temptation to kick people around.

285 The genesis of the "Rockies" speech was described by Chrétien in an interview.

287 Robert Sheppard relived his days on the referendum campaign trail during an interview with the author.

290 Claude Ryan and Chrétien both gave their own version of what happened at the federalist victory rally at the Verdun arena.

Chapter Sixteen: Father of Re-Confederation

293 For a discussion of Chrétien's lack of interest in constitutional matters, see Douglas Fisher's column in the *Toronto Sun*, April 21, 1982.

294 During an interview, Roger Tassé made the observation that Chrétien "wasn't greatly interested in the legal system."

295 Chrétien's remark that Canada was "trying hard to decentralize at any price" was reported in the *Globe and Mail*, July 13, 1978.

295 For Chrétien's testy exchange with Michael Pitfield, see *Straight from the Heart*, p. 182.

296 The description of the death of Wellie Chrétien was drawn from interviews with Jean, Michel, and Guy Chrétien. It was striking to hear Jean Chrétien talk about his father in such uncomplimentary terms. Wellie had been a major force in Jean's early career, yet he preferred to emphasize his father's less attractive features.

297 Paul Chrétien's troubles with the Peruvian justice system were recounted in an interview with Françoise Chrétien.

299 The view that Chrétien didn't really care what was in the charter, so long as he got one, came from interviews with Roger Tassé and Barry Strayer.

300 Ronald Reagan's remark that "*The Sound of Music* was on last night" was first reported by Lou Cannon of the *Washington Post*. His article was reprinted in the *Ottawa Citizen* on April 28, 1991.

302 The account of Chrétien's success at the final constitutional conference was based on interviews with Roger Tassé, Barry Strayer, John Roberts, Robert Sheppard, and Jean Chrétien. See also press reports; Robert Sheppard and Michael Valpy, *The National Deal: The Fight for a Canadian Constitution* (Toronto: Fleet Books, 1982); Clarkson and McCall, *Trudeau and Our Times*, vol. I, *The Magnificent Obsession*; Michel Vastel, *The Outsider: The Life of Pierre Elliott Trudeau*, trans. Hubert Bauch (Toronto: Macmillan, 1990); and *Straight from the Heart*.

Chapter Seventeen: Family Matters

307 The problems faced by the Chrétiens' adopted son were recounted in interviews with Maurice, Jean, Michel, Gabriel, Françoise, and Giselle Chrétien, Eddie

Goldenberg, John Rae, Judd Buchanan, and Diane Comeau.

310 Hubert Chrétien's story is drawn from interviews with Jean Chrétien, Ed Lumley, and Jean Carle.

314 For Patrick O'Callaghan's comments on the Department of Energy, see *Calgary Herald*, September 18, 1982. The full quote reads, "Chrétien, who freely admits he knows nothing about Energy, is no more than a caretaker in a department that ruthlessly wiped out a decade of Western progress." Like other commentators, O'Callaghan noticed a distinct lack of enthusiasm on Chrétien's part on being appointed to the portfolio. The publisher said he exhibited "an out-of-character fit of sulks."

314 Ed Lumley spoke of Chrétien's being strongly in favour of scaling back the NEP when he first took over the Energy portfolio. Lumley maintained that big changes of the type seen under Mulroney might have followed had the Liberals been re-elected in 1984.

318 Chrétien first used his "society of complainers" speech as early as the 1960s to complain about unappreciative Quebeckers. At the start of 1977 his rhetoric hardened, and he used the "society of bitchers" phrase.

319 Stephen Clarkson, co-author of *Trudeau and Our Times*, said in an interview that a major rift developed between Marc Lalonde and Chrétien over their differing views on the NEP. Chrétien, however, denied that any such split occurred. As with other ministers, he noted, he frequently had agreements and disagreements with Lalonde at the cabinet table.

320 Chrétien's accusation that Mulroney was only interested in pleasing his American friends was significant in that it marked the opening volley in a battle that stretched over the next decade. Mulroney's close links to the Americans became the dominant theme of Chrétien's criticisms of the Conservative leader.

321 The Canadian Press reporter who taped Chrétien's indiscreet comments about the coming Liberal leadership race was Tim Naumetz.

322 For Lise Bissonnette's remarks on Chrétien, see Linda Diebel's June 24, 1990, profile of him in the *Toronto Star*.

322 The account of the running battle between Lysiane Gagnon and Chrétien was based on interviews with Gagnon and several members of the Chrétien family.

323 Claude Ryan's observations about the "false intellectualism" of the Quebec media were made during an interview with the author.

324 For Chrétien's remarks about not wanting to put "mascara over the body," see the Diebel profile in the *Toronto Star*.

Chapter Eighteen: A Man Betrayed

326 Ed Lumley described in interviews the friendliness of his early relationship with Chrétien.

327 The story of Lumley's break with Chrétien is based on accounts from Lumley, Chrétien, John Rae, and Eddie Goldenberg.

328 Chrétien's rift with André Ouellet was described by Chrétien, Goldenberg, Roland de Corneille, and Rae.

329 Judd Buchanan recounted the story of his decision to support Turner.

330 For Chrétien's comment that he "had collected some IOUs," see Michel Grátton and Robert Fife's interview with Chrétien in the *Ottawa Sun*, June 28, 1992.

330 For Chrétien's assertion that those who deserted him were only "saving their own asses," see Norman Snider, *The Changing of the Guard: How the Liberals Fell from*

Grace and the Tories Rose to Power (Toronto: Lester & Orpen Dennys, 1985), p. 58. Snider's volume contains several scenes that vividly capture Chrétien's personality.

330 The description of the early press coverage of the leadership campaign was drawn from interviews with Hugh Winsor, John Rae, and Eddie Goldenberg. See also *Straight from the Heart*, p. 198, where Chrétien wrote, "I still maintain that if the media hadn't gone crazy for Turner that first day, I could have won the convention."

332 For Chrétien's jab that Turner was "still wearing garter belts," see Snider, *The Changing of the Guard*, p. 48.

334 Judd Buchanan recounted in an interview the conversation he had with Chrétien years after the leadership convention.

336 Chrétien's loss of perspective baffled his campaign team, who felt that while he had gained considerable ground throughout the campaign, he was still a long shot when the convention began. They couldn't convince Chrétien of this, however. He always had faith in his own instincts, which were now telling him he could win.

336 That the Chrétien family had a history of problems with dyslexia was confirmed by Maurice, Jean, and Françoise Chrétien, and Pierre Garceau.

338 For a description of the Turner camp and their magic number, see Jack Cahill, *John Turner: The Long Run* (Toronto: McClelland and Stewart, 1984), pp. 217–229.

341 Françoise Chrétien, who was present at the dinner, told the story of the normally stoic Maurice covering his face with his hands.

342 Yvon Boisvert, in describing how upset Chrétien was after his defeat, twice mentioned during an interview at his home in Shawinigan that Chrétien had cried. Hours after the interview, he caught up with the author to explain that he had been talking to his wife and that maybe the book shouldn't reveal that Chrétien was in tears. Chrétien himself has always maintained that he didn't cry after the defeat.

Chapter Nineteen: Strategic Retreat

346 Roy MacGregor's memories of spending election night with Chrétien were recounted during an interview. See also MacGregor's February 28, 1986, column in the *Ottawa Citizen*.

347 Paul Martin Jr., who lived with his father at the time, contended that, contrary to what some people have written, Paul Martin Sr. spent only a small amount of time practicing law during his years as an Opposition MP.

347 Doug Frith's remarks about Turner's low approval ratings were made during an interview.

348 In an interview, Roland de Corneille made the comment that Chrétien had ego enough for "an entire Parliament."

349 Mulroney's visit with Reagan is described in a White House memorandum that was released to the author under the U.S. Freedom of Information Act.

350 Jean Carle described his warm relationship with Chrétien during an interview.

352 For the remark that Chrétien doesn't read books, see Peter Worthington, "Chrétien after Turner's job," *Financial Post*, November 11, 1985.

355 Michel Roy made his criticisms of Chrétien in an article entitled "Le choix que doit faire Jean Chrétien," in *La Presse*, January 13, 1986.

356 Jean Carle recounted the great emotion he felt when he accompanied Chrétien to Turner's office so the former could hand in his resignation.

356 Aline Chrétien's uncharacteristic outburst was described to the author by Jason Moscovitz.

357 For an account of Chrétien describing his proudest moments, see Graham Fraser's article in the *Globe and Mail,* February 28, 1986.

357 For Chrétien's comments about Aline—"How can you be bored with a lady like that?"—see Bob Mckenzie, "Comeback still possible, Chrétien hints," *Toronto Star,* February 28, 1986.

357 For an impressive overview of Chrétien's political obituaries, see Hubert Bauch, "Chrétien spoke people's language," *Montreal Gazette,* February 28, 1986.

359 For a detailed account of the leadership review campaign, see Greg Weston, *Reign of Error: The Inside Story of John Turner's Troubled Leadership* (Toronto: McGraw-Hill Ryerson, 1988).

359 Mark Resnick recalled during an interview the paranoid atmosphere surrounding the leadership review.

361 Keith Davey's comment that his support of Turner was the one big mistake in his political career was recounted by Roland de Corneille.

362 In an interview, Eddie Goldenberg remembered Turner's sharp rebuke and his refusal to shake Goldenberg's hand.

363 For Chrétien's reflections on Nixon and others, see Joel Ruimy, "Subdued Chrétien weighs his future," *Toronto Star,* December 1, 1986.

Chapter Twenty: Poised for Power

367 Wellie told the story of falling off the podium at the insurance company banquet to Émilienne Godin, who repeated it to the author.

368 The account of Viceroy's gold strike came from Ross Fitzpatrick. Fitzpatrick explained that Chrétien didn't make as much money as he might have because he didn't quickly exercise the option on his shares.

369 Lysiane Gagnon made her remarks about Chrétien during an interview.

370 During an interview, John Rae talked about what he saw as the main difference between Chrétien and Mulroney.

370 Roger Tassé recounted Chrétien's disinterest in much of his legal work.

370 The story of Chrétien attending Shawinigan High School's fortieth anniversary came from Ole Kiar.

373 The account of Chrétien's lunch with André Ouellet was drawn from an interview with Chrétien. Despite what several of his colleagues said, Chrétien claimed he could not recall vowing never to forgive Ouellet.

374 For Mitchell Sharp's comments about Chrétien's image problem, see Ross Laver and Bruce Wallace, "Ready to Run," *Maclean's,* June 26, 1989. Sharp was less convinced than others that changes to his image were necessary. "He does not have to change his style," he told *Maclean's,* "he has to change the content."

374 Mel Hurtig recounted his session with Chrétien during an interview with the author.

374 One of Chrétien's image coaches was Montrealer André Morrow. Another who helped was George Radwanski, the former editorial page editor of the *Toronto Star.*

INDEX

Jarvis, William, 274
Johnson, Daniel, 212
Joliette seminary, 32-47
The Journal, 330-331
Joyal, Serge, 303
Justice: Chrétien as minister of (1980-
 1982), 277-290, 291-306, 310-313
Justice Committee (House of
 Commons), 313

Kaplan, Bob, 361
Katimavik, 358
Kennedy, John F., 128, 142
Kennedy, Robert F., 142
Keynesianism, 254-255
Kiar, Ole, 85, 118
Kiar, Palle, 10, 370-371
Kierans, Eric, 238
King, Mackenzie, 14, 25, 376
Kolber, Leo, 360

La Baie Shawinigan (PQ), 1, 4, 7-8
Lacoursière, Claude, 127
Ladouceur, Jean, 81
Ladouceur, Jean-Claude (Le Chat), 73-
 74, 82, 116, 122
Lafond, Gélinas (law firm), 104
Lafond, Jean, 104-105
Lafond, Joe, 104
Laforest, Martial, 136
Laing, Arthur, 192
Lajoie, Robert, 106, 250
Lalonde, Marc, 240, 341
 and Chrétien, 222, 281, 319, 328, 355
 as Energy minister, 314, 319
 as Finance minister, 315-316
 and party leadership, 328-329, 339, 340,
  360-361, 363
 and Trudeau, 185, 341
LaMarsh, Judy, 151
La Mauricie (PQ) National Park, 212-213,
 215, 275
Lambert, Roger, 187
Lamontagne, Maurice, 144, 158
Lamothe, Robert, 43, 99
Lamy, Gérard, 124, 130-136
Landry, Raymond, 105, 109-110, 113
Langevin, Raymond, 45
Lang Michener (law firm), 348, 367, 368,
 370
Lang, Otto, 242

Laniel, Gérald, 173
Lanoue, François, 35
Lapalme, Georges, 86
Lapointe, Charles, 330, 340
Laporte, Pierre, 215
Laski, Harold, 169
Latouche, Daniel, 179, 180
Laurier, Wilfrid, 6, 44, 255, 377
Laval University, 29, 73, 74, 75, 77-78,
 81-84, 91-93
Lavelle, Patrick, 334-336, 359
Lavergne, Fernand D., 100, 114-115, 129-
 130, 143, 156, 173
Lawrence, Allan, 258
Lebrun, Guy, 79-80, 122
Lefebvre, Gilles, 21
Lesage, Jean, 86, 117, 156
Lévesque, René, 119, 233, 248, 261, 282,
 286, 288, 302-303, 305
 and Chrétien, 134-135, 155-156, 274
Liberal leadership races
 in 1958 (won by Pearson), 93-94, 346-
  347
 in 1968 (won by Trudeau), 184-185
 in 1980 (irrelevant once Trudeau agrees
  to stay on), 276, 277
 in 1984 (won by Turner), 320-324, 325-
  342, 350
 in 1990 (won by Chrétien), 372-377
 and supposed tradition of *alternance*,
  321, 329, 335, 338, 342, 372
Liberal leadership review (1986), 351,
 354-363, 365
Liberals (federal)
 divisions within, 172, 347, 354, 355-356,
  365
 and party machine in Quebec, 328-329,
  340-341, 348
Liberals (Manitoba), 357-358
Liberals (Ontario), 351
Liberals (Quebec). *See* Quebec Liberals
Liddle, Clive, 157, 164, 165
Lizotte, Louis, 164
Loubier, Gabriel, 80-81, 122, 211-212, 213
Lumley, Ed, 269, 314, 316, 325, 326-328
Lynch, Charles, 242

Macaluso, Joe, 144, 145, 218
Macdonald, Donald, 145, 170, 242, 248,
 253, 268, 277, 301
MacDonald, John, 204